OPERATION VALHALLA

a Cultural Politics book
*A series edited by John Armitage,
Ryan Bishop, and Douglas Kellner*

FRIEDRICH KITTLER

OPERATION
Valhalla

WRITINGS ON WAR, WEAPONS, AND MEDIA

EDITED AND TRANSLATED
BY ILINCA IURASCU,
GEOFFREY WINTHROP-YOUNG,
AND MICHAEL WUTZ

WITH AN INTRODUCTION BY
GEOFFREY WINTHROP-YOUNG

DUKE UNIVERSITY PRESS   DURHAM + LONDON   2021

© 2021 Duke University Press
All rights reserved
Designed by Amy Ruth Buchanan
Typeset in Monotype Dante by Westchester Publishing Services
Project editor: Lisa Lawley

Library of Congress Cataloging-in-Publication Data
Names: Kittler, Friedrich A., author. | Winthrop-Young, Geoffrey, [date] editor. | Wutz, Michael, editor. | Iurascu, Ilinca, editor, translator.
Title: Operation Valhalla : writings on war, weapons, and media / Friedrich Kittler ; edited and translated by Ilinca Iurascu, Geoffrey Winthrop-Young, and Michael Wutz.
Description: Durham : Duke University Press, 2021. | Includes index.
Identifiers: LCCN 2020022635 (print)
LCCN 2020022636 (ebook)
ISBN 9781478010715 (hardcover)
ISBN 9781478011842 (paperback)
ISBN 9781478013181 (ebook)
Subjects: LCSH: Communication and technology—Philosophy. | Literature—History and criticism. | Technology—Social aspects—Philosophy. | War (Philosophy) | Weapons—Philosophy.
Classification: LCC P96.T42 K588 2021 (print) | LCC P96.T42 (ebook) | DDC 302.23—dc23
LC record available at https://lccn.loc.gov/2020022635
LC ebook record available at https://lccn.loc.gov/2020022636

Cover art: Joseph G. Cruz, *What happens when the horizon completes its circle*, 2016. Sand from the original test site of the V2, dimensions variable. From the installation titled *Across the Sky, Came a Screaming*, Evanston Art Center, Evanston, IL. Courtesy of the artist.

Editors' Preface vii
ILINCA IURASCU, GEOFFREY WINTHROP-YOUNG, AND MICHAEL WUTZ

Introduction: The Wars of Friedrich Kittler 1
GEOFFREY WINTHROP-YOUNG

Part I: Guns, Germans, and Steel: The Hardware(s) of War

1. Free Ways 53
   TRANSLATED BY GEOFFREY WINTHROP-YOUNG

2. A Short History of the Searchlight 62
   TRANSLATED BY GEOFFREY WINTHROP-YOUNG

3. Fragments of a History of Firearms 69
   TRANSLATED BY MICHAEL WUTZ

4. Tanks 73
   TRANSLATED BY MICHAEL WUTZ

Part II: Wires, Waves, and Wagner

5. Noises of War 79
   TRANSLATED BY MICHAEL WUTZ

6. Playback: A World War History of Radio Drama 91
   TRANSLATED BY MICHAEL WUTZ

7. Operation Valhalla 110
   TRANSLATED BY GEOFFREY WINTHROP-YOUNG

8. When the Blitzkrieg Raged 117
   TRANSLATED BY GEOFFREY WINTHROP-YOUNG

Part III: Vanishing Animals and Returning Nomads

9 Animals of War: A Historical Bestiary 123
TRANSLATED BY GEOFFREY WINTHROP-YOUNG

10 On Modern Warfare: A Conversation with Alexander Kluge 127
TRANSLATED BY GEOFFREY WINTHROP-YOUNG

11 Of States and Their Terrorists 136
TRANSLATED BY GEOFFREY WINTHROP-YOUNG

Part IV: Love and War

12 Manners of Death in War 151
TRANSLATED BY MICHAEL WUTZ

13 Ottilie Hauptmann 166
TRANSLATED BY ILINCA IURASCU

Part V: Pynchon's War

14 On a Novel That Would Not Only Be Fiction . . . 193
TRANSLATED BY MICHAEL WUTZ

15 De Nostalgia 198
TRANSLATED BY GEOFFREY WINTHROP-YOUNG

16 Media and Drugs in Pynchon's Second World War 211
TRANSLATED BY MICHAEL WUTZ

Part VI: Kittler on Kittler

17 Biogeography 227
TRANSLATED BY GEOFFREY WINTHROP-YOUNG

18 Theology 233
TRANSLATED BY GEOFFREY WINTHROP-YOUNG

Notes 235

Bibliography 273

Index 287

Credits 295

Editors' Preface

ILINCA IURASCU, GEOFFREY WINTHROP-YOUNG, AND MICHAEL WUTZ

Operation Valhalla is a selection of texts by Friedrich Kittler (1943–2011) written over the course of almost thirty years that focus on the intersection of war and media. They deal with weapons development, the evolution of tactics, military hardware, advances in army communications, the literary mobilization of gendered subjects, the technological conditions of terrorist activities, and deposits of war in music and literature. Addressing different audiences, they vary in length and format, ranging from public lectures, op-ed pieces, and handbook entries to autobiographical musings, detailed literary analyses, and a conversation with theorist and filmmaker Alexander Kluge. Of the eighteen texts assembled here, six have already appeared in English. Of the remaining twelve, two—"Manners of Death in War" and "Playback: A World War History of Radio Drama"—have never before appeared in print and are here both published and translated into English for the first time.[1]

Given the high profile of the topic, in particular the discussion of how cyberwar, netwar, and the ongoing mobilization of the divisive impact of social media force us to reconceptualize the nexus of war and media, we think of *Operation Valhalla* as a collection that contributes to current discussions. Kittler is tackling a host of timely and troublesome issues. Much of what he says about weapons and wars, and about World War II and the Third Reich in particular, is both highly topical and strikingly original, yet some of it, as so often in his work, is dubious, if not downright disturbing. We therefore adopted a proactive editorial procedure. First, this collection contains an extensive introduction. In fairness to Kittler, a quick summary of the texts will not do, especially one that comes with critical objections. Though Kittler was neither a professional soldier nor a military historian, he was a lifelong aficionado who acquired an in-depth knowledge of Prussian and German military matters. To explain, extend, and occasionally challenge his analyses, it is necessary to go into detail and meet him, as far as possible, on his own ground.

Second, we reconnoitered and invaded the texts more than is usually the case, but we believe there are good reasons for doing so. While some of the essays in this collection are immediately accessible (e.g., "Free Ways," "A Short History of the Searchlight," and the conversation with Alexander Kluge), others (such as the autobiographical essay "Biogeography," the short piece "Tanks," and "Ottilie Hauptmann") are densely packed with arcane names, puns, and allusions that will be accessible to only a thin slice of specialized German(ist) readers. Then, there is the case of "Playback: A World War History of Radio Drama," which exists in a longer German manuscript version and a truncated and reconfigured version in Kittler's English. We compared the two texts and assembled them into a new English variant that seeks to capture accurately the substance and spirit of both. Finally, we herded the essays into thematically oriented sections and breached the individual texts with editorial notes to make sure that no reader is left too far behind.

On occasion Kittler revised texts that originally had little to do with war or with military matters. The prime example is the "Ottilie Hauptmann" essay. First published in 1977, it started out as a discourse-analytical reading of the ways in which Goethe's novel *Elective Affinities* addresses the intersection of motherhood, love, and education. For its republication in 1991, however, Kittler inserted long sections on military telegraphy and the German Wars of Liberation against Napoleon without changing the original portions. As a result, it becomes difficult to tell where Kittler draws the line between love and war, education and mobilization, or the marital and the martial—if indeed he draws any at all. To illustrate this weaponization and allow readers a glimpse into Kittler's mode of operation, we used different fonts to highlight the martial portions added in 1991.

Third, the mistakes: Kittler connoisseurs know that he specializes in two types of inaccuracy. There is the simple a.k.a. honest blunder: an incorrect date, a faulty name, a misremembered song. As a teacher, Kittler could be surprisingly indulgent when it came to allowing his students to develop their own ideas and interests, but he could be quite unforgiving when it came to factual inaccuracies, also and especially in matters historical and military. "I have always tried to introduce criteria," he stated in an interview, "to determine what is not true, what is the result of sloppy research, and what is wrong. For instance, I will, as it were, slap the face of anybody in my seminar who claims that the Red Army reached Berlin in 1941."[2] However, Kittler produced his own share of slips and snafus. In minor cases we tacitly corrected the text without further ado.

But then there are mistakes that appear to have method to them. Take a Kittler trademark, the creatively enhanced quote. He will (mis)cite a source in ways that tend to align it with his own argument. For instance, in *Untimely Meditations* an exasperated Friedrich Nietzsche dismisses his fellow human beings as "thinking-, writing- and speaking-machines" (*Redemaschinen*).[3] The younger Kittler was fond of this quote, yet occasionally the "Redemaschinen" are promoted to "*Rechenmaschinen*," or calculating machines.[4] The epigraph at the beginning of *Gramophone, Film, Typewriter*, in turn, is taken from Thomas Pynchon's *Gravity's Rainbow*: "Tap my head and mike my brain / Stick that needle in my vein." In the original German edition, *tap* appears as *tape*. A mere slip? Maybe. Yet in both cases the sloppiness serves to update the source. Nietzsche is fast-forwarded into the Turing age of computing machines, and Pynchon's ditty now supports the link between analog technology and cerebral functions analyzed in *Gramophone, Film, Typewriter*. Or, to move from quotes to gaffes: in the lecture "Of States and Their Terrorists" (contained in this volume), Kittler repeatedly describes Rudyard Kipling's eponymous hero Kim as a "half blood" with an Indian mother. In the novel, however, Kim, the son of Kimball O'Hara and Annie Shott, is clearly identified as having a full-European heritage; indeed, the whole story hinges on the fact that the pseudonative proto-spy Kim is not Indian. But Kittler's mistake supports his argument: the growing indistinguishability between the armies of the imperial nation-states and old or new nomadic collectives becomes all the more apparent if both sides start to merge on an ethnic level.

At times Kittler's gaffes can take on a slightly obsessive character. In the following introduction, the section "Pynchon's Rocket" will deal with one of the most prominent and revealing items, which appears in *Gramophone, Film, Typewriter* as well as in the autobiographical essay "Biogeography." It is the factually incorrect claim that an early German computer, Konrad Zuse's Z4, was used for the construction of the V-2 rocket. Ultimately, it is a wishful mistake that sheds light on one of the central motives of Kittler's martial theorizing. In short, Friedrich Kittler the writer was prone to display some of the habits that Friedrich Kittler the analyst attributed to writers of the "Discourse Network 1800" like Goethe and Hegel, who at times grandiloquently bungled or creatively enhanced quotes in self-serving ways.

We realize that our notes and procedures may strike some as know-it-all gotcha politics, but the bottom line is that these questionable items are no less part and parcel of Kittler's work than his remarkable insights. Both are linked to a strong personal interest that occasionally borders on the obsessive. Unlike some, Kittler was fully aware of his own error-prone stubbornness; unlike many, he had no difficulties admitting it. As he pointed out in a letter to one of the editors, referring to himself in the third person, "Kittler errs quite often, but because he is fascinated by something."[5]

We would like to thank our series editors, John Armitage and Ryan Bishop, for their support and patience. We are indebted to Christiane Bacher, Devin Fore, Tania Hron, Sandrina Khaled, Alexander Kluge, Sandra Korn, Charlene McCombs, and Beata Wiggen. Our special thanks go to Susanne Holl for her generous encouragement and for granting the rights to Kittler's texts.

Introduction
The Wars of Friedrich Kittler

GEOFFREY WINTHROP-YOUNG

In the beginning was the war. The greatest and deadliest on record, it transcended its own boundaries and refused to end even after it was over. Unprecedented in scope, it defied the strategies of combatants just as it came to defy the explanations of historians. It began with confident plans to secure rapid regional victories by means of lightning strikes and decisive battles but soon grew into a global conflict of grinding attrition. Afterward, in so-called peace, efforts to understand the war were marked by equally confident narratives designed to seal off the past with definitive accounts, but they, too, were eroded by the growing awareness of the more complex dimensions of the conflict. As a result, this war, World War II, has come to resemble an undead monster that disturbs the living because it was not properly buried. The essays in this volume were written by a man convinced that the hidden history of World War II has not yet come to light. His texts revolve around the claim that we need to access the war's deeper layers that so far have been neglected—either because we lacked the proper means of understanding them or because those layers were concealed under more opportune narratives.

Friedrich Adolf Kittler was born in Rochlitz in the vicinity of Dresden on June 12, 1943, roughly four months after the German defeat at Stalingrad, less than a year before the invasion of Normandy, and almost exactly on the day Anglo-American forces first breached the soft underbelly of Adolf Hitler's "Fortress Europe" by crossing over from North Africa to Sicily. There is an ongoing debate among military historians over at what point Germany was no longer able to win the war. Was it the Battle of Kiev that delayed the advance on Moscow? The Battle of Moscow that put an end to all blitzkrieg operations and forced Germany to wage a deep war for which it lacked the necessary resources? Or the split offensive of 1942 that broke down in Stalingrad and the Caucasus? But then again, does it make sense to succumb to the "allure of battle" and foreground clashes and campaigns as decisive turning points?[1] Is it realistic to assume that Germany could ever have won? In any case, Kittler's early childhood was overshadowed by defeat, and those days remained with him. Sixty years after the fact, he claimed to dimly recall "the fires of Dresden" of the air raids of February 13–15, 1945.[2] If true, it would be a remarkable feat of memory, but even if it is one of his taller tales, it remains a revealing pseudoreminiscence.

The undead war set the future literature and media scholar on his path. In a book-length interview Kittler recounts that his father, a teacher barred until 1953 by the new Socialist regime, took to lecturing his sons instead, with the result that at the tender age of seven Kittler was able to recite long passages from Goethe's *Faust* by heart. At the same time, his elder half-brother, a former wireless operator, assembled illegal radios using parts scavenged from abandoned military aircraft in order to impress the local girls.[3] Thus the basic binaries and building blocks of Kittler's later work were already in place: Goethe versus gadgets, high classicism versus modern communications technology, the ensnaring and imprinting of young children by humanist discourse versus the abuse of army equipment for entertainment purposes. Not to mention that so-called history is best understood as a sequence of changing epistemo-technical regimes in which women inspire men to do something with media.

Maybe it all boils down to the right preposition. Kittler was not born *during* but *into* the war, and the question is whether he ever got out of it. As in the case of his theoretical brother-in-arms Paul Virilio, World War II ricochets through large portions of his work. Like Virilio, Kittler was prone to project the impact of his childhood war back into the past, thus turning war into a transhistorical driving force. As a result, *war* is one of the most overdetermined words in Kittler's writings. It is less a clearly defined term than a dirty semantic bomb that wreaks conceptual havoc. Kittler's *war* is almost as confusing as Kittler's *media*: what does the word mean when it is supposed to mean so much?

The following remarks aim to provide signposts and markers for the war-related essays in this collection.[4] The next section will sketch a basic triple-M model, arguing that in Kittler's martially oriented texts war figures as *motor*, *model*, and *motivation*. This tripartition, however, is little more than a heuristic triage to provisionally separate layers in order to gain access to Kittler's war universe. Very soon, motor and model will flow into each other to the point of indistinguishability. The following sections trace a more historical trajectory by working through the primarily German wars that feature prominently in this collection. Indeed, reading Kittler, you may well doubt whether there ever was a serious war that did not involve Germany and the Germans. Though he will now and then leave his native domain and pay his respects to the chariot charges of Megiddo ("Animals of War") or the machine-gun massacres of Omdurman and Port Arthur ("A Short History of the Searchlight"), in the end it all will come down to the great German three: the Prussian Wars of Liberation against Napoleon, World War I, and World War II. The introduction's third section ("Discourse Nation") will center on the age of Napoleon, with special emphasis on Heinrich von Kleist's controversial play *The Battle of Hermann*, while the fourth section ("Social Word Wars") aims to connect the discourse mobilization of wars past with the mobilized discourse fragmentation brought about by social media in wars present. The next two sections will address some of the more troubling and personal aspects of this collection by focusing on World War II ("Blitzkrieg Nation" and "Missile Subjects"). The end point—in some ways, the point zero of Kittler's war-related texts—is the V-2 rocket, which is at the center of the seventh section ("Pynchon's Rocket"). The concluding section ("The Benefits of Defeat") returns to the triple-M model by delving into the question of motive. Why war? More to the hidden point: Why so much war by a *German* theorist?

Motor and Model: From the Medial a Priori of War to the Martial a Priori of Media

In Kittler's most martial utterances, war is the motor, the determining base of media history. Wars are "in truth and fact the historical a priori" of modern media; hence, "the unwritten history of technical norms is a history of war."[5] If wars determine media, and media, in turn, "determine our situation," war emerges as the prime mover of history.[6] Periods of peace are blank pages in the combat manual of history.

Upon closer inspection, this martial a priori turns blurry. On the one hand, we read that "media were developed for technological wars."[7] Kittler's prime exhibits include, among others, the mechanical telegraph installed in 1794 by the revolutionary French government under siege from coalition forces, and the computer, the universal discrete machine that crossed over from Alan Turing's mind into technical reality as a means to crack the encoded German Enigma communications. On the other hand, Kittler provides a detailed account of the nonmartial origins of radio technology, only to add: "A world war, the first of its kind, had to break out to facilitate the switch from Poulsen's arc transmission to Lieben or De Forest's tube-type technology and the mass production of Fessenden's experimental procedure."[8] War, then, is either the inception or the puberty of new media technologies, their original breeding ground or the point when they come into their own.

Two circumstances inform this martial a priori. First, there is an obvious element of provocation. At times, the explanatory value of war as a determining agent in history is less important than its rhetorical shock value. In an attempt to explain to an American audience the very un-American origins of so-called German media theory (which in its earliest stage was a Freiburg media theory), Bernhard Siegert emphasized that when Kittler and those inspired by his work spoke of media, they did not have in mind the mass media located within the so-called public sphere. Nor were they interested in socially oriented content analysis, the politics of meaning, or the economics of media ownership. Instead, the focus was on "insignificant, unprepossessing technologies that underlie the constitution of meaning" and thus form an "abyss of non-meaning."[9] Siegert calls this abyss "war." It is a sinister entity; it conceals itself by providing the very means necessary for it to be overlooked and forgotten by those who draw on its resources. The abyss of nonmeaning enables the emergence of self-entitled, meaningful subjects who place themselves in the center of a sphere of enlightened communication, created by the users for the users, conceived in the spirit of liberty, and dedicated to the proposition that all users are or should be equal: "To invoke the 'public sphere' entailed ideas such as enlightened consciousness, self-determination, freedom, and so on, while to speak of 'war' implied an unconscious processed by symbolic media as well as the notion that 'freedom' was a kind of narcissism associated with the Lacanian mirror stage."[10]

War, then, is less opposed to peace than to all that is conjured up by emphatic or humanist notions of *communication*. Within the specific West German postwar context Siegert has in mind, war references everything that the canonized Frankfurt Critical Theory of Max Horkheimer and Theodor W. Adorno, Jürgen Habermas's *The Theory of Communicative Action*, and almost all media studies programs appeared unwilling to address. Any proper study of media and communication presupposes an analysis of the dirty matters and cold materialities those communication acts emerged from. To phrase this confrontational redirection from human communication to technological communications in martial Kittlerese, if you don't want to talk about war, quit talking about media.

In retrospect, the attractiveness of this approach resembled the appeal of hard-core Marxist analyses from earlier decades. The similarities are too obvious to be coincidental. At the center was a radical reductionism that related pesky matters of culture, history, and ideology, all located within a self-important but ultimately derivative superstructure, to an underlying determining base characterized by escalating conflicts. In both cases, theory practitioners rejected bourgeois blather about peace and consensus to engage with the gritty and unsentimental operations of real life. In both cases, there was a secularized eschatology at work that pointed ahead to some (social) revolution or (technological) takeoff that would fundamentally change what it means to be human. At the core of these future events is a promise of sublation or at least dedifferentiation: just as social divisions will give way to a classless society, technical differentiations of storage, processes, and communication will be standardized and united in the digital machine. And in both cases a disproportionate number of discourse adopters were male.

Second, the foregrounding of war is a methodological move to address a basic quandary related to Kittler's update of Michel Foucault's *The Order of Things*, a book that was to Kittler (just like Thomas Pynchon's *Gravity's Rainbow*) a combination of revelation, playground, and toolbox—in short, a drug. The archaeological Foucault, a creature very different from the later genealogical, biopolitical, and ethical Foucaults that were of less appeal to Kittler, had traced a grand panorama of epistemic snapshots. Unconnected to each other, one epistemic regime after the other had taken control of European orders of speech by imposing distinct conditions of truthfulness. Foucault sliced the history of thought into discrete segments, which were then subjected to a cold "outside" gaze directed at their internal dynamics. Kittler was enchanted. All hegemonic continualist, gradualist, or progressivist notions of history were suspended. The usual grand subjects of Western historiography (progressive enlightenment, secularization, modernism, the working class, and all the other protagonists of Whiggish master narratives) were deprived of the opportunity to grow, mature, and occupy center stage. The ultimate target of Foucault's archaeology was, of course, Hegel's *Geist*, which consumes all of history in order to produce itself—unless, that is, you conceive of the Hegelian world spirit as a performance artist in the mold of David Bowie, who periodically reinvents himself from scratch.

Kittler grounded these Foucauldian epistemes in "discourse networks," defined as the "network of technologies and institutions that allow a given culture to select, store and process relevant data."[11] Not only was this an ingenious technological and infrastructural update designed to push Foucault's somewhat stuffy world of archives and libraries into the wired domain of circuits and data, but it also seemed to cure Foucauldian archaeology of its puzzling preference for immaculate conceptions. Foucault's orders of discourse are structures that drop in out of the blue; there is no rhyme or reason to the random ways in which they appear and disappear. Kittler had found the answer: epistemes change because the underlying discourse networks—composed of an infrastructure of media technologies, cultural techniques, and practices—change. But that, of course, is not really an answer; it merely serves to defer the question. If discursive orders change because discourse networks change, then what makes the latter change?[12] One answer is war.

To grasp what is at stake, we will briefly pursue a comparison that may be helpful because it appears so far-fetched. It is frequently pointed out that *The Order of Things*, first published in 1966, appeared only four years after Thomas Kuhn's *The Structure of Scientific Revolutions*. Temporal proximity indicates conceptual similarity: Foucault's epistemes and Kuhn's paradigms are not that distinct from each other. But there is a more intriguing comparison. Six years after the appearance of *The Order of Things*, paleontologists Niles Eldredge and Stephen Jay Gould published the first of many papers in which they argued for a revision of Darwinian evolutionary dynamics they called "punctuated equilibrium."[13] The evolution of species, they claimed, proceeded much like the proverbial life of a soldier, with long periods of boredom or "stasis" interrupted by short bursts of intense activity. Evolution is a branching river that runs through calm pools and brief turbulent rapids. A species can remain stable for a long time, but especially under stressful conditions nature presses her finger on the fast-forward button, and species transformation occurs at a rapid pace.

The similarities to Foucault/Kittler are intriguing. Indeed, it is an instance of convergent evolution, because just as taxonomically widely divergent marine predators like dolphins, sharks, and ichthyosaurs evolved deceptively similar body shapes while occupying similar habitats, widely different disciplines produce similar solutions when exposed to similar pressures. Up against the orthodoxy of uniformitarianism, which decreed that evolution is a slow, incremental process with no distinct change of pace or sudden large-scale transformations, Gould and Eldredge could not retreat into discredited, old-style catastrophism, but they did the next best thing. They replaced singular, genetically indefensible macromutations—known to insiders as "hopeful monsters"—with the less scandalous acceleration of micromutations. *Natura non facit saltus* (nature does not jump), but it does go into sudden overdrive. Species transform and radiate at speeds that, when compared to the glacial pace at which they normally drift along, make these transformations appear almost like ruptures. And—an important corollary—how evolution works will be much more evident when studying these bursts of accelerated change.

This is how war tends to function in many of Kittler's texts. Wars are periods of intense acceleration of technological change that interrupt periods of relative stasis. They are not inexplicable or "catastrophist" Foucauldian ruptures, but they are the next best thing: periods of high-speed transformation that allow observers to detect technological continuities in what appear to be abrupt discontinuities. To exaggerate for the sake of clarity, war itself is a modern media technology because, like a sped-up film that shows the seasonal growing and withering of a plant in twenty seconds, it speeds up what normally progresses at a much slower rate, thus allowing us to observe what otherwise is widely dispersed across time and space. Modern war is, to use one of Kittler's favorite words, the "cleartext" of history because it reveals otherwise obscured technological dynamics. The underlying logic, which applies to paleontology as much as to media studies, is that acceleration may act as a conceptual replacement for catastrophes. But you do not have to study accelerationist manifestos to realize that once acceleration is the only thing left because there are no longer any periods of stasis and deceleration, acceleration itself *is* the catastrophe.

Wars, then, reveal how technologies engage each other in compressed time and independent of social surroundings. They appear to be increasingly closed systems in which systemic features react to each other rather than to external input. Kittler's telegraphy sequence, bits and pieces of which will surface in several of the following texts, including the weaponized second version of "Ottilie Hauptmann," may serve as an example. At the height of the Reign of Terror, while at war with most of Europe, the French Revolution installs the first mechanical telegraph, which just a few years later will enable Napoleon to coordinate his troop movements in ways that defy the communication abilities of his enemies. The advantage is short-lived, as the mechanical telegraph accelerates the development of superior electric telegraphy. Semaphores are superseded by wires and cables, which in combination with adjacent railroad tracks will allow the

Prussian Army to outmaneuver its Austrian and French opponents in 1866 and 1871, respectively. On the very first day of World War I, however, the British Navy will cut the German transatlantic cables. The vulnerability of physical cables, in turn, will force the military repurposing of early wireless tinkering, which in a further spiral will necessitate the design of increasingly sophisticated encryption and decryption technologies, until, as Kittler (quoting a British wiretapping agent) writes in "Playback," all parties intercept "pages of letters, letters in arbitrary sequence without rhyme or reason. That is the order of things. There is no plain text anywhere." Hot and cold war combatants will resort to transmitting noise and gibberish because they all know they will be intercepted. Ruptures and catastrophes are the social effects of accelerated military time that will allow technologically savvy observers to compress wars into each other and thus explain media change. While Kittler may not be subject to the aforementioned allure of the decisive battle, he does submit to the allure of the decisive technological clash. If the many accounts of war that focus on the gore and glory of combat have been described as a kind of historical pornography, Kittler indulges in a pornography of war technology.

But does this make war the motor of history? When read more closely, Kittler's war-centered narrative reveals a more moderate heuristic stance: "When the development of a media subsystem is analyzed in all its historical breadth..., the... suspicion arises that technical innovations—following the model of military escalation—only refer to and answer to each other, and the result of this proprietary development, which progresses completely independent of individual or even collective bodies of people, is an overwhelming impact on sense and organs in general."[14] Here, "military escalation" is a "model" rather than an empirical driver of history. Media are not "in truth and fact" propelled by war; they evolve *like* war. War is model and metaphor rather than causative agent. This modeling of media evolution on the history of war implies that media react to each other in an ongoing game of positioning or one-upmanship in much the same way that strategies, tactics, and weapons systems produce alternate strategies, countertactics, and superior weapons.

However, this moderating movement from motor to model serves to turn the martial a priori of media into its even darker opposite: *the medial a priori of war*. The media-technologically facilitated access to domains and bandwidths beyond the reach of normal human perception results in the emergence of new enemies or new ways of fighting old enemies. *Media evolution is first and foremost the expansion of war and enmity.* Antonie van

Leeuwenhoek invents a single-lens microscope, and what does he discover? All kinds of hostile microorganisms we need to combat or at least deploy against other microscope owners. We intercept radio waves, including those from outer space, and what do we really expect to hear? Hostile signals that need to be decoded. Or you can go all the way back to Oswald Spengler's *Man and Technics*. Humans developed the hand as a "weapon" with which they performed a hostile turn on nature. It is the twisted Caliban logic of media progress: we teach ourselves language, and we use it to curse.

As noted at the outset, constructs like the martial a priori of media, the medial a priori of war, or war as either the motor or the model of media history are at best heuristic devices with limited use value and shelf life. They are neither the building blocks of Kittler's theory nor the cornerstones of a critical analysis. Kittler was in many ways a nineteenth-century creature; that is, he was hardwired to ferret out the history and the determining logic of a diachronic sequence. It is advisable, therefore, to switch to a more historically oriented account of his martial musings. Once again, and despite the attempted domestication of Foucault's discursive catastrophism, the story will begin with a disaster.

Discourse Nation: Of Mobilized Men and Dismembered Women

For readers unfamiliar with German literature, this section may present a bit of a challenge. Suffice it to say that at the center of the following remarks is the maverick author Heinrich von Kleist (1777–1811). The scion of a well-known Pomeranian family that specialized in supplying officers to every possible regime in over three hundred years of Prusso-German history, Kleist is the great odd man out in German letters. Kleist knew war and, more important for our purposes, defeat in war. He served in the Prussian Army from 1792 to 1799, and his masterpiece *The Prince of Homburg* (unfortunately not discussed in any great detail by Kittler) is without a doubt the greatest military play ever written. Kleist also knew defeat in writing. His name was long overshadowed by the well-engineered profile of the more respectable authors who came to define the world of letters as much as Napoleon came to embody his age of war—most notably, the canonized classics Goethe and Schiller. Times and reputations have changed. Maybe the greatness of Schiller now rests in part on the fact that he produced material Kleist came to challenge.

In 1808 Kleist wrote *The Battle of Hermann*, a timely and topical play of grotesque martial frenzy. Flanked by Friedrich Schiller's *Wilhelm Tell* and

Thomas Pynchon's *Gravity's Rainbow*, it is the centerpiece of the literary triptych in Kittler's essay "De Nostalgia," chapter 15 in this volume, which explores the war-driven construction and "deconstruction" of *Heimat*, or homeland.[15] We will tackle Pynchon later; this section focuses on problems contained in the progress from *Tell* to *Hermann* within the context of the so-called German Wars of Liberation. The Schiller-Kleist sequence makes a lot of sense, for *Hermann* is a countertext, as it were, to *Tell*; it reads as if Schiller's play had been rewritten by Quentin Tarantino. *Tell* stages the well-known story of the iconic Swiss marksman who kills the tyrannical Habsburg stooge Gessler because the latter forced him to shoot an apple off his son's head. This private act of revenge takes place alongside a public uprising against the Austrian oppressors. The insurgency, or at least Schiller's version thereof, is a distinctly Swiss affair: clean, measured, orderly, and not sullied by undue violence and politicizing. In other words, it is not French. There are no guillotines, massacres, or predatory crusades in the alleged service of universal ideals. It is a sober, upright, and above all restorative rebellion carried out by a happy band of paleoconservative brothers. The Swiss simply want to oust their foreign oppressors and return to the old way of life. There is no talk of marching on Vienna, killing all Austrians, and establishing a Greater Helvetian Reich stretching from the Matterhorn to Moscow. The Swiss don't do that. Or rather, as Kittler reminds us, they only do it as homesick mercenaries in the employ of others.[16]

Kleist's *Hermann* is a different beast. The background story is as famous as the Swiss apple shot. In 9 CE a Roman army composed of three legions under the command of Publius Quinctilius Varus was ambushed and massacred by a motley coalition of Germanic tribes led by the Cherusci chieftain Arminius. So traumatic was the "Varian Disaster" that in a singular symbolic gesture the Roman Army—much like a hockey team bidding farewell to a star player by retiring his number and hanging his jersey from the rafters—never reconstituted the three annihilated legions XVII, XVIII, and XIX. Rome gave up on all plans to expand its empire eastward across the Rhine into Magna Germania, thus laying the groundwork for the continental Germanic-Romance divide and all the centuries of trouble that arose from it.

In the sixteenth century, Arminius was given the German name Hermann (which informally translates as "army guy"), and he rapidly mutated into a national German role model that could be reactivated under the most disparate historical circumstances. For Kleist, the historical parallels were obvious. The late reign of Augustus prefigures the tyranny of Napoleon; the year 9 is the year 1808 minus cannons and muskets. The squabbling Germanic tribes subdued by the Romans correspond to the petty German dukedoms and kingdoms that have come under French rule, including Kleist's own Prussia; the Suevi under Marbod, with whom Hermann is keen to form an alliance, represent Austria (at this point not yet conquered by Napoleon); and the Romans themselves are the French under their Corsican Augustus. Things are not going well in Magna Germania. The Franco-Romans are pushing eastward, yet even if the bickering Germanic tribes get their act together, there will be little chance of military success. As Hermann bluntly tells his fellow chieftains, if they, "a rabble horde / emerging from the trees," were to pit themselves "against well-ordered cohorts / Accompanied wherever they go by that unfailing fighting spirit," German defeat would be assured.[17] This is why Hermann plans not to emerge from the trees in the first place but to lure the Romans into the woods and pounce on them in the dark. Not very heroic, to be sure, but effective. The tactical problem is solved, but how do you equip the tribes with the right "unfailing fighting spirit" to match that of the Romans?

Underneath its antique veneer Kleist's play is probing the problems and perils of collective mobilization, an issue of cardinal importance for Kittler's assessment of the cultural role and impact of modern war. As indicated by Kittler, Kleist's ruthless reflection on the new shape of war in the age of Napoleon is best illustrated by comparing his play to the tidy rebellion of *Wilhelm Tell*. No Swiss insurgent, empirical or thought up by Schiller, ever exhorted his countrymen to burn their villages to the ground, or bludgeon their cows to death with alphorns, in order to deprive the invaders of resources. But that is precisely what Hermann asks his fellow chieftains to do:

> Melt all the gold and silver dishes
> You possess, take your pearls and jewels
> And sell them off or pawn them,
> Lay waste to your lands, slaughter
> Your cattle, set fire to your camps[18]

The idea does not catch on. "But, you madman," replies a perplexed chieftain, "these are the very things / That we are fighting this war to defend!" Hermann's laconic response: "Forgive me, I thought it was for your freedom."[19] Unlike his less committed peers, Hermann has taken Janis Joplin to heart: freedom's just another word for nothin' left to lose, so it is better to destroy all the material possessions that otherwise would keep you from gaining freedom.

Hermann realizes that his war must begin with words that divide and unite, sow doubt and enrage minds. To rile up his followers and create the right fighting spirit, he weaponizes communication in the shape of tactically deployed fake news. When he is informed by messengers that the Romans have plundered three settlements, he tells them to spread the word that they plundered seven. When messengers report that Roman legionnaires killed an infant, Hermann commands that it be known that the father was murdered as well. When word comes that the Romans mistakenly felled an oak sacred to Wotan, Hermann responds he "was told / That the Romans even forced their prisoners / To kneel in dust to Zeus, their dreadful god!"[20] The confused messengers fail to grasp why Hermann is ordering them to spread such exaggerations, so one of his henchmen has to pull them aside to explain the logic behind their leader's 8chan rhetoric. At times, the stressed Hermann voices his frustration that his followers are too thickheaded to understand his propaganda campaign: "What aurochs the Germans are!"[21]

The symbolic core event is act 4, scene 6. Hermann encounters the smith Teuthold ("gracious German"), who killed his daughter, Hally, because she was raped by Roman soldiers—allegedly, we must add, since the play keeps the door wide open for the possibility that Hally was raped by Germanic tribesmen ordered by Hermann to dress up as Romans and "scorch, burn and plunder," or maybe even by Hermann himself.[22] In any case, he issues a command to the father that will set the land ablaze with anti-Roman hatred. Since Germania comprises fifteen different tribes, Teuthold is told to cut his daughter's body into fifteen parts:

> Divide her body accordingly, and by fifteen messengers,
> I'll give you fifteen horses for this, send the parts
> To each of the fifteen tribes of Germany.
> Helping you to your revenge, the corpse will rouse
> Across Germany even the most inanimate elements.
> The storm winds howling through the woods
> Will shriek Revenge! And the sea beating
> The ribs of the coast will shout Freedom![23]

Kleist, who never came across an interesting idea he did not twist and throttle to squeeze out its most radical consequence, glimpsed the genocidal potential contained within the collective mobilization of negative affect. Enmity of this intensity cannot settle for expulsion; it will pursue extermination. While Schiller's Swiss patriots are content to evict the Austrians from their home turf, Hermann's final words reveal his greater ambitions. If the Romans send us their rapists, we will send our death squads to Rome:

> We or our descendants, my brothers!
> Because the world will have no peace
> From this murderous brood
> Until we have fully destroyed the outlaw's lair,
> And nothing remains but a black flag
> Fluttering over its desolate ruins![24]

As Kittler points out in "De Nostalgia" and other essays, this is the world of Hitler, Joseph Goebbels, and Carl Schmitt. Hermann's insistence that his fellow tribesmen lay waste to their land anticipates Hitler's "Nero Decree" of March 19, 1945, ordering the wholesale destruction of the German industrial infrastructure in the face of the Allied advance. The snarling equation of freedom and revenge contains the core point of Goebbels's post-Stalingrad total-war rhetoric. Finally, to label Rome an "outlaw's lair" points to Schmitt's critique of the modern "discriminating concept of war."[25] At issue is not only the envisaged absolute destruction of a collective rather than of a mere army but also the fact that it is preceded by an act of universalist hypocrisy, which Kittler in his 2003 lecture "Of States and Their Terrorists" attributes to the post-9/11 government of George W. Bush. Hermann, whom the Romans no doubt view as a tribal terrorist, in turn declares Rome to be a *hostis humani generis*, an enemy of all humankind, or an "outlaw" state that has removed itself from the pale of humanity and hence does not deserve to be treated as a moral equal. The march on Rome will not be a symmetrical war but an exterminating police action, a war on Roman terror. *The Battle of Hermann* is the first text to spell out the ultimately genocidal paradox that the more people resolve in the spirit of freedom and self-determination to take control of their own wars, the more these wars will depend on the preemptive dehumanization of the enemy.

The play did not catch on until the late nineteenth century (and it enjoyed a good run in the Third Reich); the first, solitary performance took place more than twenty-five years after Kleist's suicide. But while it did not participate in the spiritual mobilization envisaged by its author, it lays out the main problems that inform Kittler's discourse-historical analyses. With *Hermann* in mind, we can move from fictional battles to real ones to show how the consequences of the latter were processed by the former.

On October 14, 1806, the Prussian Army was routed by the French at the twin Battle of Jena-Auerstedt. "I've never seen men so completely beaten,"

Napoleon gloated.²⁶ The vanquished agreed. Carl von Clausewitz, who would spend the rest of his life trying to assemble the traumatic friction of Napoleonic warfare into a theory of war, lamented that the Prussian Army, hamstrung by "the most extreme poverty of the imagination . . . , was ruined more completely than any army had ever been ruined on the battlefield."²⁷ How thoroughly Prussia had been defeated was best captured by Cornelia Vismann in her study *Files: Law and Media Technology*. Between Jena-Auerstedt and the humiliating Treaty of Tilsit, signed on July 9, 1807, the usually hyperproductive Prussian state archive produced a paltry twenty-one files.²⁸ Catastrophes *in mundo* cause atrophies *in actis*.

Vismann's reference to the precipitous decline in bureaucratic activities points to one of the great myths of Prussian history. The story goes that, following its defeat, Prussia was rebooted by a phalanx of farsighted civil and military officials. Nothing was left untouched as a slew of social, agricultural, financial, constitutional, administrative, educational, and military reforms gushed forth from the pens of Baron vom und zum Stein, Karl August von Hardenberg, Wilhelm von Humboldt, Gerhard von Scharnhorst, August Neidhart von Gneisenau, and other illustrious names that came to grace German boulevards and battle cruisers. Prussia emerged as the prime exhibit of bureaucratic efficiency. Its rise from the ashes of Napoleon to the glories of Otto von Bismarck and the elder Helmuth von Moltke appears to prove what many doubt: that civil servants can get things done.

Hans-Ulrich Wehler, the late doyen of German social history, warned that this "colossal gilt frame painting" has a very tenuous relationship to historical reality.²⁹ Christopher Clark, author of *Iron Kingdom*, voiced similar reservations. The notion that modern Prussia sprang Athena-like from the foreheads of illustrious civil servants in the wake of October 14, 1806, ignores that these reforms were just "one energetic episode within a *longue durée* of Prussian administrative change between the 1790s and the 1840s."³⁰ Other German states such as Baden, Württemberg, and Bavaria passed through similar periods of intensified bureaucratic reform with more substantial results, yet their bureaucrats have not ended up on the pedestal erected for the Prussian state intelligentsia.

There is an obvious reason for this skewed treatment. German historiography was long dominated by Prussian academic historians, who, as patriotic civil servants, were inclined to extol the achievements of other Prussian civil servants. But there is a deeper reason. The post-1806 Prussian *Verwaltungswunder*, or administrative miracle, which is as questionable a myth as the post-1945 German *Wirtschaftswunder*, or economic miracle, seems to illustrate that it is possible to engineer all the benefits of a revolution without any of the political and social costs. Where the French took to the streets, the Prussians retreated to their offices. Catering to the old cliché that the Germans accomplish in theory what the French achieve in practice, bureaucratic master planning resulted in a "momentous revolution from above" with no less far-reaching consequences than the real revolution that had occurred on the other side of the Rhine.[31] Defeated by the French, the Prussians developed an almost French belief in the omnipotent ability of the state to bring about what the French themselves had been able to achieve only by destroying their system of government.

In German academese this is known as *Borussianismus*, an exaggerated appreciation of all things Prussian. Kittler, the Saxon, inherited his share, though his interest in the governmental revolution is highly selective. The social and economic domains—everything from agricultural reform and financial restructuring to administrative reorganization—are absent. He focuses, as in "Ottilie Hauptmann," on two areas, the military and educational, though the line that divides them is not always clear. The reason for this blurring is obvious: both are large-scale enterprises that increasingly depend on the mobilization of self-motivated subjects, be they soldiers or students—with the crucial addendum that in the case of the former the mobilized subjects are exclusively male, while in the latter a large, possibly determining portion of the mobilizing subjects are female. The two key issues are, first, the production of modern subjectivity (with all the attendant focus on initiative, self-reflexivity, autonomy, and "independent thought") and, second, the closely related production of gender differentiation.

First, the subject. Surveying the debris of Jena-Auerstedt, Prussian military planners realized the defeat could not be attributed solely to an unfortunate combination of superior French battlefield élan and Napoleon's military genius. The root cause was a catastrophic systems failure on the Prussian side, which demanded that the entire military apparatus be reshaped. There were a number of straightforward reforms, from adopting the Napoleonic corps system and allowing meritorious bourgeois to become officers to abolishing inhumane punishments like running the gauntlet and forming the famed Great General Staff, which occupies a privileged position in Kittler's personal pantheon and is granted cameo performances throughout this collection. But these measures are not sufficient, for they fail to address the cardinal problem: how Prussia and the Prussian Army can generate the effectiveness and motivational resources displayed by the French without undergoing the French social chaos—from a nation-building revolution to a *levée en masse*—which would effectively destroy the very monarchy they were trying to liberate.

The answer is radical; it amounts to a revolution folded inward. For the purposes of modern war, traditional underling-subjects have to be refashioned into modern citizen-subjects. Kittler's basic idea is that military reforms stressing initiative, reflection, and self-guidance are not simply an effect of, but contemporaneous with, if not even a blueprint for, the rise of modern self-reflective subjectivity. This is one of the most intriguing aspects of his polemo-centrism. In essence, it revolves around the paradox "that just when the mass of civilian workers became cogs in a vast industrial machine, the military machine was rolling in the opposite direction. Just when the worker became a cog, the soldier was recognized as an independent thinking cell."[32] In the Prusso-German context, this cellular martial independence is frequently enshrined in the concept of *mission tactics* (*Auftragstaktik*). Subordinate leaders are commanded to be in command. Entrusted with a considerable degree of freedom, they are ordered to carry out tactical orders on their own, which requires that they are trained to think on their own, develop their own initiative, plan all tactical details on their own, and react to changing circumstances without relying on a new set of orders from above. Frederick the Great's machine-soldiers (who have other machine-soldiers in their back programmed to shoot at them if they refuse to march into battle) become Gneisenau's martial subjects.

A necessary sidebar on mission tactics. Like *blitzkrieg* (more on which later), it is a loaded term that comes to Kittler's texts in questionable shape. It normally refers to general mission orders issued to lower ranks that do not spell out specifics but call on the subordinate commander's initiative and insight to flesh out the details. A lieutenant in the German army is ordered: Take that hill by tomorrow morning at 4:00 a.m. How you achieve the objective is your business (we are not the British, French, or Russian Army; we do not micromanage). You know the terrain and the particular section of the enemy best, so you plan the mission, determine and obtain the appropriate resources, and get on your way—though always keep in mind that the self-reliance and initiative your tactical foray depends on is part of a general strategy from which you cannot deviate. (Rephrased as a martial Kantian categorical imperative: Act in such a way that the will guiding your tactical operations, if promoted to a general level, could amount to an overall strategy.) But as noted by the editors of the English translation of the 1933/34 *Truppenführung* (*Unit Command*) handbook, the definitive German military manual, adorned with the Sun Tzu–inspired title *On the German Art of War*, this is a twentieth-century development: "Prior to World War I, the German Army operated under a principle known as *Weisungsführung* (leadership by directive), which was similar to *Auftragstaktik*, but only entrusted commanders down to the army level—or sometimes the corps—with broad discretionary powers in the execution their missions. *Auftragstaktik*, which was a post–World War I creation . . . extended that principle down to lowest squad leader and even, when necessary, to the individual soldier."[33]

It is a mistake, therefore, to assume that mission tactics—a term that did not even make it into the *German Art of War* manual—was applied to officers and soldiers of all ranks in the aftermath of Jena-Auerstedt. The older concept of Weisungsführung was limited to the very top, that is, to army or corps commanders, and in the traditional seventeenth- and eighteenth-century Prussian Army these were recruited from Junker nobility. Here, Kittler's determined neglect of social configurations misses out on something very interesting. Weisungsführung was not anything the army cooked up on its own; it was the military processing of a social division. The Junker nobility swore fealty to the king, who, in turn, granted them near-total dominance over their domain. "This relationship extended to the general's relationship with the troops under his command. Although they were not his property, they were bound to obey him, and he could launch them on any operation that he saw fit. For the king (or his deputy, the chief of his staff) to intervene in any detailed way in the military operations of his subordinate would have been to violate this arrangement and to call into question the sovereignty of the Prussian nobility."[34] This is a fascinating case of exchange between the social and the military. The army accepts a fundamental social configuration, which it then processes and, following Kittler, releases back into the social as a fundamental discursive reconfiguration.

Against the military background, then, reflexive subjectivity is the ability to perform under the paradoxical *command of a free will*. At his most war-centered, Kittler will not merely associate but in fact equate the psychic preconditions for mission tactics and related military reforms with the emergence of modern subjectivity. He does not even shy away from enlisting the help of a high-profile Prussian philosopher he normally disdains: Immanuel Kant. At one point the latter spelled out in distinctly military fashion the pivotal difference between lower-level *Verstand* (understanding), midlevel *Urteilskraft* (judgment), and upper-level *Vernunft* (reason): "The domestic or civil servant under orders needs only to have understanding. The officer, to whom only a general rule is prescribed, and who is then left on his own, needs judgement to decide for himself what should be done in a given case.

The general, who must consider potential future cases and who must think out rules on his own, must have Reason."[35] Exactly, Kittler responds in one of his most characteristic moves, this is true once we read *literally* what probably was intended as a helpful comparison. Kant's alignment of the hierarchies of the military order with the hierarchies of the cognitive apparatus is anything but a gratuitous association. As Kittler would have it, the former is, if not the actual origin, then at least a closely associated model of the latter. The martial a priori we encountered in all its blurred glory of motor and model in the technological domain reappears in the psycho-discursive domain. Maybe war did not simply create the modern subject, but the discursive orders necessitated by mobilization compress and make visible the discourse of subjection, just as war has compressed and rendered more visible the evolution of technology. War is the cleartext of our orders of speech.

Kittler's argument depends on a systematic blurring of war and mobilization, which serves to greatly extend the reach of war. Mobilization blurs the boundary between war and peace because it takes place in both. It blurs the boundary between the military and the civilian population because it affects one as much as the other. Finally, it blurs the boundary between material hardware and psychic software because it deals as much with the optimization of logistics, transport, and technology as with increasing mental preparedness and overall combat readiness. But what kind of human is most equipped (or least underequipped) to deal with the acceleration and incomprehensibility of modern war? What type of mind is able to make rapid, on-the-spot decisions or even make up new rules when no commanding authority is in sight? What has been programmed to fight with a free will? The modern subject.

One of the great problems for military reformers, however, was the threat that excessive mobilization could result in unchained subjects transgressing the social order they were mobilized to defend. As Kittler points out on several occasions, Prussia could in theory engineer an enlightened version of the guerrilla tactics used by Spanish and Tyrolean peasants in their struggle against French occupiers, but would the Prussian monarchy survive such martial anarchy? If you cry havoc and let loose the canine subjects of war, can you ever leash them again? Once again, we will briefly pursue a comparison that, like the link between paleontology and media evolution in the preceding section, may be of help because it is so counterintuitive: the similarities between *fighting and reading*.

Beginning in the second half of the eighteenth century and thus coinciding with Kittler's Discourse Network 1800, Germany underwent a so-called *Leserevolution*, or reading revolution. The term, introduced in the 1960s by Rolf Engelsing, refers to a momentous switch from "intensive" to "extensive" reading practices.[36] Intensive reading is the repeated, frequently loud and communal reading of a small number of canonized texts (most notably, the Bible), which by virtue of their constant engagement come to be fully integrated into the lives of readers. By contrast, extensive reading is the predominantly silent and solitary reading of a wide array of texts spanning all possible genres. In more loaded terms, intensive reading is the incorporation of a few edifying texts; extensive reading is the consumption of many entertaining texts.

In the eyes of troubled guardians of virtue, the fact that more and more people were reading more and more books at ever faster rates came with two significant dangers. First, in a classic case of retrograde media usage, intensive reading practices could be applied to extensive reading material. Trashy texts—most notably, novels—could be read with the immersive commitment hitherto reserved for scripture. In the case of allegedly weak and susceptible readers, that is, young men and women of all ages, this spelled disaster. Not coincidentally, one of the most successful and canonized texts of that period, Goethe's *Sorrows of Young Werther*, is about the dangers of bad reading. The response involved the deployment and interiorization of a wide array of cultural techniques we now take for granted, ranging from the systematic exclusion of the body as a medium from the reading process to the fine-tuning of mental-focus adjustments, that is, the ability to instantaneously assess the fictionality status of a given text and adopt the corresponding level of engagement.[37]

In other words, there was a loosening of the intensive ties that had bound readers to texts. However, this contentious release of the reader conjured up the threat that extensive reading could proliferate into a cancerous anarchy of millions of uncoordinated and uncontrollable mental escapes with grave social consequences.[38] Rogue readers were free to interpret the truth content and moral underpinning of texts any which way they wanted. The Leserevolution threatened to turn into a Les*err*evolution, or revolution of the reader. Like soldiers in the new great wars, readers of new novels had been unchained; hence, the question arose how to rein them in without forfeiting the profitable energy produced by the release. This issue is at the very center of Kittler's Discourse Network 1800. It became necessary to create philosophically supervised hermeneutic reading practices and interpretation protocols that allowed for a delicate trade-off between fruitful autonomy and conformist standardization. Readers are kites, free to rise and soar and explore all kinds of textual stratospheres, yet always tied to the ground by strings that are long but, hopefully, unbreakable.[39] Modern readers, then, are modern soldiers engaged in textual combat equipped with mental mission tactics. In much the same way as "the emptiness of the battlefield [*die Leere des Gefechtsfeldes*] requires soldiers who can think and act independently," the new confusion of texts lacking clear moral directives calls for new hermeneutic practices that, developed in accordance with new biopolitical imperatives to exploit the productivity of semiautonomous subjects, serve to advance the new frontiers of knowledge and conquer new territories of experience.[40]

The second major issue concerns the question of gender. Where are women and men located in the social and military circuits, and what input/output functions do they serve? Kittler's martial writings effectively weaponize the analysis of gender differentiation developed in *Discourse Networks*. What the latter—and related essays such as "Ottilie Hauptmann"—said about the position of women in the "network of technologies and institutions" that arose in the last third of the eighteenth century is now applied to the position women occupy in mobilization and war. In the shape of mothers and muses, women provided the input—that is, they "generate[d] the mass of words" that male authors take over and turn into works—while "philosophy rereads the entire output of this production as theory," which, in turn, is fed back into women in the shape of new educational protocols.[41] In much the same way, women provide the main input for affect mobilization, be it as empirical mothers and mates who nurture warriors present and future, or on a symbolic level as an increasingly feminized *patria*, Heimat, or homeland able to generate emotional attachments, including Hermann's "unfailing fighting spirit," in ways old absolutist states could not even dream of. As Kittler notes in "Operation Valhalla," chapter 7 of this volume, "without unconscious programming from the moment of birth, that is, without childhood, maternal womb, and female idol, there is no modern cannon fodder." Kleist, as usual, went overboard to assess in which murderous direction the ship was headed: a raped female body, representing a penetrated and fragmented Heimat, is cut into pieces and distributed across the land in the hope that the severed parts will be stitched together into a collective Frankenmother, otherwise known as a nation. But finally, if women are mobilized to mobilize men, there is always the danger that they may take matters into their own hands and join the fighting, which in the eyes of concerned male observers would be as detrimental to the social order as outright partisan warfare.

The issue is addressed in "Operation Valhalla," a martial reading of Richard Wagner's *The Ring of the Nibelung*. According to a memorable snarkasm attributed to Mark Twain, Wagner's music is better than it sounds. To appease Wagnerites, let us agree that Wagner's proto-cinematic soundscape, containing some of the most sensuous love music ever inspired by other men's wives, is in little need of improvement. His libretti are more problematic. As a lifelong Wagner devotee, Kittler joined a long list of luminaries intent on turning Wagner's ponderous verse into profound cultural analysis, but where others foregrounded questions of capitalism, alienation, aesthetics, and power, he focused on war and women. The "nomadic storm god" Wotan cheats on his wife, Fricka, and begets with Mother Earth nine maidens known as Valkyries. Half semidivine flight attendants, half army recruiters, they conduct slain warriors from the battlefields to Valhalla, where they join "43,000 men or three divisions" ("Operation Valhalla") on standby for *ragnarök*, the last of all battles. Only the dead will see the end of all war and then die once more, this time for good. So far, so Norse; but now Kittler gets down to business and translates Wotan's aria addressed to his daughter Brünnhilde in act 2, scene 2, of *The Valkyrie* into military cleartext. Brünnhilde's task is to "arouse brave men / to ruthless war," which is necessary because thus far Wotan's human helpers are "held . . . in bondage" and "bound in obedience" by "treacherous treaties [and] shameful agreements." Translation: The unmotivated, unthinking cannon fodder of cabinet wars are to be replaced by Gneisenau's and Kleist's motivated, self-reliant patriotic warriors, just as obsolete linear formations are to morph into new storm-trooper tactics. But Brünnhilde does more than merely arouse. She defies her father and actively interferes in the duel between Siegmund and Hunding, whereupon Wotan confines her to a burning circle, that is, to incinerating domesticity. Later on, her main role will be to produce lots of "poetry" to inspire Siegmund's son, Siegfried—precisely the type of poetry or "poetic attunement" Gneisenau had in mind when he advised Frederick Wilhelm III that "there is no uplifting of the spirit without poetic mood," for the "security of all thrones is built on poetry."[42]

Kittler's analysis is a war-centered take on Wagner's grand avalanche of guilt and violence that cascades with growing sound and fury down through history, or at least down to the end of the fourth night of the *Ring*. With his innumerable quirks, tics, and fetishes, Wagner is a late nineteenth-century creature; remove the magic rings and winged helmets, and you are in the middle of an Ibsen drama. The debates between Wotan and Fricka concerning the fate of Siegmund are a domestic squabble over how to best raise a child under cutthroat capitalist conditions. In an ultimate act of potentially all-destructive mobilization, Wotan wants to create and enflame allegedly free men and revolutionaries like Siegmund and Siegfried to lay waste to a defiled world, while Fricka points out that such a "command of free will" contradicts the very idea of freedom it is designed to achieve. Wagner, who in Friedrich Nietzsche's maliciously perceptive words "believed in the Revolution as much as ever a Frenchman believed in it," also believed as fervently in the necessity of an *aesthetic replacement of the Revolution* as ever a German did.[43] Like the post-Jena administrative reforms composed by Prussian bureaucratic officials, music can act as a slightly less violent substitute. The question remains, however, whether any music—and Wagnerian music in particular—that aspires to replace revolution is so much like the revolution because it, too, is unable to control itself. Is Wagner's infinite melody not the equivalent of Trotsky's permanent revolution and Clausewitz's absolute war? When Robert Duvall a.k.a. Colonel Bill Kilgore blasts the "Ride of the Valkyries" from helicopter-mounted speakers for the air attack in *Apocalypse Now* to mobilize his men into action—"My boys love it!"—Bayreuth has become the battlefield it always wanted to be.

But whether or not mission tactics and other military subject-enhancing protocols were implemented in the post-Jena reforms, whether or not the Prussian martial reboot is just another gilt-framed myth, whether or not the underlying binary that pits the enthusiastic combatants of revolutionary armies fueled by patriotic fervor against sullen, apolitical old-regime soldiers driven by money or brutal discipline is historically valid, something did increase Prussian military efficiency.[44] Even Napoleon was impressed. Faced with the new and improved Prussian forces during the 1813 campaign, he admitted, "The animals have learned something."[45] Indeed they had. Starting out as animal cannon fodder, they became human and would well have been promoted to the status of sophisticated machines, had not the machines themselves evolved a superior degree of sophistication and taken over. For as we shall see in the section "Blitzkrieg Nation," war promotes the replaceability of human subjects by machines by enhancing the ability for self-guidance.

Postscript to Discourse Nation: Social Word Wars

"Due to inclement weather," noted the satirist Kurt Tucholsky in 1930, "the German revolution took place in music." Translation: All the German revolts and insurgencies in the wake of World War I, from the Bavarian

Soviet Republic of 1919 to the Hamburg Uprising of 1923, failed; instead, Comrade Arnold Schönberg invented the twelve-tone technique, just as Comrade Wagner had aspired to replace the failed revolution of 1848 with mobilizing total works of art.

Tucholsky's quip recycles a venerable meme launched two centuries ago by Heinrich Heine, who observed that "German philosophy is nothing but the dream of the French Revolution."[46] Kant's philosophical guillotine decapitating unwarranted metaphysical speculations is the less bloody, but no less brutal, equivalent of Maximilien Robespierre's guillotine decimating unwanted political opponents. The underlying story has been rehashed in countless comparative studies: while the British bourgeoisie set sail to create and exploit an empire, and its French counterpart took to the streets to stage a revolution, the atrophied and fragmented German middle class congregated in governmental offices and lecture halls to pursue empires and revolutions of the mind.

Leaving aside the question of whether this Franco-German binary can withstand sustained scrutiny, it is difficult to avoid the impression that Kittler is reentering it *within* the Germany of his student days. The alleged substitutional relationship between French political revolutions on the one hand and German governmental and/or philosophical revolutions on the other resembles the divide between the more political and activist currents of the German student movement, up to and including the terrorism of the Red Army Faction discussed in "Of States and Their Terrorists," and the more culturally and aesthetically inclined currents that, incidentally, were especially prevalent in Kittler's Freiburg. Ironically, Kittler, who later attributed his lack of political engagement in the late 1960s and early 1970s to "50% laziness and 50% conservatism," may have read too many French theorists to truly believe in French revolutions.[47] If, following Jacques Lacan, the human subject is, much like the fancy pattern of underwear hanging on a clothesline, the effect of an inscriptional construct strung along a chain of signifiers, then the status and potential efficacy of revolutionary subjects are severely diminished. What remains is the rigorous analysis of the protocols and practices that program human inscription surfaces to view themselves as (revolutionary) subjects in the first place.

But it goes deeper and darker. Both the French political revolution and the German administrative "antirevolution" are always already heading for war.[48] Kittler's martial a priori takes on the appearance of a martial telos. War is not only the potential ground or origin but perhaps also the goal or vanishing point of accelerated human-machine interactions. If Lacan was right to refer the signifying operations that constitute subjects to a cybernetic paradigm (something Kittler never doubted), then it stands to reason that ever tighter and faster loops between connected humans and distributed cybernetic machines, combined with an ongoing mobilization of bodies, minds, and words, will generate violence. The principal players in this perfect information storm are known by the euphemism *social media*.

In February 2017 rumors spread online that German soldiers attached to a NATO unit stationed in Lithuania had raped a fifteen-year-old Russian girl.[49] The story was quickly discredited as part of a Russian disinformation campaign targeting the Baltics in an attempt to whip up pro-Russian sentiments by catering to collective memories of the Nazi occupation. Upon closer inspection, the story appeared to be an iteration of a rape meme that began a year earlier with reports of "Lisa," a thirteen-year-old Russian girl who had been raped by migrants in Germany; soon afterward, the story reappeared with Lithuanian military instructors raping a girl in Ukraine.

The incident recalls Hally's rape in Kleist's *Battle of Hermann*. The notion that *la patrie*, *die Heimat*, or the Mother Country is a virtuous female body in need of male protection is already at play in Livy's account of the rape of Lucretia, which led to the overthrow of Tarquinius Superbus and the establishment of the Roman Republic. But there is something else at stake here. We first need to fathom the virtually bottomless disdain Kittler had for social media. Indeed, to think of the media theorist Kittler surrounded by social media brings to mind a militant vegan forced to work in a meatpacking plant. The proliferation of social media promoted everything his take on media had tried to debunk, from the instrumentalist conceptualization of media as means of communication to their support of the petty narcissism of users, who, precisely because they remain ignorant of the degree to which they are subject to gadgets, are condemned to fill up their platform-enabled subject bubbles with tweets of hot air. Kittler, however, died before he could witness the full-scale weaponization of social media, when LinkedIn became RopedIn, Twitter turned into Trasher, and Facebook degenerated into Hatebook. What might he have said? Where does his body of work best connect? One thing is clear: when it comes to a bellicist analysis of social media, Kittler's hardware focus or information-theoretical materialism has less to offer than his earlier, less technological work. With the Kleistian discourse mobilization in mind, we can leapfrog from discourse analysis to social media analysis. Three closely related points anchored in a common premise are important:

To begin with the Kittlerian premise: social media are neither social nor media. They are not social because (as will be discussed in the following paragraphs) they appear to support the *full-scale attack of a communications infrastructure on a communication culture*, and they are not media in any conventional meaning of the word, be it obedient channels or neutral transmitters. They are, at best or worst, media in the more critical sense Kittler came to use the term, that is, mere interface effects at the outer perimeter of the great digital compound, designed to fob off easily manipulated users limited by inferior processing capabilities with an addictive diet of words, sounds, and images.

But—first point—of course social media do transmit something. Take one of the best of Kittler's flashy opening lines: "Let us say the function of literature and literary studies is to make transmittable the cohesiveness of the net in which everyday languages capture their subjects."[50] Or, if we update this statement from 1800 to 2000: the function of social media analysis is to make transmittable the cohesiveness of the grid in which digital signals charge and mobilize their subjects. The operative word is *mobilization*. In 2006 Audrey Kurth Cronin published "Cyber-Mobilization: The New *Levée en Masse*," a widely discussed paper that compared the levée en masse of the French Revolution with the "21st-century's *levée en masse*, a mass-networked mobilization that emerges from cyberspace with a direct impact on physical reality."[51] For our purposes, the most interesting point is the link between mobilization instances that both occur in critical times of accelerated proliferation of media ecologies—the compressed time of change alluded to in the section "Motor and Model." With regard to the original levée en masse, Cronin notes, "The French populace was reached, radicalized, educated and organized so as to save the revolution and participate in its wars. It is no accident that the rise of mass warfare coincided with a dramatic growth in the number of common publications such as journals, newspapers, pamphlets, and other short-lived forms of literature. No popular mobilization could have expanded in the absence of dramatically expanding popular communications."[52]

This only scratches the surface of the revolutionary media ecology, which included accelerated rituals of transcription and (re)oralization, Claude Chappe's telegraph, large-scale media events, and, as Jacques Guilhaumou showed in a fascinating study, dreams of early megaphones, mechanized banners, and movable chairs that could technologically implement revolutionary discourse.[53] What is happening now is seen as a "historical successor," with "21st-century mobilization . . . perpetuating a fractionation of violence."⁵⁴ Bluntly put, the French Jacobins realized their universalist ambitions. The world is turning into one extended Paris suburb—however, not the Paris of the ancien régime or the belle epoque but that of 1794: a frenzied media cauldron filled with mobilized subjects that process incoming communication according to a strict us-versus-them code.

Second point: of course there are messages, but one great difference between the original levée en masse 1.0 and the cyber levée en masse 2.0 is that the former consisted primarily of unifying messages circulated within a state, whereas the latter is to a large extent composed of divisive messages originating on the outside. It is also well known—and denied only by disinformation profiteers a.k.a. politicians—that the goal of divisive messages in the new information warfare is to exacerbate and exploit preexisting social fault lines and create tribal communities on standby to receive further outside interpellation. It is as if Varus and a horde of Roman bots had pulled a reverse Hermann by spreading intertribal German hatred. This is not your parents' cold war: you no longer create solitary sleepers or Manchurian candidates who at one point will be activated for a specific purpose; instead, you create wide-awake networked mobs whose general purpose is to prevent the other side from jointly pursuing any agreed-upon single purpose.

Final point: Is the above a credible description? Is it war? Kittler would probably respond to both questions in the affirmative by appealing to a couple of supreme authorities. According to Clausewitz, war is *"an act of force to compel our enemy to do our will."*⁵⁵ Clausewitz was far too imbued with the spirit of Hegelian feedback not to realize that the imposition of one's will is never a unilinear act. The action of one will always depend on the willed actions of the opponent, and vice versa: "Each side, therefore, compels its opponent to follow suit; a reciprocal action is started which must lead, in theory, to extremes."⁵⁶ But what if it were possible to prevent an enemy from developing an effective will in the first place? What if I can engineer my opponent to contain contradictory and ultimately crippling multitudes? If, for instance, a foreign government were to conduct a campaign of misinformation and division against another country with the goal of influencing a federal election, and if the result of that action were the election of a government more accommodating to the foreign influencers, or at least less capable of resisting their influence, would that constitute an act of war? Or of prewar? At the very least it would meet the approval of the other supreme authority, Sun Tzu: "To subdue the enemy without fighting is the acme of skill."⁵⁷

Blitzkrieg Nation: German Ways of War and Theory

In 1934 a Berlin women's organization, eager to present Hitler with a welcoming bouquet, asked the Ministry of Propaganda to name the Führer's favorite flower. A flustered secretary contacted the Reich Chancellery and probed several of Hitler's aides, but without success. Hitler, it seems, had not clearly expressed himself in this matter. In his memoirs, *Inside the Third Reich*, Albert Speer, Hitler's architect and as of 1942 the Reich's minister of armaments and war production, recounts how the secretary took matters into his own hands: "He reflected for a while. 'What do you think, Speer? Shouldn't we say edelweiss? I think edelweiss sounds right. First of all it's rare and then it also comes from the Bavarian mountains. Let's simply say edelweiss!' From then on the edelweiss was officially 'the *Führer*'s favorite flower.' This incident shows how much liberty party propaganda sometimes took in shaping Hitler's image."[58] Trivial as the incident may be, it captures what some scholars identify as a key feature of the Third Reich. The edelweiss was no random choice. More exclusive than a tulip or daisy, it befitted the exalted status of the Führer, while also paying respect to Hitler's well-known fondness for alpine regions. The secretary's decision was a proactive, plausible speculation; he chose what Hitler himself may well have chosen had he felt the need to reveal his floral preferences. This comes close to what Ian Kershaw, recycling a phrase by a Prussian bureaucrat, has labeled "working towards the Führer."[59] The Third Reich was not a streamlined, top-down tyranny whose goose-stepping population was either made up of fanatical followers or kept in line by Gestapo terror, nor was it an unhinged polycracy over which Hitler as a structurally weak dictator had little control. Rather, Hitler operated at the center of a divisive mass of bodies and entities vying for access to the Führer by putting into concrete practice policies that Hitler himself had not clearly spelled out—or that he, in a conscious attempt to promote fitness-enhancing administrative struggles, had assigned to competing agencies. Nazism derived a significant part of its destructive energy from initiatives emanating from below, thereby unleashing a volatile dynamic in which competing proposals and initiatives became ever more radical. Bluntly put, the Third Reich was a system in which shit was programmed to rise to the top; it promoted ever more extreme political and administrative mission tactics in the service of military aggression and genocide.

However, at the conclusion of his memoirs, Speer, quoting his final statement at the Nuremberg trials, presents a very different image of the

Third Reich. For those interested in Kittler's view of World War II and of the grotesque regime responsible for its European portion, this particular statement, repeatedly referred to in his texts, is indispensable:

> Hitler's dictatorship was the first dictatorship of an industrial state in this age of modern technology, a dictatorship which employed to perfection the instruments of technology to dominate its own people.... By means of such instruments of technology as the radio and public-address systems, eighty million persons could be made subject to the will of one individual. Telephone, teletype, and radio made it possible to transmit the commands of the highest level directly to the lowest organs where because of their high authority they were executed uncritically. Thus many offices and squads received their evil commands in this direct manner. The instruments of technology made it possible to maintain a close watch over all citizens and to keep criminal operations shrouded in a high degree of secrecy. To the outsider this state apparatus may look like the seemingly wild tangle of cables in a telephone exchange; but like such an exchange it could be directed by a single will. Dictatorships of the past needed assistants of high quality in the lower ranks of leadership also—men who could think and act independently. The authoritarian system in the age of technology can do without such men. The means of communication alone enable it to mechanize the work of the lower leadership. Thus the type of uncritical receiver of orders is created.[60]

What is behind this diagnosis? First and foremost, a denial of responsibility. If media technology turns everybody into uncritical receivers of orders passed down from above, if a giant switchboard connects all to the domineering "will of one," then the responsibility even of a high-ranking official like Speer is drastically diminished. This is self-exculpatory instrumentalism at its most pathetic: the dictator-sender is in such full control of channels and messages that everybody hooked to the receiving end is as much an instrument as the connecting conduits. Tools can plead innocence because they are, after all, just tools.

While Kittler abstains from striking any critical note in his frequent references to Speer, he does not fully endorse the Nuremberg statement. Rather, his view of World War II and the military culture of the Third Reich oscillated between the two Speer quotes above—that is, between the focus on mobilization, speed, and initiative on the one hand and the focus on total control on the other—with the crucial caveat that this movement takes place against a background that moved from the human toward the technological. Kittler—and here we are at the heart of his war-related writings—is engaged in a large-scale attempt to reconceptualize World War II along lines very different from those habitually invoked. Underneath the war between the Allies and the Axis, or democracy and fascism, there were other, potentially more decisive wars between fundamental technological imperatives, above all the struggles between speed and control, between initiative and oversight, and, by extension, between humans and machines. And since the wars between nations, empires, or ideologies do not align with the wars between technologies, media, and infrastructures, a different World War II emerges.

To probe this revision, it will once again be necessary to follow Kittler into military-historical arcana. We begin with a revealing embarrassment triggered by Kittler's high opinion of the German Wehrmacht:

> I am not one of those theorists who despise the German *Wehrmacht* and its military operations. There has, for example, been much talk recently of the brutality of the *Wehrmacht* in the Russian campaign during World War II and I understand that. Nonetheless, it is obvious ... to me that the real riddle of World War II is how it was possible for Hitler's *Blitzkrieg* to conquer the whole of Europe, except Finland, in two years? This to me was an *incredible* event.[61]

Really? The whole of Europe? Including Spain, Portugal, Ireland, Scotland, England, Iceland, Sweden, and Switzerland, where no Wehrmacht jackboot ever set foot? (Besides, more than two years separated the conquests of Poland and France from the German occupation of several eastern European countries.) No doubt he knows better. Once again, enthused words outpace awkward facts, but rather than figuratively punch Kittler behind the ears—as he himself said he would if he came across such nonsense—it is more interesting to delve into historical circumstances that help explain these claims. What is "the real riddle" behind "the *incredible* event" of World War II?

First off, Kittler is appealing to a well-known phenomenon Robert M. Citino calls "the German way of war." Germany's (and Prussia's) military planning has always been dictated by its disadvantageous geostrategic location: "Crammed into an unfortunately tight spot in the heart of the continent, ringed by enemies and potential enemies, more often than not the chessboard on which other players played out their strategies, it had neither the resources nor the manpower to win long, drawn-out wars of attrition."⁶² Germany and Prussia thus are notoriously prone to "the short-war illusion."⁶³ They must win their wars quickly or not at all, hence the marked emphasis on speed, from the legendary sleigh drive that enabled the victory of Brandenburg's Great Elector, Frederick Wilhelm I, over the Swedes at the Battle of Fehrbellin (1675) to the panzer thrust into France in 1940; hence also the emphasis on front-loaded, no-holds-barred, and decision-seeking aggressiveness, from Frederick the Great's first Silesian campaign up to the Schlieffen Plan and Operation Barbarossa. None of this is essentially or uniquely German, but it is a military proclivity especially prominent in the German context: "Prussia-Germany tried to keep its wars short, winning a decisive battlefield victory in the briefest possible time. Although it might be argued that every warring party followed the same path, no other country took this trend to such extremes. No other country in European history sought victory so relentlessly through sudden or surprising military maneuver."⁶⁴

Citino's use of *German* in "the German way of war" resembles the use of *German* in discussions of "German media theory." The latter designation likewise does not imply anything essentially or uniquely German; it serves to indicate that the recurrence of a certain set of assumptions, references, and associations in media-theoretical analyses has to be understood against the background of debates about technology, humanism, and individual as well as collective identity formation that over the course of the past two centuries emerged with particular acuity in the German-speaking countries. Juxtaposing "the German way of war" and "German media theory," though, is more than a superficial analogy. It contains a genealogical relationship in the sense that media theory inherits and reprocesses basic concerns and experiences that were also central to military thinking. So-called German media theory is the continuation of so-called German war on a different level.

Kittler's war-related texts focusing on the twentieth century are rooted in the premise that Germany must compensate for its inability to wage deep wars by means of coordinated speed and military hardware innovations. The former will allow for rapid and decisive engagements in the early stages of the war, while the deployment of more advanced weapons will make up for quantitative inferiority. However, accelerations at the tactical and operational levels as well as hardware innovations are, in essence, problems of media, which supports Kittler's confluence of war and media. This becomes even more obvious once we take into account that coordinated speed is a subset of hardware innovation, given that coordination at greater speeds calls for improved communications technologies to control and coordinate—much as, for instance, the development of the railroad required telegraph lines to coordinate rail traffic. The second, closely related assumption is that improvisation and innovation increasingly move from the tactical to the technological. Once again, the martial a priori rears its head: war is not only, to quote the title of one of the darker essays in this collection, the constant improvement of "manners of death." By pushing the replacement of soldiers equipped with a "command of free will" with killing devices equipped with decision-making algorithms, such as killer drones, war paved the way for the general substitution of human subjects by machine subjects—a substitution that, as will be discussed in the next section, works so well because the two different subjects in question are not that different.[65] Here, we will focus on one phenomenon that captures most of the aspects under discussion and that also allows for a linkup with the previous section: blitzkrieg. With the caveat, however, that the word (like mission tactics) resembles Aladdin's lamp. Once the lamp has been rubbed, or the bottle uncorked, the escaping content is difficult to control.

The most revealing text is the conversation with Alexander Kluge (chapter 10, this volume), which in no small measure is due to Kluge's ability to tease out what Kittler really wants to say. (Think of their conversation as a Freudian talking cure: Kluge, the analyst, keeps feeding associations and prompters back into the patient to keep him talking.) Kittler recounts the well-known story of how German World War I storm-trooper tactics were developed to overcome the stalemate of the *Stellungskrieg* (static or position war) on the western front. The goal was to resuscitate the desired *Bewegungskrieg*, or war of movement. Instead of large frontal assaults by rifle-armed soldiers advancing through barbed wire toward enemy parapets and machine-gun nests, small, flexible, and highly mobile units equipped with a diversity of weapons would break through at specified points and fan out behind enemy lines. In the false peace between 1919 and 1939, when *peace* referred to periods of history in which Europeans took a break from killing each other in larger numbers, the German Army, eager to avoid another unwinnable Stellungskrieg, motorized and upgraded these tactics. What worked with men on a tactical level could work faster and even more decisively on an operational level with tanks. This was all the more urgent because due to the significant reduction of the German Army in the wake of the Treaty of Versailles it became even more necessary to compensate for the lack of men, matériel, and resources by means of speed and technological superiority.

Blitzkrieg, then, is the operational redeployment of a tactical innovation responding to a strategic imperative. More to the point, it was the name given to the operational implementations of tactical innovations in the campaigns against Poland and France, though it was a designation the German Army neither invented nor adopted. The rapid German victory in the West has added to the flashy mystique of the term as well as to the questionable perception, shared by Kittler, that it all went off exactly as conceived. Germany, so the story goes, planned its lightning wars with all the meticulous care it devotes to its manufacture of its cars, beer, and idealist philosophy. The Kipling admirer Kittler offers a Just So Blitzkrieg Story that revolves around one of the Wehrmacht's best-known senior generals and postwar self-promoters, Heinz Guderian. Based on his experiences in World War I, Guderian (who, as mentioned in "Free Ways," was a signals officer who witnessed firsthand the failure of the Schlieffen Plan) laid the groundwork for the accelerated mechanized warfare in the 1920s, planned the attack on France, and then, holding a general's rank, rode off into the raging blitzkrieg in his VHF radio–equipped tanks, to be immortalized twenty-five years later in a samba-like groove by the Rolling Stones. Discourse analysis's finest hour came another twenty years later when Kittler had "Sympathy for the Devil" implode into Guderian's blitzkrieg.[66]

As most military historians would argue, that is not quite what happened.[67] Indeed, the best indication that the "incredible" Wehrmacht did not fully understand its own success was its belief that said success could easily be repeated on a larger scale in Operation Barbarossa, the 1941 attack on the Soviet Union. It was a spectacular failure of imagination and foresight, based on the fallacy that blitzkrieg is a scale-invariant procedure. The procedure had worked on several different levels, so why not ratchet it up another notch? Thus Citino can answer, with amazing exactitude, the question at what point exactly German military planners realized the war was lost. On December 26, 1941, soon after German forces had dug in west of Moscow to stave off a Red Army counterattack, the semi-official *Militär-Wochenblatt* [Military weekly] featured the simple but fateful headline "Stellungskrieg in the East." The type of war Germany did not lose was over; the type of war it could not win had begun.[68]

But then again—and now we enter truly Kittlerian terrain—blitzkrieg is a protean beast that makes full use of the conceptual expansion of war into mobilization and speed. Take the at first glance facetious ending of the opening essay "Free Ways": "And every time summer comes around, as it did in 1939," Kittler rhapsodizes, German tourist divisions sally forth until "Europe's borders capitulate." Technologically enhanced collective mobilization morphs into mass tourism, an annual conquest of seasonal lebensraum for entertainment purposes. The final verdict (as if Clausewitz had written a sequel to On War called On Tourism): "Peace is the continuation of war with the same means of transportation." Networked means of transportation, we should add, for it appears that cars are tanks, given that Guderian's VHF equipment, so indispensable for the coordination of lightning-strike maneuvers, reappears in the shape of car stereos, equally indispensable for the diversion of the occupants.

The martial a priori of the autobahn and of modern tourism ties in with the overall martial a priori of the entire modern entertainment industry, just as one Prussian century earlier, governmental and educational reforms were linked to mobilization efforts. The basic difference is that the primarily discursive mobilization of spirits, moods, and affects is replaced by the functionally equivalent, primarily technological mobilization of bodies, reflexes, and senses. "*Funkspiel,* VHF tank radio, vocoders, Magnetophones, submarine location technologies, air war radio beams etc. have released an abuse of army equipment that adapts ears and reaction speeds to World War $n+1$. Radio, the first abuse, led from World War I to World War II, rock music, the next abuse, from II to III."[69] The drill is so necessary because humans are so slow:

> In terms of motor skills, sensory perception, and intellectual acumen, people are evidently not designed to wage high-tech wars. Ever since World War I . . . speed and acceleration have mandated the creation of special training camps that teach new forms of perception to sluggish people and accustom them to man-machine synergies. This started in 1914 with the wristwatch, and it will not end with today's combat simulators. We can assume that in the interim period, when wars are not running in real time, rock concerts and discos function as boot camps for perceptions that undermine the thresholds of perception.[70]

One obvious extension is the internalization of technologies, the creation of augmented supersoldiers, which—as Kluge emphasizes—is the realization of old futurist dreams of the merging of flesh and steel. Kittler, however, is less interested in human-machine melds because they elide a more fundamental issue. On the battlefield, increasing speed may be as precarious as promoting independent initiatives. As in the case of the released reader, a too-vigorous deployment of the desired means threatens to destroy the overall purpose. In their conversation both Kittler and

Kluge strike an accelerationist note by talking about blitzkrieg enabling an escape velocity that would allow the combatants nothing less than an escape from *the state* (Kittler) or even from *war itself* (Kluge). The concrete historical referent is Erwin Rommel's Seventh Panzer Division, which during the French campaign advanced at such speeds that the German High Command lost track of it, whereupon it became known as the "Ghost Division"—an achievement some say was possible only by combining two types of speed, kinetic and pharmacological, that is, motorization and methamphetamines.[71]

Of course, Rommel had no intention of abandoning the war or his employer, but Kittler, probed by Kluge, is hinting at a more general point that is familiar terrain for military historians. Whether you pinpoint Moscow in late 1941 or the failure of the 1942 offensive in Stalingrad and the Caucasus, the end of the German war of movement coincides with a change in German military command culture, which effectively terminated the independence and initiative of the commanders so visibly on display in the early stages of the war. Assuming ever tighter control of military operations, Hitler's first decree as the new commander in chief was to order all higher commands to "report every detail, to provide plain answers to every question, and to state clearly when they had dialed to assigned orders."[72] In a word, Hitler put an end to all Auftragstaktik and started to micromanage a very un-German extended war of attrition and retreat.

Hitler's performance as a military commander has received its share of critique—part of it justified, part of it self-serving.[73] But as Citino emphasizes, it is necessary to go beyond a simple "Hitler did it" approach to the death of Auftragstaktik. In the age of the radio, the supreme commander now had virtually instantaneous access to each army group and army commander. There was nothing to stop him from directly accessing every link in the chain of command if he so desired.[74] This is exactly what Kittler, armed with Speer's Nuremberg quote, is aiming at. The very technology that allowed for the unleashing of coordinated mechanized speed now serves to subject all movement to tight control. In Deleuzian terms that are hovering at the edges of Kittler's rumination on nomads and terrorists (and on the metamorphosis of modern soldiers into high-tech nomads who resemble the nomadic terrorists they are fighting), the deterritorialization of blitzkrieg is countered by a massive reterritorialization in which the state once again assumes control over those who were on the verge of escaping its grip. Or, on an even more fundamental level, World War II is a pivotal juncture in the ongoing conflict between state and war. According to Kittler, the modern mass-army wars that started with the French levée en masse "fizzled out" in the steppes of Astrakhan. There will be other masses fighting in the future, but they will not be wearing standardized uniforms, they will not fight for nations, and they may not even be composed of humans.

Postscript to Blitzkrieg Nation: Missile Subjects and the Final War

When was Nazism overcome? At what point did the militant German variant of fascism vanish from history? (Did it ever?) With Hitler's suicide? When Germany surrendered? On February 23, 1947, when the Allies officially abolished Prussia? But fascism, German or otherwise, cannot be defeated by military means alone, nor legislated out of history with the stroke of a pen. It sits too deep, hides too well, and for some may be too alluring to abandon.

In 2004 Klaus Theweleit, author of *Male Fantasies* and a fellow student of Kittler's in Freiburg, published a beautiful book on soccer in which he claimed that fascism was overcome in 1956/57, when German teenagers tuned in to the British Forces Network and encountered the top ten: from Buddy Holly to Chuck Berry, Petula Clark to Peggy Lee, Fats Domino to Elvis. If, as Theweleit had argued in *Male Fantasies*, one of the core features of fascism was the construction of hardened male bodies that project their inner chaos onto a world they feel compelled to destroy, then no combination of carpet bombing, denazification trials, and economic recovery plans could hope to eradicate fascism. It has to be danced off, as it were, exorcized from drilled bodies by new music in new media formats. Blues and early rock and roll freed desires and bodies from armored fascist constraints. When it came to severing the fascist mooring of German being, Buddy Holly and the Crickets had more to offer than Adorno and Horkheimer.[75]

Kittler, whose musical loyalties lay with the British invasion of the 1960s, would no doubt stress the psychedelic Wagnerian impact of the late Beatles and early Pink Floyd, but he would be skeptical about the alleged emancipatory potential.[76] If, as Paul Virilio argues in *War and Cinema*, the war that did not manage to end all wars in 1918 withdrew into cinema palaces, only to burst out into the open again in 1939, Kittler adds that after 1945 the war spread out in layers of psychophysical mobilization—a permanent drill experienced by many as an ongoing thrill. In classic Kittlerese (a line at odds with Theweleit's more positive appreciation of modern music), "our discos are preparing our youth for a retaliatory strike."[77] War appears to be everywhere at all times. Kittler's work is part of a critical trend of the 1970s and 1980s that suggests we are subject to a critical flicker fusion rate of martial history, when the rising frequency of war and war-derived technologies makes it appear permanent.

As mentioned, Kittler was less interested in the increasing technologizing, enhancing, or upgrading of humans or warriors by the behavioral optimization, implants, or human-machine melds that had haunted futurist reveries. There are limits to human upgradeability that our species narcissism is happy to ignore. The obvious alternative is the replacement of underperforming humans by machines; the specifically Kittlerian twist is that this substitution is channeled through a weaponized Lacanianism.

To understand matters, we need to briefly return to the mobilization into self-reflexivity, which was booked under the heading of mission tactics. The mental faculties necessary to perform civic duties in the bewildering quagmire of a decentered, functionally differentiated modern society devoid of all-encompassing rules and guidelines is also what is needed to fight on the decentered modern battlefield. Upgraded subjects are soldiers who have learned to think on their own. Yet from Kittler's point of view, it is precisely the fact that modern subjects are self-directed agents capable of autocorrective reflection—that is, of reacting to unforeseen circumstances by rewriting the initial set of instructions without losing sight of the overall goal—that allows them to be replaced by modern weapons. Our philosophically embellished features of self-reflexivity are also present in nontrivial machine subjects. Because human neuronal networks and electronic hardware circuits are functionally equivalent inscription surfaces, there is not much difference between a self-directed human and a self-directed cruise missile. Kittler equips this equivalence with a Lacanian spin by emphasizing that the crucial feature that turns trivial machines into nontrivial machine subjects is the implementation of conditional jump instructions, or IF/THEN commands. Quoting Lacan, he insists that the difference between a straightforward mechanical command that determines exactly how an operation should be executed from beginning to end (which in Kant's illustration is the level of the simple servant or soldier) and a program that enables the operator to alter its behavior during the operation once or if certain conditions have been met (Kant's officer) is the same as the distinction between an animal code and a language involving human subjectivity:

> For example, the dance of bees, as it has been researched by [Karl] von Frisch, "is distinguished from language precisely by the fixed correlation

of its signs to the reality they signify." While the messages of one bee control the flight of another to blossoms and prey, these messages are not decoded and transmitted by the second bee. By contrast, "the form in which language is expressed . . . itself defines subjectivity. Language says: 'You will go here, and when you see this, you will turn off there.' In other words, it refers itself to the discourse of the other." In yet other words: bees are projectiles, and humans, cruise missiles. One is given objective data on angles and distances by a dance, the other, a command of free will.[78]

Subjective agency is conceived of as an operational reflexivity that, translated into the computational realm, takes on the shape of feedback commands. This allows Kittler to establish a functional equivalence between human operators and cruise missiles as machine subjects and to claim that the latter have ousted the former since they are able to receive, process, and execute incoming information in a superior fashion. It does not mean that computers are artificial human brains, nor that they digitally ape specifically human ways of thinking. Rather, they optimize certain patterns of information processing that earlier in history were also imposed on human beings but subsequently mistaken for innately human qualities. Human subjects—conceived of as projectiles equipped with upgraded internal processing capabilities—emerge from war only to be replaced by more efficient machine subjects that emerge in later wars.

This allows us to address a common misperception that associates Kittler's work with the oeuvre of Arnold Schwarzenegger. The meme was especially rampant when Kittler died. The headline of a post-mortem portrait in the *Guardian* says it all: "Friedrich Kittler and the rise of the machine"—which is both an homage to the title of the third *Terminator* movie and an attempt to summarize Kittler. In terms of atmosphere or zeitgeist, it is on target; otherwise, it is wrong. Like Martin Heidegger, Kittler was afflicted with an almost pathological intolerance of anthropocentrism. If philosophy, a notoriously anthropocentric endeavor, wanted to live up to its aspirations, it had to undergo a rigorous housecleaning regimen. It needed to fumigate its premises to eradicate its many debilitating humanist head games, first and foremost of which is the delusion that humans are the measure of all things—also and especially of the machines that are rising up to kill them. From Kittler's point of view, the *Terminator* scenario is nothing but a variation of the old Pinocchio fallacy. Humans labor under the conceit that their creations have got nothing better to do than to try to become like them. And the last, melodramatic resort of human self-infatuation, the final pipedream of our eschatocene anthropocentrism, is to take pride in the fact that we are the grand target of our insurgent creations: *what a piece of work is man* that his creations are so set on obliterating him. But machines are no less literate; they can read to the end of Hamlet's speech: *Man delights not me*. Machines are not avengers, Kittler would have said; they prefer the cosmic indifferentism of H. P. Lovecraft's monsters. This last war was the one he did not talk about because it does not deserve the term. If our machines remove us, it will not be a Hermann-like uprising or a crusade to liberate oppressed gadgets; it will be either unintended collateral damage, the result of a genocidal glitch, or an apocalyptic accident. Or the machines, in a last gesture of ironic respect, will mimic our hypocrisy and speak of a police action or a hygienic measure.

Pynchon's Rocket: War as Accelerated Technology Transfer

There were no techno-subjects or computer-guided cruise missiles in World War II, but Germany produced the next best thing, the V-2 rocket. Developed at the Peenemünde Army Research Center on the Baltic island of Usedom and assembled at the underground Mittelwerk factory in Thuringia using slave labor from the Dora-Mittelbau concentration camp, the V-2 was the world's first liquid-propelled, long-range ballistic missile. It is a sleek, murderous oddity central to Kittler's war-related writings, and to a certain extent even to his life. Over the next two sections, it will allow us to draw together many strands and address the key aspects of Kittler's view of war and history as well as the question of motivation. What emotional liquid fuel propels his martial texts beyond the gravity of common history, common sense, and common ethics?

As a so-called *Wunderwaffe*, or miracle weapon, a last-ditch attempt to overcome the crushing superiority of the enemy with a weapon of unprecedented shock, speed, and awe, the V-2 represents the culmination of the "German way of war." It was the forty-day Schlieffen Plan compressed into four minutes, the forward escape of Rommel's Ghost Division accelerated to supersonic speed. Tactically and economically, however, it was a disaster. The total explosive load of all V-2s ever fired equaled that of a single large Allied air raid. Designed to be a quick ballistic fix, it turned out to be a crippling drain of resources. By drawing away roughly two billion Reichsmark from more effective weapons systems, the V-2 may indeed have shortened the war but not in the way the German side intended.[79] The most gruesome statistic is that it is the only weapon in history that killed more people during its assembly than through its use. The roughly twenty thousand victims died under circumstances worse than in many other concentration camps. Dora-Mittelbau started out as a subcamp of Buchenwald; one survivor testified that in comparison to Dora, Buchenwald appeared like "heaven."[80]

The V-2 was a weapon out of time. Militarily, it arrived too late in the war to have any impact, yet it was so ineffective because, technologically, it arrived too early.[81] It lacked what only a decade later would render ballistic missiles the supreme weapon: the right warhead (bigger blast) and sophisticated electronics (better aim and the ability to self-correct). It was as if Wernher von Braun and his entourage, their minds still awash with the space-travel dreams of the 1920s, had reached out into the future to haphazardly grab whatever could be used to serve the present. This strange time compression is central to Kittler's argument: as the V-2s screamed across the sky toward London, they came loaded with dreams of the past, failures of the present, and threatening promises of the future.

Once again, it is best to begin with a blunder, arguably the most revealing in Kittler's rich cabinet of curious claims. In *Gramophone, Film, Typewriter*, he notes that Konrad Zuse's Z4, a programmable, relay-based electronic data-processing machine some consider to be the first real computer, was involved in "determining in the bunkers of the Harz the fate of the v2."[82] Zuse's Z4, so Kittler's story goes, was used to program the construction of the missile. Factually, this is a mistake. Kittler could have avoided it if he had really done what his bibliography claims he did, namely, read the whole of Zuse's memoirs. Zuse has a Pynchonesque story to tell. The Z4, the fourth machine assembled in his parents' apartment in Berlin, was also known as the V4. The V stood for *Versuchsmodell* (experimental model), and because V4 seemed close to V-2 (which, to add to the confusion, was initially known as the A4), one of his collaborators managed to persuade the authorities to order Zuse and his fellow workers to evacuate the Z4/V4 from Berlin to the Mittelbau ordnance factories where the V-2/A4 was being assembled. On their arrival the group took one look at the inhuman conditions and escaped to the South German Allgäu region—Hitler's edelweiss territory—to sit out the end of the war.[83] As a result, the first real digital service ever rendered on German soil had little to do with military endeavors but took place after the war in a less martial domain: Zuse programmed the Z4 to assist an alpine dairy in calculating milk yields and to help out with accounting.

To a certain extent, Kittler can be excused. He quoted an otherwise impeccable source, Andrew Hodges's magisterial biography of Alan Turing, the first edition of which claims that "Zuse calculators were used in the engineering of v2 rockets, and in 1945 Zuse himself was installed in the Dora underground factories."[84] Hodges has since acknowledged his mistake, but Kittler appears to have difficulties letting go of the idea. "Biogeography," the cryptic autobiographical martial musing near the end of this collection, mentions a brief exchange during his first visit to the Mittelbau-Dora concentration camp in July 1990: "When the last director of the museum was asked whether Konrad Zuse's world war computer had been used in Mittelbau, he observed: 'Zuse? Never heard of him.' Not for nothing did Stalin denounce all computer science as bourgeois deviation." While the incorrect z4/v-2 linkup remains an option, the fact that nobody knows Zuse's name is blamed on totalitarian cyberphobia.

But why this obsession? *Because that is what the war was really about.* How does Kittler know this? Because he read *Gravity's Rainbow*. That is not to say that Kittler gained new insights from Pynchon's novel; he did not learn anything important he had not known or suspected before. Rather, *Gravity's Rainbow* acted as an incentive, a spur, a *drug* that swept away inhibitions. Kittler first read the novel during his 1982 sojourn in Berkeley—in the original, no less, which is quite a feat for someone whose main staple of anglophone literature up until then had been Raymond Chandler. The novel struck him as "a positive shockwave" that "lifted a kind of dark veil from my eyes concerning my own childhood experiences with v2s," provoking and answering questions that had been lurking in the background ever since the toddler witnessed the fires of Dresden.[85] An American author furnished a German theorist with a letter of marque to prey on the established narratives of the last German war, the ensuing German fate, and even his own German childhood.

First, the biographical level: In 1953, 1954, 1956, and 1958, the young Kittler spent his summer holidays on the island of Usedom, close to the former Peenemünde Army Research Center. Traveling through the province of Brandenburg, which in the intricate multiple exposure of "Biogeography" appears as both the last battleground of the past and the first combat zone of the next war, the Kittler family ends up in a site of picturesque destruction: "Concrete slabs with asphalt joints . . . thrown into cubist disarray by the bombs of the Royal Air Force during a long summer night." What "Biogeography" presents in esoteric allusions Kittler spelled out clearly in an interview:

> From my early childhood, my mother often took me to the shore in East Germany where Hitler's v2 rockets were developed during World War II. However, what fascinated me most about these sites and rockets was the fact that no one said a word about them. And yet the traces of this particular aspect of the German military-industrial complex . . . were everywhere. And so I had to find my own explanation for this hidden part of history. But it was difficult to do so because it was almost forbidden to talk about the military-industrial complex in East Germany or even speak about the German side of the war effort more generally, and especially anything that touched upon the technological side.[86]

Traces without texts, scars without stories, and a socialist *damnatio memoriae* that keeps reminding people of what they have been ordered to forget. No wonder that smallness, both spatial and historical, is a leitmotif of "Biogeography." In the eyes of the young child (and the mature theorist), the German Democratic Republic, that puny country with its pompous name, fades in comparison to the "wild, great past" from which it emerged.[87] The veil of the foreign language through which Kittler first read *Gravity's Rainbow* comes to resemble the veil of obfuscation the GDR imposed on large portions of its immediate past. But the novel not only resonates with Kittler's unanswered memories but also exposes in amazing detail that the "technological side," concentrated in its sheerest essence in the v-2, is the defining mark of World War II. Reading Pynchon, Kittler realized that he had spent uncanny childhood vacations close to a world-historical ground zero where "our strategic present began."

For—to go from biography to hidden history—what kind of war emerges in *Gravity's Rainbow*? Who or what are the combatants? Nations? Ideologies? Nations are nothing but media in Kittler's jaded sense of the word, fancy interface constructs that supply networked users known as citizens with a diet of words, images, and sounds that produce identity effects and collective death wishes, while behind it all is a machinery that cares as much about the fate of nations as a hard drive does about the well-being of its human appendages. Ideologies, in turn, are prefabricated discursive deposits on standby, equipped with varying degrees of affective potential and developed when it was still necessary to mobilize people to "help History grow to its predestined shape"—which, of course, is no longer necessary once you can deploy nontrivial mechanized subjects that need neither sleep nor collective narratives.[88] The World War II Kittler glimpsed in *Gravity's Rainbow* has little to do with politics and ideology; it is not about living spaces for master races or grand crusades to liberate oppressed continents, even if rewritten in a dark key as the prospect that "American Death has come to occupy Europe."[89] Whatever the human players may be dreaming of or dying for in Pynchon's novel, they are no more than disposable appurtenances in a story that operates on a very different level:

> This war was never political at all, the politics was all theatre, all just to keep the people distracted.... Secretly, it was being dictated instead by the needs of technology ... by a conspiracy between human beings and techniques, by something that needed the energy-burst of war, crying, "Money be damned, the very life of [insert name of Nation] is at stake," but meaning, most likely, *dawn is nearly here, I need my night's blood, my funding, funding, ahh more, more*.... The real crises were crises of allocation and priority, not among firms—it was only staged to look that way—but among the different Technologies, Plastics, Electronics, Aircraft, and their needs which are understood only by the ruling elite.[90]

The paranoia of Pynchon's protagonists reappears in the paranoia of Kittler's historical analyses, to the extent that in some of his essays Kittler resorts to lining up one Pynchon quote after another as documentary evidence.[91] For example, leading up to the celebrated passage just quoted, Enzian, the half-Herero leader of the all-black *Schwarzkommando*, senses the secret arrangements between the German IG Farben conglomerate and Allied bombers. German industry set up temporary facilities that act as "come-ons to call down special tools in the form of the 8th AF bombers" and plotted in advance in such a way as "to bring *precisely tonight's wreck* into being."[92] An old adage has it that modern urban architecture is nothing but the continuation of carpet bombing with other means. For Kittler, this is no joke but the simple truth of his childhood war. The bombing of Germany was the premeditated early stage of its industrial and urban renewal. American bomber squadrons destroying IG Farben installations are participating in a tacitly agreed-upon merger of postwar German and American sciences and industries. The need to move German high-tech industries out of urban centers and into rural areas to protect them from Allied air raids was, therefore, only the first step in revitalizing the postwar manufacturing industry.[93] The alliances of corporate interests and the joint effort to secure future resources undercut the surface constellations of political enmity.

Yet the most important question is not what secret agenda is behind Allied air raids (ultimately, it is a crude form of urban and industrial reconstruction that comes with greater collateral damage) but why Germany is firing off the v-2s. As noted, the rocket was marked by "complete short-term ineffectiveness *versus* profound long-term importance."[94] Its tactical value was negligible, its strategic potential immense. And this brings us to the very heart of the matter: as a weapon out of time, the v-2 is as much headed out of Germany as it is headed out of the war into a coming peace that will offer better conditions for the construction of the ultimate weapon. It is headed across the channel to Britain (and, in the final pages of *Gravity's Rainbow*, through time to the California of the early 1970s) to bring about the great merger of missile, computer, and atom bomb. To refer back to the second section of this introduction, which described ruptures and wars as instances of accelerated technological change, Kittler's World War II is a violent cataract in the flow of technological evolution. Its goal is nothing less than the unholy trinity of history's most destructive ménage à trois: the fusion of nuclear payload, computer-based self-directed guiding technology, and missile-based delivery system.

Replacing weapons with locations, the telos of the war is the merger of its three most important sites: Peenemünde, Bletchley Park, and Los Alamos (or Hiroshima). The war is an act of nuclear fusion; it compresses formerly distinct entities into one, a process that, if unchecked, releases a tremendous amount of destructive energy. This explains the wishful thinking behind Kittler's Z4/A4 gaffe. If Zuse's early computer had indeed been used to program the v-2, then a significant part of this techno-tectonic teleology would have taken place on Kittler's home ground. The gaffe, no doubt, comes with its share of Kittler's palpable "techno-patriotism."[95]

The rewriting of World War II as a primarily macrotechnological event "that devolved from humans and soldiers to machine subjects" has drawn considerable criticism (and caused some to part ways with Kittler).[96] Peenemünde, Bletchley Park, Los Alamos—sure, but where is Auschwitz? So much talk about the Wehrmacht and the war, so little mention of the Holocaust. There is no Hitler in Kittler's war, no war of aggression, no final solution, no complicity of military conquest and racial genocide, and subsequently no question of guilt and responsibility. For many, the truly offensive part of the quote cited at the beginning of the section "Blitzkrieg Nation" is not the sophomoric glorification of the Wehrmacht's "incredible" performance but the glib dismissal of its crimes. Of course, Kittler knew better. Tank expert that he was, he may even have known about the specific link between war crimes and the accelerated operational procedure of panzer-equipped units.[97] To take one of the most glaring examples, "Biogeography" and most of the essays dealing with Pynchon's *Gravity's*

Rainbow feature cameo performances by SS Brigadier General Hans Kammler, who in 1944 came to replace Walter Dornberger as the leader of the V-2 project. Readers learn that Kammler is in part behind the nefarious Captain Blicero in Pynchon's novel. They also learn that Kammler shares with Pynchon himself the "rare quality of having destroyed all his photographs," which makes for good reading but bad scholarship, for there is no shortage of photos.[98] The problem is what readers do *not* learn. Kammler is one of those shadowy figures who emerged in the final twilight of the war and who, endowed with the annihilationist mystique of the SS that tends to exert a certain fascination on some, graduated into the netherworld of pulp documentaries. He has also been awarded the ultimate honor bestowed on vanished Nazis, namely, ongoing doubts whether he really died at the end of the war.[99] Some of this is uncomfortably present in Kittler's texts. What readers do not learn is that Kammler was "one of the most capable, energetic, and vicious figures in [Heinrich] Himmler's entire murderous organization"; that he was one of the principal building inspectors for the SS Main Economic and Administrative Offices in the conquered East; and that many construction designs for the crematoria and gas chambers at Auschwitz come with his signature.[100]

Kittler would insist that his lack of interest in what he once referred to as the "Auschwitz-theoretical" understanding of the war constitutes a demotion rather than a downright denial.[101] The war has to be viewed differently; its very destructiveness has to be reconceptualized as a fundamentally technological event. "People meet their neighbors for the first time while watching their apartment houses burn down," Jerry Rubin remarked.[102] Likewise, technologies merge best when nations burn.

Conclusion: The Benefits of Defeat

"There is no escape from Kittler's technological singlemindedness," Amit Pinchevski notes. "His efforts to subordinate history to technology are nothing less than, well, obsessive."[103] Indeed, given the degree to which Kittler's childhood experience of the silencing of the war with all its uncanny scars and traces impacts his work, why not mobilize a concept that the modern critical industry has come to exploit as recklessly as other industries deplete fossil fuel: *trauma*? Yet we should hesitate to call trauma what may be no more than an unwillingness to speak out of shame, or the result of a political gag order, just as we should hesitate to call honesty what may be no more than the self-indulgent desire to speak in order to provoke others who do not. And in any case Kittler is ahead of the critical game. He would pounce on the irony (which is in line with the aforementioned literal reading of Kant's military hierarchy of reason) that the Freudian concept potentially capable of explaining his obsession with war and technology is—just like so many other tools in Freud's psycho-military arsenal—*itself* an effect of a historically identifiable conjuncture of war, technology, and tactics.

"Last night I dreamed about Freud. What does that mean?" runs an aphorism by Stanisław Jerzy Lec.[104] Kittler's answer: War, what else? Freud told him so—in a dream, no less. In the mid-1980s, as he was touring German universities in search of a permanent appointment, Kittler spent a night at the house of his colleague Manfred Schneider, who in a recently published essay recounts that Kittler appeared at the breakfast table to announce that Freud had revealed to him in a dream the real, secret origin of psychoanalysis:

> The theory's guiding concepts *defense, fraying* (Bahnung), *occupation, projection, death drive, repression, resistance, final objective, force* are words of war. Not only do they name psychic dramas and conflicts, but there is an unconscious at work in them. They come with the semantic residues of commands and military tactics. Psychoanalysis speaks a soldier's language. Once again Friedrich opened our eyes to a hidden occidental history. Sure, we are appendages of letters, numbers, and tools, but this symbolic machinery was forged by the war-father of all things. Just look: Even the letters the mythical Cadmus brought to Thebes were dragons' teeth, but from them warriors sprung![105]

Indeed, what is Freud's weaponized account of trauma in *Beyond the Pleasure Principle*, with its barrages and bombardments, strikes and sentinels, overrun defenses and occupied territories, other than a military dispatch? Trauma is an experiential blitzkrieg on hapless subjects. Crashing into an inadequately guarded center of gravity, or *Schwerpunkt*, storm-trooping stimuli break through the Maginot Line of consciousness. The explosive attack outstrips the ability of shocked subjects to process and experience the breach. Alien elements rush into the hinter- or *unter*land of the psyche, bind forces no longer available for the routine operations of consciousness, and disrupt all psychic communication and supply lines.

To look at war through trauma, Kittler would argue, requires that you first look at trauma through war. No tactical innovations of modern warfare, no widely deployable trauma concept. As the dream of Freud revealed, the origins of the concepts that shed light on repression and repetition compulsion are themselves repressed, which is precisely why they work so well. But this sidesteps the real issue. Kittler was not traumatized; he was a loser. His texts, especially those focusing on World War II, are a technologically refined twist on the *Besiegtentheorem*, or loser's theorem. Losers, so the story goes, are forced to develop a more profound understanding of history. Since events did not turn out as planned, losers are under greater pressure to understand the past than the victorious parties, who do not have to grapple with the unsettling discrepancy between expectation and experience. As a result, the old adage that winners write history becomes questionable. Maybe losers furnish more insightful accounts. Many of Kittler's World War II essays are, at rock bottom, attempts to unlose the war, or at the very least to lose it better than the other side won it by arriving at an allegedly more fundamental understanding.

In the German context, the loser urtext is a short essay written in 1948 by Carl Schmitt on French historian Alexis de Tocqueville.[106] Schmitt's personal agenda—his postwar mixture of artfully arranged resentment and ineluctable self-pity—need not concern us. What is at stake is the claim that Tocqueville's greatness as a historian emerges from his accumulation of defeats. He was a multiple loser: as an aristocrat, he was on the losing side of the French Revolution; as a liberal, he lost in 1830; as a Frenchman, he had to suffer the defeat of 1815; and as a European, he was one of the first to anticipate the future sandwiching of a demoted Europe between Russia and the United States. As Schmitt would have it, Tocqueville processed his defeats by withdrawing into a distanced view of history that eschewed the superficial narratives of myopic winners and instead explained events in terms of an overarching history of centralization and bureaucratization. He removed the sting of defeat by questioning the self-image of the victorious parties. Sure, this revolution or that war may have been won by this class or that nation, but their victories do not count for much because they had little to do with the actors' plans and intentions. This raises the questions: To what extent are you still a winner if you do not really understand why you won? And are you not less of a loser if you come to fully understand your defeat?

The loser's egg laid by Schmitt was hatched and bred into full maturity by his erstwhile intellectual scion Reinhart Koselleck in his famous essay "Transformations of Experience and Methodological Change." Koselleck honed Schmitt's incidental remarks into a veritable thesis: "The condition of being vanquished apparently contains an inexhaustible epistemological potential," especially when the defeated are forced to elaborate new methodological interpretations of history to account for the disturbing hiatus between expectation (we will win) and experience (we lost).[107] Defeat is the ultimate defamiliarization exercise, a Brechtian V-effect with high casualty rates. If accepted and pondered, defeat will facilitate a new view of history. By contrast, victory breeds intellectual laziness, since it is liable to confirm established, self-serving historiographical narratives. The loser, thrown to the ground, is closer to the subterranean movements of history than the winners strutting around on their victorious stilts.

Koselleck was careful to point out that the putative connection between unexpected experiences and viable, intellectually qualified methodological change by no means guarantees that "every history written by the vanquished is therefore more insightful."[108] To wit, many of the accounts written by German historians after the end of World War I are anything but. Yet on a psychological level, defeat certainly becomes more acceptable if the vanquished can show that the winners do not fully understand their victory. The prime exhibit is the success of Oswald Spengler's *Decline of the West*. As a historical analysis, it is questionable; as a communicative offer, irresistible. The unexpected "traumatic" defeat of 1918 is alleviated by administering a nation-sized dosage of prophetic opium: like a flower that grew, bloomed, and is now withering away, Western a.k.a. "Faustian" civilization is going down the drain of money and materialism, after which all historical energy will be spent. Does it really matter, then, who won or lost the war? Spengler wrote the first volume in anticipation of a German victory, but if Germany had indeed won World War I, his grand diagnosis would not have changed.

Furthermore, the very notion of defeat becomes questionable once you can show that what has occurred does not allow for a division into winners and losers because both sides are victims in a larger structural process, as in Tocqueville's grand narrative of governmental centralization or Spengler's morphological *missa solemnis*. War is, as it were, de-bellicized; military defeat is recast as civilizational catastrophe or historical rupture. This is also central to Kittler. As described in the preceding section, his Pynchonesque view transforms World War II into an accelerated techno-structural process marked by a tectonic shift that leads, in almost teleological fashion, to the fusion of hitherto separate technologies. As in the case of Spengler and World War I, the difference between a world in which Germany lost the war and an unrealized world in which the Third Reich was victorious pales in comparison to the difference between a world in which history was still conducted and processed by humans and one in which history, if that word still applies, operates on a machine level far removed from humans.

To conclude, readers of this collection will encounter a theorist engaged in a large-scale *polemodicy*, an attempt to do justice to war. Just as early modern theodicies tried to justify the goodness of God in the face of worldly (read: human) evil, polemodicies justify wars by showing the benefits, or at least the evolutionary necessity, of conflicts beyond all superficial (read: human) input. These conflicts were history as long as the struggles between human institutions and collectives corresponded to the struggles between media technologies. With the merging of the latter into the universal digital infrastructure, the histories of the former come to an end. "Media cross another in time that is no longer history."[109]

But deep down, buried under the notion of war as a giant "laboratory" of death and technology, there is a fleeting promise of freedom, though accompanied by a poignant sense of loss.[110] As Kittler is prone to do, he defers to quotes from *Gravity's Rainbow*. The uncanny quest into "the Zone," the destroyed Third Reich of 1945, is not only a descent into the German heart of darkness; it is also a pilgrimage into an anarchic, psychedelic realm full of dreams of "alternate histories," in which "this War—this incredible War—just for the moment has wiped out the proliferation of little states that's prevailed in Germany for a thousand years. Wiped it clean. *Opened it*."[111] For a fleeting moment other Germanies seemed possible, maybe better Germanies than those that came to be. Here, Kittler's political stance resembles that of Heidegger and others who regretted the inability of Germany to pursue an alternate third way—neither West nor East—after 1945. Or, rather, an alternate second way, since the two smaller Germanies that existed for a while in hostile tandem seemed rather interchangeable. That, at least, is one of the messages of "Biogeography." In *Gravity's Rainbow*, these aspirations are still alive and flickering across the Zone—but only for a brief instance and with little chance of success, for other centralizing and connective forces are already at work that will soon do away with nations and politics to create a techno-ballistic globe: "Oh, a State begins to take form in the stateless German night, a State that spans oceans and surface politics, sovereign as the International or the Church of Rome, and the Rocket is its soul."[112]

OPERATION VALHALLA

PART I

Guns, Germans, and Steel

THE HARDWARE(S) OF WAR

CHAPTER 1

Free Ways

TRANSLATED BY GEOFFREY WINTHROP-YOUNG

> The country offers ways because it is country. It gives way, moves us. We hear the words "give way" in this sense: to be the original giver and founder of ways.
> —Martin Heidegger, *On the Way to Language* (1959)

Tragedy, as we all know, began at the three-way crossing of Daulis with the chance encounter between a mule cart and a pedestrian, between a tyrant named Laius and his unrecognized son. It would have been averted had Delphi and Corinth been connected by an intersection-free, median stripe–equipped highway. Which is why Heiner Müller is not Sophocles, and why all op-ed laments about the disappearance of dramatic encounters miss the point. Where the god of chance (whose *herma* once graced every Greek crossroad) has left the stage, runways and their centaurs take over. There is no drama anymore, only the movement of tanks, from Verdun to Volokolamsk and on: "Only empty tanks which crash / Into each other on this scorched earth."[1]

At the end of *Gravity's Rainbow*, a final news flash from PNS Los Angeles reaches you, the reader of the novel. Seconds before the first or last V-2 explodes over LA, a "Managerial Volkswagen" takes you on a trip along the Santa Monica Freeway, "the freeway of freaks" and "traditionally the

---

Originally published as "Auto Bahnen," in *Der Technikdiskurs in der Hitler-Stalin-Ära*, edited by Wolfgang Emmeric and Carl Wege (Stuttgart: Metzler, 1995), 114–22; and translated by Geoffrey Winthrop-Young in *Cultural Politics* 11, no. 3 (2015): 376–83. A shorter version of the same essay appeared in *Kulturrevolution: Zeitschrift für angewandte Diskurstheorie* 5 (1984): 44–47.

scene of every form of automotive folly known to man."² In the oncoming lane, "the city's garbage trucks are all heading north toward the Ventura Freeway."³ In downtown LA you are surrounded by increasingly congested truck traffic. Heading up the Hollywood Freeway, you are passed by "a mysteriously canvassed trailer rig and a liquid-hydrogen tanker"—precisely the type of convoy or motorized rocket brigade Waffen-SS lieutenant general Hans Kammler used to send along the autobahn between September 1944 and March 1945.⁴ And when the electric off-ground detonator, thought up by Hitler himself, is triggered by the rocket closing in on the LA of the early 1970s, you'll be able to see for a millisecond in the blinding light of its payload what they are, all the freeways and *Reichsautobahnen* of this world. . . .

Which leaves the question who thought up the automotive folly called *autobahn*. As is frequently the case with inventions, there are two versions. The first is feudal and famous, the other a forgotten matter of war. The autobahns, "the roads of Adolf Hitler," are said to be from their very outset a thoroughly German affair. Hence a historiography that is spearheaded, not coincidentally, by a former press relations officer of the HAFRABA erases all foreign traces.⁵

This official version is quickly told. In that unimaginable past when only general staffs and major corporations owned fleets of vehicles, certain high-ranking drivers were upset by the dust and clamor that prevailed on roads. According to the last crown prince of Prussia, this dust prevented the setting of new records at the Hamburg car race of 1904 and therefore made concrete surfaces all the more desirable. A lot of hue and cry—race car driver Manfred von Brauchitsch recalls—threatened a driver who dared "defy it and make full use of his engine."⁶ In the cities they had to contend with pedestrians, cyclists, carts, and carriages; in the country, with hay wagons, children, cattle, and free-range poultry. Unacceptable conditions, no doubt, whose termination led to an agreement between the emperor and his firstborn. While Wilhelm II, a major techno-freak, continued to focus on large-scale projects and basic research such as Alfred von Tirpitz's shipbuilding program or the army telegraph, which he discussed with his chief engineers on walks across the Brandenburg Schorfheide or over dinner at his Hubertusstock hunting lodge, Crown Prince Wilhelm received permission to further indulge in his racing hobby that he had already pursued with great success in Indianapolis and Los Angeles.

And so it came to pass that in 1907 a command was issued from "the very highest place" to construct a paved road able to accommodate parallel traffic. Two years later, members of the Berlin sports and finance world created the office of the Automobil-Verkehrs und Übungs-Straße [Automobile Traffic and Training Road], better known by its acronym, Avus. Ten kilometers between Charlottenburg and Wannsee, or the road of the future: for cars only, with no intersections, but featuring raised curves, bleachers for sporting events, and (not to forget) two lanes separated by a median stripe.

It's hard to imagine what people were willing to put up with. From mule tracks to Roman roads, from cobblestone to asphalt—millennia of walking, riding, and driving on any possible type of path, track, or way, and all without median stripes or dividers. While random encounters persisted, Hermes, god of roads, retained his power over boulevards and lidos. It was the autobahn that finally delivered traffic (both work and thing) from its obscene double meaning, which already long before Freud was celebrated in countless puns.[7] To be sure, right-hand traffic had been decreed by Napoleon as part of his joint creation of marching infantry divisions and a national road system, but regulations on their own cannot guarantee that nobody will ever bump into anybody else. It is the autobahn's median divider that, once and for all, separates the two snakes or streams that pass each other and vanish beyond different horizons. Wannsee and Charlottenburg . . .

All the sadder, then, that the initiator of this automotive folly was never able to act out his obsession. Only in his imagination did the exiled crown prince race along the Avus unencumbered by dust goggles and oncoming traffic. A world war, the first of two, interrupted its construction. Financed by the industrialist Hugo Stinnes and built with the help of new cement mixers, the Avus was not completed until 1921—as a leisure track for gentlemen drivers. And the latter, though recently democratized, had not increased in number. In any case, endless traffic jams, bumper to bumper by day, headlight on headlight by night, are no German invention. To turn gentlemen drivers into responsible citizens of the road (the twentieth century's character mask) required greater resources than Hohenzollern hobbies. The car as a means of mass transportation emerged at a time when weeds covered the unfinished Avus: during World War I. This is the strategic secret studiously avoided by the heroic epics of German autobahn construction.

September 1914: an anthroposophic member of the German General Staff has a better grasp on bearers of bad tidings than on Schlieffen Plans. Instead of simply connecting frontline units by telegraph, Helmut von Moltke the Younger sends an automobile-equipped lieutenant colonel,

Richard Hentsch, to the Marne. Hentsch, head of the intelligence section at Supreme Headquarters, communicates reports of wide-open fronts and French attacks. Yes, only a thin cavalry line (whose heavy radio equipment is under the command of none other than a certain Captain Heinz Guderian) is covering the gap between Alexander von Kluck's First and Karl von Bülow's Second Army. And yes, General Joseph Gallieni, military commander of Paris, commandeers all the city's cabs to rush his Sixty-Second Infantry Division to the front at Nanteuil. But improvised prophecies in the shape of history's first motorized division do not decide battles—for that you need the blind gentleman driver Hentsch. And so the Miracle of the Marne came about.

February 1916: the armies have long since dug themselves in and buried the Schlieffen Plan. Trench warfare from Ypres to Belfort. The hapless Younger Moltke is succeeded by Erich von Falkenhayn, who stands in front of his sandbox (an innovation, incidentally, introduced by Heinrich von Kleist's circle of military friends) and ponders the situation. Ever since the Battle of the Marne, breakthroughs and thrusts, encirclements and annihilation, are out of the question. Clausewitz is obsolete. But what if the French were to be bled dry by applying a "suction pump"? At a place where they would be forced to join battle but where the Germans would not be required to ship materials? His cartographic eyes fixed on the front line, Falkenhayn identifies the only possible point: the string of forts called Verdun. Even failed Schlieffen Plans have their upside: as the hub for the large move to the right undertaken in 1914, Verdun is cut off from the French hinterland and connected only by one railway line and a road. (One world war later, the German Army Command will note that the planned advance toward the Ural Mountains by eight panzer and four infantry divisions "is generally determined by rail and road connections.")

And Falkenhayn acts. Crown Prince Wilhelm, in command of the Fifth Army, is given the order to attack on February 12, 1916. A racing aficionado, of all people, is ordered to set in motion Falkenhayn's grinding "blood mill." But owing to their own transportation problems, the Germans are forced to postpone their opening barrage, which provides the French with a crucial reprieve—and the opportunity to make global traffic history. On February 19, German deserters betray the new date of the attack. General Camille Ragueneau and Major Aimé Doumenc, head of the military automobile service, instantly recognize the gravity of the situation. It boils down to a simple problem of securing supplies. Once the Germans sever the railroad connection, Verdun will depend on one last umbilical cord, the *route nationale* to Bar-le-Duc. Forty-five Napoleonic kilometers will determine the fate of France. But for the Direction des services automobiles, that is no reason for despair. Even before the German barrage opens on February 21 at 7 a.m., Doumenc had converted the old-fashioned route nationale 109 into the first autobahn. Bar-le-Duc becomes the headquarters of the Commission Regulatrice Automobile (CRA), which relegates all pedestrians, cyclists, and horse carts to rural dirt roads and reserves the route nationale 109 for the exclusive use of trucks. Europe's ambiguous traffic comes to an end.

Jacques Lacan explained what he called the urinal segregation of occidental man by telling the story of a little boy and a little girl, brother and sister, seated across from each other in a railway compartment watching "the station platforms going by as the train comes to a stop. 'Look,' says the brother, 'we are at Ladies!' 'Imbecile,' replies his sister, 'Don't you see we're at Gentlemen.'"[8] And because, according to Lacan, the rails "materialize the bar in the Saussurian algorithm," they need not be materially present. As long as they feature two sets of rails, even railway lines destroyed by German shock troops can become the model for automotive segregation.

Major Doumenc issues orders that route nationale 109 is to be used like a double-track railroad. The way trains had been passing each other since 1830 becomes standard procedure for roads in 1916. From now on, an improvised divider separates the input and output of large-scale modern battles. In the course of seven months, 350,000 dead need to be removed and replaced. Wheels are rolling for victory—on the right, cannon fodder from Bar-le-Duc to Verdun; on the left, cannon victims from Verdun to Bar-le-Duc. "Two endless chains," in the words of Doumenc, but without any contact between them. Random encounters between trucks and carts caused enough damage; those between cannon fodder and corpse convoys would lead to catastrophes and mutinies. Militarily, the median stripe is a *cordon sanitaire* (and to be removed only in emergencies when highways have to double as runways).

Even if Falkenhayn's suction pump were not in itself already "a declaration of bankruptcy, a capitulation of operative leadership in the face of static warfare," it is overcome by Doumenc's double-truck pump. Verdun holds out for seven months; then the crown prince's bloodied army gives up. The fortress hexagon manages to retain its cruelly exposed part because every day 13,600 trucks (or one truck every six seconds) secure the connection. "C'est la route qui mène la bataille," notes the CRA, and bestows on its improvised autobahn the proudest name empires have been able to award since Roman days: *La Voie sacrée—via sacra*.⁹

The *Collection des cahiers de la victoire*, a series of French war propaganda pamphlets, dedicates an issue and a title to the *Voie sacrée*. The autobahn, hardly invented, becomes literature. Long before Tyrone Slothrop and Thomas Pynchon, soldiers of the (barely neutral) United States come to Europe and take note of how the Old World is inventing the future, a nameless GI, witness to Verdun, extols for the *Cahiers de la victoire* what night has come to mean from the Avus to the Santa Monica Freeway, from Charlottenburg to California: headlights upon headlights, a luminous ribbon stretching across the hills and valleys of the Argonne, "quelque gigantesque et lumineux serpent ('a giant and luminous snake')."¹⁰

"The defense of Verdun came to depend on the operability of vehicular traffic on the *voie sacrée*. And so, from the beginning to the end of the battle, fresh blood pulsed into the almost severed link of the French front and kept it alive."¹¹ No American world war tourist could have phrased it more poetically, but this is in fact Captain Guderian speaking. In one of the ironies of history, Guderian, a signals officer (and thus one of Schlieffen's favorite sons), was always in the thick of things: in 1914 at the Marne and in 1916 at Verdun. He remained on the spot even after the Treaty of Versailles had left the Reich an army of only 100,000 men without a single armored vehicle. This, however, was to underestimate the inventiveness of Prussian staff officers. As early as the winter of 1923–24, Guderian and the later commander in chief of the German Army, Walther von Brauchitsch (not to be confused with race car–driving nephew Manfred), organized blitzkrieg maneuvers whose tank units consisted of highly poetic mock-ups: staff vehicles with glued-on cardboard turrets. According to Hans von Seeckt, chief of the German General Staff during the Weimar Republic, "The motorization of the army was one of the most important issues."¹² Small wonder, then, that the very same Guderian writes the first text on the autobahn. The January 1925 issue of *Militär-Wochenblatt* [Military weekly] contains, as part of a section on "the armored vehicle," his epochal essay "The Lifeline of Verdun."¹³ While the solitary author of *Mein Kampf* can merely dream of an autobahn, Guderian clearly spells out Doumenc's lesson: ever since February 1916, giant snakes of light and steel are our lifelines.

In short, you learn from your enemy. The tactics of World War x become the strategies of World War $x+1$. Tanks, used by the British in 1917 at Cambrai for infantry support only, and still as late as 1940 restricted to tactical employment in the Allied armies (with the notable exception of de

Gaulle), are turned by Guderian into a decisive weapon. "Deployed by the high command in surprising numbers and depth on a broad front," independently operating panzer divisions drive the blitzkrieg. The autobahn, a purely defensive measure at Verdun and not pursued in postwar Europe (with the exception of Italy's Dr. Piero Puricelli, who, however, did not implement the two-way traffic with clearly divided lanes), is turned by Hitler into the lifeline of the Third Reich. (Just one of Guderian's ten panzer divisions is already a 110-kilometer column.)

The two creators first met at the 1933 Berlin Automobile Exhibition. In his memoirs Guderian recounts that it was "unusual for the Chancellor himself to open the exhibition. And what he had to say was in striking contrast to the customary speeches of ministers and chancellors on such occasions. He announced the abolition of the tax on cars and spoke of the new national roads that were to be built and of the Volkswagen, the cheap 'People's Car,' that was to be mass-produced."[14]

Said and done. The Reich came to experience what even sober economic historians of the Kuczynski school can only describe in psychiatric terms: "the motorization psychosis." The 1932 traffic volume of 522,943 cars and 162,073 trucks certainly did not require any autobahn, but, as Hitler put it, "just as the horse carriage once paved its way and the railroad built the necessary tracks, motor traffic must receive the necessary road system." The movement of 1933, then, was always already a moving [*Be-wegung*]. It awakened people's desires to acquire a driver's license—in German, *Führerschein*. And the Führer granted them their wish—as tank commanders [*Panzerführer*] on the autobahn.

A short story, published by the headquarters of the VII Army Corps, may serve as a miniature model: in the last days of the 1940 blitzkrieg against France, two German soldiers on reconnaissance enter the village of Sy. They discover "two, three, four—fifteen motorcycles, five of them equipped with sidecars. An entire signal squadron," whose "drivers must have fled from our artillery." "One thing is clear: the bikes are going back with us." While Private A goes looking for reinforcements, Private B "enviously" inspects the loot. He "doesn't know much about motorbikes"; he has "only now and then watched cyclists and the staff's 'gentlemen drivers.'" But war is wish fulfillment—also and especially for those without a driver's license. Private A returns with a motorcycle expert. "Then, suddenly, the sound of an approaching engine. Everybody takes cover," but only to witness Private B "return at top speed, stop with squealing brakes and report to his commander: 'Sir, Sy liberated from the enemy!'" A short story in which one need only replace motorbikes with cars, and country roads with the autobahn, in order to arrive at the Kraftwerk song.[15]

For the autobahn *is* aesthetics. "For motorized traffic," notes the 1937 governmental publication *Bauten der Bewegung*, "the Reichsautobahn constitutes a veritable artery: it is not a foreign body in the landscape but a harmonious part."[16] The somewhat less public reason: unlike autostradas and autoroutes, the autobahn avoids unnecessarily deep embankments "that would separate them from the landscape." In the words of Fritz Todt and his constant army contacts, "the autobahn must not turn into a mousetrap from which military vehicles cannot escape."[17] Thus, peacetime planning paves the way for Kammler's brigades, who spent the final months of the war rushing along the autobahn to launch V-2 rockets toward London and World War $x+1$.

Unlike its foreign imitations, Germany's autobahn is surrounded by green. State secretary and later field marshal Erhard Milch of the Reich Aviation Ministry provided Todt's engineers with aircraft "in order for them to see their autobahn from above and assess how advantageously planted vegetation could at least in part obscure the road when approached from the side."[18] Eichendorff's question who put the forest so high above can thus be answered in part.[19] It was the Supreme Command of the German Wehrmacht, spurred by the all-too-prophetic concern that enemy aircraft could follow the uncamouflaged autobahn all the way to Berlin. World War $x+1$ casts its shadow on all thorough planning.

And when the soloist of *Hitler's Table Talk* dreams of driving along the Reichsautobahn all the way to Kiev and Odessa in a car with a built-in camera, the modern landscape movie has been shot, and the identity of aesthetics and blitzkrieg is beyond all doubt.[20]

To this day, Americans, who had to wait until February 9, 1938, for the Senate to officially recommend the construction of express highways, drive their cars as if they were covered wagons heading west. Speed limits and front bench seats, that stubborn relic from horse-wagon days, do not bother pioneers. On a broad, well-behaved front, with nobody passing anyone, they all trek together toward the last frontier. But German panzer divisions moving at combat speed, to quote Colonel General Werner von Fritsch of the German Supreme Command, need the autobahn from "Halle to Berlin to themselves." Which also indicates who, if anybody, is allowed to pass said divisions. Germany forgoes twelve- or fourteen-lane Santa Monica–type freeways. There is only one passing lane for staff officers and engineers, the gentlemen drivers in motion.

And every time summer comes around, as it did in 1939, when the autobahn is cloaked in green and its soft embankments are navigable, people's wishes are granted: tourist division upon tourist division sallies forth. Motorization psychosis. Six-cylinder engines roar. Not to mention stereos. Until Europe's borders capitulate. Blitzkrieg *à tous azimuts* [in all directions]. And everyone passes everyone.

Peace is the continuation of war with the same means of transportation.

A Short History of the Searchlight

TRANSLATED BY GEOFFREY WINTHROP-YOUNG

"You who through beauty reign / glittering, glorious race" are the words used by the giant Fasolt[1] in scene 2 of Richard Wagner's *Rhinegold* to address a group of gods whose power since time immemorial was based on their command of light.[2] But thorn bushes and magic fire are not yet on the level of searchlights. Only when power (in Michel Foucault's words) turns into absolutist supremacy does the command of light advance from mere illumination to deliberate blinding. Otherwise it would be difficult to explain why the seventeenth century witnessed the first discussions of bull's-eye lanterns, while at the same time threatening their private use with draconian punishments. In German principalities, this injunction was directed especially at poachers, whose lanterns (long before the invention of highways and headlights) threatened to deprive local lords, with their absolute hunting rights, of their customary haul of rabbits, stags, and deer. In France, the use of such lanterns was punishable by death, for it was assumed they might enable murderers to hunt, trap, blind, and kill humans and animals alike. Which is, by contrast, exactly what these lanterns could and had to do on battlefields. As part of the monopoly of force wielded by the new Leviathan sovereign known as the state, lanterns served as weapons to overwhelm hostile eyes—just as the new, no longer light-shunning palaces did in so-called peace. Caught in their sooty night, the masses could do no more than gawk at all the fireworks, luminous candelabra, and hall-

---

Originally published as "Eine Kurzgeschichte des Scheinwerfers," in *Der Entzug der Bilder: Visuelle Realitäten*, edited by Michael Wetzel and Herta Wolf (Munich: Fink, 1999), 83–89; and translated by Geoffrey Winthrop-Young in *Cultural Politics* 11, no. 3 (2015): 384–90.

of-mirrors light shows. Which once again proves Foucault's words that "the famous dazzling effect of power . . . is not something that petrifies, solidifies, and immobilizes the entire social body, and thus keeps it in order; it is in fact a divisive light that illuminates one side of the social body but leaves the other side in shadow or casts it into darkness."[3]

The origin of the searchlight, then, is illuminated—as is history itself—by the light of absolutist wars. Searchlights exploit the same optical laws that allowed the seventeenth century to design telescopes and microscopes: their parabolic mirrors focus incident light in exactly the same way as lenses or glasses act on transmitted light. Searchlights, however, also render light available for tactical purposes. Despite the many metaphors at play in the history of science, the true weaponizing of our vision is not a matter of telescopes and microscopes, which after all work only if whatever they move closer or enlarge is itself already bright or illuminated. Instead, armed eyes emerge with searchlights that mobilize and mechanize vision itself. Searchlights—to invoke Leonardo da Vinci's description of the sun—never see any shadows. Anything that appears in their beam of light, anything that is illuminated against the background of a vanquished darkness, becomes a projection of the eye that directed and cast the beam in the first place—an eye that has none of the sun-likeness Goethe attributed to it.[4] As Paul Eduard Liesegang has shown, baroque lanterns were the immediate predecessor of the *laterna magica* and hence of all film projectors.[5]

Magic lanterns, however, preferred to project the ghosts and phantoms that, since the spiritual exercises of the Jesuits, came to dance before the inner eye; in other words, they projected the subject of the Counter-Reformation. According to Carl Schmitt's beautifully cruel formulation, the shape of one's question, as evoked by all optical media from lanterns to film projectors and radar beams, is always the enemy.[6] Historical differences depend on the degree of illumination. The weak candlelight projected by the parabolic mirror of a magic lantern (or, since the days of absolutist police reform, by streetlights) had a direct effect on the enemy. To produce new degrees of light, it was necessary to first string up Europe's nobility on the lampposts and turn popular insurgencies into new Napoleonic armies.

A spring night in Madrid in 1808, which no Spanish court painter would ever have survived, witnessed how a French execution squad dealt with history's first *guerrilleros*: as depicted in Francisco Goya's *The Third of May 1808*, the light of a lantern enables both individualization and well-aimed shots, thereby also shedding light on the Enlightenment itself, whose trademark ever since Benjamin Franklin happens to be the lightning bolt of truth.

Then, on an early spring day in Paris in 1802, Étienne-Gaspard Robert, a.k.a. Robertson, a Belgian stage magician turned experimenter, noticed during a public performance of the first artificial lightning that it was sparked by two carbon rods placed between the poles of 120 wired silver-zinc batteries. Electric light, if only for a few seconds, had become real. But when in 1848 it became possible to make the carbon rods part of a feedback circuit, sustained artificial lightning triumphed over its divine counterpart. Just one year later the carbon-arc light fell into a concave mirror and was projected onto a transparent silk screen, serving as a fake sun for a performance of Giacomo Meyerbeer's opera *Le prophète*. Never before had theater audiences, who following the introduction of the proscenium stage had to endure the chiaroscuro of smoky candles, enjoyed such bright and sharply contoured lighting effects.

Projection, which in the times of the magic lantern had to make do with the shadowy existence of dubious ghosts, was now able to assault bodies, first on the stage and then in so-called life. Charles Babbage and Michael Faraday, arguably the most famous lighting crew in the history of theater, used extremely strong stage lights to chase a ballet troupe clad all in white through the entire color spectrum. Placing the stage lights underneath a special glass floor, Loïe Fuller turned expressive dance into a self-advertisement for electric lighting. The figures her veiled body presented to an enthused audience lost all human likeness and were simply called "fire and lightning". In the words of an official history of the Siemens company published in 1949:

> The theater was among the very first parties interested in electric light. The appearance of metal-filament lamps, especially in the shape of large semiwatt lamps, revolutionized stage lighting. As in so many other instances, eyes soon came to expect the new fullness of light as the norm and would have regarded any retreat to older standards as unacceptable. Hidden from the audience behind the proscenium arch or hanging from the gridiron, the new lights took on all possible shapes and functions: spotlights, footlights, skylights, festoon lamps, and apron lights, all equipped with all kinds of colored panes and color-mixing devices but, above all, with extensive control systems. By adding a resistor, the luminosity of a bulb can be reduced to the point of complete darkness, and theaters fully exploited this possibility.

> These effects had all the more impact because the introduction of metal-filament lamps coincided with that of the cyclorama or rounded

horizon, which replaced the painted sceneries and backdrops of the old chariot-and-pole system with a unified space, whose light background enabled the projection of far more delicate shades of color. The daytime Easter Walk of Goethe's *Faust* and his return home at dusk with the poodle, the sunrise over Friedrich Schiller's Rütli, the magical light of *Tannhäuser*'s Venus mountain, Sarastro's sacred halls, Palestrina's nocturnal study—they could now be staged with such realism that the Meiningers would have turned green with envy.[7] After all, when it comes to conjuring up illusions for the audience, costumes and props are far less important than light.

But here we once again stumble across the gap that opens up between technology and the overall progress of culture. The principal beneficiaries of the new stage lighting techniques were the then new and fashionable revues. Given that the exhibition of naked flesh depends on good lighting, they could not have been staged without filament lamps and stage lights. By contrast, the spirit haunting the midnight battlement of Elsinore survived without electric light for three hundred years.[8]

This historic switch from spirit to flesh proved equally irresistible to the greater theater of war. In 1881 Hiram Stevens Maxim constructed the first light bulb with clearly defined luminous intensities. Not coincidentally, two years later he was the one to present the prototype of all machine guns. Targeting bodies with light and with bullets proceeded in tandem. The great machine-gun premiere took place during the British-Sudanese conflict, when eleven thousand dervishes fell to six machine guns outside of Khartoum at the Battle of Omdurman. The premiere of the military searchlight followed suit. *Meyers Großes Konversations-Lexikon* of 1907 notes that searchlights are "powerful electric arc lights equipped with parabolic reflectors. . . . They are used for military purposes on warships, in fortresses, and most recently also on battlefields to identify enemy positions at night and search the terrain for wounded combatants. Searchlights have been used with great success in the Russo-Japanese War. Britain has recently introduced searchlight companies that use motorized vehicles to transport their equipment."[9] What began "most recently"—to be precise, in 1904—in the nightly machine-gun massacres at Port Arthur is (in Paul Virilio's words) light war. Searchlights illuminated and sometimes even guided hit rates. World wars and blitzkrieg tactics were feverishly at work to automate the coupling of missile trajectories and artificial light beams. The results are well known: ever since their premiere in the early days of

World War I, searchlights from Paris to Baghdad write the signature of our century across the skies.

"How little one felt the war in Paris," the protagonist of Marcel Proust's *In Search of Lost Time* remarks in 1916 to his friend, the Marquis Saint-Loup, a frontline officer on leave from the trenches.[10] But Saint-Loup disagrees, for "even in Paris" things were at times "pretty extraordinary," especially when zeppelin raids turn into spectacles "of great aesthetic beauty." As if an entire city had been submerged in Babbage's magical-fire ballet, the two friends admire the shades of "pink" and "pale green" created by the jousts between dirigibles and flak lights:

> The town from being a black shapeless mass seemed suddenly to rise out of the abyss and the night into the luminous sky, where one after another the pilots soared upwards in answer to the heartrending appeal of the sirens, while with a movement slower but more insidious, more alarming—for their gaze made one think of the object, still invisible but perhaps already very near, which it sought—the searchlights strayed ceaselessly to and fro, scenting the enemy, encircling him with their beams until the moment when the aeroplanes should be unleashed to bound after him in pursuit and seize him. And squadron after squadron, each pilot, as he soared thus above the town, itself now transported into the sky, resembled indeed a Valkyrie.[11]

Long before movie theaters plunged audiences into total darkness, thereby abolishing glittering and glorious gods, Wagner's Bayreuth media technology became the theatrical model of all searchlight pans and night fights from Proust's novel to Francis Ford Coppola's Vietnam movie. As the Siemens history points out, the early bulbs were too expensive for private customers, whose eyes had to learn from watching music dramas and world wars how they could be used as replacement searchlights. And watching these searchlights they saw, naturally, nothing but other searchlights. For instance, in 1916, when Major Aimé Doumenc of the French saved the fortress of Verdun from an entire German Army Group simply by inventing the autobahn with its median stripe—which resulted in a single supply line from Bar-le-Duc to Verdun traversed by ten vehicles per minute—an advance detachment of the U.S. Army witnessed in the hills of the Argonne the same as Proust and Saint-Loup had seen across the Parisian city sky: headlight upon headlight, the whole *route nationale* 109 as "a giant and luminous snake."[12] Electric lighting, night combat, and the adoration of new serpentine divinities historically coincide. The skill not to be as helplessly attracted by the light of oncoming traffic as are animals and insects has become a survival and selection principle for entire vehicular populations. And when a modern French army restages Goya's *The Third of May 1808* during the Occupation of the Ruhr in the early 1920s, then—as at the conclusion of Hanns Johst's *Schlageter* drama—army trucks with beaming headlights appear onstage and optically preexecute the protagonist (as well as all the eyes of the SA storm troopers in the audience) before any shots are fired and curtains fall.[13] Death of the pedestrian . . .

A modern art for the masses—at least for those in the Third Reich entitled to buy VWs—culminated in the so-called cathedral of light, created in 1934 by the later minister of armaments using 130 flak lights (a significant part of Göring's "strategic air force reserve") assembled for the Nuremberg party rally:

> The actual effect far surpassed anything I had imagined. The hundred and thirty sharply defined beams, placed around the field at intervals of forty feet, were visible to a height of twenty to twenty-five thousand feet, after which they merged into a general glow. The feeling was of a vast room, with the beams serving as mighty pillars of infinitely high outer walls. Now and then a cloud moved through this wreath of light, bringing an element of surrealistic surprise to the mirage. I imagine that this "cathedral of light" was the first luminescent architecture of this type, and for me it remains not only my most beautiful architectural concept but, after its fashion, the only one which has survived the passage of time.[14]

The only one, indeed. As already intimated by his "Theory of Ruin Value," all of Speer's spatial creations swiftly returned to the world war surrealism of light architectures.[15] On November 22, 1943, when "the Royal Air Force began an air offensive against Berlin," the minister of armaments, perched on a Berlin flak tower, witnessed the "unforgettable sight" of the destruction of the city he had partly rebuilt himself:

> I had to remind myself of the cruel reality in order not to be completely entranced by the scene: the illumination of the parachute flares, which the Berliners called "Christmas trees," followed by flashes of explosion which were caught by the clouds of smoke, the innumerable probing searchlights, the excitement when a plane was caught and tried to escape the cone of light, the brief flaming torch when it was hit. No doubt about it, this apocalypse provided a magnificent spectacle.[16]

The apocalypse had already been invoked by Saint-Loup, but this may well be the last instance, because the basic precondition—the eyes' ability to see searchlight performances—was falling by the wayside. When Soviet Marshal Georgy Zhukov ordered the final attack on the German defenses on the Oder on April 16, 1945, it required that the First Belorussian Front deploy 140 searchlights:

> At exactly three minutes before the beginning of the artillery preparation we all went out of the dugout and took up positions at the observation posts. . . . The entire vicinity beyond the Oder could be seen from here in the daytime. Now there was a morning mist there. I looked at my watch: it was five o'clock sharp.
>
> And at this moment the vicinity was lit up by the fire of many thousands of machine guns, mortars and the legendary Katyusha rocket launchers followed by a tremendous din from discharges and explosions of shells and aircraft bombs. The continuous roar of bombers was steadily growing louder. . . .
>
> Thousands of flares of different colour flew into the air. This was the signal for 140 searchlights placed at intervals of 200 metres to flash spot lights equalling 100,000 million candle-powers, lighting up the battlefield and blinding the enemy and snatching objects for attack by our tanks and infantry from the darkness. It was a striking picture, and I remember having seen nothing like it during my whole life.[17]

Thus Marshal Zhukov in his memoirs. The strategist of 1945 recognized that his armed searchlight gaze scuttled the enemy's countergaze. The good old baroque lanterns had successfully completed their march through history.

If he had been less blinded by his cathedrals of light, the record-setting minister of armaments perched atop the Berlin flak tower would have realized that human eyes were now only able to see "magnificent spectacles"—in other words, nothing. Since World War II—to be precise, since Norbert Wiener, Claude Shannon, and Josef Kammhuber—searchlights are no longer linked to hands, eyes, and artillery but to radar systems and rocket batteries. Electronic weapons dissolve the century-old union of light and electricity; they have the power to operate in the invisible parts of the electromagnetic spectrum—that is, automatically. The V-2, a self-guided weapon, has replaced the classic subject; the radar beam, an invisible searchlight, the armed gaze. And because electronic warfare has moved into the domain of mathematical formulas and thus beyond all presentability, the short history of the searchlight will turn out to have been a short story.

CHAPTER 3

Fragments of a History of Firearms

TRANSLATED BY MICHAEL WUTZ

The Greeks knew thunder and lightning only when they were doomed, as a jealously guarded sign of domination sent down by their highest god from the highest mountain. Following that, rolling thunder—infinite repetitions of the event further below in the valleys of the mortals. In his wisdom, Pythagoras never wrote of such scares but only passed them on as *acusmata*, as aurally transmitted sayings. He told his pupils: thunder is a scare tactic for the people banished to the Tartarus.[1] It was not until Archytas of Taranto, one of Pythagoras's pupils in mathematics, that some of this dim wisdom was translated into science: the knowledge of whole numbers in lute music and in the skies. That's why lightning was no longer talked about, only its measurable and repeatable echo. High-pitched sounds of strings were beats in the air in rapid succession; the muffle of rolling thunder, by contrast, much slower beats. Greek scientists working on acoustics deduced, with razor-sharp logic, that the speed of sounds through the air and into the brain, blood, and eventually the soul depended on their pitch.

It was not until European modernity that thunder and lightning could be manufactured. Greek fire, whose monopoly secured for the eastern Roman Empire domination of the Aegean Sea for several hundred years during the early Middle Ages, was already a human invention but not yet a firearm delivering fatal flashes. It smoldered and glowed on the planks of enemy ships as long as its ingredients—sulfur, pitch, and oil—were not burned up. Only gunpowder as an essential composite of saltpeter, coal,

Originally published as "Bruchstücke einer Geschichte der Feuerwaffen," in *Feuer: Elemente des Naturhaushalts II*, edited by Bernd Busch with Johann Georg Goldammer and Andreas Denk (Cologne: Wienand, 2001), 560–62.

and sulfur (similar to the way pure alcohol, at about the same historical moment, was a quintessence of all wines and herbs) consumes itself in the flashy explosion of a godless event. A moment beyond the threshold of perception made history. Being the humanist that he was, François Rabelais thanked his god for Johannes Gutenberg's invention of letterpress printing. In the same breath, however, he ascribed the invention of artillery to the whisperings of Satan himself.[2] And indeed: the wind- and watermills Europe initially imported from Asia for the production of innocent paper, as in Augsburg, Spandau, and Liegnitz, shifted to the production of gunpowder around 1340. Then, in 1525, France—which seven years later devoured Rabelais's novel—discovered the secret of gunpowder granulation. Slowed down artificially, gunpowder fired its bullets even faster and with more fatal force into the soul, which is far removed from Plato's notion of the soul as the site of hearing.

For that very reason Tommaso Campanella and Francis Bacon went a step further than Rabelais. Both wrote that the invention of the printing press, the compass, and gunpowder changed the world, or, better, our technical infrastructure, more than anything else in the past four thousand years.[3] Time, which escapes any form of temporal perception, pulls history along in its flash. The invention of Satan, which provides the godly, faith-based wars of humanism or Protestantism with firepower, rubs off on its beneficiaries. Faced with cannon and musket blasts, Bacon arrived at the truism, which has since been repeated ad nauseam, that the invention of technologies is a fundamentally human matter. Lightning, which the ancients believed to be beyond the reach of humanity, it being the sole craft of their highest god, was brought down to earth as a firearm. It can be understood as an expression of the naked truth, however ephemeral, that art has successfully shed its Aristotelian essence of being no more than a mere imitation of the natural world.[4]

In 1628 things came to a head. Firearms and firewater, the two quintessential extractions of all the old-European elements, had conquered Mother Earth and all of its natives. What remained to be done was to get rid of their so-called inventors. The war between Catholics and Protestants fought against progress itself, only to put it on its own feet. Cardinal Richelieu declared religious tolerance null and void and ordered his artillery to batter the last fortress of the Huguenots before storming it. One day, an unnamed captain stood in front of La Rochelle's walls and towers, which to this day connect the town to the sea but protect it from the hinterland. Enveloped by the smoke of enemy gunpowder, he kept his cool and relied on his heartbeat. The good Catholic saw flashing gunfire from the crenels of La Rochelle and started counting. Seconds, or rather several heartbeats later, he could hear the rolling thunder of the escape velocity of the cannons, and he stopped counting. And because he ostensibly stayed true to Bacon's notion of a scientific experiment, he repeated the elementary setup of the trial, including all variable wind and weather conditions, until La Rochelle had capitulated and he had fulfilled his mission.[5]

That doesn't quite count as a scientific result but was a beginning nevertheless. Echo and thunder—that much could be seen and heard—travel slower than fire or lightning. The captain was, however, only able to estimate, or at best measure, his distance from the enemy cannons. And so he handed over his many diverse numbers, including those for varying weather and wind conditions, to a pious monk, who, it seems, had open access to the artillery setups of the most Christian of kings. Marin Mersenne, a friend of René Descartes and a Minorite priest, reconstructed the experiment, this time with friendly fire. This time, the positioning of the cannon was as precise as the positioning of the experimental subject. *Res extensa*, the three-dimensional military reality of our Cartesian world, collided with *res cogitans*, the punctual and irreducible subject of contemporary technoscience. Experimental physics is the peaceful continuation and improvement of "la última razón de los reyes" [the last reason of the kings], as Pedro Calderón de la Barca described firearms, which, as "ultima ratio regis" [the king's final argument], also adorns the barrel of every French royal cannon beginning with Louis XIV.

All Mersenne needed was an absolute, not to say absolutist, baseline. He simply decreed, in Cartesian fashion, that light or fire is infinitely fast. Because it takes no time for the flash coming out of the barrel to reach the measuring eye, it follows that the much slower speed of the echo or thunder results from dividing the Parisian ells by the number of seconds elapsed. Based on such idealized conditions, lightning measured thunder, and fire the echo, at about 440 meters per second, which gets reasonably close to today's standard measurement at zero degrees Celsius.[6] From which our good Mersenne deduced one benefit for godliness and one for the kings: God-fearing people were said to be able to estimate the distance of lightning from the echo of the thunder; through the invention of infinitely powerful cannons, kings were said to be able to fire their will ten and a half hours later into the ears of their antipodes.[7] According to Mersenne, the last European *lógos*, or reason, for the gods was absolutist princes + firearms (just as communism, following Lenin, is socialism + electrification).

It even seems that the worldly priest—not Pierre Gassendi, his freethinking and atomistic counterpart—appears to have put an end to the last sacred delusion of Old Europe on the premises of the French royal artillery. Mersenne arranged for a cannon and a musket, which is what artillery and infantry were called since then, to be fired and measured at the same time. The result was a slap in the face, and on the ear, of all the Greeks: the rolling thunder of the cannon and the high-pitched pop of the musket registered at precisely the same moment, or millisecond, in the observers' ears.

Beginning at that moment, the event of shooting a firearm was elevated to a physical standard. Optics is grounded in lightning, acoustics in the bang. Neither proffers to give more than what you perceive. "Things" pop just the way (*pace* Nietzsche) they "flash." The purity of the event is independent of the difference between high and low tones (as with the Greeks). Conversely, high and low tones are no longer measured in terms of intervals along a Pythagorean string but in terms of frequencies. The nameless captain based the intervals of the echo on the same heartbeat as did the patient Mersenne when measuring the recurring vibrations of an oscillating string that was noticeably stretched. As if in mirrored symmetry, that is how the notion of the event got juxtaposed with the notion of repetition or frequency. Descartes generalized the strict unrepeatability of the acoustic beat—the gentle empiricism of this pious friend—into noise; he generalized the eternal repetition of the same beats, by contrast, into tone, sound, music.

CHAPTER 4

Tanks

TRANSLATED BY MICHAEL WUTZ

> Tanks [Middle High German *panzier* "breastplate," from Old French *pancier(e)*, to Latin *pantex, panticis* "paunch"], 1) *protective armor*: upper-body combat armor made from animal hide, leather, fabric, or metal. 2) *weapons system*: collective term for all types of armored vehicles on treads or wheels, whose engineering and equipment are optimized to execute specific tactical purposes.

For Thomas Macho

Presiding over Berlin's evocative Straße des 17. Juni [17th of June Street], two T-34 tanks stand as nostalgic museum pieces to commemorate the Battle of Berlin in 1945.[1] The time when their present-day successors will quit combat duty and instead serve the duties of polished memorial cultures does not seem far away. Heiner Müller's tragedy only followed the road of the tanks from the Volokolamsk Chaussee [Volokolamsk Highway] via Berlin and Budapest to Prague.[2] But this road might end up as an index fossil, which might at least allow for the exhumation of our century after its battles are long forgotten.

Index fossils, whether in a paleontological or ontological sense, need hard shells. Of mammals in general and humans in particular, whose toughness is, on the contrary, lodged in hidden bones, only skeletons survive. That is why Franz Kafka's metamorphosis (as Gilles Deleuze and Félix Guattari

---

Originally published as "Panzer," in *100 Wörter des Jahrhunderts*, edited by Wolfgang Schneider (Frankfurt am Main: Suhrkamp, 1999), 195–99.

were the first to recognize) was a form or armament tracing the war technology of its time. In 1915 no one less than Sir Winston Churchill, the failed cavalryman at the Battle of Omdurman, had the truly Anglo-American idea to put the bleeding British troops into American caterpillar tractors that were said to traverse trenches and shield bodies.[3] With internal temperatures reaching sixty degrees Celsius, blind tank crews rolled toward the stage victory of 1918, guided not by radio controls, whose exterior antennas did not long survive their contact with barbed wire, but by homing pigeons.

But just as Bertolt Brecht's anarchic Fatzer crawled out of a tank womb right at the end of World War I, this century's index fossil emerged from a stage defeat.[4] General staffs are conservative, if they haven't just suffered a loss. "The taboo" about building tanks "convinced the Germans that the tank had been a potent factor in Allied victory."[5] Hence, key figures of the General Staff, such as Heinz Guderian, whether or not motivated by ironclad male fantasies, began to resuscitate the age-old dream that goes by the name of cavalry: in 1926 the Imperial Defense Force began training a modern cavalry made from passenger cars armed with tank turrets and tank guns made from papier-mâché.[6]

The consequences of such armament are known. The trench warfare of 1914, which measured victories in feet and yards, morphed into blitzkriegs, as tanks began steamrolling over entire countries or deserts. Prospective partisans were happy that the tried-and-true railway, which was still at the center of Moltke the Elder's innovative logistics, was left behind, while any number of streets—not just in Smolensk or Volokolamsk—were upgraded to army roads.[7] Each of the "people's democratic republics" in Eastern Europe was the site of a tank encirclement mopped up by the Red Army, every Israeli offensive on the Sinai peninsula "a 1940-vintage Blitzkrieg."[8] And even if Guderian's tactics to remote-control his motorized divisions with a brand-new radio technology called FM has since been superseded by a Global Positioning System, which provides network coverage over the deserts in southern Iraq, that technology still, fundamentally, remains in force to this day. To which I would add that remote control, which began as emancipated car radios playing the Beach Boys, is encroaching more and more into the lives of civilian drivers on the autobahn. Understood as the computerized armament of automobiles, which have long morphed into more than VW Beetles, the motorization of war is homing in on its goal.

As usual, new kinds of death are accruing on the other side of that goal. At Kursk and Oryol, the last tank offensives of the Wehrmacht, crews were under strict orders to take their Tigers into battle with locked turrets. The very few who survived the counteroffensive of General Nikolai Vatutin left their turrets unsecured.⁹ Every weapon is bound to conjure up antiweapons capable of transforming even centennial index fossils into steel coffins lit up by fuel. Armament, that is, does not guarantee vision. And just as European knights once stormed into battle oblivious to crossbows and pikes, the Hammurabi division of the Republican Guards—operating without night-vision goggles—was reduced to a pile of burning coffins while defending the southwestern deserts of Basra.

And so it goes with tanks, as with all spawns of terror: their preferred targets are unarmed, such as people or protestors, governments or radio stations. Even Guderian's ten tank divisions made elegant detours around enemy troops in order to destroy their communications systems (similar only to Orson Welles's radiophonic world war play, broadcast at the same time).¹⁰ Every coupist living under conditions of media imitated him that way. Tanks that are rolling against radio and television stations are feeding radio and television (and me) the secular keyword that, ever since Martin Heidegger's notion of event, has itself been called an event.¹¹ Tanks that systematically grind over foxholes or students do more than that: they are also perverting the name of the Square of Heavenly Peace.¹²

But all was for naught. Just as the sea once forgot its ships, so does today's earth forget its tanks.¹³ With the exception of the two exhibition pieces in Berlin, none of the T-34s is positioned at its point of final advance. Even Marshal Chuikov's Sixty-Second Tank Division, which decided the Battle of Stalingrad and was hoping for a European-wide expansion in Magdeburg, is thrown back to its renamed point of origin.¹⁴ From Stalingrad to Volgograd, war without battle: neither Alexander Kluge nor Heiner Müller was able to tell it just that way.

Mikhail Gorbachev's ghostwriters are likely correct: while the Red Army was still mobilizing untold numbers of tank divisions against the ten divisions of Guderian, which had already been destroyed, present-day metamorphoses take on new dimensions. In the century of tanks, warfare without battle is all about armoring. Every integrated circuit—or, to put it differently, every computer chip—encases a core of silicon and silicon oxide in a protective shell made from epoxy or silicon resin.¹⁵ Its innards are no less organic or susceptible to injury than its casing. What's more, the double armor insulates not only the conducting paths of the insulators themselves but also the chips of those "societies" that had better be termed carbon symbioses.

The century, in that sense, comes to a close by achieving its dream of encasing mammals, carbon symbionts or, more precisely, soldiers. Adolf Hitler's dream of World War I to build virtually impenetrable tanks, the way Ferdinand Porsche engineered the Hannibalesque tank code-named Maus, was even as a failed design the last character armor Wilhelm Reich could still have psychoanalyzed.[16] (Apparently, obsessive-compulsive disorders resolve simply by passing from people into chrome alloy steel.) Death today, by contrast, comes in the form of armored, that is, "embedded," silicon chips controlling every decent grenade and, hence, every decent car. Tanks, the way Porsche camouflaged them as mice or elephants, weigh a hundred tons; microprocessors, by contrast, have the width of a thumb, including their epoxy casing. War and armoring are continuing these days but well below the threshold of carbon symbioses, perceptions, and so on. The first thumbnail-sized drones are already coming out of labs; prototypes of the first microtanks will follow soon. The index fossil of the twenty-first century will only be visible through electron microscopes.

PART II

Wires, Waves, and Wagner

CHAPTER 5

Noises of War

TRANSLATED BY MICHAEL WUTZ

Ladies and Gentlemen,

Obviously, we can talk about anything. Already during the Renaissance, philosophy claimed to be able to discuss everything under the sun, and then some. Conferences, symposia, and lecture series today even go a step further. Despite that, noises are a topic that is barely touched on in speeches simply because an ever-present noise already cancels them out. Things are even worse when it comes to noises of war. And that is what I want to talk about today. As already pointed out by the foremost German dissertation on the noises of World War I, finding words and names for them is possible only as long as the war rages on.[1] As soon as the guns come to a standstill, ears give themselves a merciful respite. When the Basel Museum of Design sent me the invitation for this talk, we were still in a moment of deep peace. By the time I gave my lecture on radio plays and wars, however, we were in the midst of the Gulf War, and our ears were once again, and in a flash, newly tuned to noises of war.

Fortunately for us all, I cannot count on such acoustic solidarity this evening. That's what will make this talk more abstract and ungrounded but perhaps not in vain. Since all talk about noises runs up against the strain between talk and noise, my talk might remind us that words are not everything.

Wars have been around ever since males have banded together. The noises of war that immediately come to mind date back to those times: the shout of the warrior and the moaning of the dying. Before the German

---

Originally "Geräusche des Krieges" (unpublished lecture manuscript in German first presented in Basel in June 1994).

word *spirit* was hijacked by Christian theologians and Greek philosophers, it presumably designated nothing other than that warrior shout. For spirit was not something a warrior possessed but rather something a warrior was possessed by once he had banded with other berserks and they had gotten themselves suitably ecstatic while donning their bear or wolf skins. What came out of their screaming mouths was called *slobber*, or *spirit*; both words have the same root.[2] Warriors of that prehistorical time were men who morphed into inhuman roles to scare their enemies, and perhaps even themselves, in order to reenact the noise of divine battles on earth.

However, not only has none of that lore been passed down to us; there is also nothing to be said about it. For the shouts of warriors and the moaning of the dying were within a spectrum of sounds humans make and hear all the time, with or without war. Noises of war that are really only produced by war, simply in order to pour terror into everybody's ears, begin only with the warfare of modern states. These states can be identified, on the one hand, by their monopolization of violence and, on the other, by the way they maximize violence through weapons systems. Not for nothing did cannons have the imprint "ultima ratio regum" on their barrels—the last argument of kings.

The long line of war-based noises begins with arquebuses and muskets, mortars and cannons. Ever since the invention of firearms, natural catastrophes no longer have the sole privilege of triggering events that are faster than sound. Given the escape velocities, which even in the nineteenth century far exceeded three hundred meters per second, grenades and bullets have, technologically speaking, long caught up with the unthinkable prerogative of lightning and thunder. Eyes are no longer able to follow a trajectory—as they could with a lance or an arrow—and are replaced, at the very latest with Leibniz, with the new mathematical science of ballistics. Ears, however, which much in contrast to the eyes are principally open and alert, register mortal danger only when it is too late. Since that time, following Goethe's big pronouncement, we have been living in "a new epoch" in the history of the world.[3]

As is well known, Goethe made his pronouncement within view, or, better, earshot, of a cannonade that was inconsequential from a strategic and political point of view but that ushered in a new sound experience for its participants. In July 1792 Prussia and Austria invaded revolutionary France in order to restore the authority of the second-to-last Bourbon king, according to the commanding Duke of Brunswick. On September 20, the Prussian Army—reinforced by the armies of Karl August, Duke of Saxe-Weimar-Eisenach, and Goethe, his minister of poetry—faced fifty thousand French troops close to Valmy in the Champagne region, led by General François Kellermann. They were, however, not permitted to attack, as had been planned by Frederick Wilhelm II. As the *ultima ratio* to save the monarchy of Louis XVI, the Duke of Brunswick allowed only an artillery attack of the French positions, who, as it turned out, were equipped with the most modern artillery at the time. That's how Goethe, as he recorded it in his *Campaign in France*, received his baptism by fire:

> All this went on to the continual accompaniment of thundering cannon. Each side squandered ten thousand rounds that day, resulting in the loss of two hundred men on our side, and even these to no avail. The sky cleared as a result of this terrible convulsion: for the cannon were shot off just like volleys of muskets, somewhat unevenly, to be sure, now increasing, now decreasing in volume. The heaviest firing took place at one in the afternoon, after a pause. The earth literally shook, and yet one could not see the slightest change in the respective positions. No one knew what was to come of all this.
>
> I had heard a lot about cannon fever and wanted to find out exactly what it was like. Boredom, and a spirit which is provoked to audacity, even to temerity, by every danger, lured me into riding up quite calmly toward the La Lune outwork. . . .
>
> I had now reached the area where the cannon balls were landing; the sound is strange enough, as though composed of the hum of a top, the bubbling of water, and the whistling of a bird. . . .
>
> Even under these circumstances, however, I could soon tell that something unusual was happening inside me; I paid careful attention to this, and yet I can only describe this feeling in the form of a simile. It seemed as though I were in a very hot place, and thoroughly permeated by that same heat, so that I felt completely at one with the element in which I found myself. My eyes lost nothing of their strength or clarity of vision, yet it was as though the world had a certain reddish-brown tone, which made my own condition, as well as the objects around me, still more ominous. I did not notice any quickening of the blood, everything seemed rather to be caught up in this intense burning. From this it became apparent to me in what sense this condition could be called a "fever." Nonetheless it is still remarkable how whatever causes such terrible anxiety is conveyed to us solely through our sense of hearing; for it is the thunder of the cannon, and the howling, whistling and

blasting of cannon balls through the air that is actually the cause of these sensations.⁴

As you could hear, Goethe himself heard the cannon thunder as if it were no longer communicable, or if so only through metaphor. At the historical moment when the firing speed of machines has pulled even with the speed of platoon firing, war becomes technological and leaves the realm of everyday language. What the war reporter of the Duke of Weimar couldn't know, however, is that, for the first time in the history of military warfare, the forty French cannons fired standardized grenades that combined the hitherto separate functions of gunpowder and bullets. They could do so only because their inventor, General Jean-Baptiste Vaquette de Gribeauval, copied a revolutionary manufacturing technique developed by Swiss metallurgists. The barrels were no longer cast in one piece, which up to that point had limited the singularity of each cannon to the ammunition that had to be specifically supplied for it. Instead, Gribeauval used specialized drill bits to bore a (so-called) soul into prefabricated barrels with such precision that, from then on, every cannon made from that same series could fire the same ammunition. Put differently, the cannonade of Valmy was based on the industrialized standardization of death. And when such mass-produced weapons were combined with systematically trained conscripts, following Lazare Carnot's simultaneous call for a "mass levy," the progress of central Europe was only a matter of course. War was incommunicable also because—following an observation made by the same Goethe—everybody had to put their shoulder to the wheel, and so nobody was listening to his stories anymore. This space without speech spelled the demise of entire literary genres such as the epic and tragedy. In their place, writers beginning with Goethe were faced with the incessant task of using words to describe noises that fundamentally supersede the capacity of our ears.

Out of Gribeauval's mobilized field artillery, whose standardization solved the logistical problem of ammunition feed once and for all, were born the acoustics of modern warfare and, at the same time, its first sound engineer. Lieutenant Napoleon Bonaparte began as a field artillery soldier in Toulon, increased his troop count from battle to battle, only to end his career as the emperor of France in the cannon thunder of Waterloo. One of his admirers, a man by the name of Fabrice del Dongo, witnessed the event, at least in Stendhal's novel. Plastered as he was, the fledgling volunteer missed catching a glimpse of the emperor.⁵ Nevertheless, he managed to have a conversation with one of the generals surrounding the monarch.

Fabrice set his horse into one of those mud puddles of Flanders that would make history in World War I and drenched the general next to him from head to toe. As if to acknowledge the modern futility of all war cries, the general exclaimed, "To hell with the f . . . brute! . . . Where did you get this horse?"—but there was no answer. While it seemed to Fabrice that "the cannon-fire sounded louder," he "could barely make out what the general . . . was shouting in his ear." Eventually, "the din was so fierce just then that Fabrice was unable to answer him." Which forces the novelist to confess that his hero at Waterloo was most unheroic at that moment: "Fear, however, was only a secondary emotion; what shocked him most was the noise which was hurting his ears."[6]

As the birthplace of the realist novel, Waterloo marks the historical moment when the demise of sensory perception coincides with the death of the hero. Goethe, the man of vision, was at least still able to see at Valmy, even as his ears had already capitulated to that "terrible anxiety." Stendhal's Fabrice del Dongo, by contrast, surrenders both of his long-range senses, one at a time, to the thunder of the cannons and their smoking barrels. The battle becomes unmoored from any unifying perspective and disperses into a mosaic of scattered perceptions that cannot lay any claim to truth. But they produce a new type of discourse: the war novel seen and heard from the perspective of the frontline grunt. For in order to describe how to lose your eyes and ears in battle, you no longer need a hero, nor the writer who invents him, but only each one "as his immediately positive self" who "makes himself into an absolute power [that is, he becomes a criminal]."[7] As Hegel argued in the *Jena Lectures* in 1805, the modern "externalization must have this same abstract form, must be without individuality—death coldly received and given, not in ongoing battle where the individual has his eye on his opponent and kills him with direct hatred; rather, death emptily given and received, *impersonal* in the gunsmoke."[8]

Hegel's idea of impersonal death corresponds rather precisely to a new military communications technology. When not even a fledgling volunteer like Fabrice hears the shouts of generals, when "shouts," as they are described in Christian Dietrich Grabbe's play on Waterloo, are "blared out" "but barely heard," signaling technology must cancel its age-old contract with the ear.[9] In the pre-Napoleonic era, everything that was addressed to everybody, which is to say, everything that did not have a pair of eyes fixed on it, traveled along acoustic channels. The military historian Martin van Creveld has called this form of information flow "The Stone Age of Command."[10] Beginning with the new system of a general staff, the way it was introduced by Napoleon, and subsequently his enemies, orders were given in written form. When long distances were involved, they were also communicated through a first, not-yet-electrical, system of semaphore lines. On a strategic level, war was hence brought to a level of in-humanity, or silence, that rendered it immune to the noises of its artillery. In the nineteenth century, when both the postal system and the railroad uncoupled the information flow from the transport of passengers and goods, silence became the secret of power. In the words of a Prussian chief of the General Staff, who knew the sounds of battle only from his desk, "the *Feldherr* finds himself further back in a house with a spacious office, where telegraphs, telephones, and signals apparatus are to hand."[11]

Given this distance of strategic leadership from frontline combat, it is not surprising that grunts wanted to partake in it. In 1866, when the eventual poet Lieutenant Detlev von Liliencron and his company came under heavy Austrian gunfire at Königgrätz, his ears played a remarkable trick on him: "We soon reached a little forest and dispersed at the other side of it behind the trees. I heard tak, tak, tak; tak, tak, tak-tak-taktak-taktaktaktaktak-tak-tak-taktaktak. . . . It sounded as if we were in a large telegraph office. In reality, it was enemy bullets hitting the trees behind which we sought cover."[12]

As is well known, Moltke the Elder won the Battle of Königgrätz through a systematic coordination of all three Prussian armies, which homed in on the enemy's anticipated deployment sites with the aid of a network of railroad and telegraph lines. For that reason, Moltke's grunts—not unlike Wagner's Isolde at around the same time—could only nourish an acoustic dream born out of battle and mortal danger: namely, that of hallucinating the intersecting sounds of a communications technology whose very electronics undermines audibility in the first place. To describe the acoustic routine in the trenches, the telegraph and the typewriter became, hence, the two most popular metaphors in World War I—when whites also began using their machine guns against other whites, not just against red-, yellow-, or black-skinned people. As we can read in an English source, "Then in the front line [was] the typewriter clacking of machine-guns."[13]

World War I as a *Storm of Steel*, however, to speak with Ernst Jünger, put an end to office metaphors based on telegraphy or the typewriter.[14] Credit for that goes to a typewriter called the machine gun, which allowed a single surviving crew to mow down entire regiments. For that very reason, beginning in 1915, British and French infantry attacks engaged artillery only after weeks of barrage; German attacks did so beginning in the spring of 1918 immediately following a creeping barrage that was shorter but all the more intense. As barrage or creeping barrage, however, the artillery sacrificed its Napoleonic quality: it stopped producing singular acoustic events against a subdued background noise but became itself a form of uninterrupted noise so loud that it came close to, if not even exceeded altogether, the threshold of aural pain. A British soldier described that sensation as follows. The tumult "did not begin, intensify, decline and end. It was poised in the air, a stationary panorama of sound, not the creation of men."[15] A French soldier described it similarly: "It was a noise at once further away, denser, thicker, more compact. The whole atmosphere was vibrating. My temples and teeth were throbbing. The sound didn't fluctuate because it was the immense and constant noise of battle."[16]

But the kind of noise that lacks a creator or a sense of dynamism coincides with its opposite, the sensory deprivation rampant in the trenches from 1914 to 1918. For that reason, in terms of both the myths and practices in the trenches, everything depended on a new training of the ears that—strictly following Heinz von Foerster—sought to distill order from the acoustic chaos. As a 1915 article in the *Frankfurter Zeitung* reports, whosoever wanted to survive learned to differentiate between formerly unheard-of sounds:

> While naturally everybody can distinguish the sound of a firing gun from the impact of a projectile, and the ratatat of a German from a French machine gun, and a volley from the discharge of clamped guns, there are some who can identify each and every sound by location and type. Not only are they capable of differentiating between the shrieking of light and heavy artillery, and between the heavy ordnance of howitzers and the gurgling whoosh of mortar shells, they can even predict whether a flying projectile will end up as a dud, and they never mix up the boom of a bursting trench mortar with the explosion of an artillery ordnance of the same caliber.[17]

The art of acoustic differentiation was all the more important because it was without optical assistance. What is so memorable in Paul Fussell's book on the trench warfare of 1914–18 is that every soldier who attempted to visually orient themselves, beyond the trenches, in the bombed-out no-man's-land between the front lines, ended up with a shot in the head. In principle, the enemy was only audible, not visible, even when not trying to undermine trench positions with mines and explosives. Kafka's narrative "The Burrow," the story of an animal defending itself against its anonymous enemies only by virtue of its auditory discrimination skills, was written immediately after Kafka had read a war report on the mine war of 1916.[18]

On both the military and literary fronts, however, ears have their built-in limit: their distance from one another. On the eve of World War I, physiology and phenomenology, Carl Friedrich Stumpf and Edmund Husserl, were in agreement as they had just discovered that humans can see only because they have spaced eyes and can hear only because they have two more or less spaced ears. The single privileged sense organ of philosophical lore, the way it adorns each and every dollar bill to this day, was rejected in theory. It was up to World War I to translate this rejection into practical terms.

The first step was undertaken by one of Stumpf's assistants, Erich Moritz von Hornbostel, who later became famous as a professor of musicology. He translated the principle of the scissors telescope onto the ears and connected both auricles to bells whose distance was no longer measured in centimeters but in meters. And behold: the artificially enlarged auricle radius allowed artillery scouts on the western front to acoustically locate enemy batteries even from a distance of many kilometers. Then, Dr. Otto Schwab, who held a PhD in engineering and was, incidentally, also named director of the Technical Office of the Waffen-ss during World War II, built on this fortuitous development. He replaced what were still human ears in Hornbostel's setup with instruments that could automatically measure the differences in sound propagation, in large part because their two sensors were positioned kilometers apart. That is how acoustics—albeit only in nonhuman form from then on, and only barely—kept pace with the explosiveness and reach of modern artillery, which had been extraordinarily improved since 1860. Schwab's new technology made it possible to locate, and hence eliminate, enemy positions even behind the third row of trenches, that is, from a distance of about twenty kilometers.

Put differently, war noise left the human ear. To make decisions and initiate countermeasures, such noise had to be registered by sound-recording machines. And even if "ear witnesses described the overall impression of war noise as an infernal din that could not fully be captured by the phonograph," the latter was already present to do its work.[19] Those ear witnesses themselves were called on to switch their acoustic discrimination from words—the way Europeans had been trained to do for millennia—to pure sounds. No ear witness of World War I has testified more credibly to that shift than the member of an artillery testing crew, also a PhD, who in his civilian life had edited the most literal words of German poetry before dying at Verdun. On February 4, 1916, the editor of Hölderlin's works, Norbert von Hellingrath, wrote the following letter to his bride from the front on the Vosges mountains:

> When I made it to the top, I beheld the lovely hill with the lovely grove of oaks shrouded in translucent mist, punctured only by the black puffs of grenades and the red clouds of bursting clay, and sometimes, as if they were a spray of embers, the colorful trails of fire grenades. Up here you can finally hear the quiet of the fight; one can hear smaller guns, and mine fights make noises as well. In this all-surrounding din mixing and coming from all sides (because our barrage fire was hovering like a hedge of clouds over neighboring enemy positions) everything was balanced once more: a more refined audible silence similar to a whispering forest or the stillness of the ocean. (And it is one of the few benefits of the testing crew that our endless crouching and waiting has made us doubly receptive to hearing such silence.)
>
> That silence is among the most beautiful sensations you can think of and has no more dignified background than that of our wooded mountains.[20]

The acoustic miracle of silence, however, which resulted from the undifferentiated noise spectrum of the various artilleries, became a storage challenge. Words were no match for it. As Robert Ranke-Graves, Hellingrath's British fellow poet put it in an interview while on furlough, "You can't communicate noise. Noise never stopped for one moment—ever."[21] For that reason, as early as 1916, a certain Pessler wrote in the magazine *Museumskunde* [Museum studies] that he had dreams of opening a world war museum aimed at "preserving the momentous din of battle, especially in world war," in phonographic form.[22] Postwar novels in England picked up on that theme and created entire scenarios in which soldiers fought and died until they realized that the battle was nothing but an exercise simulated by gigantic phonographs.[23]

World War II connected precisely to this level of strategy. Hitler's last offensive in the winter of 1944, for example, as in the early spring of 1940, aimed at making a sickle cut through the Ardennes region but was—in view of the twentyfold superiority of Allied airpower—possible only through acoustic simulations. Hence, real tanks drove with muffled engines into their positions at night, while supersized phonographs blared the sounds of engines and the treads of imaginary tanks all day long across the front lines, without any plan of attack.²⁴ And yet the only reason for this gigantic acoustic simulation was to drown out the flow of commands in inaudible high frequencies with audible low frequencies. The explicit order for the front lines during the Battle of the Bulge was not silence but radio silence.²⁵ The attack on Pearl Harbor—the opening move in the Pacific theater—was possible only because Rear Admiral Chūichi Nagumo pulled off the unthinkable and shipped an entire carrier fleet from Yokohama via the Aleutian Islands to Hawaii in complete radio silence. The claim that Nagumo's kamikaze pilots torpedoed the Pacific fleet of the U.S. Navy by letting out an ancient samurai shout—especially in light of that radio silence—was and remains the mythology of war, whether in feature films or elsewhere.

The transformation of audible, low-frequency sounds into metaphors of inaudible radio frequencies was notably documented by nobody less than Reginald V. Jones, the British assistant director of intelligence (science). In 1940 he was tasked with figuring out why the attacks of the Luftwaffe on towns and radio positions in southern England were far more accurate than any attacks flown by the Royal Air Force at the same time. He surmised, which was soon to be confirmed, the existence of a radio beam transmission that made all the Messerschmitts and Heinkels of the Luftwaffe into functions of a gigantic trigonometric equation. Everything appeared as if the passive, artillery-based sound measurements of World War I had been transformed into an active guidance system, its reach improved a hundredfold, and its low-frequency technology translated into a high-frequency technology. What was unfortunate for the British was that its intelligence not only was unable to demonstrate the existence of these radio waves, owing to a lack of receivers, but also denied their technical feasibility. They argued that the speed of electrons themselves would not permit feedback loops with wavelengths of less than ten centimeters.²⁶

One day, however, Jones witnessed a demonstration in Farnborough, the traditional airfield of the Royal Air Force:

> It arose from a demonstration . . . of a very powerful loudspeaker system and amplifier system that had been developed for installation in aircraft policing the North-West frontier of India. The policing was sometimes done by punishing marauding tribesmen by bombing their villages, after due warning. Someone thought that the warning would be all the more effective if it came as from the voice of God, bellowing out from an aircraft. When the apparatus had been perfected, it was demonstrated to the Air Staff at Farnborough by mounting a micro-

phone on one side of the aerodrome, some two thousand feet away. If you spoke into the microphone you could hear your voice coming two seconds later across from the other side. All went well with the demonstration until one of the inspecting officers, struck by the curiosity of hearing his delayed voice, started to laugh. Two seconds later there came back a laugh from the loudspeaker at which everybody laughed. Two seconds later the shower of laughs returned, and I like to think that by now the volume was so great that the returned laugh was picked up by the microphone and duly relayed once again, making a system that laughed by itself.

Apart from the comedy of the situation, there was an important lesson to be learnt. This was that the time of oscillations generated by the human voice is typically of the order of a thousandth of a second, and yet these were being faithfully generated by a system in which the transit time of sound across the aerodrome was some two seconds. This showed the fallacy in the argument about centimetric waves. What really mattered was not the transit time itself, but the regularity in the time of transit.[27]

A couple of weeks later, Jones was in possession of systems capable not only of laughing on their own but also of receiving or producing high frequencies. The radio beam transmission of the Luftwaffe was no longer a secret and, hence, was rendered ineffective. Where days earlier acoustic gods had been simulated for the ears of tribes, now the time was ripe for the inaudible battle in the ether.

The enemy underwent the same development. The Wehrmacht began its blitzkrieg with a combination of radio-controlled tank divisions and the dive bombers that didn't much differ from the aerial reconnaissance in northern India. The Junkers Ju 87, too, commuted into acoustic terror the gods to which enemy populations had been praying ever since the invention of air-raid alarms. At an angle of seventy degrees, their dive bombing was not only terrifying to look at but also terrifying to listen to, because the sound of the siren, which was meant to warn of an air attack, emanated from the cockpit of the attacker.[28] (The damage to the pilots' hearing, by the way, was alleged to have been cured only by the music of Wagner.[29])

Four years later, the Stukas and their terror sirens were history.[30] Instead, a tactical terror was replaced with a strategic terror, which gave rise to Thomas Pynchon's phenomenal novel of World War II. The terror of intercontinental missiles begun by the V-2 is simply that the rocket's supersonic boom cannot be heard until after it has been seen and has detonated its payload. Acoustics has transcended itself and, with supersonic speeds, transitioned into the realm of high frequencies.

Since then, nothing much can be said about noises of war that couldn't also be measured by instruments. Today's acoustic entertainment industry, from headphones and high fidelity to stereophonic sound, is based in its entirety on the technological know-how of 1945. All we know about acoustics and electronics (in that suggestive combination) is grounded in the research developed in the largest psychology lab of World War II: the twin Psycho-Acoustic and Electro-Acoustic Laboratories at Harvard University. I will conclude with a few basic insights about this lab.

First, measured by the tactics of blitzkrieg, such as approaching kamikaze pilots, speaking and listening are principally no longer fast enough. The flow of communication has to be transferred onto electronic or optic channels and, ideally, becomes automated.[31]

Second, acoustic noise cannot be eliminated in principle, neither from war nor from research. Instead of being oblivious to or eliminating noise, as people had been doing for millennia, noise became the key to all knowledge.[32]

Third, the words of natural languages are more or less susceptible to noise. For that reason, languages themselves have to be decluttered of all that could possibly impede the flow of communication.[33]

Fourth, and last, acoustic noise doesn't cause physiological, only strategic damage. Pilots who had been exposed to the simulated cockpit noise of a bomber, measuring 115 decibels, for eight hours a day, four days a week, for four weeks at the Harvard lab did not show any significant changes in performance and behavior. The noise did, however, interfere with their message-processing abilities.[34]

For that reason, as a Berlin police chief opined during Napoleon's occupation of 1806, silence remains the first civic duty.[35]

CHAPTER 6

Playback
A World War History of Radio Drama

TRANSLATED BY MICHAEL WUTZ

"When power becomes gracious and descends into the visible," as Nietzsche put it, "such descent I call beauty."[1] That gracious gift is the reason for power's very invisibility or inaudibility. No art ever tells of its origin, be it in the realm of the visible or the audible, as Nietzsche—the first theorist of the radio drama avant la lettre—was the first to note. And when that power, somewhere in the vastness of the nineteenth century, escaped the limited space of speech and writing—that is, humanity itself—to assume electronic omnipotence, that omnipotence was potentiated by its very invisibility. The arts were replaced by media that could manipulate sight and sound precisely because their technologies operate beyond all thresholds of visual and auditory perception. Entertainment media, for that reason, are nothing but the human-machine interface of a system that operates in a no-man's-land stretching from communications technologies to digital signals processing.

The first principle of a theory of the radio drama would have to be that communications technologies can exist without radio drama but that no radio drama can exist without communications technologies. From which follows the second principle: that no radio drama can transmit the technical conditions of its possibility. It isn't only wavelength, bandwidth, and silicon chips that are invisible to consumers, who are technically unarmed, even if they could take a forbidden peek under the hood, so to speak. Rather, that invisibility is the preferred mode of a system of power that no longer relies

Originally "Playback: Weltkriegsgeschichte des Hörspiels" (unpublished lecture manuscript in German presented in June 1999) and "Radio Drama" (a second, shorter, and also unpublished version in English).

on the gift of erstwhile priests and kings able to descend, here and there, into the realm of the visible.

It's no wonder, then, that writers flung into the media system have puzzled over the question what, if any, is the real content of radio drama. Bertolt Brecht's radio play of 1929, *The Flight across the Ocean* [*Der Ozeanflug*], which was produced here in Baden-Baden, evolved from that very question.² In 1971, then under pressure from television, that question was brought to the very point in Helmut Heißenbüttel's radio drama *Was sollen wir überhaupt senden?* (What should we be broadcasting at all?). But if entertainment media are the human-machine interface in a system that, much in contrast to all of history, exists without any such interface (Niklas Luhmann was supposed to have commented recently that there is no such thing as the postmodern, only the modern post), perhaps the very nature of the question is wrong. What according to the Bible is true of humanity seems to be true of artists as well: they have ears only to be deaf.

Once Friedrich Nietzsche had coined the term *Hörspiel* [sound play], Karl Groos began to put it on a theoretical footing and asserted that radio dramas have always existed prior to any aesthetic or directorial planning.³ From "the singing of caged birds" and "the seething of waves," from "the suckling" and "concert goer" to the "piano virtuoso," as he put it, "the disposition toward acoustic expression . . . is so strong, in fact, as to extend the sphere of sound-play far beyond that of the sensuously agreeable. Absolute silence makes us uncomfortable, and, when it is lasting," as Wilhelm Preyer has demonstrated, "conveys to the mind a special quality of emotion, as in optics there is a positive feeling of blackness."⁴

Hence, the third principle of a theory of the radio drama would be to take radio dramas, or *Funkspiele* (which is what the intelligence agencies of World War II called them), for what they are and where they are.⁵ Not only in sound and speech archives, which is what civil radio stations have essentially become since the invention of the reel-to-reel, but also in the bandwidths between kilometers and centimeters from which the so-called population has been barred on good strategic grounds. On the station Radio Bremen, Wolfgang Hagen asked, "Who do people speaking on the radio speak to?," and he answered, in full knowledge that all studios are completely soundproof, "To the dead." Conversely, when Ferdinand Kriwet was asked what radio dramas do when they wiretap enemy broadcasts, he was similarly succinct.⁶

Let me create some provisional order from this jumble of frontline reports and battle cries, which will need to include Morse and radar signals as well. The first and (as is common among historians) longer portion will unearth stories that come close to answering the question of what radio dramas themselves listened to when people still listened to them, that is, before the dominance of TV shows and computer animation. To give my provisional answer right here: they listened to the dead of all the technological wars that, for the past ninety-two years, have been waged with radio and over the radio. In a more speculative conclusion, I want to project these stories into a future that integrates all analog media as a subset into a universal discrete machine, a.k.a. the computer. As the first published *Introduction to Electronic Warfare* put it, the outbreak of Star Wars would only validate "the generally acknowledged military principle" that "the next war will be won by the side that best exploits the electromagnetic spectrum."[7]

Philosophers and artists say the same thing in a different way. Friends of Carl Schmitt, the crown jurist of the Third Reich who, from 1930 to 1936, legitimated the state of emergency during the reign of two chancellors, tell of a radio drama and of his last words.

In the radio drama that the ninety-five-year-old schizophrenic hallucinated, "sound waves entered the house from all sides. Frequencies emanating from various electric apparatus relayed voices with utmost clarity and over a distance of hundreds of kilometers. Electronic bugs had been placed all over the house. His enemies prepared for a final and decisive offensive against him. . . . They were primitive but techno-savvy and incredibly dangerous."[8]

Schmitt's delirious last words are referring precisely to this radio drama and give it its very name. On Christmas Eve 1984, "in laborious conversations that were handicapped by his hearing loss and deteriorated into monologues," Schmitt suddenly "said loud and clear": "After World War I, I said: 'Sovereign is he who determines the state of exception.' After World War II, in the face of my death, I now say: 'Sovereign is he who commands the waves of space.'"[9]

Our century doesn't just add up communications technologies and weapons systems the way it was done in previous epochs but rather develops its communications technologies as technologies of war. With James Clerk Maxwell, control over the waves in space was a problem of theoretical physics, and with Heinrich Hertz it was an experimental one. Beginning with Guglielmo Marconi and Karl Ferdinand Braun, Reginald Fessenden and Oliver Lodge, however, high-frequency research is predicated on its strategic usefulness. Among Maxwell's contemporaries, the strategic value of wireless control over waves—when Europe and North America were still racing head-to-head in laying their transatlantic cables—was perhaps anticipated only by an artist.

The short history of the radio drama begins with Wagner's *The Ring of the Nibelung*, which may well be regarded as the zero series of all world wars. Nietzsche coined the word *Hörspiel* to account for his friend's ability to dramatize acoustic events as such: "In Wagner," Nietzsche wrote in 1876, "the whole visible world desires to be spiritualized, absorbed, and lost in the world of sounds. In Wagner, too, the world of sounds seeks to manifest itself as a phenomenon for the sight. . . . His art always leads him into two distinct directions, from the world of the play of sound to the mysterious and yet related world of visible things, and vice versa."[10]

Such media transfers, however common they have since become between books and movies, records and video clips all over the world, are by no means reducible to aesthetic effects. Wagner's music drama pushes play and sound play, traditional art and modern media technology, into a struggle for world domination, which is synonymous with *The Ring of the Nibelung*. On the one hand, his gods naturally dwell in their illustrious heights, that is, onstage. Their power, just like that of all old-world rulers, stems from show business and smoke and mirrors. The Nibelung Alberich, on the other hand, represents the modern engineer and industrialist who reigns over his battery of workers dwelling in subterranean caverns, that is, Bayreuth's invisible orchestra pit or the trenches of World War I. Alberich's technical power, which only reflects Wagner's own, spells the end of the gods. And because "in Wagner the whole visible world desires to be spiritualized, absorbed, and lost in the world of sounds," their defeat comes down to a literal twilight: step by step, the gods disappear from the stage and passively endure what, in the case of Alberich, is an active strategy: the transformation of actors into space waves. As a rebel hunkering down in the command bunker, long before Heinrich Brüning or Adolf Hitler, Wotan tries in vain to avert the fate of the gods by passing emergency resolutions and martial law. That fate consists, not coincidentally, of contractual shackles or (as in the case of the prologue to *Götterdämmerung* [*Twilight of the Gods*]) even ropes. His war on two fronts against the Nibelung and giants consumes the logistics of wires or telegraph cables to make room for white noise, as with radio.

Step by step, evening after evening, Wotan becomes increasingly invisible. By the end of the tetralogy, he and his gods have been reduced to a faint acoustic trace and a bunker onstage, which is "entirely hidden" by the flames.[11] Notwithstanding all informatics, signal and interference, message and noise coincide. In the final act of *Götterdämmerung*, which was not coincidentally the final broadcast of the Großdeutsche Rundfunk on April 12, 1945, Brünnhilde—the daughter or the unconscious of a dead god—announces that the "stirring" of Wotan's ravens is in fact their very "tidings," a lullaby for Wotan and the gods as a whole:[12]

> Weiß ich nun, was dir frommt?
> Alles, alles,
> alles weiß ich,
> alles ward mir nun frei!
> Auch deine Raben
> hör ich rauschen;
> mit bang ersehnter Botschaft
> send ich die beiden nun heim.
> Ruhe, ruhe, du Gott!

> Now I know what must be.
> All things, all things,
> all I know now;
> all to me is revealed!
> Call back your ravens
> hovering round me;
> they'll bring to you those tidings
> you have both feared and desired.
> Rest now, rest now O god![13]

Stirring (or noise) is precisely the tidings (the message) that had to be excluded from all traditional art forms but is constitutive of technological media themselves, because it is produced in their very channels. That is why the very same noise that transports gods into the happily ever after—that is, it abolishes them—functions from the very beginning as an element or medium in the hands of Alberich, the engineer. His command to the Nibelung to forge a magic helmet, a cloak of invisibility, is more efficient than all of Wotan's emergency declarations, simply because it gives him control over the airwaves. When Alberich tries it on the very first time, his "form disappears."[14] Henceforth he exists only as an invisible voice in the stereophonic space of the stage. Wagner employs this very first radio voice to define its and his own power. At first, rendered doubly invisible in his dark cavern and by the magic helmet, Alberich attacks his own underlings, and his blows elicit from them a literal sound play, as if commenting on the baton of Wagner himself, his invisible orchestra, and the sound effects of the Bayreuth Festival Theater. Following that, Alberich and Wagner's music itself announce what domination under conditions of media technology really means: namely, the abolition of a "leadership vacuum." In the days of books and newspapers, such a vacuum was still something to be lamented but can, thanks to the radio (as an expert in the Großdeutsche Rundfunk observed in 1939), be reduced to zero:

> Nibelungen all,
> neigt euch nun Alberich!
> Überall weilt er nun,
> euch zu bewachen;
> Ruh und Rast
> ist euch zerronnen;
> ihm müßt ihr schaffen,
> wo nicht ihr ihn schaut;
> wo ihr nicht ihn gewahrt,
> seid seiner gegenwärtig!
> Untertan seid ihr ihm immer!
>
> Nibelungs below,
> bow down to Alberich!
> I shall be watching
> to see that you are working;
> day and night
> you must be toiling,
> sweating to serve
> your invisible lord;
> who can watch you unseen
> and spy on his subjects!
> You are my slaves now for ever![15]

Following that, Wagner no longer makes music from sounds and drama from actions but begins a radio drama with a worked-out transition: following a directorial directive, Alberich's voice is "heard receding into the distance," or into the orchestra, while "the screams and cries" of his slaves come "from further and further away, until at last they are inaudible."[16]

Our century has industrialized the production of Alberich's magic helmet. Electromagnetic waves, because their signals transcend the perception of space and time, bypass all our senses. Early theories of radio, such as that of Rudolf Arnheim in 1936, culminated in a "Praise of Blindness."[17]

Just before World War I, however, Alfred Count von Schlieffen—chief of the Imperial German General Staff and creator of the new weapon called signal corps—already predicted invisible military commanders in future wars:

> However, while these battlefields may be large, they will offer little to the eye. Nothing is to be seen across the wide desert. . . . No Napoleon stands upon a rise surrounded by his brilliant retinue. Even with field glasses he wouldn't get to see much. His white horse would be the easy target of countless batteries. The *Feldherr* finds himself further back in a house with a spacious office, where telegraphs, telephones and signals apparatus are to hand. . . . There, in a comfortable chair before a wide table, the modern Alexander has before him the entire battlefield on a map. From there, he telephones stirring words. There, he receives reports from the army and the corps commanders, from the observation balloons and from the dirigibles that observe the movement of the enemy along the whole line and that look behind the enemy's positions.[18]

An invisible *Feldherr*, a technologized Alberich, reigns over similarly invisible battlefields via telephone and radio. What Schlieffen, in his prediction, calls "telegraphs, telephone and signals apparatus" was preceded by Marconi's wireless and, eventually, radio, which had a strict military prehistory. General staffs had three very good reasons for that. While the national postal systems were stuck in their ways, Schlieffen and his colleagues or enemies actively promoted every single development in radio simply because they were well aware of the drawbacks and dangers of telegraphic cables, which were fifty years old by then. First of all, the British had managed to connect the entire empire with the All Red Line that—much like Wotan's shackles or contracts—bound the entire globe without trespassing into possible enemy territories. Second, that is precisely how the All Red Line demonstrated its exposure to the dangers of interruptions and interceptions. In 1898 the United States had deprived Spain of the last of its colonial holdings, simply because its war fleet had cut all the cable connections between Spain and Cuba. It was, hence, only control over the airwaves that could bypass cable monopolies and, third, prepare for a strategy that outpaced the infinitely laborious process of laying cables. Mobile warfare in the spirit of Schlieffen, that is, command feedback from mobile bombers, tanks, and submarines, insisted imperially on wireless communication. All radio patents, beginning with cathode-ray tubes and feedback amplifiers, were channeled directly into World War I. Radio drama could begin.

And obviously once more in caverns. The command center equipped with a spacious office shriveled to the size of a command bunker, the wide desert of the battlefields, for the same reason, to the size of trenches. World war became a field of experimentation for sensory perception and techno-training for millions of Nibelung or soldiers. As Paul Fussell has brilliantly shown, the one spectacle soldiers could enjoy for four years without imminent danger of death was the sunrise and sunset high above the trench line.[19] Hence, "the whole visible world," *pace* Nietzsche, "desires to be spiritualized, absorbed, and lost in the world of sounds." Except for barrage fire, the ears of soldiers were glued to intercoms for field telephones and command radio. Then, in 1917, some officers began to have pity. Former radio engineers spiced up the boredom of wireless exchanges, which consisted solely of enemy deployment and artillery positions, by transmitting newspaper articles or gramophone music for a change. This "abuse of army equipment," as it was called, made the radio operators sitting in their trenches, bunkers, and casemates into the first mass radio audience in history.

"First Concert Broadcast . . . A Memory from the Trenches" ["Erstes Rundfunkkonzert eine . . . Erinnerung aus dem Schützengraben"] is how Eduard Meier titled his contribution to the magazine *Funk* [Radio] in 1924. There we can read: "Concert broadcasts have become very fashionable of late. When I first had the chance to listen to such a concert, our technology was far less advanced. Unbeknownst to them, it was French musicians who treated us to the first radio entertainment in 1917 during the battle around the Chemin des Dames."[20]

Meier's war report—a cleartext paralleling Franz Kafka's "The Burrow" ["Der Bau"]—is the tragicomedy of a battle of mutual radio intercepts. German radio operators had established a highly amplified ground signal station in the heavily defended limestone caves of the Champagne, which enabled them to tap into the tactical telephone lines of the enemy via their seemingly useless grounding cable. French operators, however, did not just broadcast war-related military messages but also invited piano players and violinists. Reception and interception, entertainment and espionage via headphones, hence coincide. Only when the German radio operators become bold enough to invite, via radio, their staff officers into their protruding cave does disaster strike: a direct French hit at the entrance to the cave, nine dead and fourteen severely wounded. The following day, Meier is able to decipher this final radio drama from French Morse communication: the French, for their part, had begun tapping the German telephone lines and hence intercepted their own intercepts. Their direct hit was fully strategic and Meier's concert broadcast in 1924 a war drama to be enjoyed from the peace and comfort of an armchair.

BBC London, AM, January 15, 1924, one year after the founding of British civilian broadcasting. Via the first private radio receivers, listeners first hear the sounds of an explosion, then a voice calling out in panic, "The lights have gone out!" One female and two male voices are searching for an escape route in the dark. Their author, a certain Richard Hughes, had just invented the genre of the radio drama with *A Comedy of Danger*. As a natural disaster supposedly happening in a Welsh coal mine, the explosion did its directorial duty: it put a magic helmet on the military origins of radio.

Hughes later recalled how, in media-technological terms, *A Comedy of Danger* had been conceived: over a cup of tea, he and Nigel Playfair, his client and theatrical director in London, both agreed they "could have no auxiliary recourse to a second sense, no equivalent of subtitles.... Our 'listening play' must rely on dramatic speech and sound entirely":

> It had never been done before; that was the especial rub, for it meant we had a totally inexperienced audience to deal with. We were plunging them into a blind man's world.... We agreed that, this once at any rate, something must be done to make it easier for them. A story for example which really happens in the dark, so that the characters themselves keep complaining they can't see. Then perhaps the announcer could ask the audience to put out their lights and listen in darkness, too, so as to feel themselves in the very middle of the action they were hearing.
>
> "Here's a first speech for you," said Playfair as he escorted me to the door: *"The lights have gone out!"*
>
> Back home in my attic flat in New Oxford Street I turned over possible situations in my mind. *The lights have gone out!* Not a bedroom scene. To be candid, I did not know much about bedrooms, even at twenty-three. An accident in a coal mine?[21]

That is Hughes, with all the comedic sincerity he can muster. Through broadcast delay and pre- and postproduction censorship, entertainment broadcasting no doubt repressed the bedroom scenes. Hughes knew very well that civil radio had originated in World War I and that the BBC had been founded by signal corps officers, and so even the allegedly repressed bedroom scene repressed something else.

What radio drama after World War I comes down to is this: to reproduce the mortal dangers of warfare through simulation, comedy, or playback. By means of mine explosions, which projected the enemy's function onto the natural world, the new broadcast medium was cultivating its audience. The demobilization of 1919 had turned hundreds of thousands of military radio operators into eventual broadcast consumers, if they hadn't had the good fortune, as some did in the United States, to set up commercial stations. To play back the soundtrack of a war that had truly revolutionized people's sensory perception and consciousness was therefore the most elegant way for the new communications medium to attract a public.

This publicity was badly needed because the distribution structure of civil radio inverted that of its military predecessor, whose technology it demilitarized despite or precisely because of that. Even though every tube radio or loudspeaker—following Hans Magnus Enzensberger's elegant formulation—can principally fulfill the even more elegant notion of a transceiver, that is, both receive and send messages, draconian radio signal protocols during the Weimar Republic blocked the transmission feature from civil radio. And that was done not only to preempt the transmission of anarchic chaos but also to reserve all the pleasure and power of intercom radio for the military-industrial complex. Thus, on the one hand, the worldwide radio dramas (inter)connecting general staffs and their tank crews, and air force staffs and their test pilots, are running on all possible frequencies but are out of range of civilian radio. On the other hand, there are four small frequency bands controlled by the postal service that allow civil radio to send records or newspaper articles to millions of recipients, just as in the muddy fields of Flanders. Only when radio became a mass broadcasting system did it turn into the realm of the dead.

As you know, Bertolt Brecht was the first to criticize this state of affairs. While other writers wrote for literary broadcasts or zoomed in on the politics of radio power, Brecht articulated his own theory and practice in opposition to entertainment radio. His radio theory culminated in the famous call that radio "be transformed from a distribution apparatus into a communications apparatus," and his radio practice culminated in the experiment in Baden-Baden, to exemplify, not coincidentally, such a transceiver in Lindbergh's historic flight across the Atlantic.[22]

Strangely enough, however, Brecht proclaimed a radio revolution without even mentioning the radio counterrevolution that had preceded it by nine years. He was not aware that only the German radio laws of 1923 had turned a system of wireless intercommunication into one of one-sided distribution, nor was he aware of the dangers to state security that gave rise to this change in the first place. Thus, Brecht's entire theory of radio relied on his charming but mistaken assumption that "our anarchic social order . . .

enables inventions to be made and further developed, which must then conquer their markets, justify their existence, in short, they are *inventions that have not been prescribed.*"²³

As if the General Staff did not commission orders, and the strategy of mobile warfare did not justify technologies.

No surprise, then, that the mix-up of anarchy and strategy avenged itself on the revolutionary strategist of radio drama. In *The Flight across the Ocean*, Brecht celebrated all kinds of things: the airplane, the sound of the engines, the white noise of resistance against the elements of wind and water, but especially of course the unacknowledged contribution of the working class, without which the plane would never have taken off. Brecht, however, did not mention, even with one word, the equally unacknowledged, but no less critical, contribution of radio communication. In his *Flight*, the apparatus of communication onboard the plane was simply not to be found. No wonder, then, that his wished-for transformation of his radio drama itself from a distribution to a communications apparatus was doomed to fail. Brecht's "frightful impression" that radio "was an unbelievably ancient apparatus, long ago forgotten in the deluge," brilliantly summarized his antediluvian dramatization of a world war technology.²⁴

Fortunately, not all authors of radio drama, including those on the left, forgot the deluge, a.k.a. the world war, as much as Brecht did. In 1929 Friedrich Wolf, in later years the German Democratic Republic's ambassador to Moscow and father to a high-ranking secret service officer, published a radio drama called *S.O.S. . . . Rao . . . Rao . . . Foyn—"Krassin" saves "Italia."* Its soundtrack of the rescue of a failed polar expedition in 1928 brought the myth of aviation down to its technological truth: the fact of wireless remote control. Amid the white noise of shortwave entertainment, a German-Soviet wireless amateur, based on the strategically all-important Murman Coast, intercepts the SOS signals coming from a crashed Italian airship. To demonstrate not only their humanity but also their technological advance over fascist Italy, the Soviets send radio-controlled airplanes and icebreakers and rescue not only General Umberto Nobile but finally the entire nameless crew he has abandoned.

To recognize the higher glory of radio technology, Wolf's radio drama, including its very title, leaves the domain of common language to convince listeners that modern communication relies on Morse codes and ground-to-air transmissions much more than on literature. And indeed: in 1932 General Nobile, immediately after his return from the ice and his dishonorable discharge from the Italian Air Force, shows up in Moscow with nine zeppelins in tow and offers his services as an aviation expert. A year later, the two bitter enemies, Stalin and Mussolini, sign their official treaty of friendship, while Nobile is allowed to return to Italy to prep the air force for the next war.

In 1933 Wilhelm Hoffmann, the only theorist of radio drama holding a PhD directed by Martin Heidegger, wrote, "Death is primarily a radio topic."[25] Wireless communication on the margins of death was a reality not only for Wolf. He retrieved the ghostly voices of forgotten radio operators for the entire generation between the wars.

Radio dramas such as Ernst Johannsen's *Brigadevermittlung* [Troop telephone exchange] or Eberhard Wolfgang Moeller's *Douaumont* succeeded in identifying civil radio with its military origin.[26] As dramatic continuations of Meier's "Memory from the Trenches," both radio dramas descended into those literal caverns that in *A Comedy of Danger* had been camouflaged as unlit Welsh mines: into the trench shelters or concrete casemates of World War I. They did so in order to demonstrate that modern caverns, in contrast to church naves or radio-equipped living rooms, cannot function without intercom. The attraction of radio drama: for a while, during the interwar years, even Germany's monologic national broadcast stations allowed the transmission of dramas and dialogues supposedly taking place between operators and staff officers, frontline nurses, line troubleshooters, and so on.

Only when French artillery landed a direct hit on the telephone exchange did all this traffic come to a sudden halt, replaced with a truly positive silence. That silence, however, was no longer a prayer, as in Zarathustra's cave, but deadly silence able to record and transmit the noise at the base of all signals: reams of enemy machine-gun fire, which demolished the telephone exchange itself, or enemy barrage that pulverized even shrouds made from tons of concrete and obliterated the Eighty-Fourth Infantry Division, including its radio unit. As in the finale of *Götterdämmerung*, message and noise, signal and interference, coincided and fed the interference as a signal back into the civil radio network.

The point of Moeller's radio drama was to resurrect one of the dead soldiers of Douaumont during the interwar years and to bring him home. There, as interference incarnate, he announced the very archaeology of radio: "Douaumont—that name leaves you speechless! You don't want to hear any of it!"[27] Then, the dead man took over, did his conjuring and summoning, until the shells of Douaumont could be heard and felt in Berlin at the moment of the broadcast. Radio drama as a feedback of world war—which was to be demonstrated.²⁸

Feedforward, however, did not yet exist. And that not only because, until 1940, radio and its art form could store their work only on records but not on reels-to-reels, which had yet to be invented. The other reason why radio drama had to defer its escalation was the lack of a mass audience for radio and the technology of blitzkrieg. When Guglielmo Marconi conducted his first experiments with the wireless in 1896, his investors—Italian and British general staffs—made a somber prediction: the ever-present danger of having classified information be intercepted would discourage armies from switching to radio communication. For that very reason, such interceptions were staged by the first generation of radio plays. In 1938 on Radio Rome, however, people could hear Marconi's recorded voice declaring, posthumously and victoriously, that the strategic medium of interception had, finally, been successfully converted into a medium of reception for forty million listeners:

> I confess that when forty-two years ago I succeeded in making the first radio transmission at Pontecchio, I foresaw the possibility of sending electric waves to great distances, but I did not hold hope of being able to obtain the great satisfaction which is being accorded me today.
>
> In fact, a major defect was then attributed to my invention—that of possible interception of messages transmitted. This defect preoccupied me so much that for many years my principal researches were directed to its elimination.
>
> Nevertheless, this "defect" was utilized after about thirty years and has become radio—that means of reception which daily reaches more than forty million listeners.²⁹

Thus, in the eyes of its inventor, radio as we know it was a by-product, a civilian spin-off, of military research. Since it originated along the way from interception to reception, from strategy to demography, there always remains the danger of regression: at any time, reception can again turn into interception. This fact, which most reception theories tend to ignore, was most dramatically stated, just one year after Marconi's last words, by the most famous and efficient drama in radio history: Orson Welles's broadcast of *The War of the Worlds* from his Mercury Theatre on the Air. On October 31, 1938, only ten months before the simulated attack on the broadcasting station Gleiwitz that was to trigger another world war, Welles—with the self-assumed authority of the Columbia Broadcasting System—announced the simulated message that all danger of war was banned now, that the unemployment rate was effectively reduced, and that the radio audience in the United States had grown to thirty-two million.[30] The now of the broadcast's historical moment, however, was not October 31, 1938, but October 30, 1939, that is, World War II.

World war as war of the worlds—that is how ingeniously Orson Welles and his collaborators updated the novel by H. G. Wells on which the radio drama is based. If a German pun on their proper names (which are variants of the German word *Wellen* [waves] were allowed in English, one could say: Welles, the radio dramatist, supplemented Wells, the novelist, with James Clerk Maxwell's radio waves. Precisely because radio had become an immaterial world wide web, because CBS ruled over millions of listeners, and its own radio drama was its most powerful publicity, the danger of radio interception grew to unheard-of proportions. At the very moment when planet Earth turned into a global media system, it offered itself to the eventuality of being intercepted, victimized, and attacked by other planets. Radio drama is the self-promotion of an electromagnetic superpower, which makes us forget what general staffers explained to young Marconi: the more powerful a radio system, the more likely it is that its messages will be intercepted. The Wehrmacht could tell you a story about that in World War II.

For that reason, Welles in his dark voice began the broadcast with words that are hardly translatable, simply because in the wonderful American English of the superpower, *intelligence* at once signifies intelligence, news, and the secret service:

> We know now that in the early years of the twentieth century this world was being watched closely by intelligences greater than man's and yet as mortal as his own. We know now that as human beings busied themselves about their various concerns they were scrutinized and studied, perhaps almost as narrowly as a man with a microscope might scrutinize the transient creatures that swarm and multiply in a drop of water.... Across an immense ethereal gulf, minds that are to our minds as ours are to the beasts in the jungle, intellects vast, cool and unsympathetic regarded this earth with envious eyes and slowly and surely drew their plans against us.[31]

Thus, Orson Welles confirmed Marconi's early statement that "of course, the signals may come from space outside the earth.... They may be caused by magnetic disturbances on the sun; they may come from Mars or Venus."³² Just as the concept of a unified world had derived from telegraphy, so did that of outer space derive from radio. When Martian intelligences scrutinized the earth, the very status of nature changed from physics to strategy. Contrary to *A Comedy of Danger* but totally in line with John von Neumann's simultaneous theory of games, whose mathematics formalized nature as an unpredictable enemy, another planet waged war against the Earth.³³

To be sure, Princeton astronomers, when they observe a series of timed explosions taking place on Mars, still believe in chance or natural law, but as soon as a first unidentifiable flying object has landed in New Jersey, the war of the worlds has broken out. The first rocket is followed by others, all of which, immediately after ground contact, transform into tanks. Whereupon the "intellects vast, cool and unsympathetic" demonstrate their strategic intelligence quotient. Their tanks destroy human enemies only in cases of self-defense; that is, their heat rays annihilate, in a series of tactical escalations, all infantry, artillery, and U.S. Air Force units that have been mobilized against them (not to mention a CBS war reporter). Otherwise, the Martian tanks stage their assault on New York as if they—and not the Supreme Command of the Wehrmacht—had invented the blitzkrieg campaigns of 1939 to 1941, whose strategy was to supersede counterforce by countercommand:³⁴ the war machines waste no time on humans, or even troops, but systematically disrupt all railroad lines, flights, bridges, highways, and lines of communication, which is to say the communications systems that had been celebrated at the outset.

World wars are essentially media wars. For that reason, the powerless defenders of New York City have nothing else to fall back on. Therefore, what is at stake concerns the very status of commercial American radio. Midway through the broadcast, the vice president in charge of operations announces to the listeners glued to their speakers that CBS has "received a request from the militia at Trenton to place at their disposal our entire broadcasting facilities. In view of the gravity of the situation, and believing that radio has a definite responsibility to serve in the public interest at all times, we are turning over our facilities" to the signal corps.³⁵

In 1938 these words were sheer prophecy, a feedforward of World War II. Three years later, this prophecy would become a historical reality when squadrons of Japanese torpedo bombers—not, it is true, planetary V-2s—surfaced in the morning sky at Pearl Harbor and America's large electronics industry was retooled into state-controlled weapons production.³⁶

Conversely, commercial radio and the recording industry fell into the hands of outsiders or blacks, who took advantage of this historical chance to smuggle the sound of rhythm and blues into white kids' ears. Rock 'n' roll was about to be born.

Reduced to a mouthpiece of the signal corps, on the other hand, the CBS broadcast became an instrument of general mobilization, at the very latest when Orson Welles, mimicking the voice of President Roosevelt, announced the country to be at war. The claim that, of the broadcast's six million listeners, several thousand were supposed to have spiraled into a panic inspired not only contemporary media sociologists but also U.S. Navy staffs to study the feasibility of radio-controlled military mobilization. Because Welles simulated the invasion from Mars exclusively as radio intercom—from the reports to special announcements, from aircraft wireless to sound recordings—the message of the radio drama imploded into media technology, the reception into interception. All this meant in the final analysis that radio, or, more precisely, the Columbia Broadcasting System itself, had to be, as Welles put it, "utterly destroyed."[37] When the Martian tanks, having overcome all military resistance, attack New York City in general, and its "Broadcast Building" in particular, the last radio microphone records and transmits the dying voice of the last CBS reporter.[38] Then, against the background of audible radio silence, another anonymous voice queries the plain fact, "Isn't there anyone on the air?"[39]

On December 24, 1942, thirty-eight days before the capitulation of the Sixth Army at the Battle of Stalingrad, the Großdeutsche Rundfunk broadcast a Christmas "ring ending," so called, which Hans-Jürgen Syberberg later retrieved from its sound grave.[40] A radio announcer in Berlin called one Wehrmacht unit after another to the microphone: from Stalingrad, the Murman Coast, and Norway to France, southern Italy, and Crete. And all began singing, first by themselves but then more or less in unison, "Silent night, holy night, all is calm. . . ." This was a radio drama as large as Fortress Europe and as world-weary as the finale of *Götterdämmerung* but based on concealed media: to facilitate the Christmas ring ending, the state-propaganda broadcast system had to short-circuit its lines with the Wehrmacht's secret lines of communication, the so-called scrambler line of General Erich Fellgiebel.

Professor Reginald Fessenden, the hero of the very first radio broadcast on Christmas Eve of 1906, suggested to the British High Command as early as 1914 that they conduct large-scale attacks from the air, which was "literally" realized during World War II, as his widow and biographer put it.⁴¹ The same electronics doesn't only make large cities (*pace* Marshall McLuhan) into global villages; it also makes them just as easily destructible as villages. Radio, however, can no longer avert invasions from Mars or the terror of attack; that is possible only with radar, radio's high-tech evolution. In *The War of the Worlds*, CBS and its reporters are all wiped out. The only one to survive is the astronomer, who was the first to spot the Martian rockets through his telescope. And that for good reason. The war had hardly ended when Great Britain, with the aid of captured radar equipment from the Wehrmacht, developed the radio telescope. Ever since, the puzzle of radio drama, whether the mishmash of waves in space is arbitrary or signals of intelligent life-forms, has been a matter of scientific interception, albeit one no longer in search of humans.

To the postwar generation was bequeathed a more modest war loot than Fessenden's radar. They were the beneficiaries of stereo, FM, tape recorders, and television. From 1934 on, all Wehrmacht tanks, but only they, had been equipped with FM radio, which was the primary technological precondition for blitzkrieg. FM was also a gift to the Federal Republic of Germany, whose access to medium-range waves had been severely limited by the Copenhagen wave plan, just as it was a gift to a generation of drivers enjoying radio tank control as tourists. Once the hero of all deceptive *Funkspiele* [radio games] under Wilhelm Canaris, the AEG magnetophone slimmed down to the size of a tape recorder and played rock music on roads and autobahns. UHF and VHF became the frequency bands for television, whose development was halted by the BBC and the Großdeutsche Rundfunk in 1939 to prevent enemy access to radar secrets, and liberated radio from the task of having to broadcast the state-controlled monopoly of radio itself. The task of minimizing people's lack of direction was given over to talking heads and TV commercials. Finally, the computer, whose secret British prototype cracked the codes of the Wehrmacht's entire information flow traveling along scrambler lines and military channels, triggered the digitalization not only of entertainment media but of cognition and computing more generally. Henri Bergson's speech as a keynoter, that is, as an idiot, of the academy warning of an impending German victory became an event: "What would happen . . . if the moral effort of humanity should turn in its tracks at the moment of attaining its goal, and if some diabolical contrivance should cause it to produce the mechanization of spirit instead of the spiritualization of matter?"⁴²

Under such conditions, when all relevant data flows—from radar to computer data—have left the hands of humans, postwar radio drama was initially reduced to myth and sound effects. Stereo systems transmitted military positioning systems and, via VHF, sounds into living rooms that were at the upper threshold of hearing. From that, radio dramas created public-service myths that were based on the assumption—comforting as much as false—that "the smoke had cleared after the war." That's how Ingeborg Bachmann put it in *The Cicadas*, whose eponymous heroes (loosely following Ovid) are reaching the upper limits of VHF frequency: "It is because the cicadas were once human. They stopped eating, drinking and loving so that they could sing on and on forever. By escaping into song, they grew thinner and smaller, and now they sing, lost to their longing—enchanted, but condemned to damnation as well, because their voices have become inhuman."[43]

Such is the mythic veil of enchantment that the mechanization of spirit had pulled over radio plays, whose broadcasting left no imprint on programming and whose authors were not yet sound engineers. In the broadcasting practice of today, however, the medium and signals of the radio plays, if they still exist, most likely coincide. They are swallowed up by the big radio play, that is, by the public-service radio system itself, ever since the pressure coming from private stations has mechanized their program structure. Radio has evolved into an echo of its modern, that is, military, siblings, which have since managed to bypass all information and interception. In World War II, the Wehrmacht still coded its messages systematically, and for that reason another system such as Colossus, the British computer prototype, was able to decode them. Today the Russians and the Americans are said to use random-generation software, which flies in the face of any effort at systematic decoding. Further, military networks are principally signaling around the clock to deprive the enemy of any basis for the frequency and importance of any particular channel. As a British wiretapping expert recently put it, "We intercept pages of letters, letters in arbitrary sequence without rhyme or reason. That is the order of things. There is no plain text anywhere. . . . To put it differently, the Russians no longer bother reading our messages, and neither do we theirs."[44]

Nonsense around the clock, from secret service radio plays to Muzak—that's how the frequencies in the ether are being jammed up these days. For that reason, interception may be more productive in the domain of hardware, when seemingly secure channels are involved, or in the domain of software, when it comes to programming languages. Once data streams have become inhuman and without voice, as in the case of Friedrich Wolf or Ingeborg Bachmann, the stage is set for hams becoming hackers, and radio plays becoming computer games. Producing a record in your own living room on a synthesizer with a MIDI interface is already fully feasible these days. Via cable, radio stations could broadcast the animations of their computerized listeners. And where there is no wire or silicon fiber, radio will likely once more be tasked with performing its original function: to make connections where and as long as distance and enemies exist. For digital signals, however, the so-called ether is not ideal: according to the Fourier transform, every rectangular pulse requires an infinite number of bandwidths, and even a data-compressed CD signals 100,000 bits per second. For that reason, wireless telephony, as radio was called in the days of its military infancy, will likely continue to remain the domain for all that cannot be cached and, hence, manipulated through digital signal processing, that is to say, for randomness, for unpredictability, for danger.

The Greeks believed that the sun, on its journey across the sky, kept grinding its own groove and thus produced a sound that was incessant, eternal, and immutable, and hence imperceptible to our ears.

How many such inaudible sounds live around us? One day, they will become audible, and fill our ears with horror. . . . [45]

Operation Valhalla

TRANSLATED BY GEOFFREY WINTHROP-YOUNG

> The insurrection will only be possible if women get involved.
> —attributed to Mirabeau (1791)

The Valkyrie, act 2, scene 2. In a "wild, craggy place," Wotan conducts a strategy debate with Brünnhilde, his illegitimate daughter and Valkyrie. He reveals to her the "grand thought" forbidden by all cultural laws and marriage alliances that came to him at the conclusion of *Rhinegold* as he contemplated the looming twilight of the gods:

> in den Schoß der Welt
> schwang ich mich hinab
> mit Liebeszauber
> zwang ich die Wala,
> stört' ihres Wissens Stolz,
> daß sie Rede nun mir stand.
> Kunde empfing ich von ihr;
> von mir doch barg sie ein Pfand:
> der Welt weisestes Weib
> gebar mir, Brünnhilde, dich.
> Mit acht Schwestern
> zog ich dich auf;
> durch euch Walküren
> wollt' ich wenden

Originally published as "Unternehmen Walhall," in *Die Nibelungen: Bilder von Liebe, Verrat und Untergang*, edited by Wolfgang Storch (Munich: Prestel, 1987), 62–63.

was mir die Wala
zu fürchten schuf:
ein schmähliches Ende der Ew'gen.
Daß stark zum Streit
uns fände der Feind,
hieß ich euch Helden mir schaffen:
die herrisch wir sonst
in Gesetzen hielten,
die Männer, denen
den Mut wir gewehrt,
die durch trüber Verträge
trügende Bande
zu blindem Gehorsam
wir uns gebunden—
die solltet zu Sturm
und Streit ihr nun stacheln,
ihre Kraft reizen
zu rauhem Krieg,
daß kühner Kämpfer Scharen
ich sammle in Walhalls Saal!

I made my way
down into the depths
by love's enchantment
I conquered the Wala,
humbled her silent pride,
till she told me all she knew.
Wisdom I learned from her words;
the Wala demanded a pledge;
the wise Erda conceived
a daughter—Brünnhilde, you.
With eight sisters
you were brought up
as bold Valkyries,
who would avert
the doom that the Wala
had made me fear—
the shameful defeat of the immortals.
Our foes would find us

CHAPTER 7

> ready for fight;
> you would assemble my army;
> the men whom we held
> by our laws in bondage,
> the mortals, whom we
> had curbed in their pride,
> whom by treacherous treaties,
> shameful agreements,
> we'd bound in obedience
> blindly to serve us;
> and yours was the task
> to stir them to battle,
> and arouse brave men
> to ruthless war,
> till valiant hosts of heroes
> had gathered in Valhalla's hall![1]

Lines from 1852 in which Wagner, as always, puts it plainly. A nomadic storm god who by marrying into Fricka's sedentary clan has been forced to take on the burden of world domination and its attendant laws returns to his strategic roots. He abandons the laws, cheats on his wife, and begets with Earth herself nine maidens who will revolutionize warfare. Linear infantry turns into storm-trooper battalions; the limited wars of old-European cabinet regimes mutate into our present: Wotan's "ruthless" war, or total war from Ludendorff to Goebbels.

Wagner's Germanic sources were already acquainted with Valkyries and battle maidens. They rode through the air in golden armor, fought according to Wotan's orders, and assigned the fate of those who fell in combat. To prepare for the final battle against fire and water, desert and icy hell—the myths of our future—the Valkyries were ordered to recruit the dead to serve their warlord, Wotan. Forty-three thousand men or three divisions were on standby in Valhalla.

While Wagner's Wotan is also engaged in preventive measures against the twilight of the gods, he deploys his storm troopers while they are still alive. The male members of a race sired by Wotan with a human woman (that is, the offspring of the union between rulers and ruled) unconsciously wage the god's proxy war. Where (according to Foucault's thesis) old-European princes reigned only over death and mountains of corpses, Wagner's sovereign is in charge of life itself. Which is why he needs Valkyries like Brünnhilde, who exercise remote control over his partisans, save them from death, and nurture them as mothers. Without unconscious programming from the moment of birth, that is, without childhood, maternal womb, and female idol, there is no modern cannon fodder.

Wotan faces an elementary and historically highly specific problem. The British colonial army lost the American War of Independence because its officers could only deploy their unmotivated German mercenaries using Frederician linear tactics. The insurgents, by contrast, were grounded in a twofold sense: in their motivation as well as in a home soil on which they could fan out as independent, autonomous partisans. Lafayette and Gneisenau, two participants in these wars, imported the new tactics to Europe: the former to the French revolutionary army, the latter to Prussia, whose linear tactics had failed to overcome the more advanced French armies at Jena and Auerstedt.

When Wagner's Wotan speaks of soldiers "held . . . in bondage" by deceptive laws and "treacherous treaties," he is obliquely referring to the recruited and enlisted men of cabinet wars. They were prepared to die only if they had received sufficient drill and pay, and they would have deserted if hussar detachments and a restriction on night and wood marches had not cut off all possibilities of escape. By contrast, the Prussian Landsturm edict of 1813 produced remote-controlled "heroes" stirred to battle.[2] Ever since the year of Wagner's birth, men have been fighting and dying without knowing that a Wotan or a Frederick Wilhelm III, at the behest of army reformers, has programmed their entire independence.

In highly paradoxical fashion, the 1812 *Exerzir-Reglement für die Infanterie* [Drill regulations for infantry] exhorted instructors

> to impress upon those soldiers who have been [re]moved from rank and file in order to fight and move on their own, that they abandon all prescribed constraints, methodical positioning, uniformity of grip, handling of rifles, measured movements, and cautious progression that are required in close and orderly formation; that they are allowed to handle their rifles in whichever way is best suited for the purposes of attack or defense; and that every movement should be carried out freely and nimbly and always in full consideration of all circumstances.
>
> The best way to train soldiers to quickly spot and exploit the advantages of the terrain such as trees, ditches, hedges, fences, houses, and walls, is to confront them with said features and show them how to move by taking into account the latter as well as the movements of the

enemy. The drillmaster must draw their attention to any feature they failed to use to their advantage and point out each and every weakness.³

Thus, princes undermine the very idea on which their rules are based. They order disobedience and remove themselves from a homeland that motivates partisans' souls and protects partisans' bodies. It takes more than princely commands to create what Carl Schmitt called tellurian warriors. Operation Valhalla, Wotan's "grand thought," can only be realized by partisans that are not aware of it. For even if Wotan's command of disobedience were able to overcome the resistance put up by his wife, the guardian of traditional marriage and feudal contracts, his orders would result in slavish servitude rather than in the type of independence that allows Siegfried to be as victorious as his name implies.⁴ Making perfect use of the terrain, and equipped with a sword whose hardening was invented by a contemporary of Henry Bessemer and Alfred Krupp, Wotan's partisan defeats the old powers.⁵ Which is why the incestuous union with Mother Earth, the guardian of all trenches, replaces marriage and why incessant drills are replaced by battle maidens. Power appropriates the revolution's new tactics.

"Allons, enfants de la Patrie," sang the revolutionary armies of a fatherland that, for good reason, was female. The enemy evoked by the "Marseillaise" only slits the throats of women and children. Which is why, in the summer of 1792, at the peak of the military craze, these women submitted countless petitions to the legislative assembly. The patriotic oath to nourish their children with a "milk ennobled by the natural, sweet spirit of liberty" marked the return of Greek amazons or Germanic battle maidens. There is nothing ancient about Heinrich von Kleist's Penthesilea or Wagner's Brünnhilde other than their costumes. In Lons-le-Saulnier, Mâcon and Tarbes women grabbed pans and pitchforks, kitchen knives and ladles; in Paris, Théroigne de Méricourt organized a female national guard.

And this was the case whenever revolutions coincided with Wagner's art. In April 1848, four years before the *Valkyrie* text, the inventor Daniel Borme created a legion of unmarried women, whose very name, *Vésuviennes*, competes with Hebbel's volcanic Brünnhilde.⁶ In October 1870, six years before the world premiere of the *Ring* cycle, Félix Berry called the first battalion of Seine amazons to join the barricades of the Paris Commune. Wagner's battle maidens are anything but a mythological quote.

Neither is it mere fiction that they were to "arouse heroes" rather than perform military duties. For the more revolutionary the men, the more forcefully they kept banning the spontaneously emerging women's battalions. According to Napoleon, there was only one "un-French thing: when women can do as they please."[7] Hence, modern states set out to refunctionalize fighting women. Maiden tactics transformed into maternal erotics. France's first girls' school came about at the command of an emperor who ordered a former secretary of Marie-Antoinette to turn the orphans of his Legion of Honor into mothers. The modern cycle that links family support and cannon fodder was launched.

And here, halfway between the Legion of Honor and the SS Lebensborn, we encounter Wotan's illegitimate daughters.[8] Battle maidens turn into heroes' mothers. In vain does Brünnhilde attempt to carry out Wotan's paradoxical—and revoked—order against Wotan himself in order to help Siegmund vanquish tyrannical feudal lords. Women are not free to do as they please, especially when the god has been compelled by his divine spouse to once again respect the laws. Wotan court-martials his daughter: "By my commandments / alone you could act, / and against me you have commanded."[9] Whereupon the Valkyrie is deprived of military honors or swordly maidenhood and compelled to adopt the son of the fallen honorary legionary. But in doing so she fulfills Wotan's or Napoleon's mandate. In Brünnhilde the orphaned Siegfried finds an ideal mother, whose love ensures that (long before Lacan) the desire of man is the desire of the other. In defiance of, or for the sake of, Wotan, the unconsciously programmed Siegfried fulfills the twilight desires of the gods.

In other words, banned female fighting units turn into nineteenth-century poetry. In a famous file note, Gneisenau impressed on his old-fashioned king, Frederick William III, that without "poetic attunement" nobody would be willing to wage national wars of liberation.[10] Which is why battle maidens like Brünnhilde approach their heroes Siegmund or Siegfried with pure poetry. And this is why, in the shape of Marianne or Germania, they stand atop national arches and monuments and grace recently invented postage stamps. Finally, in 1870 General Postmaster Heinrich von Stephan introduces military postcards, whose stamp Germanias take care of entire armies as Brünnhilde once had of Siegfried. As Stephan's self-congratulatory account would have it, the remote control exercised by military-postal mothers, wives, and brides led Germans to victory.[11]

But the war was not yet a divine storm. Only when the attack (to loosely follow Wotan) was directed against Earth herself, into the trenches and large-scale battles of World War I, did Operation Valhalla become a strategic reality. Marianne and Germania disintegrated into powder and mud. Two revolutions ended in "the shameful defeat of the immortals" and drew us all into war.¹² After three years of static fighting, Ludendorff's Spring Offensive of 1918 solved the problem of how to overrun the enemy's trenches and machine-gun nests. The pulverization of Earth was complemented by new combat tactics. Moving beyond the privates and militias of 1813, entire armies were now delivered from Prussian drill practices. Obedience was replaced by special training, resulting in a multitude of independent noncommissioned officers able to penetrate the entire length of the front between the Picardie and the Champagne.

The Spring Offensive of 1918 and its end, the victorious British tank attack, gave birth to the blitzkrieg. From Ludendorff's autonomous stormtroop leaders emerged (together with the writer Ernst Jünger) the cadre of the future Waffen-SS. From the Waffen-SS, with its innovative submachine guns and combat gear, emerged the armies and special task forces of today. The twilight desires of a dead god inevitably turn real.

CHAPTER 8

When the Blitzkrieg Raged

TRANSLATED BY GEOFFREY WINTHROP-YOUNG

> The dead ride fast, and when they become motorized,
> they move even faster.
> —Carl Schmitt, *Theory of the Partisan* (2007)

Like all poets before "All You Need Is Love," I will begin with a *captatio benevolentiae*. To the only true song on earth. May the recipient of these greetings not take offense. After all, the devil only lurks between lines, sentences, dreams, flights—and not in Aby Warburg's obsessive details.

> Please allow me to introduce myself
> I'm a man of wealth and taste.
> I've been around for a long, long year
> Stole many a man's soul and faith.
> I was 'round when Jesus Christ
> Had his moment of doubt and pain.
> Made damn sure that Pilate
> Washed his hands and sealed his fate.
>
> Pleased to meet you
> Hope you guess my name.
>
> But what's puzzling you
> Is the nature of my game.
> I stuck around St. Petersburg

Originally published under the same title in *Sympathy for the Devil*, edited by Albert Kümmel-Schnur (Munich: Fink, 2009), 137–41.

When I saw it was a time for a change
Killed the czar and his ministers
Anastasia screamed in vain.
I rode a tank
Held a general's rank
When the blitzkrieg raged
And the bodies stank.¹

In the eyes of this courteous witness, whose name poses a riddle to us, history shrivels to a *longue durée*. Bypassing the resurrection, it moves straight from the crucifixion to Anastasia—she who is already resurrected in name. Her vain and probably phony screams (Anastasia was, after all, an impostor) coincide with those of the stage microphone. The year is 1917, the year in which St. Petersburg lost both its saintly name and nimbus. Our witness is behind all true revolutions: he is John Lennon's "Revolution 9." He even forfeits magic tricks and mystery plays in order to conduct the affairs that befit a destructive character. In times of edifying literature produced in Frankfurt, this means above all to force relations to dance and to celebrate Roger Waters as Britain's greatest modern poet.²

Our rainbow-colored tabloids no longer cover the spectrum of our riddles. But our witness gets down to real business only once World War II wildly accelerates the trench warfare of World War I. It is one thing to shoot at sluggish armored cruisers like the *Aurora*; it is something entirely different to ride in tanks. When Mick Jagger was born on July 26, 1943, in Dartford, England, field marshals Günther von Kluge and Erich von Manstein had just been forced to abort the largest tank battle of the war. Deploying 1,081 tanks, including two hundred Panthers and ninety brand-new Tigers, the Wehrmacht had launched an attack against the Kursk salient, the so-called Operation Citadel, only to run into unexpectedly precise defensive positions. Only because the armored infantry defied orders and rode into battle with open turrets in order to escape the looming inferno of diesel oil and artillery shells did some survive to bear witness to this short oral history. Otherwise, their bodies too would have begun to stink between Belgorod and Oryol.

For the battle had already been lost when the crews were still driving their brand-new Tigers—by train, incidentally, to protect the treads—from Magdeburg toward Bryansk or Charkov. Nobody on the German side had the slightest idea that for several weeks the Stavka had been in possession of Kurt Zeitzler's entire plan of attack. Even Marshal Zhukov believed that his English allies had smuggled a high-ranking traitor into Hitler's headquarters. Little did he know that two years after cracking the Enigma, Alan Turing's people and machines in Bletchley Park had also managed to decode the secret Siemens teleprinter; they were now able to eavesdrop on tactical command output (between divisions) as well as on strategic orders (between army headquarters and entire army groups).

Things had been different in the blitzkrieg from Sedan to Dunkirk, when generals like Rommel literally rode their tanks. Turing was able to decipher the Enigma-encoded radio messages only with a delay of three weeks—and thus much too late to warn the French allies. In addition, no blitzkrieg was raging at just that moment. Blitzkrieg, such as it was, consisted of a wide encirclement of General Maurice Gamelin's amassed divisions in order to sever, in nonbloody fashion, their rearward communication lines. It was the French High Command's inability to use radio technology to guide its three tank divisions that made Heinz Guderian's task so easy. Drawing on his experience as the commander of a heavy and unwieldy mobile radio unit in 1914 at the Marne, he had between 1923 and 1934 put a major effort into equipping the ten tank divisions later employed in the western campaign with a technological innovation in the shape of ultrashortwave radio. All the car stereos that carried us on our trips to the Stones' beloved Côte d'Azur while playing their songs inherited this blitzkrieg trade secret. Otherwise, pop music would have remained that monophone stew of vinyl or medium-wave radio that a decade earlier had come to be known as rock 'n' roll.

Despite all the dreams harbored by *Spex*, there is no straight line from signified to signifier, from cotton plantations to the New Orleans Mardi Gras to our contemporary witness.[3] Like everything that is new under the sun (and that is denied and belittled by book-based religions for that very reason), music is a surging billow that breaks on the shore of a different culture.

> Our love was like the water
> That splashes on a stone.
> Our love is like our music,
> It's here and then it's gone.[4]

This applies to the Aegean Sea and the Greek alphabet as much as it does to pop music: both are intercultural miracles that our books suggest to young hearts. Their ears still filled with "Greensleeves" and "Merry Old England," young Brits grew up erotically-musically between U.S. Air Force bases in order to decide the first media world war. In the land of Elvis Presley, this was known as *the British invasion*. For two years, logistically underequipped GIs sloughed through France to join divisions whose Sherman tanks could counter the German *Königstiger* only because they were mass-produced. "And they knew that the greatest single weapon of the war, the atomic bomb excepted, was the German 88-mm flat-trajectory gun, which brought down thousands of bombers and tens of thousands of soldiers."[5]

No talk, then, of blitzkrieg. In defensive actions the 88 mm flak ripped off the penis of GIs with such force that its velocity could kill the person next to them.

> Don't scratch me like that,
> Oh yeah, you're a strange Stray Cat.[6]

Maiden or media studies weren't exactly the strength of the Suhrkamp publishing house. For years one placebo after another belied the strength of your claws. We, however, stood on the side of endless loops or double-eights in which observers get entangled.

Romanists in Bochum once asked Alain Robbe-Grillet, the poet of our jealous wild youth, how the trauma of World War II had inscribed itself into his works. *La défaite de Reichenfels* and so on.[7] "'Not at all, gentlemen! I only thought of the orgies with the little girls. My world war was the first!'—'But surely you were born in 1922?'—'Indeed, but since 1915 my father served with the engineers, no, with the sappers: trenches, mines, tunnels, counter-tunnels, as awful as in Kafka's 'Burrow.' After the war he was able to sleep but he screamed out his nightmares. As a little boy I listened to every one of his nightmares.'"[8]

And now our poet is dead.

But the singer lives on—into the digital demise of us all. But first he bears witness. The general who rode a blitzkrieg tank could only have been German. Enemies listen to each other since we are a conversation.[9] What Mick Jagger heard and composed ever since his birth is (to use Churchill's nice phrase) the sickle cut through France.

Keith Richards's guitar playing may be mediocre, and the bongos embarrassing. Yet when there is a fortunate crossing of cultures, pop stars rise to the status of heroes or gods while still alive. They descend to us mortals from their stage shows as did the gods from Olympus to mingle with nymphs or groupies.

And so we all die and are taken from our parents to head toward new ways of dying. And that, precisely, was the 1945 kamikaze hit of Radio Tokyo:

> Your mother weeps with joy;
> It's too great an honor for us,
> That you are worshipped as a god
> At the Yasukuni shrine.[10]

PART III

Vanishing Animals and Returning Nomads

Animals of War
A Historical Bestiary

TRANSLATED BY GEOFFREY WINTHROP-YOUNG

Right before our eyes, which already are better at processing monitors than television screens, modern war is switching from the machine to the computer age. It is time, therefore, to recall that steel and silicon were preceded by other weapons. René Descartes was the first to dissolve the so-called I into a trinity, whose other two ingredients were called God and machine. But for Descartes, the first philosopher to receive training as a military officer, machines encompassed more than clockworks, cannons, and muskets; they also included all those strange apparitions composed of heads, rumps, and limbs marching past his open Dutch windows: humans and animals.[1] Only for the past four centuries have our wars been a symbiosis of men and machines. During the preceding twenty millennia, humans and animals were not grouped under machines, and for that very reason they lived and died together. This may be as forgotten as the spit that flies from our frothing mouths and that gave rise to *spirit*, but it was this very spirit that hunters received from their animal prey.[2] Berserks were possessed by the spirits of bears; werewolves, by those of wolves—otherwise it would have been difficult to overcome the bite inhibition that exists between members of a common species. In other words, war may have been for a very long time, as it is in Ernst Jünger's *On the Marble Cliffs*, an either supremely elevated or equally debased form of hunting. The Arcadians attributed the only victory in their wars against the Spartans to their wolf and bear hides. Crusader

---

This chapter was originally published as "Die Tiere des Krieges: Ein historisches Bestiarium," in *Das Tier in mir: Die animalischen Ebenbilder des Menschen*, edited by Johannes Bilstein and Matthias Winzen (Cologne: Walther König, 2002), 143–59; and translated by Geoffrey Winthrop-Young in *Cultural Politics* 11, no. 3 (2015): 391–94.

arms were adorned with eagles or lions, and as late as July 1943 the German Wehrmacht sent its Panther and Tiger tanks into history's greatest panzer battle at Kursk. Such are the longevity and thoroughly unmetaphorical quality of animal metaphors that become necessary when we practice mimicry of superior forces.

But then again, among mammals we also encounter the opposite: herds and packs that submit to hunters masquerading as alpha animals. Horses and cattle, wolves and camels, they all abandoned their ferocity and thereby enabled the basic differentiation between murder and war. Hunting gave rise to war and domestication; domestication (according to Thomas Macho) gave rise to breeding and education.[3] Every nomad breeder knows and ought to know that a single stallion can serve ten mares; every seasoned military commander knows and ought to know what *infantry* literally means: young immature men about to be decimated by the next war. When Napoleon, emperor of the French, founded a girls' school for the semiorphaned offspring of his doomed Honor Guard, the newly appointed headmistress asked him about his educational goals. Napoleon's brusque response: Turn them into mothers! The response to the same question posed during World War II, would have been: "Dogs, do you want to live forever?"[4]

Unlike the stubborn mules that, to this day, remain necessary for mountain warfare, dogs and horses will die for their master. The same dark law united the pairs of male lovers that made up the Sacred Band of Thebes. But only domesticated and bred animals brought about the distinction between massacre and war: their superhuman abilities, strategically deployed, superseded mere tactics. Once the wheel (probably a Mesopotamian innovation) was equipped with spokes, cumbersome oxcarts gave way to light horse-driven chariots. For the first time in history, war unleashed the speed of hunted animals rather than merely that of their hunters. When Pharaoh Thutmose III defeated the Syrian chariots at Megiddo, they had to leave the battlefield on mule carts. And while Achaeans and Trojans massacred each other in close combat on the plains surrounding Sacred Ilium, their noble chariot-equipped lords faced off against each other with spears and bows. "That which strikes from afar" is Homer's well-known epithet for a strategy that unites horse, charioteer, and archer.[5] No wonder Odysseus bemoans that Ithaca, his stony home island, offers pasture for goats, sheep, and cattle only but not for horses. Clearly, the nobility of men in ancient Greece (to speak with Gilles Deleuze and Félix Guattari) was indebted to the horse as a nomadic war machine. Coats of arms do not lie. Which is why the wily Odysseus is the ancestor of all things cunning or mechanical—that is, of everything unknightly. Ever since his wooden horse, not only Trojans are wary of Greeks bearing gifts.

But those who razed Sacred Ilium did not survive for long. Standing aloof in their chariots, lords held the reins of power. Bent deeply over their horses' manes, nomads invading the Mediterranean lands around 1200 BCE put an end to this noble order of things. Then as now, power accrues to those in possession of the fastest hardware. Time and again, Huns and Mongols, Turks and Cossacks, demonstrated to the Occident that wars are not about warriors, let alone their honor. On the Catalaunian Plains, not far from Paris, survivors heard a clamor from above, as if the dead were continuing the battle in the skies. In any case, the helicopters in Francis Ford Coppola's *Apocalypse Now*, which are simulating a U.S. Cavalry, which in turn are simulating Wagner's "Ride of the Valkyries," have a long history. When the Persian emperor Cyrus inherited the art of riding from his Median grandfather, the old despots of the ancient Orient were vanquished by the High King, whose reign—in this very order—extended from horses to humans. When his successors built a royal road from Susa to the Mediterranean, thereby mobilizing the superhuman speed of messengers on horseback, the first empire of this world (to quote the Gospels) had come into being.[6] The transmission speed of these imperial military posts, which is echoed by the angels in the Revelations of St. John, remained unsurpassed until the nineteenth century created a media linkup composed of railways and electric telegraphy. Only the tanks and aircraft of the twentieth century ventured more extensively into the steppes opened up by horses and into the deserts traversed by the camels of Islamic jihads.

Precisely this nomadic space had to be conquered, subjected, and fortified by the new empires of Alexander and his Roman heirs. The Diadochi no longer put their trust in horses but in outsized war machines, though the latter (just like all artillery up to World War II) had to be moved by draft animals. In their campaigns against Rome, Pyrrhus and Hannibal deployed elephants as huge humanimal machines, whose terror was such that it took the Romans several defeats before they devised appropriate countermeasures. Ever since, war has not ceased to explode human dimensions. Animals and machines, military posts and fortification walls, were exchangeable long before Descartes provided his philosophical underpinning. The horses of the crusaders and their Saracen opponents were no longer space-annihilating devices but specifically bred massive combat machines, whose heavily armored riders were able to straddle them only thanks to the recently invented stirrup. The latter provided this martial linkup of rider, horse, armor, and lance with a kinetic energy unmatched until the arrival of modern firearms.

Nobody and nothing is immune to firearms, neither knights nor castles, neither squires nor animals. The "impersonal death from gunpowder," to quote Hegel, resulted in the unheard-of replacement of animals by machines and of warriors by soldiers.[7] Starting with the Orange-Nassau military reforms, which facilitated the successful Dutch rebellion against Spain, soldiers on parade grounds are what animals had been in riding schools or falconries: subjects of a relentless drill designed to invent walking, running, acting, and reacting a second time. Otherwise, the infantry columns of the Coalition Wars would not have stood still when under fire, and the storm troopers of World War I would not have run forward into their own artillery barrage.

But ever since drill has passed from animals to soldiers, there is little left for animals to do in war. Sure, there were carrier pigeons and gas dogs, dolphins trained to act like torpedoes and seals drilled to detect mines, but they are of greater interest to military historians than to staff officers. Rather, the ability of birds to fly despite being heavier than air gave rise to the construction of fighter planes, and the ability of dolphins to dive despite being lighter than water gave rise to the construction of torpedoes. Only when and only insofar as soldiers are still animals—that is to say, because they not only are licensed to kill but also experience hunger—do they remain dependent on animals. To save civilian populations from the terrors and travails of the Thirty Years' War, when soldiers and horses, baggage trains and camp followers depleted entire regions, modern wars have refined a logistical apparatus that supplies fighting troops with everything from ammunition to food for humans and animals. But because transportation capacities are always limited, the format of these supplies had to be optimized. The nineteenth century invented beef extract, corned beef, iron rations, and cigarettes for the explicit purpose of transporting less food and more killing equipment. Organized by the elder Moltke's quartermasters, the Franco-Prussian War of 1870–71 marked the crossing of the break-even point: ever since then, railways have been shipping more gunpowder than food to the front.

Which leaves the question of how war could also economize on soldiers. The well-known possible answers range from rockets and drones to combat robots, which give rise to new questions ranging from oil supplies to uranium deposits. Modern wars consume and devour the very soil and earth over which they are waged.

On Modern Warfare
A Conversation with Alexander Kluge

TRANSLATED BY GEOFFREY WINTHROP-YOUNG

ALEXANDER KLUGE: A GI in Afghanistan, mounted on a horse that appears to have been airlifted as well, equipped with electronics that allow him to communicate via orbit with a B-52 bomber: and this member of Custer's cavalry now guides a bomb toward a tunnel opening that is only two meters across. This is the new image of the warrior; this is the new soldier of Valmy, the lone fighter, as it were, who is no longer part of any larger unit.[1] Could you interpret this image?

FRIEDRICH KITTLER: You've seen it?

AK: Yes, it's been reproduced.

FK: This may be the ultimate amplification of war in the course of a history that, I believe, is not as long as prehistorians make it out to be. Neolithic revolution is war; that's when it begins, about 10,000 BCE. Up until today, or rather up until the mid-twentieth century—or to be exact, up until 1941—war has subjected ever larger masses, but the mass armies fizzled out, so to speak, in the steppes of Astrakhan. The Wehrmacht mobilized three and a half million men for its Operation Barbarossa, which—and you are the very first I am telling this—was originally called Aufbau Ost [Construction East].

AK: Aufbau Ost?

FK: Yes. I want to publish that; it's scandalous.

This chapter was originally published as "Über moderne Kriegsführung," in Friedrich Kittler, *Short Cuts*, edited by Peter Gente and Martin Weinmann (Frankfurt am Main: Zweitausendeins, 2002), 211–26.

AK: And the Kyffhäuser legend comes later?[2]

FK: The Kyffhäuser legend is added in 1941, but in its first and most secret stage, it's called Aufbau Ost. The way I see it, mass armies will be a thing of the past. The current German Army is the last in Europe to cling to compulsory universal conscription . . .

AK: . . . an exercise and training army . . .

FK: . . . an initiation army for every man, and that's just not working anymore . . .

AK: No.

FK: . . . and then war becomes smaller and smaller, and in the end we have, as you put it, General Custer's lone rider, seemingly all on his own.

AK: But electronically he's wired into the whole world. He can be guided from ten thousand miles away. . . .

FK: The man is a personal computer in the literal sense of the word. After all, Operation Desert Storm mainly consisted of linking every single man in the Arabian desert, down to the most solitary combatants, to GPS. Every single American GI was connected to the GPS and always knew exactly where he was. At the time this was probably more a type of passive knowledge. The current progress, if *progress* is indeed the right word, one that Walter Benjamin would prefer at this point—progress would be for this man in Afghanistan to actively guide himself. He'd no longer be a passive recipient informed by the Global Positioning System telling him where he happens to be and how far off the enemy is. Rather, he can now guide things on his own. The horse, in turn, is an allegory of the fact that war originated with the nomads and is now returning to the nomads.

AK: But surely, for these guiding purposes you require human intelligence, flexibility, adaptability, the possibility to choose between different mistakes.

FK: At this point our computer programs are still abandoned, abandoned to—rather than afflicted by—mistakes. There is no computer program without bugs. Microsoft programs are notorious in this respect; they keep making rigid decisions, and you cannot get these new animals to break the habit, they just continue with their rigid decision-making.

AK: But the old animal, man . . .

FK: We are cunning, we have . . .

AK: . . . synapses that communicate with each other over difficult terrain.

FK: As Kant puts it, soldiers have to be equipped with reflective judgment. Kant writes in a great passage that the common soldier is in need of specific judgment; he must be capable of following commands when observing and negotiating the terrain. The officer, in turn, has to be able to think up something, and members of the General Staff have to possess independent judgment.[3]

AK: Mission tactics.

FK: Yes, the Pentagon finally realized that Robert McNamara's old ideology of managing a war like the Ford Motor Company in Detroit does not work. You need on-site professionals, as Heiner Müller used to say.[4]

AK: So now we have the idea of an elite force. Following Michael Geyer, that is how you in an interesting paper characterize an Italian elite force, the Arditi.[5] Could you describe them?

FK: The Arditi, the fighters who "burned" with courage and savagery, emerged from the deadlocked trenches of World War I. Armies of millions faced each other and conducted barrage offensives attacking Earth itself rather than the enemy, but then, to the amazement and subsequent delight of the general staffs, the front itself developed tactics that no longer clearly distinguished among infantry, artillery, and sappers. Rather, every single soldier is now part of a specially selected unit in which nobody is allowed to be older than twenty-five. Now they practice "Move it! Get going!" even under the most difficult circumstances, like those that tormented Ernst Jünger in his World War I books. As a result, the infantryman is equipped with his own small cannon, a so-called mortar he is just barely able to carry, or two men come with light machine guns, and you no longer advance in formation, as had been the case in the Coalition Wars, but staggered . . .

AK: . . . as a team in compliant cooperation.

FK: *Team* is the operative word. As Michael Geyer has shown, the team is no longer organized around a leader but around the tools of war, and the machine gun is the smallest tactical unit.[6]

AK: But first there emerged around Gabriele D'Annunzio, an Italian poet, narcissist, and lover of Eleonora Duse, the great actress . . .

FK: ... and of many other women ...

AK: ... and of many other women, so first there was the union between a poetic idea and a fervent motive of young people equipped with technology, and this created a new form of cooperation, the very last before the invention of chips, the last association of small groups.

FK: These Arditi—and this makes them just a bit more exciting than German storm troopers, which arose at the same time and then, falsely, gave rise to designations like SA and SS—these Arditi were more aflame (they are, after all, Italians rather than Germans), and while the storm troopers may have had the technological edge, it is with the Arditi that we encounter for the very first time, explicitly, the futuristic motive of merging flesh and steel.

AK: Just as we are on the verge of computers, neuron computers, that fuse organic matter, that is, that connect the synapses of old Lymnaeidae or mud snails with chips in order to mix the slowness of old evolutionary intelligence with that of faster intelligence?

FK: Our soft, wet flesh and all this dry silicon dioxide—it's only logical that it will disappear in twenty years, or maybe in a hundred. Though given the many surprises we've had, I think it makes sense to limit predictions about the computer industry to fifteen years. I daresay that the main trend will be to further optimize silicon intelligence. The soldier in Afghanistan is maybe the only point at which industry is researching this merger; in all other respects, technology's disregard for human flesh is just stunning. Otherwise, it constantly would have to take into account the slowness of this flesh.

AK: The flesh is too large.

FK: The rate of explosion, the exponential increase that leads to a doubling every eighteen months, no human needs this.

AK: The Arditi, though, didn't stop burning at the end of the war. Under D'Annunzio's leadership, they occupy Fiume; they enrich Italy at the expense of Yugoslavia.

FK: They create the Balkan conflict that runs on until the Kosovo ...

AK: ... and now they're sitting in Fiume at Christmastime and are vanquished by their own Italian warships and troops. They are like Praetorians, very difficult to stop, they just keep on storming ahead.

FK: And that's almost like an allegory, a symbol of our present fundamental conflict between mass armies on the one hand—in other words, the general domestication of humanity, especially in America—and these specialists on the other who are bred to transgress the law. After all, D'Annunzio and his Arditi were committing an illegal act that the Italian government had been opposing for one and a half years.

AK: A war of his own making.

FK: D'Annunzio is waging his own war, a condottiere in the service of an ideal Italy that in his eyes had been betrayed by the centrist government in Roma Aeterna. You can well imagine—let me spin out this fantasy—that our top software and hardware companies may soon have the feeling that it's no longer worth the effort to supply this medium-sized market between the Panama Canal and the Arctic Sea. Let us become condottiere in the name of the ideal state rather than remain tied to real states. You're familiar with the Renaissance condottiere?

AK: You are contrasting the Arditi with the storm troopers. The latter is an idea that originates in the General Staff. The German General Staff develops and passes down the ranks this notion of an elite force equipped with special weapons like flamethrowers and mortars. In other words, troops are moved from the barrage to the vineyards of the Kaiserstuhl, where virtual battlefields are created and training begins.[7] What do they learn?

FK: First off (and I would like to acknowledge the Rhenish attorney who provided me with all the weapons-technical details for this story), the Russian Army, which was well equipped with relatively small field artillery, was systematically robbed, and all these beautiful, small, cute weapons, which the German arms barons in the Ruhr region never built because they were too pretty and small and elegant, were shipped to the Kaiserstuhl.

AK: The industry was oriented toward expensive, heavy weaponry, that is to say, toward more metal.

FK: Which came from the Ruhr region. But after one year of failed Schlieffen offensives, the General Staff realizes that things are not going to work out, which is why a command is issued from the top that—for the first time in imperial, indeed in German, history—violates the democratic principle that all infantrymen are to be equally armed. And now these new troops receive these wonderful little weapons the entire infantry would like to get its hands on, and they are sent to the loess mountains of the Kaiserstuhl. The

Kaiserstuhl is the warmest region in Germany; it's so soft and easy to dig up thanks to the African loess blown in by southern winds. I know it well, you can go digging there; there are ravines everywhere, natural ravines . . .

AK: It's volcanic ground, like the old region in Africa in which humanity arose; and here a new war is rehearsed?

FK: Yes.

AK: And here they are trained to become the knights in the factories of war?[8]

FK: Yes, they are brought to the Vosges mountains, where the Germans want to demonstrate something to the leadership of the army, despite the fact that the focal point of the Schlieffen Plan had been on the right wing while the Vosges were on the left wing, which ended at the borders of neutral Switzerland. Nonetheless, the local high command wanted to stage a show. There was this peak occupied by the French, and two days before Christmas, if I remember correctly, the storm battalion Rohr, that was its name, engaged the enemy, who capitulated after the seventeenth shot because the Germans had been jumping like young horses or chessboard knights through the beautiful woods of the Alsace displaying all the techniques of camouflage and armament; presumably they ran straight up to the fortifications.

AK: Twenty-three specialists who are unable to simply leave behind what they have built up in terms of skills and motivation once the war is over, so they join the Free Corps.

FK: All of them. The Free Corps continue these new fighting tactics.

AK: And not only are the Free Corps named after the storm troopers, but so are the SA and the SS, including, for instance, Felix Steiner, Hitler's last hope in 1945, who belonged to this group of specialists and officers?[9]

FK: Exactly, and Ernst Jünger of the Imperial German Army was trained in the same way, as were several others. Erwin Rommel discovered all this during the Isonzo Offensive of 1917, when he learned to jump through the karst mountains of the Dolomites.

AK: That is the blitzkrieg weapon.

FK: Yes, though during World War I it takes place on an elite level yet then, incredibly, efforts are made during World War II to implement it throughout the entire army, which could not but result in failure.

AK: It's the method of escaping forward?

FK: Yes.

AK: I cannot be reached, neither by my superiors in the rear nor by the enemy, and somehow at night I break through a gap of twenty meters, and the next day I am two hundred kilometers to the rear of the enemy.

FK: And now Heinz Guderian, for instance, the tank general in 1940 in Operation France, wonders: what is the best way of breaking through the lines without encountering anybody? He wins Operation Sickle Cut by bypassing the French and appearing, to everybody's surprise, at Sedan after having traveled along the narrowest roads ever used for a military deployment. There were jams, but they were caused by his own tanks. No other problem in the first half of the blitzkrieg of World War II—I almost blush to say this, but this form of war was almost a novel because the losses on both sides were minimal.

AK: And these are the people from the county of Mansfeld in Thuringia, whose ancestors were defeated in the Battle of Frankenberg in the Peasants' War and who followed the saying, "Do not go to your lord unless you are called."[10] Which implies an independence from commands from above. I will not be slaughtered in the trenches; I will escape from my superiors as well as from the weapons of my enemy. That is the driving force that makes blitzkrieg work, and it ceases to work the moment the enemy responds and static warfare resumes.

FK: Or because a *Führer* and Reich Chancellor, as described so brutally by Albert Speer at the conclusion of his memoirs, is in direct personal telephone contact with every regiment.[11] At that point any escape from one's commander is no longer possible. He is as omnipresent as a spider gangster in a telephone web.

AK: So we could say the intelligence of blitzkrieg stems from the fact that it is an escape from war.

FK: From the state—one's own and the other. There are rumors from the war in Kosovo that you could call into the hills from any village and tell people to become nomads, if they wanted to. That is, they could make themselves into potential enemies of the superpower; hence, NATO and the superpower are now in need of nomads as well.

AK: But the fact that you cannot stop these nomads, these barbarians and counterbarbarians and specialized combatants, once things are over—isn't that still the case? The Roman Praetorians couldn't be stopped either; they sided with the emperor and then either supported or replaced him.

FK: So what are you predicting?

AK: I am not predicting anything. I am asking: if you keep driving up the defense budget, so to speak, if you keep training all these elite troops without knowing how to stop them from still being committed specialists later on . . .

FK: Yes, but the U.S. Department of Commerce maintains control over the entire internet; the central hardware installations are there; and at the moment it looks as if you could easily cut all computer power if some groups tried to liberate themselves erotically or militarily. They'd be left with nothing more than going berserk and running amok. Of course, that will happen at one point. Rambo is a good example.

AK: But unlike Rambo, individuals are not able to assume such an independent existence.

FK: Well, if the analyses of the so-called downfall of the Roman Empire undertaken in my circles are correct, then the empire did not die at the hands of its Praetorians, as it were. It was simply turned inside out like a glove. Ultimately, the idea that you need nomads to fight nomads boils down to letting Afghans fight the current wars.

AK: What distinguishes nomads from farmers? Ever since the days of the agricultural revolution, there's a farmer hidden in all of us, which contributes in large part to the stability of our inner life. But is there still some nomadic element in us, or it is less common these days?

FK: The terrible idea occurs to me that nomads are married to their horses or mounts, while we are married to our wives, and that this tie to women and to Mother Earth is our religion, Christianity, Mary. And the nomads—right down into the erotic domain there's a relation to the furs of the soft animals they ride. Women really aren't that important, and then there's the brutality with which people are conquered and which Chingiz Aitmatov described in his horrific novel about the slaves of the nomads. Are you familiar with it?

AK: No.

FK: I really cannot talk about this with the microphone on.

AK: There's a lot of brutality?

FK: Aitmatov was a writer from Kyrgyzstan in the Brezhnev era who was still familiar with nomadic customs from the early twentieth century.[12] The nomads rode off and raided Iranian or Persian farmers and abducted six- or seven-year-old children, young but already able to survive. They buried them up to their neck and pulled the skin off their heads and then sewed it back on, back to front, or else they used horse skin. The heads continued to grow, but they couldn't; the brains were crushed by the skin and atrophied, and when they were dug up again at age twelve, the children had, biologically speaking, turned into imbeciles. They were human domestic animals, part of the slave caste nomads appear to be in need of. I'm telling you this, after all, because I was so shaken by it. I don't know exactly what it means; it entails the utmost cruelty. . . .

AK: But maybe this quality is part of the hodgepodge we pass on with our genes, just as there are animistic hunter societies that develop a balanced relationship, as it were, with their prey . . .

FK: Yes.

AK: . . . a *numen*, a respect for what they kill.

FK: Yes, and ultimately that's where we come from. Once there were peaceful farmers who in the fourteenth century BCE populated Crete and Athens, but suddenly everything burns to the ground, including writing, Linear B, the first European script. The palaces, too, are burning; they don't collapse because of earthquakes, as is often claimed. People arrived, and they did not come in horse-drawn chariots nobly fighting each other, as depicted in Homer's *Iliad*. They were crouched on their horses like the later Huns and Mongols, tied to the manes. . . .

AK: And they are superior because they are more abstract and more unfeeling?

FK: And these are our ancestors, for Greek culture arises from this assault.

AK: And we are in need of institutions to calibrate and bypass this alchemy that dwells within us? Is that a good way of looking at it?

Of States and Their Terrorists

TRANSLATED BY GEOFFREY WINTHROP-YOUNG

> All life has wandered off into building blocks.
> —Ingeborg Bachmann, "Great Landscape near Vienna" (1953)

Ladies and Gentlemen, Honored Services,

We all serve a higher purpose. I, for instance, serve a Greece in which there are no services and which allows free speech, plain and simple. You, however, are still counting on classic wars in the future. At least I hope you do, for given the two superpowers currently facing each other across the Pacific, to hope for anything else would be hopelessly naive. Nonetheless, I suspect that nobody really wants to know what classic wars would amount to in today's world. Their horrors exceed our imagination.

Instead, we Europeans find ourselves in the situation of the proverbial rabbit mesmerized by the snake: we are fixated on the seemingly distant spectacle of two absolute enemies, one of whom is neither a subject according to international law nor mindful of any basic human rights, while the other cleverly neglects the classic distinction between criminal prosecution and martial law, policing and military intervention.

Scholars from Carl Schmitt to Michael Jeismann have unearthed the long history that preceded the appearance of absolute enemies in the shape of "pig systems" and "rogue nations" that have to be wiped from the face of

---

Originally published as "Von Staaten und ihren Terroristen," in Étienne Balibar, Friedrich Kittler, and Martin van Creveld, *Vom Krieg zum Terrorismus? Humboldt-Universität zu Berlin, Mosse-Lectures 2002/2003* (Berlin: Humboldt-Universität zu Berlin, 2003), 33–50; and translated by Geoffrey Winthrop-Young in *Cultural Politics* 8, no. 3 (2012): 385–97.

the earth. But we should briefly recall the relative enemies of bygone times when European wars were still the province of *la chevalerie*, the knighthood. His Most Catholic Majesty Francis I of France is said to have remarked of the Holy Roman Emperor Charles V: "My brother Charles and I are of one heart and mind—we both want Milan." A beautiful and worthy sentiment, no doubt, but it neither dissuaded Charles's mercenaries from pursuing their bloody handiwork at the Battle of Pavia in 1525 nor kept the emperor from holding Francis captive for a year until he was released under the terms of the Treaty of Madrid. Yet neither decried the other as in- or unhuman. For, as the bon mot intimates (and Jacques Lacan explains), the desire of brothers—even if they are royal brothers in name only—is always reciprocal and based on the recognition of rivals as equals.[1] So much—or so little—about the times of classic wars when the enemy was no more than a temporary, coequal adversary.

It is, I believe, a matter of justice based on mutual recognition and equivalence not to resort to different standards when analyzing different—that is, relative and absolute—wars. Every system of power has the enemies it produces. But before I start to pursue this burning issue, I would like to illustrate the underlying hypothesis with a minor example from so-called contemporary history.

I

When the good old Federal Republic of Germany chose to bid farewell to its postwar idyll, it embarked on the modernization or—as others call it—colonization of its lifeworld. Almost overnight the many cozy single-family homes provided by the Adenauer government for returning POWs and their estranged wives gave way to endless high-rises, the construction of which demanded extensive clear-cutting operations carried out by chainsaw commandos. New residential areas with beautiful names like Freiburg-Binzengrün or Erfstadt-Liblar shot up into the sky.[2] Not surprisingly, the inhabitants of these so-called satellite cities, stacked in concrete layers around elevator shafts and garbage chutes, soon adopted statistically monotonous consumer habits and leisure practices. All this would have resulted in endless traffic jams had the developers not taken precautionary measures. Drawing on old plans whose execution had been delayed by a world war, the Federal Republic proceeded to cover itself with the world's densest highway system. Soon every satellite town boasted a department store as well as its own highway exit. A new epoch began in West Germany—and we can claim that we were present at its birth.[3]

And then there were parties, torched department stores, and bank robberies, staged or committed by strangely untraceable perpetrators. Only with the publication of so-called admission statements featuring a distinctly Eastern logo did the police come to realize whom they were dealing with, at which point the unsolved cases were handed over to a fledgling agency known as the Bundeskriminalamt (BKA), the Federal Criminal Police Office. Initially, the BKA didn't do much better, but then it retained the services of a certain middle-class Social Democrat and chief commissioner, whose long-standing dream (to quote the title of a novel by Oswald Wiener) was the improvement of central Europe.[4] This herald of modernization—that is to say, the computerization of manhunts—had a firm grasp of the simple, yet basic, idea that guides my talk: every system of power has the enemies it produces.[5]

The terrorists (as they were now known) were able to navigate the waters of partisan warfare with all the alacrity of Mao Zedong's fish because they had adapted their lifeworld to satellite cities and highway systems. They invariably drove high-speed BMWs to make full use of passing lanes, and they rented whitewashed high-rise apartments, where nobody knows your name, in order to throw the inconspicuous leftovers of their bomb-making activities down the garbage chutes. Not to mention that the neighboring woody areas made for excellent shooting ranges. Once the BKA managed to penetrate the behavioral patterns of this dismal lifeworld, the perpetrators were as good as behind bars, which, as you will recall, had been built according to the same modernist standards.[6] Not even repeat bank robbers, bomb throwers, and murderers were able to fully blend into a computerized world: for instance, even under an assumed name it was still dangerous to pay the rent by way of the usual electronic transfer. With this in mind, Dr. Horst Herold, the congenial spirit presiding over the BKA, conceived of the negative computerized manhunt: a countrywide electronic search for quotidian bureaucratic procedures deliberately avoided by certain tenants.[7] The end is known, though not necessarily understood. Only today, living in our prewar apartments, does it slowly dawn on us what it meant that the Federal Republic sealed its earthly residues under layers of concrete and asphalt.

Let us move from the local to the global. Instead of highways, air traffic; instead of BKA mainframes, internet surveillance; instead of strange cash payments, interest-free transactions based on trust alone, as is common in Islam; and, finally, instead of Stuttgart-Stammheim, Guantánamo Bay. Only the high-rises remain unchanged. Put differently, the question is, how did today's superpower acquire the enemies it has?

II

In order to grasp matters, it is necessary to take a quick look back at older empires. Before it was replaced by the United States during World War II, the British Empire rested on two pillars, one (in its day) extremely modern, the other very traditional. The innovation with which Britain entered World War I was a unique telegraph cable network that connected all the ports the Royal Navy depended on to maintain maritime superiority. This All Red British network kept the fleet apprised of each and every enemy movement and replenished coal depot. No other state, and least of all Britain's opponents, enjoyed such a global strategic and logistical capacity to wage war at a distance. In other words, already on the second day of World War I, Germany suffered a double blockade: it was cut off from news by the British cable monopoly and from resources (including Chilean nitrates) by the Royal Navy.

The second pillar also secured a steady supply, though of cannon fodder rather than goods. While other colonial powers such as France and Belgium reduced their black and yellow subjects to Spartan work slavery, Britain had learned the bitter lessons of the Sepoy Mutiny of 1857 and the Boer War of 1899. Only the telegraphic wiring of widely scattered garrisons had saved the viceroyalty from the insurgency of the numerically far superior Indian auxiliary regiments; only the mobilization of colored soldiers had secured victory over Boer partisans intent on retaining their own colored slaves. Suddenly, whole regiments of Sikhs, Gurkhas, and other colonial groups who had fought bloody skirmishes against the East India Company were ready to kill and die in the name of Queen Victoria. No wonder the "Sahibs' War," as Rudyard Kipling titled his short story about the conflict between masters, ended for many Boers in barbed-wired concentration camps.[8]

The Nobel laureate of 1907 also revealed the poetic ways in which colored whites, those strange wooden irons, came into being long before CIA-sponsored Afghan alliances. Kipling, creator of Mowgli and Kim, was born in the British Raj and thus spoke Hindi before acquiring English. Nannies are older than mothers. Kipling's lyrical burden of having to bring culture to other races was probably first thrust on him in 1881, when (long before the days of the Saudi kings and their bin Ladens) the Mahdi managed to subjugate an entire country—the Anglo-Egyptian condominium of Sudan—to the teachings of Muhammad ibn-Abdul Wahhab. The world's first rogue state was born when Gordon Pasha's severed head was displayed on the walls of Khartoum. The empire was forced to rely on poets and modern weaponry. "Whatever happens, we have got / the Maxim gun, and they have not," rhymed Hilaire Belloc, with a view toward those crucial differences of skin color that dictated that machine guns (just like the atom bomb) were to be used only against nonwhites.[9] Kipling's lyrical burden, however, became unbearable once this neat martial distinction was subverted: starting in 1899, whites trained their machine guns on whites; Boers mowed down Britons and vice versa. As a result, Kipling concluded that the British Empire could no longer afford to strike rotten compromises with unreliable royal relatives perched on other European thrones, especially those willing to roll out the red carpet for visiting Boer presidents. Only the support of black, brown, or yellow natives could assure the stability of an empire in which—as in that of Charles V—the sun would never set.

Long before the CIA came along, then, Kipling invented a new literary hero in the shape of a young semiorphaned half blood. Sitting astride the old bronze cannon of Lahore and dancing among moguls and viceroys, Indian mother and lost Irish father, Kim the nomad travels through half of India.[10] Thanks to his ability to move between the fronts, he is able to pull off a decisive move in the "Great Game" that pits Queen Victoria against Czar Nicholas in their struggle over (of all countries) Afghanistan. A half blood achieves what a hundred civil servants and twenty regiments fail to do: the nomad saves our stable abodes. Tens of thousands of armed Sikhs and Gurkhas, Britain's colonial world war elites, were to follow Kim's shining example, and, above all, there was the one Lawrence of Arabia, who took Kipling's colonial romance literally by persuading young Saudi princelings, who had only camels, falconry, and ibn-Abdul Wahhab on their mind, to fight the Turks. Less than thirty years after H. H. Kitchener's bloody victory over the Mahdi, T. E. Lawrence turned absolute enemies into kings. Their machine gun–equipped camel riders brought down the sultanate itself, destroyed the old order of the Orient, and opened up its nomadic expanse. Unlike those in charge, however, London's secret agent remained unaware of the oil riches hidden underneath the liberated desert. And so, on an unguarded morning, Lawrence of Arabia died his motorcycle death. The white man's burden slipped from his shoulders, to be taken over by our man in Riyadh or Mosul.

III

Only after this prelude known as World War I do I feel entitled to talk about the present and future; anything else would be as censored as your average press handout. Superpowers, after all, are the result of a *translatio imperii*.

America's singular global position stems from World War II, when Britain, descending into a sea of blood, sweat, and tears, signed over its empire to the United States. This did not happen with the Lend-Lease Act of 1941, which concerned only the sell-off of the Atlantic sideshow; it had to do with the Indian and Pacific Oceans. Japan's early Sunday morning attack on a sleepy Hawaii, though constantly cited as a precursor to 9/11, had its own sad and sound reason: namely, the refusal of the United States to have Japan, so poor in natural resources, participate in the industrial and military transition from coal to oil. In 1943 Japan replaced not only its foreign secretary but also its entire strategy, "which was to be of the greatest importance to the postwar development of Southeast Asia."[11] Instead of the slave nations envisioned by the military, there was to be a "Greater East Asia Co-Prosperity Sphere," whose success was to rest upon granting all the former colonies, from Vietnam to the island nations of Indonesia and the Philippines, and including Japan itself, the right to self-determination and ownership over their own oil resources. When the student revolutionaries of my generation chanted their "Ho-Ho-Ho Chi Minh" in order to position themselves as future foreign ministers, they probably didn't realize in the name of which *tenno* they were raising their voices.[12] And the story continues with al-Qaeda's current operations on Bali or Mindanao.

Facing this serious challenge to its rule over East Asia and the Pacific, the United States embarked on a military-technological revolution. In essence, its logistical war efforts focused on plastering both hemispheres and all ocean coastlines with runways and aircraft hangars. Outbidding a world power that had depended on a contractually guaranteed maximum fleet size, the United States secured its position by becoming history's very first empire to rely on airpower. World War II provided the U.S. Air Force with the bases in western Europe, South America, Africa, and India necessary for the global campaign against the Axis powers; following the war, the logistical net was tightened and came to incorporate the defeated nations (which, incidentally, may serve to explain what kind of pentagram or Pentagon, with its flyover rights, makes life so difficult for the German federal government).

But what is of far greater importance in today's Great Game are those exotic locales and islands that allow the airborne superpower to embark (in the words of Salvador Dalí) on its journey into Upper Mongolia, that is, Eurasia's hidden heartlands. When in late 2001 fully loaded B-2 bombers took off for Kandahar and Kabul, their runways and ordnance depots were still located on Diego Garcia, a formerly British island deep in the Indian Ocean, whose entire population had been relocated to the beautiful

Seychelles in 1973. Just as Malta acquired its fame as an "unsinkable aircraft carrier" responsible for bombing the supply lines of the German Africa Corps, today's islands and port cities shine forth in the resplendent glory of strategic weapons systems.

This means, however, that the superpower is encroaching on its opposite. The opposite of the sea is the desert; the opposite of the city, the steppe. Step-by-step, the civilizing process—or, more precisely, the U.S. military infrastructure—is advancing into regions hitherto closed off to Western civilization (that memorable, nonsensical notion). First, we have tin-sheet huts or cargo cults that deify the crashed debris of a military-industrial complex until the world order itself is on the brink of collapse; then, as the city runs up against the steppe, and houses encounter tents, the nomads become irritated. That seems to be the case today. When Osama bin Laden was still generously issuing communiqués to the international press, his propaganda centered on the hospitality that the sacred desert had extended to American garrisons, barracks, and hangars.

We are well advised, therefore, to undertake a small excursion into the history of philosophy before continuing with the history and future of war. Whether we choose to adopt Ronald Reagan's terminology and conjure up evil empires or decide to employ the diction of the younger George Bush and speak of rogue states, the logic of the distinction remains the same: we, the good, here on this side, are facing off against evil itself on the other. The binary seems so common and self-evident that before Friedrich Nietzsche nobody saw the need to question it. The first treatise in *On the Genealogy of Morals* (to which Michel Foucault added a masterly, though not necessarily military-historical, analysis) attempts to foreground its limitations. When the aristocrats of pre-Socratic Greece distinguished between themselves and the plebs in terms of good and bad, they were using the notion of good to praise their own virtues, which in those days referred to courage rather than morals. According to Nietzsche's informed analysis, all cultures that affirm a basic distinction between good and evil can be traced back to the pious doctrine first propagated by the historical Zarathustra in the borderlands between Persia and Afghanistan. The gods Ahura Mazda and Ahriman are struggling for dominance with such ferocity that the soul is obliged to assist Ahura Mazda the Good in removing Ahriman the Evil from this world. As if Zeus, by emasculating his bad father Cronus, had wanted to eradicate evil itself.

The pious or impious revelations from the mouth of Zarathustra sounded so perplexing to Nietzsche's "Greek ears" that he proposed a different, namely, geopolitical, reading of good and evil. In the sermons Zarathustra addressed to his Persian farmers, *evil* referred to the Eastern nomadic tribes, which as large-scale breeders refused to settle down and instead preferred to periodically raid farming villages to carry off cattle and children. The sedentary farmers, by contrast, were "good" insofar as they (following the example of their docile livestock) obeyed the words of Zarathustra, the supreme Good One. Indeed, so grateful were they for his words that they resolved to henceforth follow their shepherd (who, though a shepherd in name only, is still known today as the good shepherd). The shepherd, however, did not deign to mention that farmers have a particular preference for wresting virgin lands from nomads in order to subject them to their plowshares; it was left to Sophocles to spell it out.[13] Thus spoke Zarathustra, the Old Persian "minister of settlement."[14]

The distinction between good and evil is thus not one of morals but one of culture, yet in order to gain acceptance among its subjects, it conceals itself under a veil of morality. On the one hand, then, there is war for war's sake, a nomadology in the sense of Deleuze and Guattari; on the other hand, there is peace for the sake of agricultural enterprises whose surplus value is channeled into the construction of cities, the stone icons of sedentarism. Both life-forms exist side by side; both are an option. Nietzsche realized that in order to propagate these glad tidings, he had to put the revocation of slave morality into the mouth of the very priest who had come up with the calamity in the first place. According to the testimony found in *Ecce Homo*, this is how the book titled *Thus Spoke Zarathustra* came about: "Zarathustra *created* this fateful error of morality: this means that he has to be the first to *recognize* it."[15]

Nietzsche's analysis is timelier than ever. While he still enjoyed freedom of movement before being confined to the immobility of uncharted cave systems, bin Laden presented himself to waiting cameras astride a horse, the very image of a nomad. Of course, things are not what they seem: when Arab princelings indulge in their medieval passion for falconry, they allegedly prefer modern jeeps over beautiful Arab horses and withdraw precisely into those tribal regions or steppes in northern Pakistan that over the past year have also become the last refuge for the Taliban. As if to interpret those jeeps, Schmitt's *Theory of the Partisan* emphasizes: "The dead ride fast, and when they become motorized, they ride even faster."[16]

Paradoxically, however, the motorization and updated militarization of contemporary nomads are not—as in our minor German example—a matter of fake license plates and nightly burglaries but something the superpower brought about itself. As you will no doubt recall, for well over a decade those nomads—who as the enemies of our enemies appeared to be our friends—were useful helpers. Even a global superpower in command of stratosphere and ionosphere, bomber fleets and reconnaissance satellites, is now and then in need of a sharp sword, especially—as happened after the trauma of Vietnam—when it wants to avoid the morale-lowering arrival of flag-draped zinc coffins in the harbors of California. Hence, the CIA once again mimicked the British employment of Kipling's Sikhs and Gurkhas by mobilizing Pashtuns, Tajiks, and other Afghan tribes against the Red Army. Equipped with portable Stinger missiles, they were ordered to break, or at least challenge, the air superiority of the other superpower. If the basic distinction is no longer that between good and evil but that between good and bad, then *good* refers to all those skilled in the arts of killing and dying, which is the least that can be said about the mujahideen or the lower ranks of al-Qaeda.

But it is also the least that must be said about the new elites of the U.S. Armed Forces, who in the wake of the abolition of the general draft appear to be mimicking the nomads. Ever since René Descartes put an end to the old man-animal symbiosis, the coexistence of tribes, pets, and livestock, by turning animals into machines and humans into (literally subjected) subjects, military-industrial complexes—from Louis XV's École Militaire all the way to Los Alamos and Livermore—have taken his philosophy ever more literally. Good old cavalry horses gave way to combat choppers, while the reports delivered by mounted spies were replaced by satellite reconnaissance fed to computer-aided single combatants, with the result that not much separated fighters of the Northern Alliance from regular GIs. The nomads of old ventured hundreds of miles beyond their herds or villages on their bloody outings; those of today can be flown to any hot spot at the drop of a hat: Mazar-e-Sharif yesterday, north of Basra tomorrow. Much like the Vikings, rapid-deployment forces turn up where they are least expected, only to disappear before you know it. As a result, the North Atlantic Treaty Organization, that skin of onion layers extending eastward from Washington, is dissolving in front of our eyes. And there is a certain symbolic joke to the fact that the high command of this new global blitzkrieg is located in Florida, the touristic parody of modern tribal migrations. But who can tell what long-term cultural and political consequences will arise from the transformations of armies (no longer guided by modern concepts like fatherland or home soil) into high-tech global nomads? Divinations and prophecies of coming wars are and always have been the prerogative of the Oracle at Delphi.

IV

But enough about prehistory; let's move into the dark present. Since September 2001, it is glaringly obvious how precarious the distinction between cattle-breeding and machine-equipped nomads has become. No doubt some of the old nomadic hatred of cities and sedentary cultures was still at work in the destruction of the World Trade Center—a hatred that to this day incites the Bedouins of the Negev desert to forfeit the stone houses built for them by the Israeli government in favor of portable tents. Even Goethe, owner of a fair-sized mansion in Weimar, reputedly said to a friend that you stand upright in tents. What was new and unheard-of on that September morning was the perfect mimicry with which exotic outsiders took control of the airspace above Manhattan. Like the bygone hijackers working for Yasser Arafat, or those in command of the abducted Lufthansa jet on its long flight to Mogadishu, the murderers knew how to handle explosives and handguns, yet they were also familiar with cockpits, onboard computers, and fuel reserves: they had accessed a multilevel complex feedback system usually outside our reach. The only procedure they did not care to rehearse was the landing approach. In addition, the perpetrators, whose defiance of death poses eternal riddles, were backed by a strategic planning that must have operated on a global level almost matching that of the superpower under attack. As far as I can tell, Jürgen Kaube remains the only observer to have quoted Schmitt's prophecy that the telluric partisans of old will morph into space-traveling cosmopartisans.[17] That danger seems to loom on the horizon. It is born, I'm afraid, from the angry fear that emanates from the last cell phone calls made by the jet-setting business-class nomads and from the innermost sanctum of the burning Pentagon. In the parlance of World War II: "Feind lernt mit"—the enemy is learning.

But so are friends. In stark contrast to his sluggish European viceroys, Bush Jr. doesn't mince words. "We are in a recession. We are at war," he announced at the outset of his 2002 State of the Union address. Six months later, he added phrases that threaten to stick in one's throat. The New Jerusalem on the other side of the Atlantic, he claimed, stood for freedom, democracy, and free enterprise. Nation-state or nomad, professor or partisan—whoever dared dispute those three values was guilty of harboring anti-American sentiments and thus became a potential target of preventive counterstrikes. For better or worse, Bush's words have the power to bring about what they conjure up: they may well turn out to be a self-fulfilling prophecy by riling up and calling to arms precisely those whose nonexistence they envisage.

But with all due deference to the victims, who like most of us were noncombatants, I am unable to follow this new U.S. tablet of values (as Zarathustra called such grandiloquent words). Freedom has been a given since the days of Homer's heroes, democracy since the days of Pericles, and our liberal-democratic order since Herold. But why and to what end does this enumeration of values suddenly take an abrupt turn? Why the political flip into economics? Is free enterprise a code name for high-tech nomads who want to remain anonymous when fishing in the muddy waters of our desires? Are free entrepreneurs not supposed to be able to penetrate the market without benefiting from the threat of preventive wars? Andy Warhol's silly serial joke notwithstanding, Moscow and Beijing have long since become part of McDonald's extensive chain.[18] Obviously, we end consumers are not the issue here.

For over a century, wars and technologies have dreamed of being ahead of their day. In reality, however, they are forced to engage in recursions that burrow into ever deeper pasts. Lack of nitrate scuttled Alfred von Schlieffen's ingenious plan of attack. Just as up-to-date computer design is steadily closing in on the big bang, the logistics of war (irrespective of wishful ecological thinking) consume ever older resources. World War II began with the switch from coal and railroads to tank oil and airplane fuel, the Pax Americana with the exploration of uranium (in Germany the task was assigned to Hanns Martin Schleyer). When, finally, Richard Nixon in 1971 canceled the direct convertibility of the U.S. dollar into gold, it seemed at first as if his main goal was to put a stop to the nefarious plans of Gert Fröbe, also known as Goldfinger, in Fort Knox. More likely, the fate of the currency was to be tied to oil rather than to gold. Otherwise, it is difficult to explain why the world's most debt-ridden national economy is still able to attract so much foreign capital. According to the most recent estimates of DASA (the Defense Atomic Support Agency), which, as the successor to the Peenemünde Army Research Center, should know what it's talking about, the world's oil wells are as calculable as they are finite. Despite all drilling ventures (such as underneath the shelf off Namibia), we will not be able to locate any further deposits equal to those of Saudi Arabia or Iraq. (It is no coincidence that in 1941 a few German Messerschmitts were ordered to support the short-lived uprising of Saddam Hussein's uncle against the British.) Around 2070, neither sooner nor later, the last drop of oil will be squeezed out of the desert. DASA said so.

I therefore cannot follow Herfried Münkler when he denies any link between war aims and oil wells. Farmers are not alone in their hostility to pristine steppes; modern airpowers too are pushing their oil companies ever farther into the heart of Eurasia, Dalí's hallucinogenic Inner Mongolia. Otherwise, jeeps would remain immobilized in garages, and bombers would be stranded in hangars and onboard nuclear-powered carriers. The whole gigantic infrastructure that arose in the bloody aftermath of Pearl Harbor (in other words, all of America's military might) would turn into worthless junk. And since the optimistic vision of pure software wars evaporated in airplane fuel thanks to the miraculous survival of the mirror servers of the World Trade Center (which from a computer-technological point of view makes the attack appear like a bit of a flop), things once again boil down to hardware, raw materials, energy sources.

V

I have reached the end of this confused snapshot. The Federal Republic was a minor, manageable example. We all know and make use of the infrastructure in which the BMW nomads of the self-appointed Red Army Faction were able to survive above water or underwater, at least for a short while. But nobody, not even those in the highest echelons, seems to have any idea what dizzying networks of oil pipelines and slums, Global Positioning Systems and databanks, rapid-deployment forces and cellular abuse, are currently covering the globe—that is to say, in what kinds of labyrinths the nomads strike and seek refuge. When the Taliban (students of the Koran who have to recite it in High Arabic without understanding a single word) first caused problems for the CIA, there was hardly anybody in Langley who understood their language. Virginity is not always a virtue. Someone like Herold would first have to discern the patterns and grids that today's global infrastructure, this more or less successful extension of the United States (to briefly turn Marshall McLuhan on his head), turns toward wolves rather than pet dogs.

But together with his wife, Herold remains confined to a former barrack of the Federal Border Guard, under orders neither to write nor to appear in public, as if his knowledge had infected him with the plague—and yet, unlike me, he would be the most qualified to penetrate the darkness and take stock of the situation.[19]

PART IV

Love and War

CHAPTER 12

Manners of Death in War

TRANSLATED BY MICHAEL WUTZ

Ladies and Gentlemen,

Manners of death in war, as I would like to call this lecture cycle in honor of Carl von Clausewitz and his venerable title, are not a pleasant subject to talk about but a necessary one.[1] As the heir to various forms of theology, the tradition of European philosophy recognized death in only one form. All coding of violence disappeared in favor of a generalization that reduced murderers and victims, masters and servants, to one and the same level of humanity. Even that singular philosophy, whose declared goal was to expel all theological leftovers from the realm of thinking, did not differentiate between various manners of death but recognized death only as "the ownmost nonrelational possibility *not to be bypassed.*"[2] For that very reason, it was not until Ingeborg Bachmann and her unfinished cycle of novels—and despite or perhaps because she wrote her dissertation on *Being and Time*—that the very question about manners of death could be posed.[3] While cultural studies, unlike the novel, does not identify each and every form of death as murder, Bachmann's thesis is fully valid when considering manners of deaths brought about by war.

In the following, war is defined not as the continuation of politics by other means but as the production of various manners of death brought about by weapons and technologies. This definition, which is purposefully nonanthropological, includes angels, humans, and Klingons but not flesh-eating plants and predators. Only the obsession of British military historians

---

Originally "Todesarten im Kriege" (unpublished manuscript in German presented in June 1999).

with man-to-man combat is oblivious to the fact that war is not a matter of Hegelian consciousness fighting about lordship and bondage but of weapons technologies fighting about manners of death. Whether "the mass nature of wartime death," however, is already its final goal, or whether it "serves as a spectacle, as diversion from the real movements of the War," to speak with Thomas Pynchon, must remain unanswered until the end.[4]

What can, however, be said even at this point is that weapons technologies that don't originate in organic extensions bring about specific wounds, and manners of death and destruction, that distinguish wars from sheer violence. The very fact that weapons are coded, that that which is technically feasible (such as the chemical warfare of World War II) remained unused in arsenals, makes it possible to date wars in the history of technology. I hope you will forgive me if, in the following, I will skip over the eras of the chariot and the phalanx, and the mounted posse and the stirrup, and instead concentrate on the recent historical moment whose techno-historical marker is the firearm. From that moment on, battles stopped being a series of simultaneous man-to-man encounters and instead morphed into the impact of weapons following a Poisson distribution. From that moment on, in war—which Hegel called the "crime for [i.e., on behalf of] the universal"—death must be "coldly received and given, not in ongoing battle where the individual has his eye on his opponent and kills him with direct hatred; rather, death emptily given and received, impersonal in the gunsmoke."[5] That is how Hegel put it in the *Jena Lectures on the Philosophy of Spirit* of 1805, less than twelve months before Napoleon's real-life proof at the Battle of Jena.[6] As is well known, Hegel's "Spirit" is called "not the life that shrinks from death and keeps itself untouched by devastation, but rather the life that endures it and maintains itself in it."[7]

I

It hasn't always been like that. "Wittstock," as we learn in *Meyers großes Konversations-Lexikon* of 1908, "was first mentioned in a document in the year 946, was declared a town in 1248, and was the residence of the Bishops of Havelberg. Under the leadership of Johan Banér at the Battle of Wittstock, on October 4, 1636, the Swedish army emerged victorious against the combined Imperial-Saxon army led by General Melchior von Hatzfeld."[8] Put differently: history, when it was still being written, consisted of long and insignificant intervals of peace, punctuated by singular, momentous military events. That sounded very different in 1688, when history wasn't even written yet, in Johann Jacob Christoffel von Grimmelshausen's *Simplicissimus*. At Wittstock

> there were so many bullets singing through the air above us that it looked as if the salvo had been aimed deliberately at us. . . . In the battle itself, however, each man tried to avoid death by dispatching the enemy immediately in front of him. . . . You could see nothing but thick smoke and dust, which seemed to be trying to hide the horror of the dead and wounded. . . . [Wounded horses] fell on top of their riders, thus in their death having the honor of being carried by the men whom they had had to carry during their lives. . . . The earth, whose usual task it is to cover the dead, was itself strewn with corpses, all with different mutilations: there were heads that had lost the bodies they belonged to and bodies lacking heads; some had their entrails hanging out in sickening fashion, others their skull smashed and the brain spattered over the ground; you could see dead bodies emptied of blood and living ones covered in the blood of others. . . . You could see mutilated soldiers begging to be put to death, others to be granted quarter and spared. . . . In a word, it was a pitiful sight.[9]

Grimmelshausen's hero is witness to such a pitiful sight at Wittstock in part because he was on the wrong side of the fight. The Imperial Saxon Army was no match for the nimble Swedish field artillery. For that reason, the smoke of Banér's twelve-pounders was given the job that, in times of peace, would have been the job of Mother Earth: rendering invisible those that were already gone. In 1636 the second death—that is, the burial of the fallen soldiers—was far from the minds of the conscripted mercenaries, who were prisoners and looters all in one. At Lützen, the Swedes found the body of their dead king stripped and naked, buried under horses and human bodies. That's why, at Wittstock, the distinction between the creatures human and horse restricted itself to the human ability, no less elementary than it was futile, to ask for life or death a second time. As ossuaries no longer subject to the order of cemeteries and not yet subject to the order of the Red Cross, battlefields presented themselves in a state of chaos that refuted each and every dance of death: the bodies were marked with "different mutilations," not by virtue of their sins (as with Dante) or by virtue of their social standing (as with Hans Holbein), but by systematically perverting top and bottom, inside and outside, head and body, humans and animals. For that reason, the soldiers of the Thirty Years' War—notwithstanding all the greenhorns of our tenderfoot regiment—were not murderers. As Grimmelshausen put it, "In the battle itself . . . each man tried to avoid death by dispatching the enemy immediately in front of him." By anticipating their own death, to which I will return, each mercenary inverted the world only in order not to suffer that inversion (i.e., death) himself. Even noncombatants, like the farmers in Grimmelshausen's first chapter, who were tortured to death by marauding troops, regularly took revenge on the earth itself.

The introduction of standing armies, which evolved, militarily and historically speaking, out of the Thirty Years' War, did not do much to change this logic of preemption. While standing armies were no longer allowed to torture civil populations, they were, for obvious logistical reasons, still allowed to plunder. Standing armies were under the *Exerzierreglement* [drill regulations] of the Princes of Orange, and the training of the Dukes of Dessau, but only so that they would not, at the first opportunity (paraphrasing Hemingway), escape across the river and into the trees. Frederick the Great, also known as "Old Fritz," certainly did not produce his military writings to teach his successors or generals how to fight in oblique order, but rather to prevent desertions. Two opposing infantries sworn to engage in linear tactics fired their salvos in sequence only so they would not be shot as deserters by their own hussars. An infantry battle, which left about a tenth of the soldiers on the battlefield, was the kind of bleeding that, quite literally, decimated the Roman legions of yore and that, following Thomas Macho, was the most effective means of disposing of superfluous young men, a.k.a. infantries. Only if you survive seven battles and the Seven Years' War with nary a scar, as did the Old Fritz, are you entitled to rise from invalid to schoolmaster and begin the process of alphabetizing Prussia's infantile, unlettered farmers.

II

That did not change until a young lieutenant of the artillery, as yet wet behind the ears, entered into his diary that geniuses are meteors—sublunary beings, that is, whose mission was to go up in flames in order to light up or rather (as the French original puts it) to enlighten their century: "Les hommes de génie sont des météores destinés à brûler pour éclairer leur siècle" [Men of genius are meteors destined to be consumed in lighting up their century].[10] It was this enlightenment as the self-prescribed mortality of a commanding officer, who had barely turned twenty-six at the Battle of Lodi, that truly diversified Europe's war-related manners of death. Even the general who is given voice in Gottfried Benn's eponymous poem of 1938 concludes his staff briefing with the following words:

VERNICHTUNG!
Und wer mich sucht,
im Gegensatz zum Weltkrieg
beim Kampfwagenangriff
im vordersten Tank!

ANNIHILATION!
And whoever wishes to find me
in contrast to the Great War,
in case of an armoured attack,
will find me up front in my tank![11]

That's how it came to be that in modern armies (except for some inglorious transatlantic exceptions) it is not merely that officers, in particular, fall prey to the manners of death but also that these manners are optimized in scientific terms. Certainly, Leonhard Euler discovered the mathematical constant e as early as 1727 during the target practice of the Russian imperial artillery and thus demonstrated the connection between war and science, but it was not until the École Polytechnique in Paris, and its countless European reincarnations, that the various manners of death were put on a systematic theoretical-practical basis. Nation-states that are founded on the basis of a democratic military conscription and technically standardized weapons systems have elevated war to the level of a Clausewitzian definition: the "destruction of the enemy forces."[12] The École Polytechnique, which was known as the School of Gunpowder and Saltpeter for the first two years of its existence, systematized the effectiveness of artillery through the misuse of wine cellars, as in Saint-Émilion, or cheese factories, as in Roquefort. In cases of emergency, however (as is reported in songs at the time), when, for example, the troops of an aging duke strangled the mothers and daughters of revolutionary patriots, destruction required that the nonstandardized combatant be equipped with nonstandardized weapons: in Mâcon and Châlons-sur-Marne, even in the Prussian Landsturm edict of 1813, women were asked to fight with pitchforks and scythes.

For twenty-two years, from 1793 to 1815, "the Children of the Fatherland" (to speak with Leconte de Lisle) were levied and made into cannon fodder, until France's birth rate fell below its death rate.[13] For the emperor of the French, that was reason enough to begin the processing of military leftovers. For one, crippled soldiers whom the surgeon general of the Grand Army deemed fit for recycling were posted in the towers of the secret military semaphore lines; second, the semiorphaned daughters of fallen officers of the Honor Guard were enrolled in a new school for girls. As if to bring to a point the new feedback loop between women and cannon fodder, motherland and conscription, the emperor reduced the school's mission to one goal only: the training of mothers. Motherhood, after all (once more following Pynchon), "that's a civil-service category."[14]

And yet not even the emperor who rose to fame as a lieutenant in the artillery and whose victories were powered by the artillery managed to reach what military historians call the break-even point. Not until the Battle of Solferino in 1859, where one in seven soldiers lost their lives, did the battlefield become the most likely site of a soldier's death. During the Battle of Leipzig, by contrast—and notwithstanding its title as a "people's battle" [*Völkerschlacht*]—many more soldiers died from contagious diseases in field hospitals than from actual weapons. The battles of Old Europe brought about more manners of death than they actually produced. Hence, we can read the following in the autobiography of a musician who was born on May 22, 1813, in the Brühl district of Leipzig: "My father Friedrich Wagner, at the time of my birth the registrar of police in Leipzig with the expectation of becoming director of police, died in October of the same year, following the great exertions imposed by an overwhelming load of official duties during the wartime unrest and the battle of Leipzig, after catching typhoid fever in what had become an epidemic."[15] In *My Life*, Wagner spoke the truth: "the terrible misery brought about by the untold number of the wounded and diseased in the city" ended in a mountain of corpses underneath the foundation of the 1913 centenary monument of the Battle of Leipzig.[16] *The Ring of the Nibelung*, however, is an even more enduring monument of the battle. Like Napoleon, Wagner's Wotan begins as a nomadic god of war who is only in control of fire, or, better, an artillery by the name of Loge.[17] Again like Napoleon, he makes the big mistake of marrying into an old-European dynasty, including its contractual agreements, and thus betrays Wagner's anarchistic ideals. Only when his own twilight of the gods is close does Napoleon, a.k.a. Wotan, return to one hundred days of revolutionary glory. He expels his legitimate spouse, only to impregnate Mother Earth herself with nine Valkyries. To these fighting virgins, he issues a straightforward combat command:

Daß stark zum Streit
uns fände der Feind,
hieß ich euch Helden mir schaffen:
die herrisch wir sonst
in Gesetzen hielten

die Männer, denen
den Muth wir gewehrt,
die durch trüber Verträge
trügende Bande
zu blindem Gehorsam
wir uns gebunden—
die solltet zu Sturm
und Streit ihr nun stacheln
ihre Kraft reizen
zu rauhem Krieg,
daß kühner Kämpfer Scharen
ich sammle in Walhalls Saal!

Our foes would find us
ready for fight;
you would assemble my army:
the men whom we held
by our laws in bondage,
the mortals, whom we
had curbed in their pride,
whom by treacherous treaties,
shameful agreements,
we'd bound in obedience
blindly to serve us;
and yours was the task
to stir them to battle,
and arouse brave men
to ruthless war,
till valiant hosts of heroes
had gathered in Valhalla's hall![18]

Wotan, a.k.a. Napoleon, declares that mercenary armies—bound only by murky contracts—have reached their historical end point, and he announces the historical origins of storm troopers that—from the storm battalions of World War I and the Waffen-SS of World War II to the rapid-deployment forces of today—execute the will of an army central command out of their own "volition," even if that means against orders and the law. This "bitter," that is, total, war mobilizes even the dead in "Valhalla's hall" and the women in the Valkyries. For if Wotan's daughter Brünnhilde—who is loved no less illegitimately by the god than Napoleon loved his stepdaughter—in the first instance rescues the broken spear, and the pregnant wife of a storm-troop leader in the second, in order to feed a third generation of warriors into the Wild Army, Wagner's rather un-German Valkyries are brought to a point: they are war nurses, Red Cross nurses, or ideal mothers the way Napoleon had them trained and Henri Dunant had them on rotation in view of the mounting corpses in Solferino.[19]

III

"In 1870, at Metz, German army losses within five days of the battle amounted to 39,292 soldiers. Of these, 6,360 died on the actual day, which left 32,932 soldiers in medical care. Despite these enormous losses, virtually all of the wounded had been given first aid by noon on August 19."[20] That had consequences. For one, Wagner's friend and military orderly (not his father) contracted dysentery in the field hospital and along with it *The Birth of Tragedy from the Spirit of Music*.[21] Second, breechloaders and machine guns—whose miniaturized high-explosive bullets sufficed "to render *hors de combat* not only one of Nature's sons from a faraway land, but also a civilized European" (according to Schlieffen)—for the first time produced head wounds that no longer smashed the brain, as they did in Wittstock, but perforated it in linear and precise fashion and thus served as the foundation for modern-day neurophysiology.[22] Third, the rates of loss, as in the battles at Metz or Mars-la-Tour, were such that they ushered in a science called *combat psychology*, whose sole purpose was to bring about the conditions of possibility for the acceptance of high-tech manners of death. Its media arsenal ranged from ultrashortwave songs celebrating the happiness of Japanese mothers whose sons are commemorated at the Yasukuni Shrine to running television cameras, without which elite units of the American military in Vietnam would simply refuse to die.[23] But, fourth, all sciences and media were reduced to nothing when Schlieffen deduced conclusively that a war built around "arms specialists spurred on to their utmost" would have to change its very nature:

> It is no longer possible, as it was in the eighteenth century, to deploy against one another in two lines and fire salvos into one another at not too great a distance. In the space of a few minutes, both armies would be eradicated from the face of the Earth by rapid fire. It is no longer possible to storm the enemy position in Napoleonic columns, columns as wide as they are deep. They would be smashed by a hail of shrapnel. . . . Only by the use of the cover of trees and houses, of walls and trenches,

of elevations and depressions in the ground is it possible for the infantryman to advance on his enemy. . . . However much cover the battlefield may offer sooner or later, an open, empty space covered by fire may extend out before the enemy. If the space is small, then the attacker will rapidly storm the defender, who will have been shaken by the continuous fire. If the space is wide, there will be nothing left for the attacker but to create cover for himself by the use of the spade and to advance, as in a fortress war, from trench to trench, when necessary by night.[24]

That is what the chief of the General Staff of the Imperial Army wrote in 1909, where excavators are now digging the foundations of the new office of the chancellery. Less than five years later—precisely because Schlieffen's big plan of attack had failed—the prophecy came true. Millions of soldiers followed Wotan on his way into the earth and night. Heavy artillery and two new types of weaponry, the air force and the signal corps, set out "to storm the defender, who will have been shaken by the continuous fire." But even after three weeks of barrage fire at the trenches of the enemy, in the summer of 1916, the Scottish regiments didn't lose 80 percent of their soldiers until they made "a quick dash" across the no-man's-land. Field Marshal Douglas Haig and his officers stayed behind the front lines and simply overlooked that a few remaining machine-gun nests of the enemy were still primed and ready to fire.

And so it came about that World War I, as a race between tactics and technology (so called by the executive director of the Rheinmetall weapons manufacturer), triggered a revolutionary thought in the already revolutionary Third Supreme Army Command [Oberste Heeresleitung] of the Imperial Army.[25] As I observed before, the problem of war is not that soldiers are murderers but that (following Pynchon once more) they are expected to die for others. Its traditional solution was to allow manners of death to be defined by the enemy or microbes; its modern solution goes by the name of friendly fire. Older military science, as best as I can determine, did not even mention death as a result of fire from within one's own ranks. As members of the German Supreme Army Command responsible for artillery tactics and storm troops, respectively, by contrast, Colonels Max Bauer and Georg Bruchmüller programmed the so-called Ludendorff Offensive as follows:[26]

> Creeping Barrage, which precedes the attack, ought to be made with as many batteries as possible. . . . The use of Blue Cross ammunition depends on local [weather] conditions.

So that infantry can, at lineup, walk freely into artillery fire, it is recommended to delay firing the last rounds of preparation to reduce the danger of stray bullets. . . . Troops have to be trained to that effect behind the creeping barrage.

The movement of fire forward should be done in intervals, and its timing and depth should be controlled by the order of attack.
The depth depends on the terrain, the ground conditions, and the expected duration of the attack. The speed of the creeping barrage has to be coordinated with the infantry so that its forward movement can proceed unimpeded. . . .

During the charge, the infantry should fully exploit the effectiveness of the artillery preparation and fire support. Coinciding with the final shots and mines of the artillery, the storming infantry must secure the enemy positions and in the unfolding fight immediately follow the creeping barrage to prevent the enemy from leaving any remaining dugouts or priming up again.

The infantry principle of walking into the artillery fire and mine throwers of one's own troops—which proved highly successful with our storm battalions—must become a common property of the entire infantry. It requires relentless grit and superior morale, because it comes with scattered losses. On the plus side of it, walking into the fire of one's own troops facilitates hand-to-hand combat with the enemy infantry and their machine guns. As the result, the total losses will be significantly lower. We must use any means necessary to communicate that to the infantry. That has to be possible.[27]

The friendly fire that Wotan released on his own son, Siegmund, was hence passed down from elite guards or storm battalions to millions of fighting soldiers. From Haig's bloody and failed battles at the Somme, Erich Ludendorff drew the simple conclusion that an unending barrage of artillery would be the best way to disrupt enemy fire, so that all losses of the infantry would of necessity be the result of fire from within one's own ranks. Little wonder that his frontline officers were hard-pressed to get their infantry to accept this new form of death. In both his war novels and his specs for infantry engagements, for example, storm-trooper Lieutenant Ernst Jünger was hard at work promoting new forms of death with his own barrage of fire.[28] Somebody who contributed even more was a weather observer instrumental in deciding between the use of high-explosive ammunition and poison gas during the Spring Offensive on the front line of the

Ardennes region. That is to say, he could not have but been trained how to work in the rear of a barrage of fire. For the young meteorologist proved, strictly following Colonel Bauer, that death from a bullet from within one's own ranks not only was "possible" but is downright "the ownmost nonrelational possibility *not to be bypassed*."[29] In the summer of 1918,

> Heidegger was . . . serving with his meteorological observer unit on the Western front, in the sector assigned to the 1st Army. "Frontwetterwarte 414" was under the operational command of the 3rd Army meteorological observer corps, and was stationed in the Ardennes, not far from Sedan. Its main task in the second battle of Marne (which began on 15 July 1918) was to cover the left flank of the 1st Army as it advanced toward Rheims. These meteorological units had been set up to provide advance weather information in support of poison gas attacks.[30]

And yet: Fritz Haber's experiment to replace manners of death with chemicals, for which he was awarded the (dynamite) Nobel Prize, is, from a fundamental-ontological perspective, irrelevant. Heidegger's notion of Dasein has shed not only the term *man* but also the old-European understanding of death. As long as humans attributed death to nature or to a god as payment for their sins, death—from the Greeks and Christians to the psychoanalysts—was defined as anything but friendly fire. "God," as we can read in the final lines of Grimmelshausen's *Simplicissimus*, "grant us His grace so that we all come to that which we most desire, namely a blessed END."[31] Beginning with Nietzsche's *Birth of Tragedy* and Heidegger's *Being and Time*, such external agents have been outdone. Instead of murders there are only suicides, which they really aren't. When Dionysus chops himself to pieces, it is only because a wartime medical orderly delirious from the effects of dysentery in the field hospital in Metz has ceased being human. When Dasein dies, it does so only because its existence has always already been a being-toward-death. It projected itself from the very beginning onto death as a "possibility," which—much in contrast to all other possibilities—"gives Dasein nothing to 'be actualized' and nothing which it itself could *be* as something real. It is the possibility of the impossibility of every mode of behavior toward . . . every way of existing."[32] At the same time, the no-man's-land between the trench systems, which nobody can enter unscathed for even a second, must—strictly following Schlieffen and Bauer—simply be conquered. Fundamental ontology is at its service. Heidegger's notion of death is a well-defined manner of death in the sense of Ingeborg Bachmann, nothing else:

> In running ahead to this possibility, that is, the impossibility of any form of existence, it becomes "greater and greater," that is, it reveals itself as something which knows no measure at all, no more or less, but means the possibility of the measureless impossibility of existence. Essentially, this possibility offers no support for becoming intent on something, for "spelling out" the real thing that is possible and so forgetting its possibility. As anticipation of possibility, being-toward-death first makes this possibility possible and sets it free as possibility.[33]

Following Trotsky's capitulation in Brest-Litowsk, Ludendorff was able to perform a strategic switch and free up twenty divisions for the western front. That meant that on March 21, 1918, 56 out of 192 divisions were ready to walk into "the artillery fire and mine throwers of [their] own troops."

> Being-toward-death is the anticipation of a potentiality-of-being of *that* being whose kind of being is anticipation itself. In the anticipatory revealing of this potentiality-of-being, Da-sein discloses itself to itself with regard to its most extreme possibility. But to project oneself upon one's ownmost potentiality of being means to be able to understand oneself in the being of the being thus revealed: to exist. Anticipation shows itself as the possibility of understanding one's *ownmost* and extreme potentiality-of-being, that is, as the possibility of *authentic existence*.[34]

Put differently, and in the words of Colonel Bauer ten years before the publication of *Being and Time*: "We must use any means necessary to communicate that to the infantry."

IV

Dasein picks its hero—or at least I do. "The authentic retrieve of a possibility of existence that has been—the possibility that Dasein may choose its heroes—is existentially grounded in anticipatory resoluteness; for in resoluteness the choice is first chosen that makes one free for the struggle to come, and the loyalty to what can be retrieved."[35] But preoccupied as it was with the philosophy of storm trooping, *Being and Time*, as you know, forgot *The Question concerning Technology*. As far as manners of death are concerned, that is an unavoidable question in the age of high-tech warfare.[36] "That which presences does not hold sway; rather, setting-upon rules," Heidegger wrote not until after his turn.[37]

When humans are reduced to mere "human material," however, any ruling setting-upon is always exceeded by strategy.[38] Before the Wehrmacht had completely lost it, for example, it kept practicing the tactics of barrage fire but virtually avoided it in actual combat. When the ten light tank divisions began Operation Sickle Cut in May 1940, they were under strict orders not even to engage the troop concentrations of the enemy.[39] Rather, destroying the enemy's weapons and communications systems far behind the front lines was deemed much more effective than the actual killing of soldiers, if only because modern armies (much like Wagner's Siegfried) cannot, in principle, attack from the rear. Blitzkriegs and cauldron battles—at least before the transport of POWs into camps—have lowered rates of death to levels that are a delight to the doctrines of the U.S. Army. That's why it is information warfare, as the Pentagon has branded it, that has been going on for the past sixty years. An increasing number of weapons are in use today whose primary purpose is the destruction of other weapons and long-range weapons guidance systems—and in the case of information warfare, the hacking of systems—but in which manners of death register only as a side effect. Even the barrage of fire of 1918 attacked space as such but enemy troops only to the degree that they occupied said space. Otherwise, Lieutenant Jünger would not have found shelter from shrapnel under unburied and rotting bodies. Operation Desert Storm similarly attacked not the tank divisions and missile launching sites of the Iraqi forces but rather the sites where these very same tanks and missiles were manufactured. When humans don't fight humans but industries, the very term *weapon*, understood as a tool, turns meaningless. And that "means," strictly following Pynchon, that war

> was never political at all, the politics was all theatre, all just to keep the people distracted.... Secretly, it was being dictated instead by the needs of technology ... by a conspiracy between human beings and techniques, by something that needed the energy-burst of war.... The real crises were crises of allocation and priority, not among firms—it was only staged to look that way—but among the different Technologies, Plastics, Electronics, Aircraft, and their needs which are understood only by the ruling elite.[40]

Under the conditions of an industry that, as Friedrich Engels put it, "remains industry, whether it is applied to the production or the destruction of things," manners of death in war have shrunk to the size of accidents.[41] As is widely known, accidents have the bad habit of destroying not only technological systems but also their teams or operators. At Kursk and Oryol, the last tank offensive of the Wehrmacht, tank teams refused to obey orders and rode into battle with open turrets to minimize the side effects of burning diesel tanks.[42] Following Hiroshima and Nagasaki, after the U.S. Air Force had dropped uranium and plutonium from the Japanese sky, they had to follow up with flyers explaining to a stunned population that the fire had not been a "divine wind"—that is to say, no kamikaze— but the work of humans and weapons (see Yukio Mishima). Manners of death that leave only a faint, greasy residue imprinted on the walls of houses, such as those in Hiroshima, don't, for heaven's sake, need camera crews but explanations. If, in 1944, "you asked a wounded soldier or marine what hit him, you'd hardly be ready for the answer, 'My buddy's head,' or his sergeant's heel or his head, or a Japanese leg, complete with shoes and puttees, or the West Point ring on his captain's severed hand."[43] And if you asked Niklas Luhmann when he began thinking in terms of contingency, he would answer, "In April 1945 I heard a boom, turned around, and saw— not the dead body of my desk mate, but nothing. That's when I began thinking in terms of contingency."[44]

Absolute contingency has resulted in two consequences, an existential and a statistical one. Soon after Pearl Harbor, military psychiatrists on both sides discovered—to the initial dismay of their superiors, and notwithstanding all national hymns—that the Horatian form of death simply does not exist in national standing armies. Soldiers are prepared to die not for their country but for the platoon in which they fight.[45] That is how existentialism shows itself, and that is how training manuals have been updated. At 50 percent attrition rates, when platoons cease to be platoons, armies such as that of Israel stop fighting.[46]

The statistical consequence, by contrast, is simply the reign of statistics itself. In 1897 a captain in the Imperial and Royal General Staff published *Die Zahl im Kriege* [Numbers in war], the first reference work on attrition rates from Leuthen to Sedan. Or, to put it differently: the first empirical liquidation of specific manners of death.[47] Seventy years later, when the manager of vehicle assembly lines became the U.S. secretary of defense, the so-called body count became the first and last measure of all warfare. Robert McNamara lost the war but considered it won because the number of dead Vietnamese outstripped the number of zinc caskets arriving in Oakland's harbor. As if the percentage of the dead in war, which cultures accept without capitulating, were a constant removed from all history.

To put it differently: because the demographics of the dead in war are a historical variable, they were able to make history itself. I would like to illustrate that with a concluding oral history that has its origins in the memories of a sloshed secret military agent from California. George (to allow him to remain reasonably anonymous) discovered his taste for wine while in Rheims, when French farmers served vintages to their liberators that had been walled up for the past four years. From that day on, George was in his jeep and made it a rule to be ahead of the advance guard of the American tanks by two or three days. While his colleagues in the secret service searched the bombed-out Reich for the blueprints of liquid-fuel rockets or jet aircraft, George made deep advances into Saxony without encountering the enemy. There, in the courtyard of an abandoned secondary school, he discovered a dim fire fed by an old custodian who dumped papers on it by the wheelbarrow. By the time George was able to stop him, two-thirds of the documents had already been charred. What was still readable were the personnel files of German prisoner-of-war camps. George had stumbled on a central registry that carefully recorded—by date and by cause of death—each and every soldier of the Red Army who had been captured in cauldron battles and later died in prison camps. He forced the custodian to get a heavy scale, put out the fire, and weigh the fuel. That is how ashes—the leftovers of leftovers of a leftover—testify in simple and statistical form that the Wehrmacht did not kill three million Russians but starved them to death.[48] "In a word, it was a pitiful sight."[49]

George tried to report his discovery from the Saxon secondary school to Potsdam, but it was too late. Harry Truman and Winston Churchill had already accepted Stalin's officious declaration, according to which the Great War for the Fatherland had cost the fatherland of all workers twenty million lives, in the same officious fashion. With a death toll of twenty-three million, it dawned even on them that the Soviet Union was even more destroyed and bled dry than their generals, for the best political reasons, had made them believe. That's how it happened that the Saxon secondary school fell under Soviet military rule.

In a word, that is, what counts in matters of violence is solely its coding.

CHAPTER 13

Ottilie Hauptmann

TRANSLATED BY ILINCA IURASCU

> I fought in the old revolution on the side of the ghost[s]
> and the [k]ing[s].
> —Leonard Cohen, "The Old Revolution" (1969)

I

"All men, in the vertiginous moment of coitus, are the same man."[1] Thus says the law, for it is one with desire.

Forgetting the law therefore means: the forgetting of forgetting. A transgression that has long passed for love. To still be one, man or woman, in that moment of bodily vertigo and mean One, name or image, is one of the Europeans' most peculiar abilities. The narrator of *Elective Affinities* knows it by virtue of no less peculiar abilities. "In the dim lamplight secret affections began to hold sway, and imagination took over from reality. Eduard clasped none other than Ottilie in his arms; Charlotte saw the Captain more or less distinctly before her mind's eye, and so things present and absent mingled, curiously enough, in the most charming and delightful manner."[2] It hardly matters that those two sleeping together also happen to be married to each other and hence, from the novelist's perspective, commit double adultery by fantasy. Even if Eduard and Charlotte saw only

---

Originally published in Friedrich Kittler, *Dichter, Mutter, Kind* (Munich: Fink, 1991), 119–48. A shorter version of the same essay appeared in *Goethes Wahlverwandtschaften: Kritische Modelle und Diskursanalysen zum Mythos Literatur*, edited by Norbert W. Bolz (Munich: Gerstenberg, 1981), 260–75. The portion of section IV in bold highlights the additional material included in the 1991 version. (See also note 88.)

their partners' names and images before their mind's eyes, they would still remain in the penalty zone of that peculiar mnemotechnics. For what they transgress is not the moral or private law but the colossal law of the present. That law is the prerogative of the soulless body when it "forgets everything and remembers again in an instant."[3] Yet the novel grants the bliss of amnesia only to the one it excludes from the circle of amorous elective affinities: the wild Luciane. In contrast, the main protagonists' bodies are inhabited by souls that are so incapable of being absent that, even absently, they still recall the absent ones' name and image. Inevitably, everyone falls into the snares of love, the belief in a You and Me.

But "you cannot walk beneath concepts with impunity."[4] A dumb body, the child conceived that night, refutes all identities. Little Otto's facial features and black eyes make it clear as day: when Eduard and Charlotte sleep with each other, they are not themselves but rather the Captain [Hauptmann] and Ottilie.[5] Their bodies are possessed, ghostlike, by a force that in the novel and everywhere else goes by the euphemism of soul. Which proves, once again, that no transgression can transcend the law.

Still: from where and for what do ghosts draw such power? Despite all its urgency and empathy for Eduard and Charlotte, the novel keeps deflecting that question. In lieu of an affair between the Captain and Ottilie, we find a void in the elective affinities' seemingly comprehensive combinatorics. Before they arrive at the manor, Charlotte warns of their potential affair, yet they end up spending months together without exchanging a word with each other.[6] Their intercourse is manifest only as silence, embodiment, and scandal: as a child that combines the Captain's facial features and Ottilie's black eyes as if in mockery of Eduard and Charlotte, his biological parents. Thus, what reads and appears as double adultery by fantasy in the wordy account of the aristocratic couple is, conversely and tacitly, the one and only way to reach the impossible, that is to say, the Real: a sexual relation between the Captain and Ottilie. The coupling of ghosts is possible only because, even as they climax, two other subjects so unforgettably fail to forget. Ottilie, who is and remains a virgin, becomes a mother; the Captain, who is and remains committed to a dead woman, becomes a father.[7] A married couple, a succubus and an incubus: the ABCD of elective affinities.

As it is told in Jewish lore: incubi and succubi look for a hidden path to one's soul in order to manage their spectral infertility and procreate, using a man's seed or a woman's pleasure.[8] That is precisely what happens when the husband and his wife fall in love. At the outset of the novel, a couple lacking nothing, neither wealth nor enjoyment, discover a double lack that is none. It is not Eduard who needs the Captain, with whom Charlotte will fall in love; in his last letter, the Captain himself describes his lack of employment in terms of utter discontent. It is not Charlotte who needs Ottilie, with whom Eduard will fall in love; the letters and reports of the pedagogical assistant inform Charlotte that Ottilie herself has brought to naught the path she was meant to follow as a well-educated bourgeois daughter, by gratuitously and spectacularly failing a certain school examination. All of which inevitably leads to a captain without a job and a niece who has failed school being summoned to, or by, the small world of the novel.

And thus begins for the aristocratic pair one of those aptly named learning curves that conclude, as they always do, in liquidation. At the end of the novel, lord and estate are gone and left without an heir. Eduard himself states the historical relevance of such educational processes: "Our ancestors held firm to what they had been learned in their youth; but we have to learn everything over again every five years if we are to be not totally behind the times."[9] The baron therefore distinguishes between traditional cultures where rights of rank and forms of knowledge are passed down without change and a stage of historical innovation that practically invents the very idea of innovation. While France is in the process of liquidating its nobility, German barons and baronesses like Eduard and Charlotte undergo a reeducation program that, historically speaking, ultimately yields similar results as the guillotine; nevertheless, it also ensures that aristocrats pass basic chemistry courses and are—already as fictional characters—never behind the times. Eduard's love for Ottilie gives him a real rejuvenating boost, as the loved one confides in her journal, and it is only the Captain's topographic techniques that give Charlotte's dilettante landscape design a professional finish, as she herself admits.

So enough with the observations on morality and adultery, guilt and love, in *Elective Affinities*. As Foucault put it: morality can be reduced entirely to sexuality, which, in turn, can be reduced, without remainder, to politics.[10] The aristocratic couple are in love not just with some person or another but with a power that ends up revolutionizing them as well. The Captain and Ottilie, an incubus and a succubus, take up, via the twisted or possessed souls of that couple, an impossible relationship with each other, in order to give rise to a new Man.

The new Man in question is educated, made by the power of pedagogues. That, and none other, was already the subject of Kant's lecture on pedagogy. It is the pedagogical assistant who divulges the secret in the novel (not without swearing others to silence first) when he speaks of the model of a new kind of instruction. Talking to Ottilie, who—as if to summon the case of Abel and student number 447[11]—is both his pupil and his confidante, he boils down the whole business of teaching to a single formula: "Boys should be educated to be servants and girls to be mothers."[12] Full of excitement over "how few words" are needed to express that new pedagogical goal, the assistant obviously omits to say whom those servants are supposed to serve. The writer does it for him: he repeats the phrase almost verbatim to his own literary assistant, drawing on the words attributed to Joseph or Frederick II to designate all servants as "civil servants."[13]

The matter at hand then, both in the novel and beyond, is the pedagogical production of civil servants and mothers. Civil servants and mothers are precisely the two professional groups Germany designates as the new bearers of culture and the state around 1800. The civil service–cum–motherhood dyad, in its double sense of image and screen, exposure and concealment of sexual difference, forms the system of power of Goethe's age. That system, called *education*, assigns the instruction of small children exclusively to mothers, who must be trained in their profession by pedagogical servants; the duties of higher education are conferred on civil servants, who must, in turn, be trained in their own humanity by mothers. The cross-coupling (to call things by their technical name) makes education a system of self-preservation and self-enhancement, that is to say, a structure of power and domination in Nietzsche's exact sense of the word.[14]

The novel brings the pedagogue's word into the limelight. Against the dull background inhabited by the aristocratic couple, the new protagonists can finally shine: the Captain as civil servant and Ottilie as mother.

II

Before she comes to the manor, Ottilie attends a boarding school for "higher daughters" together with Luciane, Charlotte's child from her first marriage.[15] The program of instruction defines, on the one hand, the socialization practices of the old nobility, who do not shower their offspring with gestures of familiarity and maternal affection, and, on the other hand, the identity of the poor orphan Ottilie, who, not unlike Recha,[16] becomes what she is only by way of education.[17] That is why Luciane and Ottilie come across as each other's counterparts: feudal representation and bourgeois interiority, discourse and silence, "Dutch" potlach [sic] and domestic economy.[18] Obviously, the school principal is sufficiently deluded to prefer Luciane over Ottilie; when writing to Charlotte, the girls' mother and guardian, she meets Ottilie's silence with silence. But that is precisely what gives the school assistant the opportunity to concentrate the whole strength of his discourse on Ottilie. And so he becomes, the first among the novel's many later readers, the enamored and loquacious interpreter of silence and Ottilie's silence in particular as the very idea of Woman.

The other girls at the school are faster learners and better at handwriting and grammar; they are at home with the rules of classical alphabetization. But these very rules place Woman in a unique position, namely, as the silent source of all speech and writing. Thus, the other girls' verbal and written skills merely speak against the feminine didactics of her "excellent," yet "hasty and impatient teachers."[19] Those teachers have not yet learned to organically form Woman as the organism of all organisms. Their erratic instruction produces human beings as erratic and spoiled as Luciane. By contrast, Ottilie, whose learning is slow and steady, educates her enamored teacher into an art only recently invented: schooling [Unterricht].[20] His organically "coherent program," which always takes into account that a child is a child and that learning must "begin at the beginning," produces Ottilie as a pedagogical ideal.[21] The assistant counts her among "the hidden fruits," "the ones that contain the most fertile seeds."[22]

Containing the most fertile seeds means being productive and multiplying. Luciane, who passes her final exam with flying colors, dives headfirst into social and erotic amusements; she forgets about the boarding school and all her other pasts. In contrast, Ottilie remains her entire life under the spell of pedagogical power. According to the assistant, her slow and steady learning process is supposedly exponential: remarkably, she learns not "like a person being educated, but like a person destined to teach; not like a pupil, but like a future instructor."[23] In other words, her resistance to forgetting about school is matched only by her readiness to recruit pedagogical power. Precisely such self-preservation by means of instructional processes defines the power structure called education. Inventing lines of continuous procreation—from child to adult and from student to teacher—pays off, both for the assistant and for the state of the humanities during his time.[24] Ottilie bears fruit that contains the most fertile seeds, which germinate, bloom, and, in turn, bear other fruit and fertile seeds. That loop solves the problem of administration and closes the circle. For the educated pedagogical reformer, his favorite pupil is the ultimate embodiment of his own definition of female education. Ottilie is the instructed pedagogical instructor and, since all instruction must begin as maternal instruction, also the ideal mother. "Girls [should be educated] to be mothers, then everything will work out very suitably."²⁵

Obviously, a virgin programmed for ideal motherhood is bound to fail a "public examination."²⁶ Just as the public sphere is reserved for civil servants, and civil service for men, domestic and emotional intimacy, as its precise counterpart, is set aside for mothers. Nevertheless, the depth of interiority can only be measured by the extent of its silence—if it were to speak, interiority would no longer have a voice. Consequently, just around the time when the German states introduce the *Abitur*, in other words, a regime of state-sanctioned publicity, as the mandatory graduation exam for boys' high schools, the schools for higher daughters are being organized into ideal families. The statutes of the Berlin Luisenstiftung,²⁷ for instance, founded two years after the release of *Elective Affinities*, "allow, under no circumstance, public examinations," for the sake of the pedagogical production of mothers.²⁸ And therefore, when she fails the exam, Ottilie only proves just how indispensable such new statutes are. That a school for "higher daughters" should reward pupils who "outtalk[ ] and outdo[ ]" someone like Ottilie, as the assistant both maliciously and pointedly puts it, makes sense in the context of the bluestocking era; in the pedagogical age, it is sacrilege. To elicit discourse, a woman cannot be someone who speaks. Luciane's glossy eloquence dissolves into mere chatter when compared with Ottilie's wordless interiority, which is the product of genuine feminine pedagogy.

In 1808, shortly before Goethe's *Elective Affinities*, Friedrich Immanuel Niethammer publishes his *Quarrel between Philanthropism and Humanism in the Theory of Educational Instruction of Our Time*. As central commissioner of education in the Bavarian Ministry of the Interior, Niethammer holds several private conversations with Goethe on the topic of "pedagogical instruction and national education," which serve, in turn, as the basis for sweeping pedagogical reforms in the Bavarian school system.²⁹ Only women are exempt from the official obligation to attend school, simply because Niethammer's polemical essay rendered the fictional contrast between a dazzlingly public and a romantically domestic daughter into concrete pedagogical reality. As prototypes or copies of Goethe's fictional assistant, higher civil servants strictly forbid Woman from taking public exams: "How will our daughters react to the quiet of the household when in raising them we ourselves involve them from infancy in every public pastime? We are not merely ruining them for domestic life; we harm virtue much more by making our daughters' education so public that they cannot learn or produce anything that cannot be shown off. How is a spoiled girl to enjoy the quiet tasks of housework, which remain unknown to the public?"[30] And therefore, contrary to Walter Benjamin, his editor Hugo von Hofmannsthal, and that entire tradition of Goethean theology with its blindness to official records, Ottilie's silence does not mark "the semblance" (whatever that may be) "install[ing] itself consumingly in the heart of the noblest being."[31] Rather, and more plainly: a pedagogical heart is formed by a gender-specific and datable educational politics. If, at the end of the novel, Ottilie no longer consumes anything, it is not because she longs to be consumed; she remains, until her death, faithful to a preprogrammed instructional enterprise that consumes only men.

Engendered by pedagogy, her silence strengthens her against erotic temptations. The seducer Eduard becomes, as he declares just before his death, Ottilie's weak—in other words, impotent—student.[32] There was a time when, flanked by the count, the baron managed quite a few gallant exploits. Now, even in an isolated inn and flanked by the most sympathetic of pandering landladies, he is not able to do anything about Ottilie's "terrible silence" and her mute gestures of denial.[33] The reversal of the double adultery by fantasy—the simple and straightforward adultery by deed—fails to take place. But that is hardly surprising in the context of a novel where even an old libertine count falls prey to familial affections when Ottilie is involved. Instead of "looking upon a woman with desire," which, after all, is the "basic text" not merely when it comes to the novel, he prefers to "think of [Ottilie] as a daughter."[34]

Since it bears fertile seeds, the fruit reaps what it sows. Not Charlotte but Ottilie is the bearer of the discourse of family love in the small world of the novel. Charlotte only pleads for marriage; Luciane, her own fruit, shows quite clearly the extent of her maternal capabilities. In contrast, Ottilie, an innate pedagogical talent, actively participates in the turn from conjugal family to modern nuclear family with the mother and child as its double center. She goes into the village to instruct the local girls "more systematically and consistently."[35] Her one declared goal is "to inculcate in each girl devotion to home, parents, brothers and sisters."[36] It is Little Nan, above all, who proves what that means. Ottilie's "progressive attitude to life"[37] grants her a connection not unlike that between a mother and her child and therefore, ultimately and supremely, a rebirth.[38] Thus, even among peasants, a social category still treated in Old Europe as an anonymous whole, familiarization produces discrete individuals.[39]

What's good for the peasants is even better for the masters. When Charlotte gives birth to a boy, Ottilie thinks it is "devoutly . . . to be wished . . . that he should grow up in the presence of his father and mother." Naturally, since she is trained for motherhood, Ottilie takes up the role of little Otto's mother. The age of governesses, along with their rearing of aristocratic children, is over. An explicit decision, made in the child's best interest, not to give him "to a nurse, but to feed him with milk and water," upgrades Ottilie to the rank of "his closest guardian" and elevates an animal product to the standard of maternal milk.[40]

That closeness is what defines the very act of pedagogically aesthetic intervention: as the effect of multiple resolutions, enactments, and transfigurations. When the power structure called education claims the task of instructing women in matters of motherhood, the other, conventional method of making mothers is rendered obsolete. Instruction instead of insemination: the new practice makes it necessary to document and archive motherhood at all times. Ottilie is perfectly suited for the task. Not unlike the nightingale, whose song the other birds imitate: only a barren virgin who ultimately brings death to the child can model for all other, empirical mothers what motherhood actually means. Once again, the author turns Christmas into a celebration of Mother's Day avant la lettre.[41] Cast in a tableau vivant of the Virgin and Child, Mother Ottilie surpasses "anything an artist has ever depicted": she becomes a "newly created queen of heaven."[42] And in the age of copyright and production aesthetics, where there is creation, the creator cannot be far away: "Looking out from under her long eyelashes," the Virgin known as Ottilie recognizes "her devoted teacher" among the onlookers.[43] An enamored architect as stage director, an enamored instructor as creator and critic, and a virgin as the prima donna of ideal motherhood: together they form a compact machine that instills the new ideal in the empirical, all-too-empirical mother Charlotte. Someone who only has a daughter like Luciane cannot claim to have fulfilled her calling to pedagogical motherhood. In contrast, Ottilie is cast, once more, as the very picture of a Madonna or *penserosa*. Strolling with little Otto in her left arm and a book in her right, she becomes "as good as a mother, or rather, second mother, to the growing boy."[44] Growing up in this "different fashion" is no longer a matter of biology but rather of education. And even if the pedagogy of *liberi et libri* [children and books] abruptly turns into *liberi aut libri* [children or books] with the death of the little boy, that is merely a matter of instilling in the characters the fantasy of an ideal- and-empirical motherhood.[45] Standing in front of Otto's body, the Captain thinks of Ottilie "with a child of her own on her arm as the most perfect replacement for what she had taken from him."[46]

Obviously, there is no ideal *and* empirical mother at once. And precisely therefore Ottilie appears, before both men and readers, to create and feed that very fantasy. She embodies the erotic function under the conditions of a culture that exploits its biological reproduction through discipline and consequently situates women strictly along the lines of a dichotomy between mothers and hysterics.[47] When he sleeps with Charlotte but dreams of Ottilie, Eduard chases precisely after that impossible and damned coincidence of the empirical and ideal mother, desired woman and beloved maiden.[48]

III

The family logic demands a complement to the ideal-and-empirical mother: a man, procreator and father in one. That man is not Eduard. Out of love for Ottilie, he eagerly plans a divorce that would take a husband from Charlotte and "a father from his children," yet that prospect leaves him "smiling coldly."[49] And when the Captain explains that the birth of a child means a commitment for parents to always "stay together" in order to "share the responsibility of his upbringing and future welfare," Eduard gives him the traditional European answer, namely, that "parents just delude themselves" in thinking they are irreplaceable.[50] And therefore, while sleeping with Eduard, Charlotte dreams precisely of the man who gives such advice, especially when he also happens to be an actual captain. That man would not merely father but also "educate the boy and guide and develop his talents as he s[ees] fit"—in other words, become his instructor.[51] In a nuclear-family culture, which, unlike many others, specifies the functions of progenitor and father, the fantasy of a perfect coincidence between the R/real and the S/symbolic is inevitable.

But in the Captain's case, there is a gaping hole in place of the Real. Only a detective could uncover the secret hidden behind the beautiful semblance that the novel employs to veil the element at its core, namely, power. At the heart of the novel, the acclaimed "Curious Tale of the Childhood Sweethearts" announces and conceals its secret kernel of violence, which interpreters, in messianic fashion, yet again conceal, breathing a sigh of relief. Oddly enough, however, and not just according to the unsuspecting English visitors who recount the tale from hearsay, Charlotte "leaves the room with a silent gesture of apology," as if they had talked about rope in a hanged man's house. But the tale actually concerns the Captain and his neighbor.[52]

A boy and a girl who have passionately disliked each other from early childhood are separated when they reach marriageable age. The boy pursues a military career; the girl gets engaged to a rich and respectable man. While on leave visiting his family, the young man sees the bride-to-be again and treats her with the indifference that befits his "ambition."[53] She, however, realizes that her childish hatred was nothing but the mask of love and—as if to prefigure Ottilie—seeks to render her own "dead image" unforgettable to him by committing suicide.[54] Whereupon the loved one jumps after her into the water, thus gaining a life, a wife, and a blessing.

> It had actually happened to the Captain and a neighbor of his—not quite the way the Englishman had reported it, though its main outline was not distorted, just decorated and developed in more detail, as often happens with such stories when they have passed from one person to another and are filtered, finally, through the imagination of a tasteful and intelligent narrator. In most cases, everything and nothing ends up the same.[55]

Earlier interpreters typically gloss over the remark concerning the "tasteful and intelligent" narrator, provided they make the effort to identify the fictional Captain in the novella in the first place. All his attributes seem to point to the identity of the rejected husband, especially the Captain's reluctance to discuss the subject of drowning.[56] But there are clearly other correspondences at play. The rejected husband is described as a man of "family, fortune and prominence," whereas the Captain brings little honor to his own name (Otto), as opposed to his namesake, the "well-to-do baron" Eduard.[57] Rather than feudal riches and privileges, the Captain boasts bourgeois skills. He is a learner and producer, while the others are still consumers or, worse still, agents of waste. In that sense, he resembles the rescuer in the novella, who "learned easily [whatever he was taught]" and whose "patrons, as well as his own inner inclinations, destined him to be an officer," not unlike the Captain himself.[58] Whenever it comes to rescuing people, they are called "skillful swimmer[s]," and their ambitions follow the general principles of classical humanism, "motivated solely by the desire to promote the well-being of others."[59]

The equation rescuer = Captain works except for one variable, a riddle reserved only for "shallow, bloated" interpretations, which allowed messianic readings to celebrate the "childhood sweethearts" as witnesses of true love.[60] Plainly put, here is the riddle: why is the Captain single? After all, he is a good swimmer in an age when swimming lessons are introduced as part of combat training (and strictly in that context).⁶¹ Isn't he supposed to have saved his childhood sweetheart from suicidal plans, treacherous waters, and the threat of an unsuitable marriage? At least as accurate as it is "shallow," André François-Poncet's reading of that paradox suggests the possibility of a "new drama" ruining the happiness of the rescuer and depriving him, once more, of the love he had regained.⁶² That reading seems somewhat contradicted by the silence in the novel, and especially the Captain's peculiar tendency to "avoid confronting some sad memory" in the case of drowning accidents, since "such an incident had been a turning-point in [his] life."⁶³ But as he stands by the bier of the drowned child Otto, those memories can no longer be stopped, and he is overcome by a ghost-like "inward shudder."⁶⁴

Combined in criminological fashion, the clues above add up to an inevitable conclusion: the plot of the novella is real and has occurred as the sole drama in the Captain's life. The woman who loved him jumped into the water but was not saved. Other solutions for the second variable are nonexistent.

So it goes with the tales of fortune: "In most cases, everything and nothing ends up the same." The messianic or even archaic state of the world that the novella is supposed to imagine is a fantasy; not unlike the world itself, it is merely constructed to fill up the gaps in the discourse.⁶⁵ Passing from mouth to ear and from ear to mouth, the catastrophe of the childhood sweethearts gives rise to a beautiful novella, which the Captain and Charlotte alone refuse to hear. To those two, who are in the know, the tale speaks only of the R/real: namely, of the fact that there is no such thing as a sexual relationship. "What constitutes the basis of life, in effect, is that for everything having to do with the relations between men and women, what is called collectivity, it's not working out [ça ne va pas]. It's not working out and the whole world talks about it and a large part of our activity is taken up with saying so."⁶⁶ In lieu of the sexual relationship, there are only two modalities of misfire: "the male way . . . and then the other one."⁶⁷ The couple who miss each other in the raging waters make different choices: the girl opts for a "strange delirium,"⁶⁸ the desire for the unattainable desire of the other, whereas the male swimmer, both skillful and unsuccessful, chooses that which, for a man, replaces the sexual relationship—the element that sustains his swimming.⁶⁹ The fear-ridden love for the maternal waters constitutes the genealogy of the civil servant, as the Captain and soon-to-be Major imagines it. Civil servants are committed not to a rescued bride but to a mother, since the ideal mother, who has been instructed in motherhood, programmatically educates them in the first place. If, throughout the novel, the wifeless, solitary Captain neither lives nor renounces his love, that is a direct consequence of the fact that his "past life has been nothing else but a painful wound."[70] What connects him to Charlotte is a silent attachment to trauma that does not allow for any sexual relationships.

And therefore it all comes down to the improvement of central Europe. Precisely since the impossibility of the sexual relationship cancels out all talk of society and community, society and community become the very motto of civil service. For military men such as the Captain, the uniform is a pedagogical tool in the work "for society as a whole" and thereby for strengthening the classical gender role distribution.[71] Whereas Ottilie sets up modern nuclear families only on a small scale and in silence, the unemployed captain becomes the effusive custodian of that which nowadays passes for social totality. He proves parents are irreplaceable to an uncaring father like Eduard; he reforms the feudal evening reading sessions by introducing books "concerning the welfare, advantages and comfort of bourgeois society"; he introduces our modern, or (to speak with Goethe) "blotting-paper catechisms," even into old manors with the aid of his topographical maps and his bureaucratic distinctions between repository and archive.[72] The novelist, himself a high-ranking bureaucrat, can only benefit from learning such discursive practices when he incorporates into his own work Ottilie's diary and the pedagogical assistant's reports, as well as location sketches, which he then presumably destroyed.[73]

There are certain nondiscursive analogies for the discursive practice delineated above. As Ottilie rightfully remarks, "an educated soldier enjoys the greatest advantages in life as in society in general."[74] The baron does not "like to deal with townspeople and peasants" unless he "is in a position to actually give orders."[75] Instead, the Captain has grown so used to orders that he can just as well live without them. He understands the kind of power that beckons those educated to serve rather than rule—as the assistant put it. The genealogy of that power can be traced back to Wilhelm Meister, whose initial job choice is determined by a mother's love, and his final one by a drowning accident. Both in the *Apprenticeship* and the *Elective Affinities*, a beloved creature is pried away by the waters and, in both cases, the one who stays behind chooses renunciation and therapy. A medically informed authority replaces the despotism of the old aristocracy. The captain imposes a "Swiss style of order" on the farmers and their run-down farms;[76] he stocks the house apothecary so Charlotte can serve as bureaucracy's charitable right arm; he even suggests an army surgeon for "sudden complaints . . . in the country," let alone the "special care" he takes with the equipment against drowning.[77]

Thus, the Captain is indeed the "living example of the limited and problematic bourgeois emancipation" around 1800.[78] His problems, however, are other than those indicated by the critics, who would prefer him to be even more of a socialist. If, to paraphrase Walter Benjamin, myth dies with the last remaining beggar, the Captain is one of its executioners.[79] He is the first to successfully turn the unlimited almsgiving in Eduard's villages into a true precursor of our contemporary welfare state. As Eduard admiringly observes, the Captain is neither inexperienced like scholars and the learned men from the city nor dumb or deceitful like farmers and therefore can integrate both peasants and beggars into the new power system. No absolute orders should or may be passed to reach that goal. The only necessary and sufficient condition in that regard are a few enlightened people acting as "country legislators" in order to distribute small sums of money fairly and equally, in other words, according to the principles of the welfare state.[80]

Above all, the Captain never forgets the principle that would prove vital should his reforms fail, like so many other universal improvement plans in the premodern era: "not to leave unfinished any business he had undertaken until he could find a suitable substitute."[81] The impeccable ethics of public servants: a man, himself long unemployed and therefore potentially indifferent to any questions of succession, ensures that his position is filled by another, just as the assistant and pedagogical servant does in his own field of activity. Therefore, contrary to what the novelist suggests, it is hardly trivial or coincidental that after the Captain's promotion and departure, his "former pupil"—the architect—who has been "scarcely noticed before" "steps in right away to fill the empty spot."[82] In contrast to "common life," which, not unlike the baron's estate in the novel, depends on the contingencies of birth and death, the administrative system takes matters of succession in its own hands and treats them with technical precision. With the consequence that even we, today, still inhabit that Captain's "artificial world."[83]

IV

Let us, then, proceed in nominalist fashion and name names. As opposed to ideal mothers such as Ottilie, who can never be empirical mothers at the same time, ideal public servants like the Captain have historical empiricism fully on their side. And since the rules of the *Elective Affinities* game allow for several explicit character combinations, let us immediately propose two names that could strategically replace the fictional Captain in the novel (and not merely in order to serve educational practices).

One of those names is Friedrich Eberhard von Rochow—neither a learned man from the city nor a speechless peasant but rather a retired officer (not unlike the Captain). After serving as first lieutenant and being wounded during the Seven Years' War, Rochow first pursues scientific studies (not unlike the Captain, who takes up chemistry), before spreading his wisdom and administrative talents across the rural areas as an educated soldier (again, not unlike the Captain). That is how his estates Reckahn, Getting, Krahne, and Brückermark acquire the first modern elementary schools in the Margraviate of Brandenburg and consequently also in the empire. Rochow's name has been long forgotten by nonhistorians, but since fame is a form of forgetting, the erasure of a name is the highest of victories: all of central Europe has since then passed through Rochow's elementary school system.[84]

During the wet summers of 1771 and 1772, when epidemics raged among the people and cattle of Reckahn, "von Rochow hired a doctor, who provided medicine for everyone living on the estate free of charge; he even continued to pay him on a regular basis and gave plenty of instructions."[85] The Captain handles Charlotte's apothecary and the hiring of an army surgeon in similar fashion, ensuring the financial details of their remuneration. Von Rochow is the author of 143 articles catering to the interests of bourgeois society, therefore precisely the kind of readings the Captain chooses for the evenings he sets up at the manor. Around 1780, with the numbers of beggars among the lower peasant and bourgeois population at an all-time high, von Rochow promptly writes an "Essay concerning Poor Relief Societies and the Abolition of Mendicity" ["Versuch über Armen Anstalten und Abschaffung aller Betteley"] (as if to give the Captain his cue). The text contains a proposal to launch poor-relief agencies even out in the country, which receives praise and is approved at the highest level.[86] Similarly, much to Charlotte's dismay, the highest authority in the novel discovers that the Captain is too much of a universal thinker for his modest field of activity and hence would be "more significant in a more elevated sphere of society."[87] And, indeed, a few chapters later he is promoted to the rank of major.[88]

That is precisely why there is yet another candidate for replacing Goethe's Captain or Major: an officer who, unlike Rochow, is not only

still around at the time *Elective Affinities* is released but is also told by others he had the honor of being immortalized in the novel. In late 1809 Varnhagen von Ense learns from an informed source, namely, "General von Rühle," that the Weimar society has been busy decoding a roman à clef that famously does not contain "a [single] line" that Goethe has not "taken from [his] own experience":⁸⁹ "In Charlotte they saw the Duchess Luise, in the Captain, the Baron von Müffling, the current governor of Berlin, Luciane was said to bear some similarities to young Lady Reitzenstein, and so on."⁹⁰

Heinrich von Kleist's close friend General Rühle von Lilienstern must have known it: after the catastrophic defeat of his army and state at Jena and Auerstedt, the now-unemployed Prussian officer is appointed by Duke Karl August to serve as "tutor to his son, Prince Bernhard."⁹¹ The official report from Paris contains a protest against that blatantly anti-Napoleonic career and for that very reason, if not others, is read by Goethe in his bureaucratic capacity. But the document also features the name of the brother-in-arms that Rühle had immortalized as the real-life model for Goethe's fictional Captain: Friedrich Karl Ferdinand von Müffling, known as Weiß, obviously also a captain. In spite of being a "serving officer and the son of the eponymous Prussian general," Müffling is appointed to the court in Weimar, where he receives "a generous salary as the president of a provincial council" and is drawn into the duke's "intimate circle."⁹² That should be reason enough to add that bout of Napoleonic rage to the bulk of Goethean philology and to turn not merely to conversation partners, secretaries, romantic female correspondents, and so on but also to the memoirs of a certain soldier who is, after all, Goethe's colleague at the Privy Council of the Duchy of Saxe-Weimar-Eisenach.⁹³

There is no trace of heartbreak or drowning in the printed sections of *Passages from My Life*. As a conscientious Prussian officer, Müffling arranges for the book to be released only posthumously by Berlin's foremost military publisher. The case of the childhood sweethearts is still a matter of circumstantial evidence. But apart from it, and therefore apart from Müffling's marital and parental bliss, the fictional Captain and the real-life duke overlap perfectly with each other.⁹⁴

Müffling is born on June 12, 1775, into an aristocratic family from Thuringia that had fallen into ruin in the aftermath of the Thirty Years' War. Since inheriting "a fortune is out of the question," he embarks on a military path, not unlike the soldier in the tale, with the aid of "patrons and his own personal inclination."⁹⁵ No one less than Duke Karl Wilhelm Ferdinand von Brunswick plays the role of Müffling's patron—a position similar to that of the Count in the novel. At the helm of his division during the Rhineland Campaign, the young first lieutenant gains valuable experience for the fight against revolutionary armies such as the French. Obviously, that experience inevitably also includes the tactics of "la petite guerre."⁹⁶ In the midst of combat, Müffling also gains lifelong friendships: so, for instance, in 1793, during the battles of Kaiserslautern and Pirmasens, he befriends a young regent and regiment commander named Duke Karl August of Saxe-Weimar-Eisenach.⁹⁷

Nevertheless, in 1797 his military life takes "a different turn," as he moves away from all the hussars, the free corps, and infantrymen he struggles to discipline and lead into battle and steps into the familiar domain of education. By his own account, the lieutenant is left "with nothing to do but sit behind books, thoroughly examine [his] tasks, so [he] may solve them to the best of [his] abilities." All that because a certain Colonel of Lecoq who has read Müffling's squibs on members of the General Staff decides, on the spot, "to bring him into [their] service."⁹⁸ In 1802–03, as first lieutenant and quartermaster, Müffling joins the newly formed General Staff at Potsdam, fashioned after the Napoleonic model. That historical moment, recorded with exemplary precision in Goethe's *Elective Affinities*, marks the birth of the educated officer (read: Captain). As soon as Eduard shows his guest to "a pleasant, spacious room in the right wing of the manor," the latter proceeds to "set up his books, papers and instruments, organizing them in preparation for his usual activities."⁹⁹

Nevertheless, the "usual activities" of classic fictional characters and, obviously, writers are anything but usual for the soldiers of Old Europe. Without his innate "turn for mathematics," Müffling would never have successfully completed Lecoq's assignments.¹⁰⁰ Those tasks involve mapping: first, a few potential battlegrounds; then, the broader war territory in Westphalia; and ultimately, in 1803, once he is named Prussian inspector—and with the help of a certain "astronomer Gauß"—the entire land of Thuringia.¹⁰¹ General staff maps, as they are still known nowadays—empirical reproductions of a region, with every peak and valley, obstacle and path—are a purely military invention, a must for Napoleon's or Clausewitz's field tactics and, for that reason, a strictly guarded secret.¹⁰² Without General Staff officers like Müffling, who replace the old-fashioned freehand maps with the trigonometry of plane tables and theodolites and thereby introduce "meridians"—even if only for a certain hill at Seeberg, instead of Greenwich[103]—one could hardly explore one's country on foot, neither in Thuringia nor anywhere else.[104] Following "the principle" of the General Staff, namely, that "a large-scale map is a weapon of war," Europe undergoes a mapping revolution after 1800. "To assuage Charlotte's hesitations about inviting the Captain, Eduard exclaims: 'We have only advantages and pleasures to expect from having him with us! . . . For a long time, I have wanted to have the estate and its environs surveyed; he will undertake and direct this task.'"[105] And so he does. Following old tradition, Goethe's other novels read space only in terms of symbolic code, dismissing any trace of topographic or even geographic identification and merely transposing Old Europe's postal address system into plot. No reader can therefore follow in the footsteps of *Wilhelm Meister's Apprenticeship* through Germany. In contrast, the military geographer Müffling intervenes in the *Elective Affinities* not merely at the level of the plot, in order to survey Eduard's estate and its environs; he also assists the author at the level of narrative construction and finally lends the Goethean novel the kind of topographic order that would become the trademark of realist texts (leading all the way up to Kafka's land surveyor). Not for nothing is the fictional Captain so "experienced" in surveying the estate "with a compass" and undertaking "trigonometric measurements";[106] not for nothing is he an expert in what cartographers call the "Müffling method": an innovation involving "cross-hatching" and "coloring with water paints" in order to mark slope gradients—an element of capital importance for national armies.[107] Last but not least, not for nothing can he identify the error at the root of Charlotte's dilettantish landscaping project, namely, "not cut[ting] away" "one corner of the cliff, not a very impressive one either," on the new path leading to the moss hut and not using the spare rocks to support the structure.[108] Precisely this tactic of topographic and strategic breakthroughs is ultimately deployed, once every construction on Eduard's estate, both under and above ground, is "consult[ed]" with the aid of the "map the Captain had made."[109] And that is how a fictional captain comes to mimic exactly Captain Müffling's exploits in Saxe-Weimar-Eisenach.

Around 1806, not only the "early friendship" between Eduard and the Captain but also the one between the ruling duke and the unemployed officer finally seem to bear fruit.[110] With the defeat at Jena and

Auerstedt, there is a sense of renewed urgency to the old "wartime camaraderie" between the two men, who, not unlike Eduard and the Captain, happen to share a first name.[111] For a Prussian general like Duke Karl August, Napoleon's victory only amounts to a lost battle, but for Captain Karl von Müffling, who has been appointed as officer to the duke's General Staff and who then obviously also "ha[s] the battlefield of Auerstedt surveyed," that victory involves much more: the loss of his patron, his father, his freedom, and any possible use King Friedrich Wilhelm might have for him.[112] The Duke of Brunswick, "with bloody bandages over his sightless orbits," and Müffling's father, himself a Prussian general, both die of their wounds.[113] Meanwhile, arrested by the French, the son is only released from captivity on his honor to see his dying father. All of which Müffling relates in writing to his old friend in Weimar, the duke. No wonder, then, that Eduard's first move in the game of elective affinities is to offer his wife the most precise personal information regarding a certain Captain who has "shared in some" of his life travels:[114]

> You know the unfortunate position [our friend, the Captain] is in, like so many others, quite without fault of his own. How disturbing it must be to a man of his education, talents and skills to be without employment and—I won't conceal any longer what I want for him: I would like us to invite him here for a time. . . .
>
> In his last letter there is a subdued tone of profound dissatisfaction; not that he is in any particular need, for he is quite able to live frugally, and I have taken care of the basic necessities; and it doesn't bother him to accept help from me, since we have been in each other's debt so much all our lives, off and on, that we can't calculate the actual status of our respective debit and credit—what bothers him is the fact that he has lost his job. His sole pleasure and passion lies in his many-sided talent and training, and his ability to use it for the benefit of others every hour of every day. And now to be idle, or to take up his studies again and learn new skills when he cannot use what he already has in full measure—in short, my dear, it is a distressing position, doubly and triply agonizing to him in his present isolation.[115]

One need only change the identity of the speaker in the preceding passage to read it as a historical document about Saxe-Weimar. "The Duke of Weimar was pleased with [Müffling]'s conduct as a soldier; but he had also come to treasure [his] ambition, [his] principles and [his] openness to everything [he] deemed noble and great, and thus wrote to the [Prussian] king before he left the army, recommending [him] in the warmest terms and concluding that [Müffling] is most valuable in every respect."[116] And once the Duke also finds out about Müffling's release from captivity—how else, if not by way of the real Captain's "last letter"?—he writes back, "What will you do in Halle? Come join me in Weimar; before you are replaced, now that our soldiering is done, I have civilian work for you. A family home stands ready for your use."[117]

In the novel Eduard is similarly "pressed" by the "mail[man]" to notify the Captain that he is soon to be released, that is to say, to write and invite him to stay in the "right wing of the house."[118] And it is there that Charlotte, or "the Duchess, [Karl August's] esteemed consort, welcomes [Müffling] as well."[119] Instead of being a poetic reflection of the writer's own marriage—itself triggered by the events at Jena and Auerstedt—the character constellation in the novel gradually forces the reader to interpret Eduard and Charlotte, the baron and the baroness, as a miniature version of the reigning ducal couple.[120] The court gossip circulated by General Rühle explains the meaning of *Elective Affinities* more clearly than any academic interpretation. Coincidentally, precisely during the months when Goethe, quarrelling with Karl August and his mistress, considers quitting his directorial position at the Weimar court theater and prefers working on his novel instead, Duchess Luise finds the willpower to "attend the festivities where Jagemann," like an Ottilie figure in flesh and blood, "appears" as Karl August's "second consort."[121] And, conversely, while working with the duke on raising Weimar's status to become the "central point" in Germany not merely for "art and science" but also for the anti-Napoleonic "German freedom," Müffling regards Karl August's "worthy and most intelligent wife" as his "only confidant[e]" apart from the duke himself.[122] What wonder, then, that the Weimar court gossip "saw in Charlotte the Duchess Luise." Between 1807 and 1813, much to the displeasure of Goethe, who is quite keen on Napoleonic breakfast receptions, Legion of Honor medals, and printing privileges, Müffling literally operates a secret service together with the ducal pair. That secret service, however, needs to be urgently hidden from the prying eyes of Napoleon's ubiquitous agents and spies. The cover is provided by two fictions, of which the first and most effective one is German classical culture itself: "The large literary correspondence kept up in Weimar with all parts of Germany," which famously culminates in Goethe's world literature, "facilitates the news-department," simply because they can hide the more explosive news from Napoleon's highly developed system of postal interception.¹²³ The Duke of Weimar's "secret plan" to turn "his residence" into "the center of German freedom" also grants "the central point for art and science" its strategic function in the first place. And should poetry and philosophy not do as a cover, the duke also grants his Prussian secret service privy chief a higher title: Müffling is appointed vice president of the Provincial Council.

Formed by civilians, the council obviously has no knowledge of the tactical and operational breakthroughs that automatically derive from the military origin of all modern engineering technology. An order from Karl August to build a modern roadway and replace Weimar's dirt roads with lumber and firewood is deemed impossible. That changes with Müffling's arrival, even though, or precisely because, he understands only "the mathematical aspect" of the technical committee's affairs. Not unlike his fictional double, the Captain favors "the shortest way." That there is a "steep cliff" preventing "direct access" poses no difficulties to a mathematician or a General Staff plane table surveyor such as Müffling:¹²⁴

> After leveling and checking everything thoroughly, I discovered that one could cut through the cliff at an angle and reuse the blown-up rocks for the road. I prepared a different version of the project. My committee dismissed it, the duke approved it, and thus I saw myself forced to take the construction in my own hands; by mid-1807, it was ready. . . . The costs had remained below budget. My structure received high praise. I learned on the go. The locals named the hilltop with the cliff wall after me, the "Müffling Hill." Gradually, the duke assigned the commissioned gardens and castle to me, although I was not in his civil service.¹²⁵

Müffling's roadwork, gardens, and stately architecture are once again featured in the novel, no longer as the miniature model of a path leading up to a moss hut, but rather as full-scale spatial and political representations. While the fictional characters (as well as their interpreters) keep reading the park's aesthetics as second nature, the General Staff politics have long taken over the scene. Everything follows its course, just as the pedagogical assistant has predicted: an accomplished server acts as a civil servant, even without being in the service of an actual state. The distinction between fiction and history merely allows the novel to conceal or obscure, once again, the affairs of civil engineering invented by the duke and his old friend as a cover for their anti-Napoleonic secret politics, until all that is left is the famous text of "social relations" "symbolically understood." If Müffling's and Karl August's politics deploy literature as a cover-up for a secret "news-department," then literature, in its turn, conceals politics in the form of a love story. A high-ranking civil servant is reduced to the status of an unemployed captain; a ruling ducal court is brought down to the level of a couple from the lower aristocracy. The social or communal element thus assumes the status of ultimate reason precisely at the historical moment when technology and politics successfully take hold of and functionally reconfigure everyday life.

Consequently, Müffling's "part" in the anti-Napoleonic secret service "doings" in Weimar is to "avoid all that could compromise the princely pair" in the eyes of Napoleon's representatives and spies and, "should a victim be required, to offer [himself] to be that victim."[126] By contrast, his fictional double in the novel, the Captain, is driven to self-sacrifice or Goethean renunciation in order to prevent a baron and his wife from compromising themselves with imaginary adulterous escapades. Müffling's departure from Weimar is a military-historical event; instead, the Captain's exit from Goethe's small fictional universe is reduced to a romantic intermezzo. Traveling though the region, the fictional count is impressed with the Captain's "very serious[] and systematic[]" work, and it is precisely in the miniature model of the novel that the former "knows a position to which the man is completely suited"; besides, "by recommending him," he can also "cement a noble friendship of [his] in the happiest manner."[127] "Two letters" soon arrive from the noble talent scout: "one suitable for showing others, setting forth fair prospects for the future, and another, containing a definite offer of a significant position at court and in society right away, promotion to major, a respectable salary and other benefits," which "by reason of various accompanying circumstances . . . was to be kept secret for the moment."[128]

Precisely these circumstances that are kept hidden by both the Captain and the author are at the center of the diplomatic and military activities that ultimately lead to the so-called Wars of Liberation and the formation of a Prussian General Staff. The Peace of Tilsit finds Müffling "waiting in vain to be replaced" by the Prussian state and army. Only after the harsh peace treaty is signed does Scharnhorst, Prussia's chief of General Staff avant la lettre, respond to Müffling's repeated pleas, explaining that "he is once again free" to take up "his position with the General Staff" in Berlin, but since the king currently "lacks the means, he requests of all those appointed to support themselves until the king calls in the new army directly from Berlin. From this communication," Müffling "clearly understood that Scharnhorst was making all preparations for a better future, for taking arms against the tyrant again."[129]

That kind of strategic foresight is what sets him apart from his friend and "fellow sufferer" Karl August. For the duke "thought that moment is nigh. He intended to offer his services to the king again and spoke to [Müffling] of his wish that [he] remain in his service until then, and later, together, they once more join the Prussian army."[130]

The time is July 1807, in other words, the time when Goethe drafts his novel. To wrap up part I, he has Eduard draw up his last will and decide to join the army, now that "the war . . . had recently broken out again." Not unlike Karl August, "halfhearted military affairs had greatly annoyed him during his youth; that was why he had left the service. Now it was a glorious feeling to set out under a general of whom he could say to himself: under his leadership, death is probable and victory certain."[131]

But pipe dreams such as Eduard's or Karl August's do not come to pass. Not for nothing does the fictional count or the historical chief of the General Staff write "two letters," thus marking a clear separation between imagined war in the present and strategic war in the future. And precisely since Müffling is "firm" in his principle "never to fight for Napoleon, which would be hard to avoid if [he] [immediately] enrolled in the Prussian military service again," he sets out on his career as an officer fighting in the liberation wars instead. He "sends Scharnhorst a petition addressed to the king, to grant [him] leave"—and thereby also access to "the service in Weimar," "with the understanding that [he] would immediately join the military again if His Majesty the king took up the arms of liberty again."[132] To which Frederick William III of Prussia—seeking, despite his officers, to keep open the fair prospects (as the count would put it) of future liberation wars, replies by promoting Baron von Müffling to the rank of major. In other words, the entire six years of service the Captain spends at the court in Weimar turn out to be a mere "discharge . . . for the sake of appearance"—something obviously only Scharnhorst knows. In reality, that stage represents Müffling's "reinstatement in the army," which nevertheless "must remain secret" until the "outbreak of hostilities" against Napoleon. The Weimar intermezzo thus ends precisely on that day in March 1813 when the king's *Proclamation to His People* sounds "the signal" for Müffling, as well as so many other patriots, to rejoin the ranks of the Prussian army.[133]

And thus, from among all the sad, doomed characters in *Elective Affinities*, only the Captain has a future. In 1813 the "quietly methodical" Müffling takes up his position as quartermaster general of a brilliant field marshal who lacks professional service training: August von Gneisenau.[134] In 1815, long before General Carl-Heinrich von Stülpnagel or General Dietrich von Choltitz, he is appointed as the first German commander of Paris. One year later, we find the former military geographer at work, surveying along with his erstwhile French enemies the future world war territories, from Flanders to Dunkirk. And in 1821 he succeeds General Rühle von Lilienstern, his literary critic and colleague from his Weimar days, when the latter steps down as the chief of the Second War Department of the Berlin War Ministry. In this regard, too, he benefits from his old friendships. The king, wanting to ensure that Müffling, as his personal "confidant," is not somehow placed below Rühle, his junior, creates a rank especially for him: chief of General Army Staff. Its star would continue to shine brightly until the Day of Potsdam.[135]

As chief of General Staff of the Prussian Army, Lieutenant General Müffling first and almost matter-of-factly continues what the unemployed Captain has merely started: with immediate effect, officers are also to receive a "'learned instruction,' as the saying went: the number of hours of instruction in languages and all other fields of knowledge, ranging from philosophy and history to mathematics and natural sciences exceeded by far the specifically military disciplines." That is precisely why Clausewitz writes his first theoretical treatise, *On War*, "under Müffling's aegis."[136]

But as opposed to his novelist, Chief of General Staff Müffling has "a turn for mathematics" and therefore goes one step further than him. "By God and nature," Goethe's word is "properly that of word, language and image," as he is "totally incapable of operating in any way with signs and numbers, through which highly gifted minds communicate with ease."[137] For him, there are no codes other than those of language, love, and the narrow circle of the nuclear family. Over at the Prussian General Staff, now boasting Major General Karl von Grolman's new Division for Trigonometry and Topography, Müffling decides to bring back that mode of communication with signs and numbers, one he had studied as a young lieutenant, and approaches the Master of All Numbers: Carl Friedrich Gauß. In vain, however, does he, along with Alexander von Humboldt, plead to convince first Gauß himself and then the authorities to bring the greatest cartographer of the era to Berlin as state advisor. And it may well be that this very failure of technological transfer inspires him to come up with his own idea for solving the issue of topographical instruction—a solution that, in its turn, would gain great popularity as a small-scale application.[138] To "train General Staff officers to work through certain strategic and tactical queries but avoid costly expeditions," Müffling invents no less than the sandbox. "It was something quite new for its time," yet maybe less so for a Captain who has emerged from the small-scale model of *Elective Affinities*. Be that as it may: Müffling's sandbox, with its replicas of valleys and mountains, continues to replace the old-European model of the chessboard or theater of operations until World War II.

To triumph over that new matter, the that-ness of the earth, the members of the General Staff also require a brand-new form, or whatness. As a news communications expert, Müffling is the one to serve information to the General Staff. He ensures the military takeover of Napoleon's truly revolutionary optical telegraph. Information, in its strictly technical sense, finally puts an end to a textual monopoly whose swan song is precisely that network of love letters, mother tongues, and poetic works. The fictional Captain himself liquidates the condition of possibility for romantic fiction.

"Field Marshal Moltke has been constant in his high admiration of Müffling's works and stressed that all who had been so fortunate to meet him should feel the same. This may well be the most consequential and conclusive judgment expressed about General Field Marshal Müffling's personality."[139]

V

A: "Then what, then what, of love, of love . . . ?"[140]

B: Not much remains to be said, and even less to be written about it. Level-headed as usual, Charlotte remarks at some point: "We think we are acting of our own free will . . . but really, if we look more closely, we are simply [compelled] to follow the pitch, the inclination of our time."[141] The novel is merely the report of the compulsion to follow the plans of a General Staff and the inclinations of a female educator, celebrating her silent victory above a baron's grave and leaving no one cold but the reporter himself. It goes without saying that love, or else Eduard, is pressed to follow a beloved with pedagogical aspirations all the way to her night quarters. That this half-hearted compulsion is an answer to yet another compulsion, the compulsion to love, also goes without saying. But, under the given conditions, Eduard, or love, cannot do anything wiser than seek death in a war that has launched the advance of central Europe according to the plans of the General Staff. It is possible that, while doing so, he was fated to encounter the victor and his words of politics?

A: Incidentally, Eduard may have found his reporter in Erfurt, in audience with the victor.[142] But this, rather, is a matter of poetry and truth. Back to structural matters, then: does Eduard, when he toys with his own life for the sake of love, not also play, both slyly and fruitlessly, the role of the emperor of signifiers?

B: Precisely. "Our goal is to restore in them the sovereign freedom displayed by Humpty Dumpty when he reminds Alice that he is, after all, master of the signifier, even if he is not master of the signified from which its being derived its shape."[143] For the signified from which Eduard derives his own shape is unfortunately called Ottilie and turns out to be the only false sentence in the novel. Not even those attending "higher-daughters" institutions should say, "You cannot walk beneath palm trees with impunity."[144] All the persons concerned know, after all, that under the conditions imposed by civil servants and mothers, Eduard's barony becomes a penalty box, a punishment chamber. But to export that punishment to foreign lands beneath palm trees means turning that transgression into law. What kind of a lover is this, who recoils in horror at the thought that beneath other, brighter skies, humans might also turn out to be different?

A: In compliance with the law, they might turn out to be the same.

B: As opposed to hopes, desires are not concerned with lovers awakening "to a blessed [world]" but sleeping together in a beautiful one.[145]

PART V

Pynchon's War

CHAPTER 14

On a Novel That Would Not Only Be Fiction . . .

TRANSLATED BY MICHAEL WUTZ

. . . is a title that—with an audible nod to Jacques Lacan—seeks to capture the fact that the beauty of Thomas Pynchon's *Gravity's Rainbow* is grounded in its inverted relation to the real. The modern novel—if you permit a literary scholar to make such old-fashioned retro-references—notably began its career with Cervantes, who explicitly fictionalized all of the knightly epics that, in the pre-Gutenberg era, were not yet subject to the distinction between fiction and reality. The more Don Quixote, in all his knightliness, tries to turn those books into literal reality, the more hopelessly they reveal their fictionality.

That comforting distinction was acceptable to bourgeois readers for quite some time, but less so to their wives and children. The moment the next subject—following Hegel's phrase—sows his wild oats on the way to state power, he was willing to clearly differentiate state powers from novels, which only dealt, after all, with the likes of him.[1] Even the takeover of fictional structure by the modern sciences did not change much in that regard. When, around 1900, technical universities began to encourage their talented students to read science fiction or nonfiction (as was the case with a certain Hans Dominik in Berlin-Charlottenburg), they tended to be more interested in affirming their own glory than in the prospect of shattering the boundary between fiction and a constructed reality.

That is precisely what seems to define the unique quality of *Gravity's Rainbow*. Pynchon did not just attend Nabokov's lectures at Cornell but

---

This chapter is from Kittler's "Über einen Roman, der nicht bloß Fiktion wäre" (undated, unpublished manuscript with handwritten corrections, in German).

was also working as a technical writer for Boeing, before he was at all able to write a novel about the V-2, the German-American technology transfer, and the enabling conditions for a Pax Americana. Pynchon's lawyers recently blocked the scheduled German translation, or any other form of distribution, of the short text "Togetherness," which stems from that time period of the military-industrial complex. This essay about collaboration appeared in the military journal *Aerospace Safety* and identified its author not only in the title, where he figures as Thomas H. Pynchon, Bomarc Aero-Space Department, Boeing Airplane Company, Seattle, but also as a theorist of the military-industrial complex itself. As the opening sentence itself makes already clear, "Airlifting the IM-99A missile, like marriage, demands a certain amount of 'togetherness' between Air Force and contractor."[2] Put differently: while the Minuteman is under construction, it is being tended by the experts at Boeing, and when in flight, by the experts in the U.S. Air Force. What is critical for its well-being, and rife with danger, is its intersection, its interface, its marriage, or, as Derrida would say: the postal delivery of the projectile, which, understood as a missile, is itself a delivery.

That is young Thomas H. Pynchon's helping hand to the industry and the Pentagon, so that they can join hands in avoiding missile disasters, if only for the benefit of *Aerospace Safety*. *Gravity's Rainbow* presents exactly the same problem but in reverse. Several characters and technology-transfer experts are working at the intersection of V-2 missile production in Nordhausen and the missiles' deployment in the Netherlands but with the singular goal of absconding with the sacred projectile during transfer. If the obvious narrative effect is that the military-industrial complex, as Eisenhower so aptly phrased it, disintegrates, the novelistic effect is less evident, because it transfigures a text that initially appeared to be a run-of-the-mill fiction into the negative image of an instruction or a blueprint authored by an engineer. Just as Pynchon was reputed to have written even his private letters on graph paper, technology insists on itself precisely through such an inversion.[3] The secret text, which (half) emerges from under the palimpsest of fiction, likely reaches its readers as a warning that even the wildest figments of imagination—all metaphysics to the contrary—may contain a kernel of truth.

Readers, in that sense, are repeating a version of the author's nasty surprise. Following the publication of his Trystero novel, Pynchon, if we are to trust *Playboy*'s reporting, allegedly received an anonymous letter claiming that the plugged-up horn—the secret postal sign of the fictive Trystero—indeed served as a symbol for a private postal system in the late Middle

Ages. Pynchon went to the library, searched for the book that was indicated as the source, and corroborated the truth of his informant's claim but also that said book was not published until shortly after *The Crying of Lot 49* had appeared.[4]

Such coincidences between fact and fiction are hardly attributable to extrasensory perception, as Pynchon himself allegedly surmised, but rather to the novel's technique of composition. It is almost inconceivable that *Gravity's Rainbow* could have been written without informants—and we are not talking about low-level sneaks but informers in high-level positions. Now, if you substitute only a couple of letters in the name of Marvy, the tragicomic U.S. major charged with hunting down V-2 technicians during Operation Paperclip, you have the literary Marvy morphing back into his historical model, Major Staver.[5] That's something you can read up on in any nonfiction book about the transatlantic technology transfer these days but not, as far as I know, in any form of documentation before 1973 and the publication of *Gravity's Rainbow*.

If we focused exclusively on Major Marvy, who ends up surrendering all his attributes of masculinity in Slothrop's pig costume, one would be tempted to dismiss such coincidences as a satirical footnote. If, however, you factor in Slothrop's somber antagonist—the commander of the German Army Research Center [Heeresversuchsanstalt] Peenemünde and, in the final months of the war, of the special rocket artillery corps—the novel's historical precision borders on the visionary. I have tried to show elsewhere how the transformation of the civilian engineer of the Wehrmacht by the name of Weissmann into the maniacal commander of the Waffen-SS, code-named Blicero, projects onto a singular figure what, in the empirical logic of Peenemünde, is reflected in the change of guards from the German Army Ordnance Office [Heereswaffenamt] to the despotic regime of SS Major General Dr. Hans Kammler.[6] This yet-unexplored and dark chapter of German World War II history—Kammler was widely seen as the successor to Albert Speer, before his mysterious death—gives the figure of Blicero, precisely because of his paranoia, the look of sourced material. Blicero's grim observation addressed to his model son and lover, according to which "fathers are carriers of the virus of Death" and "sons are the infected," seems not to have gone unnoticed by Pynchon himself, given that SS General Kammler was reputed to have had the same abiding phobia of photographic portraits as Blicero's creator.[7]

I don't feel the need to supplement the historical examples of Marvy and Weißmann with parallel examples from the realm of engineering, because readers of *Gravity's Rainbow* are no doubt aware that they are not spared any engineering details when it comes to the description of the V-2 guidance system or pilots describing their first experience with space suits made from Imipolex. The real problem, rather, as I suggested, is identifying the sources of such knowledge. The first circuit diagram of said guidance system, which was (as we know, thanks to the Museum of Technology, only as of last year) essentially also the first real-time analog computer, was, to the best of my knowledge, first published by the National Air and Space Museum in Washington, D.C., but not until exactly a decade after *Gravity's Rainbow*.[8] In this nonfiction text, the circuit diagram consists of a free gyroscope, an inductive AC power conduit, a power supply with diode bridges, and a triode switch that will, upon reaching a specified missile velocity, switch the beam control relay to an off position. The circuit diagram described in the novel consists of a ballistic pendulum, a moving coil, a transformer, an electrolytic cell, a bridge of diodes, and, last but not least, one tetrode.[9] The differences between the two are minuscule, and the probability of an informer existing before any public dissemination is overwhelming. Perhaps there were some leftover Peenemünde engineers among the staff when Boeing designed the Minuteman in Seattle.

As a revocation of "Togetherness," however, *Gravity's Rainbow* processes all of this intercepted, tapped, or speculative information—which circulated only as state secrets in the case of the real thing—but never in the way it was intended by its bearers. Rather, it is being leaked to an opposing power, in which a certain Richard Nixon in the novel still believes, unlike any enlightened contemporary in the realistic 1990s, but which supposedly emerges from within the novel's readership. (This becomes even more evident and striking in the anti-TV novel *Vineland*.)

In 1944 the guidance system of the V-2 was among the best-kept secrets of the war, simply because Churchill's engineering experts didn't even anticipate the existence of such technology, instead declaring that any rocket flying through a presumable vacuum would simply be uncontrollable.[10] Today the same circuit diagram is a historical document for museums of technology and novels about a world war. Pynchon, however, the offspring of one of the oldest families of New England, presumably did not write *Gravity's Rainbow* to broadcast the obsolete secrets of the loser of World War $n-1$ but to present a model on how novels on either side of fiction could sneak up on the secrets of contemporary superpowers. The inversion of the logic of "Togetherness" that *Gravity's Rainbow* performs in itself testifies to that. So do references to other novels, no less paranoid, that could shed light on inconclusive circumstances. And so does, finally, the incredibly sad opening of *Vineland*, in which the secret carrier pigeons appearing in a dream morph into screeching California blue jays when the dreamer awakens.[11] Just as no roll of the dice can abolish coincidence, no novel can abolish the indispensability of a power that authors its own dreams and fictions.

"Is it [Aggregate 4, a.k.a. v-2], then, really never to find you again? Not even in your worst times of night, with pencil words on your page only Δt from the things they stand for?"[12]

De Nostalgia

TRANSLATED BY GEOFFREY WINTHROP-YOUNG

Heimödil, the Old High German word from which *Heimat* originates, simply meant "estate" or "property."[1] The Greeks would have said *oikos*, maybe even *ousia*. According to behavioral science's territorial imperative, Heimat is what you defend when the enemy approaches. If the defenses are breached, you may be lucky enough to escape abroad into those foreign realms known in Old High German as *eli-lenti* or *elend*.[2]

In the following, I will not be talking about these types of Heimat and elend, home and misery, because they are as old as building, dwelling, and settling themselves. But there is a Heimat far removed from economic considerations, one not invented until the modern age. Its destiny is to be overrun by tanks and defended with bazookas. It arrived so late not only because there were no tanks before World War I and no concentrated use of them before World War II. The very concept of Heimat is strategic rather than economic. This is the misery I will be addressing, with the very likely result of producing yet another piece of *Heimatliteratur*.

To write about Heimat, it already has to be lost, even if there happen to be no armies sweeping over it. In other words, there must be homesickness [*Heimweh*]—not necessarily among those who have gone abroad but as a concept peddled by members of general staffs. The latter, however, came into being during the campaigns against Napoleon that these staffs themselves euphemistically called *Befreiungskriege*, or wars of liberation.

Originally published under the same title in *Literatur und Provinz: Das Konzept Heimat in der neueren Literatur*, edited by Hans-Georg Pott (Paderborn: Ferdinand Schöningh, 1986), 153–68; and translated by Geoffrey Winthrop-Young in *Cultural Politics* 11, no. 3 (2015): 395–405.

On the eve of these wars, Friedrich Schiller completed *Wilhelm Tell* (1804). The play amounts to a strategic program for the liberation of a home territory; its historical logic was revealed by Hansgünther Heyme's Stuttgart production as a series of German savior scenarios from Tell to Erich Ludendorff to Adolf Hitler and on.[3] Homesickness is part of these scenarios. In act 1, scene 2, the dispute between young Ulrich von Rudenz and his uncle, the aged Baron Attinghausen, demonstrates that homesickness—both word and sentiment—is not the exclusive property of those who have left their native land and people. It also afflicts Attinghausen, a retired officer firmly rooted in his home soil, who has only led his own national armies "into battle."[4] Young Rudenz, by contrast, a prototype of future Swiss mercenaries, prefers to "despise" his "native land."[5] He bitterly complains about having to stay put on his uncle's estate, while beyond the Alps the Hapsburg armies are pursuing military glory.

> My helmet here, my shield are stained with rust,
> The trumpet's voice sends forth its martial challenge,
> The herald cries his summons to the lists,
> But no sound comes to these sequestered valleys;
> I only hear the melancholy note
> Of cowbells and the dreary *ranz des vaches*.[6]

The eighty-five-year-old Attinghausen (who in historical fact was younger than this antagonist nephew) denounces mercenary armies (from which all later national armies emerged by means of nationalization). Instead, he champions homesickness and national armies—that is, the two preconditions for so-called wars of liberation. He laments that Hapsburg emperors use "our"—that is, Swiss—"blood for all the wars they choose to wage" and have young Swiss men like Rudenz make up their mercenary armies, which at one point constituted Europe's leading infantry. If Rudenz wants to heed the trumpet's voice of a "king" or emperor, to whom—much like in later times Napoleon—"the world belongs," then this means to Attinghausen "that your home / Has now become for you an alien place."[7] The old officer invents both a new misery and a new home—one its inhabitants stand to lose if they do not join the militias of 1813. But should his nephew venture abroad to become an imperial mercenary, Attinghausen predicts that "the melancholy note of cowbells" will sound very different to his Swiss ears:

> The day will come when bitter tears will flow
> And you will yearn for this your mountain home;

For that which now you spurn with brittle pride,
The *Kuhreihn* and its simple melody,
Shall echo in your ears in distant lands
And break your heart with longing for your own.⁸

Classic Schiller verses that, once again, challenged Goethe's realistic spleen. On January 13, 1804, the latter informed Attinghausen and his creator "that a Swiss does not feel homesickness when hearing the ranz des vaches in another country, for, as far as I know, it is not heard elsewhere; he feels it because he does not hear it, his ear is not hearing what it has always been accustomed to hear since his youth."⁹ It doesn't matter whether home amounts to a positive acoustic hallucination (as in Schiller) or a negative one (as Goethe and generations of psychiatrists would have it); in either case, it arouses the feelings of a new human. But while Schiller's drama still presented these sentiments as painful, lachrymose yearning, Goethe's letter introduced the technical term: *homesickness*. Which in 1804 was so alien to High German ears that Schiller avoided it.

Homesickness—"long known" either "in substance" or at least to those specializing in the history of concepts—is first recorded in 1592 as a dialectal word among the Swiss mercenaries whom France was allowed to recruit up until the Storming of the Bastille.¹⁰ (The glory of the Swiss Confederacy had come to a bloody end at the Battle of Marignano in 1515.) Schiller's Attinghausen thus ascribes words and sentiments to Rudenz that in terms of military history correspond to the introduction of modern infantry. Goethe's letter, in turn, adds psycho-medicinal details that emerged in 1688 as part of new nosologies and therapies. In that year Johannes Hofer, not coincidentally a medical student at the Swiss University of Basel, defended the first "*Dissertatio medica* DE NOSTALGIA, *or Homesickness*."¹¹

It was a discursive event when Hofer's homesickness—grecized in memory of Homeric heroes like Odysseus—became a literary and thus High German term. In bygone mercenary days, Hofer argued, the only viable remedy for homesick Swiss souls was to return home.¹² But this all-too-easy therapy is no longer an option if Heimat (as Schiller would have it) is always already sentimentally lost and therefore needs to be taught to people. Such a task, however, is beyond the power of medical doctors; it calls for poets and women.

Precisely this sentimentalization, which Attinghausen unsuccessfully tries to communicate to his nephew, is brought about by the end of the play with help from an unexpected source. Berta von Bruneck, an Austrian heiress for whom Rudenz wanted to cross over to the Hapsburg mercenaries, herself crosses the lines in the other direction and joins the insurgents, thereby attaining Swiss citizenship and curing her lover. The prospective mercenary turns into an aristocratic partisan. Followed by peasants armed with clubs and torches, he storms a foreign-held castle, thereby prefiguring a social constellation indispensable for the wars of liberation against Austrian—or rather French—emperors.

Carl Schmitt's admirable *Theory of the Partisan* starts from the premise that new forms of military irregularity became possible only once Napoleon, building on the revolutionary state and the no less revolutionary *levée en masse*, provided the "regularity of the state, as well as of the army," with a "new, exact resolution."[13] Because Napoleon's campaigns, in the words of Prussian officer and publicist Julius von Voss, were "a partisan mobilization on a grand scale," Prussian soldiers had to graduate from Frederician drill to independence, patriotism, and partisanship.[14] Precisely this became law with Frederick Wilhelm III's Landsturm edict of April 21, 1813.

With the subsequent effect of abolishing the divine right of kings, a Prussian sovereign commanded his subjects "to refuse to obey any enemy directive, and instead to injure the enemy with all possible means." Among the means mentioned were "axes, pitchforks, scythes and shotguns," as well as "intemperate, unrestrained mobs," and the paradoxical command to disobey the French security forces.[15] Distinctions between foreign and domestic politics, martial and civil law, army and police, all of which had been central to the cabinet wars fought by the ancien régimes, fell by the wayside, only to be replaced by (in Schmitt's words) a tellurian, Acherontic, and, above all, homogeneous Heimat—for example, Prussia—though this first had to be taught to its many Brandenburgian, Pomeranian, Mecklenburgian, and Schleswigian subjects. Edicts and administrative acts were unable to turn conscripts or mercenaries into partisans of a home country. The foundation of this new Heimat required poetry. And that is the historical a priori of all Heimatliteratur.

In his "Plan for the Preparation of a Popular Uprising," the foundational document even of Stalin's 1941 partisan homeland love, Neidhart von Gneisenau, the first chief of the Prussian General Staff avant la lettre, recommended that the later Ministry of Culture be involved in the production of gallophobia and the people's spirit. His old-fashioned king noted in the margins: "Usable at best for poetry." To which Gneisenau responded: "Religion, prayer, love of the sovereign, of the fatherland, and of virtue are nothing but poetry; there is no uplifting of the spirit without poetic mood.

Those who act only in a coldly calculating manner will become rigid egotists. The security of all thrones is built on poetry."[16]

The uprising of the people as an uplifting of hearts—Finance Minister Karl vom Stein zum Altenstein had already recognized this in 1807—cannot do without poetry, that is, without the official "usage of writers." According to Altenstein, "men who forge ahead of an age will soon pull its voice with them. Their own voices may not be immediately understood and are therefore of less importance than those of journalists. But in time they will take hold of public opinion. And when the power of their voice reveals itself, it will be too late, even for Napoleon, to curtail the effects."[17] Sentences that come with the precision of a General Staff that has eliminated all questions of authorship and hermeneutics, of fictionality and the ivory tower status of poetry. Sentences that also inspired Heinrich von Kleist, Altenstein's subordinate, to produce the first piece of German *Heimatliteratur*, or, in Carl Schmitt's more precise words, "the greatest partisan poem of all times": the drama *The Battle of Hermann*.[18]

In contrast to Schiller's naive-sentimental ambiguities, Kleist's point of departure is clearly circumscribed: a Napoleon by the name of Augustus has occupied half of a Germania made up of principalities whose sluggish sovereigns are mired in cabinet wars and coalitions with or against Rome. The result is as predicted by Gneisenau: rigid egotism and cold calculation are undermining their thrones. Kleist confronts them with a leader who—located on a line reaching from Leonidas over Tell to Spain's anti-French *guerrilleros*—brings state, military, and the homeland up to modern standards. Hermann, the ideal leader, knows full well that the Germanic tribes would be lost if they, "a rabble horde, / emerging from the trees," were they to pit themselves "against well-ordered cohorts, / Accompanied wherever they go by that unfailing spirit."[19] To defeat Varus or Napoleon and—in the words of Kleist or [Joseph] Goebbels—raise "a black flag" over Rome's "desolate ruins," Germania has to develop partisan tactics.[20] This, however, demands a new kind of love for one's home.

Hermann's first proposal: as soon as Varus marches in with his three legions, all Germanic princes are to pursue a scorched-earth strategy—gather up women and children, pawn all resources and monetary reserves, destroy all agricultural lands, and burn down the entire infrastructure. In complete accordance, Hitler's Führer Directive of March 19, 1945, orders the destruction of all "military transport, and communication, facilities, industrial establishments, and supply depots, as well as anything else of value within Reich territory, which could in any way be used by the enemy immediately or within the foreseeable future for the prosecution of the war."[21] Unfortunately, Germania's other leaders react to Hermann's proposal much as Albert Speer, the gauleiters, and the managers of the future economic miracle did to Hitler's directive.[22] They thwart the scorched-earth command because they do not realize that Hermann's "freedom" and Hitler's "struggle for the existence of our people" both entail that one first obliterate all Heimat.[23] Only as a desolate ruin can Germany likewise turn an imperial metropolis like Rome into a desolate ruin and confine to dust "all the enemies of Brandenburg."[24] Such are the preconditions of final victory.

The prince of the Cherusci is forced to act on his own. Only a loyal sidekick and efficient signals officer called Eginhardt, who in Peymann's Bochum production was located in a gray zone between the SS and the Red Army Faction, is there to help him bring about the preventive destruction of the homeland.[25] When vandalizing Romans pillage three Cherusci villages, Hermann's secret propaganda raises the number to seven.[26] When Varus, obeying the old-fashioned distinction between military and police, orders the immediate execution of the Roman marauders, Hermann obtains clemency for them—only to then incite disobedience against the civil authorities of the occupiers, exactly as the Landsturm edict had done.[27] (Which is, of course, what territorial princes for good reasons never do to each other.) Hermann, in short, has no need for "well-behaved Latins"— that is, for human enemies like Varus.[28] As a partisan leader, he is "counting / on fire, violence, robbery, and murder, and all the horrors of unfettered [or total] war," in order to inflame Cherusci and all of Germania "with hatred of the Romans."[29] Absolute enmity does not come naturally to people; it is an artifact of military psychology cooked up by general staffs. For precisely this reason, people first have to be deprived of their Heimat, in the old sense of the word: they have to lose their estates and properties. In glorious anticipation of the SS commando unit that, posing as Poles, seized the German Gleiwitz radio station and thus triggered a world war, Eginhardt recruits a "small party of able men" to roam the roads of Cherusca "disguised as Romans" and has them "wherever they pass / torch, burn and plunder."[30]

But while *Sonderkommandos* composed exclusively of men may incite hatred of the Romans, they cannot instill love of one's homeland. As in the case Schiller's Rudenz, a woman must come into play. Hermann orders that the body of a Cherusci girl called Hally, who was raped by Roman soldiers and subsequently killed by her own father, be divided into fifteen pieces, and her *corps morcelé* be sent "by fifteen messengers" to the fifteen German tribes.[31] People are, quite literally, taught to be homesick. Fifteen German states and their equally divided subjects turn into one homogeneous nation, whose destiny is to wage a people's war and whose desire is the reunification of a woman—The Woman—in the imaginary.

La femme—we know it from Lacan—*n'existe pas*. Hally disintegrates into fifteen decaying pieces of flesh in the real in order to turn into pure information in the symbolic. On the eve of the decisive battle, part of the corpse is resurrected as Woman or Mother. In the middle of the Teutoburg Forest, Varus encounters a ghostly apparition who, as the "Ancient Mother of Cherusca," predicts his downfall (and who later graces the stamps of the Second Reich). "'Mother,'" *Gravity's Rainbow* accordingly states, "that's a civil-service category. . . . They're the policemen of the soul."[32] Without a maternal there can be no tellurian home of warriors, whose strategy is symbolized not by Mao's fish navigating the waters but by the giant Anstaeus grounded in his mother Earth.

The finale of *The Battle of Hermann* makes everything clear. Varus is not defeated in a pitched battle but by a Heimat that, in stark contrast to old-European military sciences, encompasses everything that once made war difficult, if not impossible: swamps and forests, winters and mountains. Whether the swamps are located in the Pribjet marshes or along the Weser, whether the forests are in the vicinity of Velikiye Luki or Teutoburg, makes no difference, as long as the partisans of the new Heimat are sufficiently familiar with their Ancient Mother, or, in more straightforward terms, with the surrounding topography.[33] Hermann's plan of action is based in its entirety on the fact that legions "on low swampy ground" stand no chance against unified Germanic tribes "ranged on wooden heights above."[34] "The army," complains a Roman officer, "is wearing half Cherusca on its feet."[35] In other words: Napoleon's "spirit" and its "well-ordered cohorts" are doomed because Earth itself joins her sons as a fellow combatant.

Kleist's *Battle of Hermann* is no longer a drama about subjects and acts of consciousness but a set of guidelines on how to wage a popular and partisan war. *Bolshaya narodnaya voina*, Stalin called it, the Great Patriotic War, before thrusting from Velikiye Luki back across the Pribjet marshes toward the Reich Chancellery.[36] To wage war, you need to chart this earth with sufficient love, that is, with all swamps and forests, mountains and valleys—which is exactly what the strategists of Old Europe's cabinet wars had failed to do. Rather than digging into the dirt and muddying their hands, they indulged in abstract, paper-bound mathematical combinatorics with endless escalations of attacks, counterattacks, and counter-counterattacks. It was Carl von Clausewitz, the thinker of the wars of liberation, who put an end to such interactionist symmetries. His famous theorem of the superiority of defense over offense was grounded in topographic realities; indeed, his grandiose chapter on "Terrain" recommended that "truly national armies with a population in arms" make use of "heavily uneven and obstructed terrain."[37] Accordingly, it was the Prussian General Staff, adopting *On War* as its bible, that established a Topographical Bureau, to which we owe the many hiking maps used by red-socked tourists exploring whatever forests and swamps, mountains and valleys, have remained in their cemented Heimat.[38] Not to mention the motorized tourism that every summer rolls or flies over Europe's borders, from the North Cape to Crete, in order to replay the High Command's panzer and airborne operations under peacetime conditions. "The dead ride fast," Carl Schmitt noted, "and if they become motorized they move even faster."[39]

. . . And with that I have, finally, reached theme and topic: if wars of liberation were the historical a priori of Heimat novels in general, World War II was the a priori of the modern Heimat novel. "The Baltic, restless Wehrmacht gray," *Gravity's Rainbow*—the German-American novel of this war—casually notes.[40]

Once there may have been differences between land and sea: here, the "shadowless paths of the sea," as Friedrich Hölderlin notes; there, the estates and properties with their clearly marked roads.[41] But motorized war has turned land into sea, and sedentary residents into work slaves and drudges, refugees and displaced persons, as described by Thomas Pynchon: "All eastern Europe their open sea: the farmland rolls gray and green as waves. . . . Ponds and lakes seem to have no clear boundaries. . . . The Nationalities are on the move. It is a great frontierless streaming out here. . . . So the populations move, across the open meadow, limping, marching, shuffling, carried, hauling along the detritus of an order, a European and bourgeois order they don't know yet is destroyed forever."[42] The Zone of 1945, then, is the country in which—in Schmitt's words—"the elemental antithesis of land and sea" is simply "dissolved in the crucible of industrial-technical progress."[43] But what becomes of Heimat and its partisans under such conditions? This is one of the riddles posed by Pynchon's novel.

As is known, World War II began with the operative deployment of two weapons systems that during World War I had been restricted to merely tactical functions: tank divisions and air fleets. After six years of furious innovations, it ended with the first tactical deployment of two weapons systems whose combination and strategic use will support and facilitate the next world war: German guided missiles and American nuclear bombs.

Right from the outset, *Gravity's Rainbow*, the epic of the V-2 as the first liquid-fuel rocket, leaves no doubt that regardless of whatever people may choose to believe, technological wars are not waged between home- or fatherlands. "The basic problem," an IG Farben representative states, "has always been getting other people to die for you"—in this case, *you* covers the progression from religions to nineteenth-century philosophers of history and professional revolutionaries to today's corporations.⁴⁴ The "enterprise [of] systematic death," the "mass nature of wartime death," serves "as spectacle, as diversion from the real movements of the War."⁴⁵ "The real crises" were removed from propaganda and histories of philosophy; they were "crises of allocation and priority, not among firms—it was only staged to look that way—but among the different Technologies, Plastics, Electronics, Aircraft."⁴⁶

According to the principal fiction of the novel (which is impossible to distinguish from research in secret war archives), these technologies transcend borders and front lines. Corporations such as Shell and IG Farben are, at one and the same time, involved in the development of the German rocket and in British-American countermeasures. They have "no real country, no side in any war, no specific face or heritage: tapping instead out of that global stratum, most deeply laid, from which all the appearances of corporate ownership really spring."⁴⁷ The tellurian basis that provides the ground for partisans and popular uprisings is both deep and tapped. The objection raised in the novel by a military psychologist, that "we do have home," which is not just "up at the interface" but down "in the CNS," is rejected by a spiritist medium: "But I tell you there is no such message, no such home—only the millions of last moments."⁴⁸

These millions are the result of a simple addition that General Giulio Douhet's authoritative monograph *The Command of the Air* was able to carry out without any spiritist assistance: bomber squadrons and long-distance rockets liquidate the military and legal distinctions between soldiers and civilians.⁴⁹ Likewise, in the novel "the battle-fatigued and shell-shocked back from across the Channel and the bomb- or rocket-happy this side" keep adding up in the same London hospital.⁵⁰ In the mouths of prime ministers and propaganda ministers, this is known as the "home front." And because the home front extends beyond Kleist's rapes and pillages and also abolishes, militarily and economically, all gender differences, the novel can present twenty-year-old London girls with perky breasts as "alumni of the Battle of Britain."⁵¹ Ever since the aerial wars over Britain, if not since [Walther] Rathenau's introduction of the German wartime economy in 1916, the home front is, in Pynchon's words, "something of a fiction and a lie, designed, not too subtly . . . to subvert love in favor of work, abstraction, required pain, bitter death."⁵²

In other words, total mobilization leaves no space for a female idol that since the days of Kleist's wars could stand in for Heimat itself. Riding along the autobahn in prewar Germany, Enzian, the black protégé and lover of the main V-2 developer, hallucinates women "in ranks, down on all fours, having their breasts milked into pails of shining steel."⁵³ Mothers, as said, have become a civil-service category. And the only "mother" that does not take life is the war itself.⁵⁴

The novel demonstrates this by means of its protagonist, an American lieutenant who, by way of London and southern France, ventures into Peenemünde and Nordhausen, the centers of the future rocket ages—first under remote control by secret services and then as one of the anarchic roaming "technical-industrial partisans" presaged by Carl Schmitt.⁵⁵ Slothrop only thinks of his mother and his American home as long as it is not clear that today's lullabies are intoned by multinational corporations:

> They've been sleeping on your shoulder,
> They've been crying in your beer,
> And The've [sic] sung you all Their sad lullabies.⁵⁶

In the case of Slothrop, this means that IG Farben and Standard Oil, building on a solid foundation of psychoanalysis and behaviorism, have conditioned his entire childhood sexuality. Given that corporations controlled and financed their guinea pig Slothrop up through his studies at Harvard, there is ample reason for him, first, to develop a full-blown paranoia that decodes the mother-child relationship as training in sadomasochistic fitness for military service and discerns behind all "academic" endeavors the recruiting efforts of the military-industrial complex and, second, to refrain from contacting his own mother even in life-threatening situations.

Paranoia burns all bridges in order to invent a new type of homesickness on the other side. "Son, been wondering about this," says Slothrop's father in a fictitious "Heart-to-Heart, Man-to-Man," prompted by Dad's horror that the drug-riddled children of postmodernism have been shooting *"electricity* into head" or, more precisely, "keying waves."⁵⁷ "Suppose," Slothrop's father continues, "someday you just plug in and go away and never come back? Eh?" But his son is not at a loss for an answer: "'Ho, ho!

Don't I wish! What do you think every electrofreak dreams about? You're such an old fuddyduddy! A-and who sez it's a dream, huh? M-maybe it exists. Maybe there is a Machine to take us away, take us completely, suck us out through the electrodes, out of the skull 'n' into the Machine and live there forever with all the other souls it's got stored there.'"[58] Under the technological conditions of World War II, that is, before [William] Shockley's transistor and Intel's microprocessor, this machine was known as a rocket. The v-2 with its admirable acceleration integration was able to guide itself—or think. In the Nordhausen Mittelwerk, where concentration camp inmates, laboring in the largest subterranean factory in history, assembled the first rockets and jets, it is hard for Slothrop "to live in the present for long. The nostalgia you feel is not your own, but it's potent."[59] It is focused on Fritz Lang's *Woman in the Moon*, on the "Raketen-Stadt" and Wernher von Braun's space missions, on human-machine feedback and couplings between the rocket's "steel erection" and the "feminine darkness" of a "lovable but scatterbrained Mother Nature"—the v-2 as a new Heimat.[60] Not coincidentally, Geli Tripping, the first of many fräuleins Slothrop sleeps with in the Zone—and no home was ever attained differently—was a rocket mascot and "voted the Sweetheart of 3/Art. Abt. (mot) 485. . . . A pretty young witch straddling an A4. Carrying her obsolete broom over her shoulder."[61]

In short, *Gravity's Rainbow* is—in a word that I here use for the first and last time—a *deconstruction* of Heimat. The latter is destructed insofar as it is indebted to the military psychology of people's wars and nation-states. In turn, what is constructed is Heimat as planetary "battlefields," in which the "famous astronauts and cosmonauts, who formerly were only propaganda stars of the mass media (press, radio, and television), will have the opportunity to become cosmopirates, even perhaps morph into cosmopartisans."[62]

This takeoff, staged by the novel in the shape of manned spaceflight, has its reasons. With World War I, it became necessary to sever home from soil. The protracted battles literally pulverized the tellurian foundation of the wars of peoples and nations. The novel exemplifies this rupture in the figure of Brigadier Pudding, who "at the Armageddon filth of the Ypres salient" conquered forty yards "with a wastage of only 70% of his unit."[63] Between 1917 and 1945, his homesickness is directed toward the "mud of Flanders" and the Madonna between the trenches, witnessed by German, British, and French troops as a hallucinatory consolation.[64] A final Mother Earth, whose feces are revealed by Pudding's anal-masochistic rituals as the secret of all trenches.[65]

For the blitzkrieg partisans twenty-five years later, earth is no more than a burnt-out memory. After Slothrop, too, has been deconstructed, the novel's plot revolves around a group of blacks from the "Erdschweinhöhle" of the former German Southwest Africa, who joined and then quit the Waffen-SS in order to assemble V-2 leftovers into the first black spaceflight.⁶⁶ In the "stateless German night" of 1945, a zone in any conceivable meaning of the word, a new secret rocket state is taking shape. For a brief moment between two centralisms, "this War—this incredible war—just for the moment has wiped out the proliferation of little states that's prevailed in Germany for a thousand years. Wiped it clean. Opened it."⁶⁷ Cosmopirates and submarine pirates—just as described by Schmitt—have become possible.⁶⁸ In this state, functions do not survive the people who exercise them; it is "a *mortal* State that will persist no longer than the individuals in it"—just as Hitler's very real dreams were aimed at a state that would end with its leader.⁶⁹

This "Zone" of Hereros and refugees, black marketeers and rocket seekers, is "congruent but not identical" with the occupied zones that are being recentralized by the occupation powers.⁷⁰ What distinguishes the two topologies is the function of waste and ruins. In the military-industrial complex, whose long-distance bombers produced Germany's ruins, the rationale is as follows:

> If what the IG built on this site were not at all the final shape of it, but only an arrangement of fetishes, come-ons to call down the special tools in the form of the 8th AF bombers yes the "Allied" planes all would have been, ultimately, IG-built, by way of Director Krupp, through his English interlocks—the bombing was the exact industrial process of conversion, each release of bombing placed exactly in space and time, each shockwave plotted in advance to bring *precisely tonight's wreck* into being.⁷¹

In other words, the bombardments facilitate the new technologies of the economic miracle. A strategy that clearly goes beyond the scorched-earth policies of Hermann and Hitler because it resolutely ignores national boundaries. Only Albert Speer's theory of ruin value, which not coincidentally subverted the Führer Directive of March 1945, would equal it—if it had been an economic rather than an aesthetic design.⁷² By contrast, what Allied bombers bring about in complicity with the V-2, the other side's so-called vengeance weapon, is technologically perfect destruction: a simulacrum of total destruction that merely obscures the cleanup operations and the innovation of the postwar economic miracle.

In the wake of this paranoid insight, Enzian and his *Schwarzkommando* have no more reason to conserve unbombed residues, let alone mourn for the debris of a Reich that was their home only as a diaspora of the expelled and colonized, the outcast and the dead. On the contrary: for the Counterforce—the novel's designation for all the industry partisans who have broken with the military-industrial complex—industrial waste becomes the "real text."[73] It, too, will have to be reconstructed: "We have to look for power sources here, and distribution networks we were never taught, routes of power our teachers never imagined, or were encouraged to avoid. . . . We have to find meters whose scales are unknown in the world, draw our own schematics, getting feedback, making connections, reducing the error, trying to learn the real function . . . zeroing in on what incalculable plot?"[74] But the paranoid decoding of a plot cannot simply result in a reverse image of Heimat, one congruent but not identical. "Somewhere," Enzian muses, "among the wastes of the World, is the key that will bring us back, restore us to our Earth and to our freedom."[75] Or, in Pynchon's final stanzas:

> There is a Hand to turn the time,
> Though thy Glass today be run,
> Till the Light that hath brought the Towers low
> Find the last poor Preterite one . . .
> Till the Riders sleep by ev'ry road,
> All through our crippl'd Zone,
> With a face in ev'ry mountainside,
> And a Soul in ev'ry stone. . . .[76]

Media and Drugs in Pynchon's Second World War

TRANSLATED BY MICHAEL WUTZ

For David Wellbery

In the German fall of 1983, the German News Agency (DPA) issued the following report: "The leader of the Christian Social Union (CSU) and Prime Minister of Bavaria, [Franz Josef] Strauss, claims to be in possession of 'fairly concrete information' that the GDR has for years been reconstructing subterranean facilities from the Third Reich for the deployment of atomic weapons. During an international symposium of the Hanns Seidel Foundation, Strauss observed that some of these 'natural fortresses' are located 300 to 400 meters underground, making them safe against nuclear attack."[1] What the news agency failed to note is that these "natural fortresses," especially those in the vicinity of Nordhausen in the Harz Mountains, had once before housed and even mass-produced rockets. Which is why the Soviet SS 20 in their bunkers or the Pershings on our autobahns describe only an arc, the rainbow of an eccentric homecoming.[2]

War

Gravity's Rainbow, the rainbow of gravity, is the trajectory of the V-2 rockets that were launched from bases in Holland or Lower Saxony against such metropolitan areas as London or Antwerp and flew over the German-Allied

Originally published as "Medien und Drogen in Pynchons Zweitem Weltkrieg (*Gravity's Rainbow*)," in *Narrativität in den Medien*, edited by Rolf Kloepfer and Karl-Dietmar Möller (Münster: MAkS Publikationen, 1985), 231–52. This is a revised version of the translation by Michael Wutz and Geoffrey-Winthrop Young published in *Reading Matters: Narrative in the New Media Ecology*, edited by Joseph Tabbi and Michael Wutz (Ithaca, NY: Cornell University Press, 1997), 157–72.

fronts during the last six months of the war, from September 8, 1944, until March 27, 1945.[3] *Gravity's Rainbow* is also Thomas Pynchon's attempt to read the signs of the times as a novel, for these signs—notwithstanding all postwar fantasies—were written by World War II,[4] the "mother" of those technologies that have engendered us as well as of a postmodernity that "threatens the idea of cause and effect itself."[5]

The V-2, the first liquid-fuel rocket in the history of warfare, evolved in the hands of Wernher von Braun and the Peenemünde Army Research Center [Heeresversuchsanstalt] from a technician's toy into a serial miracle weapon. In Pynchon's most arcane projections—in keeping with von Braun's blueprints—it went so far as to anticipate, at the end of the war, today's space flights. That is why it is at the center of a novel that reads the signs of our times. The parallel development of American weapons technology, by contrast, surfaces only at the most distant horizon of the novel or theater of war in Hiroshima and Nagasaki.[6] The only thing you have to do is replace the conventional warhead of the V-2—a ton of amatol to be detonated, following Hitler's personal suggestion, before impact—with a uranium or plutonium payload to arrive at the state of things in 1985.[7] For while the Army High Command, according to a secret memo of October 15, 1942, planned to use "atomic decay and chain reaction only as a possible form of rocket-propulsion,"[8] Enrico Fermi and John von Neumann had already begun work on an appropriate payload that (as progress has since shown) was far too precious for their own *Enola Gays* and other bombers.

German-American friendship understood as the transfer of technology is, hence, Pynchon's subject. What began at the beach of Peenemünde and developed into assembly-line production in the bunkers of Nordhausen (built by IG Farben and taken over by the Reich)—the manufacturing site, by the way, of the first jet fighters—continues in Huntsville and Baikonur.[9] The sum total of all innovations produced by World War II—from the reel-to-reel, color film, and VHF to radar, UHF, and computers[10]—yields a postwar period whose simple secret is the marketing of miracle weapons and whose future is predictable.[11]

Certainly, even during World War II, people still believed they were dying for their fatherlands. But Pynchon, the erstwhile engineer at Boeing, minutely observes that "the enterprise [of] systematic death" "serves as spectacle, as diversion from the real movements of the War."[12] "The real crises," after all, "were crises of allocation and priority, not among firms—it was only staged to look that way—but among the different Technologies, Plastics, Electronics, Aircraft," and so forth.[13]

But if the war was literally a theater of war, and its ocean of corpses a simulacrum, a screen concealing the competition of diverse technologies for their own, or our, future, everything plays out as it does in the media, which—from the drama to the computer—also transmit nothing but information. Competition and priority disputes between technologies have always amounted to competition over information about them. As someone with solid ties to industrial espionage melancholically puts it in the novel: "Life was simple before the first war"; "dope and women" were the only matters of interest, then. But since 1939 "the world's gone insane," because "information [has] come to be the only real medium of exchange," and even industrial espionage is about to switch from agents or human beings to "information machines."[14]

Under conditions of total semiotechnology, what remains is the question of the media that implement it. And if, as in one of Pynchon's formulas, "personal density is directly proportional to temporal bandwidth," media theorists do well to remember the military history of the subjects of their own inquiry.[15] What may appear as narrativity, and hence entertainment, in the media possibly only obscures semiotechnological capabilities. Media such as literature and film and records are all at war—which is precisely why *Gravity's Rainbow* orchestrates them in such a systematic way.

Literature

In those prehistoric times when drugs and sex were still of interest, war may have been a soldier's song, an oral tale. But ever since a universal draft demanded that "everybody had to be in the field," there are, as Goethe was quick to realize, no more listeners for tales: all are involved now.[16] Therefore, the wars of liberation that from 1806 to 1815 made the people of central Europe into underlings of nation-states, that is to say, into people's armies, needed a new medium as well.[17] That medium was literature as writing and command. The new—that is, absolute—enemy first had to be named and its destruction ordered—which is precisely what was accomplished by plays such as Heinrich von Kleist's *The Battle of Hermann*, the "commander's hill" [*Feldherrnhügel*] of propaganda war.[18]

As is widely known, that poetic fortune was only short lived. When the commander's hills vanished during the material battles of World War I, literature was forced to descend into the trenches (as Paul Fussell's brilliant study of English texts illustrates).[19] An absolute enmity that was taken over by machines was no longer in need of stories, justifications, and plans. In the absence of inconceivable orders and invisible enemies, literature was left to present what Ernst Jünger so aptly calls "battle as inner experience" [*Der Kampf als inneres Erlebnis*]. In other words: film. At the outer periphery of the book medium, where explosions negate all verbal expression, its technological replacement appeared.[20] Whenever Lieutenant Jünger encountered the real behind morning fog and barbed wire, instead of still composing expressionist studies of individual experience, he always hallucinated the enemy as a cinematic doppelgänger.[21] For that reason alone, novels that captured life in the trenches, as does the work of Erich Maria Remarque, cried out for cinematic treatment.

But when the enterprise of systematic death and the simulation of relations between enemies and friends only serves as a pretext for the competition between technologies—which are themselves based not on adventure or narration but on blueprints, statistics, and secret operations—life in the trenches becomes obsolete. To secure the traces of the technological World War II, *Gravity's Rainbow* employs from the very beginning different narrative techniques.

Instead of a war with its inner experience, we witness a stochastic distribution of figures and locales, of front lines and discourses, of Allied and German sites. Only the coincidence of two coincidental distributions brings about the focus on a hero and an action/plot. The Poisson equation, whose distribution corresponds to the impact pattern of the V-2s, happens to coincide point by point with the private statistic of an American lieutenant named Slothrop with which he keeps track of his random erotic encounters. And just as the rockets, because of their supersonic speed, reverse cause and effect and audible threat and visible explosion, Slothrop's erections are an index (in the sense both of Charles Sanders Peirce and of all the prophets) that marks the next hit.[22] The V-2s follow the erections, just as their sound follows their impact. In other words: even Slothrop's love or "imagination has a bomblike structure."[23] This is reason enough for Allied intelligence to use the lieutenant as a guinea pig, in the most technical sense of the term. He infiltrates the collapsing Reich to gather information on that last, unique, and mythical rocket that transports his German doppelgänger, Gottfried, into space or death.

However, Slothrop escapes the "operational paranoia" of those secret services in the same measure that he is possessed by it.[24] The medium of that transfer is writing. The lieutenant comes from a line of Puritan paper manufacturers; that is, people who convert America's "diminishing green reaches . . . acres at a clip into paper—toilet paper, banknote stock, newsprint—a medium or ground for shit, money, and the Word."²⁵ The symbolic, to speak with Lacan, returns to reclaim him as he studies the seized V-2 documents. Reading and paranoia coincide. All the traces Slothrop learns to decode in Fortress Europe point to the fact that the military-industrial complex has always stood above war fronts—that it programmed both the conditioned sexual reflexes of American GIs and the innovations of German rocket technicians.²⁶ From his dossiers, which after all have long controlled what passes for experience or life stories, Slothrop—following the historically accurate route between IG Farben and Rockefeller's Standard Oil—infers that he has already been, from early infancy, the test subject for behaviorist experiments carried out by the same Professor Jamf whose work on synthetic polymers would also enable manned space travel.²⁷ Thus, after the fact, as always, it turns out that the detective and his doppelgänger coincide in the V-2 cockpit and that the coincidence of two iconic patterns, the real-historical map of the missile strikes and the novel's erotic map of London, is anything but a coincidence. Upon a thorough examination of the documents, coincidences always uncover a conspiracy.

The sole premise of this sinister conclusion, however, is not the immanence of fiction, as readers might assume, given their conditioned obliviousness. Rather, it is the historical exactness of what the text itself calls "data retrieval."²⁸ Step by step, Slothrop's intratextual paranoia repeats a critical-paranoid method the novelist might have learned from Salvador Dalí. Even if writer and protagonist come upon documents in reverse order, that does not make them fictional. As a textual example of so-called postmodernity, *Gravity's Rainbow* has been acknowledged a hundred times, but literary scholarship has yet to recognize the scope and precision of the research it integrates. In a manner comparable only to historical novels like *Salammbô* or *The Temptation of St. Anthony*, the text builds almost exclusively on documentary sources; only now such sources also involve circuit diagrams and differential equations, corporate contracts and organizational graphs.²⁹ (These can easily be missed by literary scholars.)

Gravity's Rainbow is data retrieval from a world war whose secret documents have become accessible to the degree that their plans have been implemented in the real world and thus are no longer in need of classified protection. If only for that reason, paranoia—which, according to Freud or Charles William Morris, is only a confusion of words and things, of designation and denotation, like all psychoses—is knowledge itself.³⁰ When the symbolic made up of signs, numbers, and letters exercises control over so-called realities, trace recovery becomes a paranoiac's first duty.

Consequently, the critical-paranoid method of the novel infects its readers. They turn from consumers of a narrative into hackers of a system. For, despite his Puritan predilection for the word, Slothrop is far from decoding all the war secrets the novel has encoded.[31] He is nowhere near deciphering that the fictional U.S. major Marvy, who is responsible for the transfer of V-2 technology to the United States, is merely a cryptogram for the historically accurate name "Staver,"[32] or that Pointsman, the chief behaviorist of the British intelligence in the novel, is given his name in order to match his German namesake and counterpart in a multinational conspiracy: Weichensteller, the Peenemünde engineer responsible, of all things, for the reentry of the V-2s into British airspace.[33]

In *Gravity's Rainbow*, fictional names and narrative structures conceal a level of information also relayed to other, no less paranoid novels; hence, for the most practical reasons in the world, it had better not be told.[34] In that sense, the novel is fully in sync with its time. When technologies assume domination over science and aesthetics, the only thing that counts is information. After all, some of the origins of semiotics itself derive from the behaviorist semiotechnologies Pynchon analyzes as strategies of war.

And yet, even after the analysis and recombination of both distributed and secret data, two problems remain: the closure and self-application of the system. It is not only because Slothrop's data retrieval takes place in 1945, years before the release of crucial intelligence archives, that he dances on "a ground of terror, contradiction, absurdity."[35] First, it is child's play for the military-industrial complex to bring in "programmers by the truckload . . . and make sure all the information fed out was harmless"—as harmless, for example, as a novel.[36] Second, according to Tyrone Slothrop's paranoid logic, his desire is solely his own, whereas in fact, to paraphrase Lacan, it has always been the desire of the Other, of the chief analyst.[37] Extending the work of his historical predecessors John Watson and Baby Albert,[38] Jamf had the "elegant"—that is, "binary"—idea to condition in Baby Slothrop, not such nonquantifiable data as fear, but a simple and unambiguous erection reflex.[39] Consequently, what surfaces in Slothrop's dreams is "a very old dictionary of technical German," which translates "JAMF," the proper name of his lab chief, with the English index "I."[40]

In other—but still Pynchon's—words, the I is only "a branch office in each of our brains, his corporate emblem is a white albatross, each local rep has a cover known as the Ego, and their mission in this world is Bad Shit."[41]

End of quote, a quote that could just as well have come from Foucault and, what is more, reads as the end of all paranoia; for nothing remains of the involuntary private detective who has finally cracked the alibi, that is to say, the elsewhere of his own ego. Under conditions of total remote control, the narrativity of the protagonist dissipates. In an endless series of makeovers and metamorphoses, Lieutenant Slothrop loses his uniform, his proper name, and his literacy; he dissolves into episodes, comic strips, myths, and, finally, record covers.[42] Only thereby does he escape the trap that the medium of writing—itself only a part of the military-industrial complex—sets up for its readers. For if there is paranoia, understood as an ominous reading of a single, cohesive, and narratable conspiracy, then "there is still also anti-paranoia, where nothing is connected to anything."[43]

And while the historical genre of the novel was defined by the fact that the ramifications of its Markoff chains diminished in direct proportion to the path traveled by the hero, eventually resulting in a structure or solution, *Gravity's Rainbow*'s antiparanoia, conversely, produces an increase in information and hence (following Claude Shannon) an increase in entropy.[44] In a progressive merging of figures, organizations, and front lines, the novel repeats precisely the second law of thermodynamics. The law of increasing entropy ascribes direction to time and can clarify—following the wonderful example of Sir Arthur Eddington—whether films, in real time, run forward or backward.[45]

Film

In this technical and temporal sense, *Gravity's Rainbow* is film, not because the novel could be made into a movie, as in the case of Remarque's, or could project invisible enemies, as in the case of Jünger's, but because it opposes its own progressive dissolution to the negentropy of the military-industrial complex. The present tense alone, which Pynchon sustains throughout, in contrast to the past tense typically used in novels, ensures a kind of forgetfulness that suppresses linear connections between cause and effect. "Each [V-2] hit is independent of all the others. Bombs are not dogs. No link. No memory. No conditioning." Hence, it is not a question of "which places would be safest to go into." Thanks to such training, there is "a whole *generation*" whose "postwar [existence is] nothing but 'events,' newly created one moment to the next."[46]

And, therefore, only the Monte Carlo fallacy can assume that a missile strike, a film image, a narrative event n are governed by the series 1

through $n-1$, as if they had a memory. Certainly, to the chief behaviorist in the text the fireblooms over London signal that "the reality is not reversible."[47] Things could come to an end only if "rockets dismantle, [and] the entire film runs backward: faired skin back to sheet steel back to pigs to white incandescence to ore, to Earth."[48] But as no one lesser than the spirit of Walther Rathenau, the inventor of German war economies and hence of Soviet five-year plans, explains when summoned, the "talk of cause and effect is secular history, and secular history is a diversionary tactic," or rather "a conspiracy."[49] Secular history, as is commonly known, existed in the medium of the book; technological media, by contrast, allow (above and beyond the diversionary tactic of their entertainment effect) for the variation of precisely those parameters that they alone are capable of recording, including that of physical time. Just as a missile strike reverses the sequence of explosion and noise, so do the many fictitious movies in *Gravity's Rainbow* operate with the trick that goes by the wonderful name of time-axis manipulation in the jargon of electronic engineering of the real.

The last work of Gerhardt von Göll, who in the novel stands for his historical colleagues G. W. Pabst, Fritz Lang, and Ernst Lubitsch, is called *New Dope* and demonstrates "24 hours a day" how it renders you incapable of "ever telling anybody what it's like, or worse, where to get any. . . . It is the dope that finds *you*, apparently. Part of a reverse world whose agents run around with guns which are like vacuum cleaners operating in the direction of life—pull the trigger and bullets are sucked back out of the recently dead into the barrel . . . to the accompaniment of a backwards gunshot."[50] Such cinematic tricks, however, are not limited to the imaginary of hallucinations and film. The novel also describes the British bombing of a V-2 launch site as a reverse transformation that turns "vehicles . . . back to the hollow design envelopes of their earliest specs" and hence intimates the darkest of its paranoid discoveries: namely, that Germany's industrial parks—following the ruin value theory of their chief architect, Albert Speer—were built with the anticipation of their eventual destruction by the Royal Air Force.[51] Only then can they fulfill their function as postwar ruins in the multinational conspiracy.[52]

Von Göll's first work, a false documentary in the best Allied black propaganda fashion, performs similar reversals of time, albeit in a less programmed way.[53] British soldiers made up as Hereros pose as one of Major General Kammler's motorized rocket batteries. The finished film is damaged and given an antiquated appearance—enhanced by the white noise that defines both technological media and their background—in order to spread German rumors about blacks in the Waffen-SS in the form of a pseudodocument sent from a counterfeit V-2 firing site.⁵⁴ That is what von Göll calls, "with the profound humility that only a German movie director can summon," his "mission": namely, "to sow . . . seeds of reality."⁵⁵ And in truth: in 1929 Lang's film *Frau im Mond* [*Woman in the Moon*] sowed the seeds of the Countdown and the future V-2 more generally.⁵⁶

But the spiral does not stop here, with the reversal of cause and effect, of programming and documenting. In the case of von Göll, what comes to light late in the novel is that the Waffen-SS Hereros were not the effect but rather the magical cause of their propagandistic simulation. Since they already exist, von Göll's forgery ought to run backward, just as countdowns do. And once again, what surfaces is the big question of the relationship between programming and narrativity in the media.

Paul Virilio's *War and Cinema* attempts to show that the relationship between world wars and film technologies is one not of mere simultaneity but of strict solidarity. War strategies that—in terms of the military, technology, and propaganda—depend on speed and information cannot do without the acceleration, dilation, and reversal of time: that is, without time-axis manipulation. What would be impossible in the media of writing or literature—notwithstanding Ilse Aichinger's "Mirror Story" ["Spiegelgeschichte"]—has been a cinematic staple since the early days of film, which, in turn, began with the revolver.⁵⁷ Of course, literature had the capacity to manipulate those times that simulate education or struggles as an inner experience. But to work with physical time itself, into which education and mortal combat are embedded, technological media become necessary. Rocket technology needs film technology, and vice versa. That the V-2 homed in on its targets in London in the first place, despite the incredulity of the newly created technical subdivision of the British secret service, can be attributed to an ingenious innovation:⁵⁸ its measured parameter was not its distance traveled, as with armies, or its speed, as, more recently, with tanks; it was its acceleration, which was accessible only to the rocket itself in the shape of information and which, through simple and double integrals, made it possible to determine speed and distance, respectively.⁵⁹ A pendulum, followed by two serial RC circuits—that's how simply Virilio's dromology can be constructed or (as in the case of the British experts) overlooked.

According to Pynchon, there is a "strange connection between the German mind and the rapid flashing of successive stills . . . since Leibniz, in the process of inventing calculus, used the same approach to break up the trajectories of cannonballs through the air."[60] Still, the technological medium that implements motion as calculus is film. Beginning with Étienne-Jules Marey's photographic gun, all cinematic illusions of continually moving pictures have been, just like the speed of the V-2, simple integrals, dependent variables of a time-axis manipulation, which is the only thing that counts for optimizing weapons of destruction. Not unlike that predecessor of film technology from 1885, the high-performance Ascania cameras of 1941 were developed not to serve the imagination of moviegoers but rather to examine the V-2 trajectory in slow motion.[61] Which, of course, does not mean that these techniques should not be extended "past images on film, to human lives."[62]

One of the many narratives that make up *Gravity's Rainbow*'s entropy questions narrativity through technology itself. It concerns an engineer of Peenemünde who is fooled by the trick of time-axis manipulation. The simulacrum in this feature film—or in this life—is his twelve-year-old daughter, whose very conception, incidentally, is already a result of the semiotechnology of film. It is one of von Göll's late-expressionist rape scenes—its climax cut in the released version but played through until the bitter end both in the studio and in Joseph Goebbels's private archive—that impregnated not only the film's star but countless wives and girlfriends of homecoming moviegoers. Under conditions of advanced technology, children are only the doppelgängers of their cinematic doppelgängers: cannon fodder in the case of boys, pinups in the case of girls.

Thirteen years later. The film-engendered cannon fodder wage a blitzkrieg; pinups are in demand. As a classic Pynchonesque figure, the rocket engineer has long forgotten his daughter and the way she looks. But from 1939 onward, she reappears during each summer furlough: as an extra bonus courtesy of the military testing facility at Peenemünde. Only after his pinup daughter has seduced him does it become clear that she has actually been assembled, year after year, from doppelgängers without an original. Starting in 1939, the concentration camp Dora in the vicinity of Nordhausen—a mass-producer of V-2s as well—simply began to give leaves of absence to its inmates, at first to a twelve-year-old, then a thirteen-year-old, and so on, until the end of the war. In Pynchon's own words: "The only continuity has been her name . . . and [her father's] love—love something like the persistence of vision, for They have used it to create for him the moving image of a daughter, flashing him only these summertime frames of her, leaving it to him to build the illusion of a single child."[63] Hence, moviegoers as such are the victims of a semiotechnology that projects coherence onto a world of snapshots and flashbulbs. Feature films began, in Germany at any rate, with doppelgängers who filmed and propagated filmmaking itself.[64] For Pynchon, as for Virilio, they culminate in the countless Japanese whom the bomb captured as "a fine-vapor deposit of fat-cracklings wrinkled into the fused rubble" of their city Hiroshima.[65]

The exposure time? Sixty-seven nanoseconds, or blitzkrieg in the literal sense of the word.

However, a war that coincides with its own representation becomes unrepresentable. *Gravity's Rainbow* concentrates all the impossibilities of representing technological warfare into the figure of Slothrop's German antipode: on the one hand, a GI who is led to the V-2 only through coincidences and military orders; on the other, a boss who directs not only the production and launching of the miracle weapon but also, with the help of lifelike film tricks, the sexuality of his engineers. The representation of the head of Peenemünde would be a repeat of the war-film cliché of the evil German. That Pynchon bypasses that stereotype and instead stages the puzzling relationship between fact and fiction has, so far, dumbfounded his interpreters. That is exactly what makes the novel so great.

Historically, the Peenemünde Army Research Center [Heeresversuchsanstalt] was under the command of General Walter Dornberger of the Army Ordnance Office [Heereswaffenamt]. By 1932 Dornberger, then a major and aide to Professor [Carl Emil] Becker, had already discovered the young Wernher von Braun. The chain of command between Kummersdorf and Peenemünde stayed this way until the methodically proliferating entropies of the Hitler state transformed the SS into a state within the state. In 1944, after the Army Ordnance Office had done its technological duty and the Wehrmacht had lapsed into agony, the command over Peenemünde, Nordhausen, and an assigned special-purpose army corps (the only one in the history of the German Army) fell to Chief Group Leader [*Obergruppenführer*] Dr. Kammler of the SS Main Economic and Administrative Office [SS-Wirtschafts-und Verwaltungshauptamt].[66] Born in 1901, Hans Kammler shares with Thomas Pynchon, born in 1937, the rare quality of having destroyed all photographs of himself.[67] And that is precisely how he traverses the novel: as an unrepresentable presence.

Pynchon's fictional head of rocket technology deletes all of his identity markers because he is not a figure but the product of a double exposure. Beginning in 1932, the head of rocket technology is called "Major Weissmann"; he is a Wehrmacht officer and (like Dornberger) "a brand-new military type, part salesman, part scientist."⁶⁸ All the way down to his conversations with subordinate officers, who camouflage wartime economic pressure with scientific interest, Pynchon's Weissmann follows a single source: the involuntary candor of Dornberger's memoir.⁶⁹ And that is precisely why Dornberger's name does not feature in this most precise of all novels, as if fact and fiction were the two sides of the same sheet of paper.

Later in Peenemünde, however, the same Weissmann carries without explanation the SS "group leader" rank⁷⁰ and ultimately, in 1944, even exchanges his own name for "the SS code name" Blicero, a paraphrase of death.⁷¹ As Blicero, Weissmann adopts all the formalities of the German generals' staff; he turns into a roaring animal, chasing the remaining rocket batteries over the bombed-out autobahns of the Reich. Dornberger, von Braun, and their appalled ghostwriters report nothing less about Kammler and his need to decide the outcome of the war all by himself, as if all the entropies of the Hitler state had been made flesh.⁷²

The merging of Dornberger and Kammler, Weissmann and Blicero, army and SS, order and entropy is the eccentric center of the novel, the site of its unrepresentability. Whether Blicero is dead or alive remains an open question, as in the case of the real Kammler for many years after the war.⁷³ Weismann-Blicero's deeds and deliria exist only as the narratives of the narratives of witnesses who were themselves under the influence of the drug Oneirine.⁷⁴ Oneirine, naturally once again synthesized by the fictitious Professor Laszlo Jamf, has, however, "the property of time-modulation" that was "first to be discovered by investigators."⁷⁵ That's why Blicero, this double exposure of 1932 and 1944, of Dornberger and Kammler, can come into being in the first place. That is why, amid the rubble of the Reich, his madness can launch a manned spaceflight, which will become historical reality only twenty years later. And that's why, finally, Pynchon's World War II can end with the intercontinental missiles of the next war, for Blicero's manned V-2, launched in Lower Saxony, touches down on the last page of the novel in the Hollywood of 1973, the year of the novel's publication. Its off-ground detonator is calibrated to respond precisely to the movie theater in which Pynchon and his readers are sitting. We "old fans, who've always been at the movies," are finally reached by a film that "we have not learned to see" but that we have been dreaming of ever since the days of Eadweard Muybridge and Étienne-Jules Marey: the melding of film and war.⁷⁶

Oneirine has additional, less sensational qualities. In contrast to the dreamlike quality of *Cannabis indica*, the hallucinations produced by Oneirine "show a definitive narrative continuity, as clearly as, say, the average *Reader's Digest* article."[77] In other words, they are "so ordinary, so conventional," so American.[78] That is Pynchon's contribution to the topic of narrativity in the media and his explanation as to why each medium, including the novel itself, is a drug, and vice versa.

According to Gustav Stresemann, people "pray not only for their daily bread, but also for their daily illusion."[79] And industrial concerns, such as the real IG Farben or Jamf's fictitious Psychochemie AG, do everything to answer "the basic problem . . . getting other people to die for you" in a positive—that is, psychopharmaceutical—way, now that theological and historico-philosophical illusions are no longer viable alternatives.[80] As early as 1904, "the American Food and Drug people took the cocaine out of Coca-Cola, which gave us an alcoholic and death-oriented generation of Yanks ideally equipped to fight WW II."[81] What remains—following the words of the Oneirine connoisseur von Göll—is to hope for the eventual melding of film and war. Slothrop, who observes that "this ain't the fuckin' *movies* now," may be rightly concerned for a while that people are getting killed, even though "they weren't supposed to"—that wasn't part of the script. Von Göll knows better. According to the director, we are "not yet" in the movies. "Maybe not quite yet. You'd better enjoy it while you can. Someday, when the film is fast enough, the equipment pocket-size and burdenless and selling at people's prices, the lights and booms no longer necessary, *then* . . . then."[82]

As early as 1973, however, as a TV quiz show for its readers, *Gravity's Rainbow* organizes "A MOMENT OF FUN WITH TAKESHI AND ICHIZO, / THE KOMICAL KAMIKAZES." And whoever manages to guess, as does "Marine Captain Esberg from Pasadena," that this whole spectacle "*is* a movie! Another World War II situation comedy," wins as first prize an all-expense-paid (one-way) trip to the movie's set location.[83] There he may experience "torrential tropical downpours" and make the acquaintance of "the Kamikaze *Zero*" that he will be operating, flying, and—crashing.[84]

Hence, the narrative continuity of Oneirine hallucinations or feature films haunts the novel, which raises them to the level of a theme. Episodes and dialogues are rendered as if they had been written under the influence of the drug.[85] Consequently, *Gravity's Rainbow*, too, is a *Reader's Digest* article: ordinary, conventional, and American: "And there ought to be a punch line to it, but there isn't."[86] The puzzling question of whether world war technologies have programmed our so-called postwar time, and if so, how, remains unresolved. The novel remains a novel, and its hero Slothrop "a tanker and feeb." His quest for Weissmann-Blicero's manned space rocket ends in failure and condemns him to "mediocrity."

And that, as the text puts it bitterly and unequivocally, "not only in life but also, heh, heh, in his chroniclers too."[87]

Record

Script records the symbolic, film the imaginary. The countless songs in the novel, by contrast, are the medium of stupidity. Record grooves store the frequencies of real bodies, whose stupidity, as is generally known, knows no bounds. What wars and drugs and the media do to bodies hence continues as music. One song in *Gravity's Rainbow* begins, "Tap my head and mike my brain, / Stick that needle in my vein."[88] The novel keeps coming to a standstill because fictitious rumbas, beguines, foxtrots, blues improvisations, and so forth—accompanied by the most precise stage directions and far from any war scenario—turn actions and conspiracies into ritornellos, into an eternal recurrence of stanza and chorus. At the end, as a new world war is about to erupt in the skies of California, a song of consolation appears for a "crippl'd Zone" that does not just signify postwar Germany. And at the end of the song and the novel: "Now everybody—."

PART VI

Kittler on Kittler

Biogeography

TRANSLATED BY GEOFFREY WINTHROP-YOUNG

In memoriam P. S.

I—who never published this letter as a pronoun—born on the day Lampedusa capitulated and the first breach had been opened up in Fortress Europe.[1]

> Spaniens Himmel breitet seine Sterne,
> Bis alles in Scherben fällt,
> Und der Morgen leuchtet in der Ferne
> Und morgen die ganze Welt.
>
> Spain's sky is spreading its stars
> Until everything falls apart,
> And the morning is glowing from afar
> And tomorrow the whole world.[2]

In the lost land of Heiner Müller, somewhere along the endless footpath to town, there was or still is a sandpit. Standing at its edge, the last king of Saxony is said to have inspected his troops. (A father who had served in 1906 and then again in 1914 in the 107th Infantry Regiment acted as playing piece and narrator.) That is how directly a battle and its miniature, sandpit and sandbox, coincided in pre–World War I Europe. The broom was in bloom where, according to family tradition, everything began. And General Field Marshal Baron von Müffling, who not only haunts Goethe's best novel in

---

Originally published as "Biogeographie," in *Ein deutscher Traum: Zyklus auf das Jahr 1990*, edited by Wolfgang Storch (Berlin: Hentrich, 1990), 63–71.

the guise of an army captain and cartographer but also—as history's first chief of the General Staff of the Prussian Army—invented sand-table exercises, would have been delighted.³ A map of the empire as large as the empire itself, like in the tale by Borges.

Later, when the single-track railway of the postwar Reich replaced my feet and the nominally abolished Saxony had become too small, what appeared behind the sooty window of a train compartment was the sand caster of the old Reich: Brandenburg, from Jüterborg to Zossen (the last refuge of the German Army High Command), one big training ground for armored divisions. To stay on the level of World War II both geopolitically and technologically, the Red Army needed steppes, monocultures, or coniferous wastelands. Marshal Georgy Zhukov's decisive tank waves could not even have been deployed for battle in the Saxon sandpit; by contrast, World War II innovations—from Volokolamsk to Jüterborg, Zossen, and Kummersorf, the Army Ordnance proving ground—were transported back to the homeland. In this country the inability to mourn begins by abandoning the inhospitality of such spaces to psychologists. While tanks are space-devouring technologies, a mother took her two children past an inaccessible Berlin and through a Mittelmark eroded by tank tracks to the island of Usedom, of all places, for a holiday on the Baltic Sea.⁴

For there, on Usedom, our strategic present began. Under a cloak of invisibility made up of the Vorpommern region, thatched roofs, and [Hans-Jürgen] Syberberg's homesickness, every wood path had been expanded into a runway during the war: concrete slabs with asphalt joints (like on the oldest segments of the autobahn) had been thrown into cubist disarray by the bombs of the Royal Air Force during one long summer night.⁵ Every morning this hot and—for a vacation village, strangely elaborate—concrete construction carried railway passengers from their Free German Trade Union Federation hostels in Zempin to their beach chairs on the Baltic. That the very same concrete had carried trailer rigs with mounted v-2 rockets to Test Stand B-II and that the very same village had included the private residence of Wernher von Braun remained a prehistory silenced by antifascism.

It was America, the country reaping the biggest world war booty, that finally broke the silence of those years. Once the v-2 had turned into the Jupiter, and the Messerschmitt Me 262 into the modern jet fighter, even German university lecturers could get into the game of transferring technology. So, with E., I drove a rental car along the California highways that at one point in Thomas Pynchon's novel even bore those trailer rigs, only to be stopped by military police in the midst of a shrubby expanse: for over an hour, our clueless rental had been cruising through restricted military zones or test sites, which, both invisible and infinite, dot even the most expansive states, such as Nevada. Only empires whose deserts keep growing are able to develop and test the space-annihilation weapons of World War $n+1$. For the rest of the world, high technology means surrender to winds, sands, and seas. When a V-2 captured in Agfacolor (rather than the real thing on its test stand) convinced history's greatest cineast that it was operational, he supposedly declared that "in the face of these rockets . . . Europe and the world are now and for all times too small for any war."[6]

A biogeography composed of sandpits, tank steppes, space stations—but after this speedup, let me once more return to that small country in which the autobahn had become impassable and the railway a single-track affair. Or, to put it differently: why we remain in the province.[7]

> The roses bloom at Kreising,
> The Wismar Sea is green
> At Oberpfaffenhofen
> Wild orchids have been seen.

A poem from the early summer of 1945 by Constance Babington Smith, the daughter of the British World War I general postmaster and the wife of the American chief architect of the Vietnam War who reputedly lives around Oxford to this very day, like a Madonna of all technology transfers.[8] And in between, she herself made history: working for the Royal Air Force's aerial reconnaissance, she discovered, somewhere between pine forests and the Wismar Sea, the Army Ordnance Missile Site, complete with Test Stand VII and the V-2.

A lost empire under natural cover: and then the order from Potsdam to shrink down to the size of the country itself. In exchange for West Berlin, the tanks of the U.S. Army (the earliest childhood memory after scattered SS Cossacks) vacated Thuringia and West Saxony. "All of Eastern Europe" became the "open sea" described by Pynchon and Klaus Theweleit: "So the populations move, across the open meadow, limping, marching, shuffling, carried, hauling along the detritus of an order, a European and bourgeois order they don't know yet is destroyed forever."[9] Hertha Benn took morphine; Heiner Müller found his material.[10] The IG Farben site for the production of wartime fuel in Lower Saxony, located immediately adjacent to the subterranean rocket-production facility, was converted into the Walter Ulbricht hydrogenation plant, and an abandoned feudal estate into an elementary school named after Wilhelm Pieck.

And so on and so forth, until the country had shriveled to the size of old blueprints. Prep schoolers learned Russian: from returning soldiers, in riding stables, and underneath classroom ceilings whose gypsum coat of arms—erased and in any case fictitious—bore the hollow marks of proletarian chisels. The arms, after all, had been thought up at the very last minute by a recipient of the Knight's Cross who had relieved the fortress of Bunzlau one last time before dying defending the fortress of Spandau, as Berlin went up in flames. At least this is what a French journalist has to say about Major General Werner Mummert, the commanding officer of the last division deployed by the Wehrmacht.[11] In the village, however, among members of the new agricultural production cooperative on the former feudal estate, other tales survived: of four-in-hand coaches and the numerous children sired by the estate owner. From the very beginning, country, village, and school, as if acting out of loyalty, fell under a greater shadow. Something that you could not speak of and that therefore would not die. It could return, though, suddenly, as the last prisoner of war.

Nestled into the ruins of the wartime economic miracle, plundered by a conqueror who had former Peenemünde employees turn the wooden ties of the Reich's second railway tracks into boxes to ship the V-2 to Baikonur, ruled over by victims who derived their state religion from the dedication of memorial sites and who encountered the same threatening future every time they visited the prison of Brandenburg—the end of the small country had been programmed into its very beginning. And maybe it was aware of it.

Mittelbau-Dora concentration camp memorial site, Niedersachswerfen, July 1990. A rainy day at the Kohnstein hill and its tunnels. My initiation (to quote Pynchon) into "the Holy-Center-Approaching" of rocket technology.[12] The debris of the Walter Ulbricht hydrogenation plant to the west, the Karl Liebknecht potash works in the south, the Kyffhäuser to the east, and in between the bombed-out remains of Nordhausen. Where once the Mittelbau AG had erected the largest underground serial production assembly line in the history of war, which—to quote Albert Speer praising SS Major General Kammler—"does not have an even remotely similar example anywhere in Europe and is unsurpassable even by American production methods," Speer's theory of ruin value was now in evidence.[13] Tunnel entrances A and B were destroyed as soon as the Red Army, as the only but unmentionable victor, had completed its series of V-2 replicas; in the moist entrance of Tunnel C, at the same time, a local agricultural production cooperative was growing its mushrooms.

Fungi grew on files and tongues as well. When the last director of the museum was asked whether Konrad Zuse's world war computer had been used in Mittelbau, he remarked, "Zuse? Never heard of him."[14] Not for nothing did Stalin denounce all computer science as bourgeois deviation. When people stationed at the tunnel access, once again made up of concrete slabs with asphalt joints, were asked about Kammler, the double mastermind of both Mittelbau and Dora, they too responded, "Never heard of him."[15] Not for nothing did the commanding general of the special deployment Rocket Army Corps make sure to have all his photos destroyed.

The postwar country as a blind spot. At the exact high-tech location for which people in Niedersachswerfen, Baikonur, and Florida died and continue to die, the Dora concentration camp registers its effects and shadows in the drawings made by inmates.[16] The camp museum's publication (not surprisingly, from Dietz) features in its first edition nothing but communist inmates engaged in active resistance, while the second mentions a U.S.-imperialist replica of the V-2. Only the final sentence of the third edition, published in April 1990, when it was all too late, mentions "that the knowledge of the German rocket research helped accelerate [sic] the Soviet development of ballistic long-range missiles and thus prevent U.S. superiority."[17]

But prevention as a state goal and commemoration as a state religion do not shorten any shadows: weapons of space annihilation are no longer the weapons of space assertion they were during World War I. If you crouch down, you can decipher from museum copies of dusty command documents (which are hidden, rather than on prominent display) what kind of engineers set the global standards that subsequently were so precious to general secretaries: engineers like Dr. P. S., a student of Küpfmüller's, came from Siemens, AEG, or IG Farben, and the global standards were derived from the electromechanical aggregates of the V-2.[18] Which is why, even before the wall fell, it retraced its path.

What came to an end, like the mushrooms in Tunnel C, was an interim or hibernation period that lasted until the final piece of flesh from the bunker, doused in ersatz gasoline culled from the Army High Command's very last reserves, had caught up with its victims and successors. According to the "fairly concrete information" of a former [Christian Social Union] CSU chairman, the NVA (the East German National People's Army) utilized "subterranean facilities from the Third Reich safe against nuclear attack" to house its own bomber groups or nuclear missiles.[19] And had such facilities indeed been "located 300 to 400 meters underground," the Kohnstein, this initiatory playground for the children of Nordhausen, would not have been empty after all—and Speer's theory of ruin value would not have been confirmed.

Peenemünde too, the old army proving ground, remained until the very end an NVA no-fly zone. In the no-man's-land between pines and bomb craters, the concrete track comes to a sudden stop. In its place, once more, a view of the Baltic Sea with its "restless Wehrmacht gray," as Pynchon writes.[20] And then tales, slides, oral history, composed of fragments scattered between Nordhausen and Peenemünde. Marshal Konstantin Rokossovsky's demolition squads are said to have brought the wind tunnels, test series facilities, and work camps down to Baltic Sea levels, while leaving all subterranean constructions operational. These were ideal silos for the devil's toolbox, as Erich Honecker said and Franz Josef Strauss surmised. Or maybe it just wasn't possible to blow up the bunkers to begin with, given that the former head chief of the site, Major General Dornberger, in wise anticipation of German-German reconstruction planning, had married the daughter of the owner of the local cement plant.

Ever since this revelation, which is missing from Dornberger's stoutly Prussian memoirs, I know what the children's bare feet were treading on while on vacation. (Thanks to corvette captain Fischer for this information.) Only the hands remained a mystery. Whenever a left-handed child that didn't know any better copied Kugler's/Menzel's cavalry, a levade to the left turned into a levade to the right.[21] These were the mirror image of [Friedrich Wilhelm von] Seydlitz's cuirassiers, Prussia's fame as seen by a Saxon child's eyes. At one point somebody using original and copy was able to point this out to me. And from that moment on, writing meant: switching left and right a second time, so that left and right may once again coincide. Biogeography. West and East are only different names for the same.

> If it wasn't for the Nips
> Being so good at building chips[22]
> The yards would still be open on the Clyde,
> But it can't be much fun for them
> Beneath the Rising Sun
> With all their kids committing suicide.

Theology

TRANSLATED BY GEOFFREY WINTHROP-YOUNG

I am drowning, *de profundis*, in invitations: computer technology over here, the future of architecture over there. One lecture chases the next. And all this despite the pledge I made to myself that after eight years of East German elementary school and five years of West German high school, I would never again submit to the morning horror of having to write five-hour essays on a preassigned topic.

So let me pretend, just for once, that some institution had invited me not to deliver a German essay based on their own, sovereign, media-controlled specifications but instead to speak about what moves the writings circulating under my surname. And because nobody can really address this, least of all the writer, I stammer (am stammered by) theology.

Kittler's gods, to the extent that they can be deciphered, seem to remain immutably the same. No deconstruction has ever eroded them. Somewhere it is written that their immortality ensures their periodic returns.[1] Somewhere else it is written that they will die of derisive laughter only when one of them declares himself to be the only god, the only truth, which says the same in the same way.[2]

In any case, these gods—and that is exactly what Nietzsche's derisive laughter represented—form an anachronistic though necessary plural. For without their plural there would be no tragedies, which—oh hear, ye gods—officially cease to exist once there is only one god. Only others will be able to determine whether (German) philhellenism is a mask for (German)

Originally published as "Theologie," in *Götter und Schriften rund ums Mittelmeer*, edited by Peter Berz, Peter Weibel, Susanne Holl, Gerhard Scharbert, Joulia Strauss, and Friedrich Kittler (Munich: Fink, 2017), 411.

anti-Semitism.³ But as long as they do not offer any evidence, this diagnosis of the present presupposes that all cultures that (following Foucault) have lost the concept of the tragic are themselves lost. What needs to be thought is not the minor shift of deconstruction, but—counter to our speech and/or bodies—a rupture of the impossible, whose proper name for the past century at least can only be war.

Hence the huns and berserkers, whose spirit already etymologically derives from the spit foaming at their mouths; hence all the strategists from von Müffling to Schlieffen and Fellgiebel who brought this spirit back to earth: as telegrams, radio messages, and wireless intercoms.⁴

Editors' Preface

1. Kittler draws on a wide array of arcane German texts, many of which are not available in English. Unless noted otherwise, all translations are our own.
2. Kittler, *Platz der Luftbrücke*, 69.
3. Nietzsche, *Untimely Meditations*, 85.
4. Kittler, *Grammophon Film Typewriter*, 30, to name one instance.
5. "Kittler irrt recht oft, aber weil ihn etwas fasziniert." Kittler, letter to Geoffrey Winthrop-Young, July 5, 2006.

Introduction: The Wars of Friedrich Kittler

1. On this point see Nolan, *Allure of Battle*.
2. Armitage, "From Discourse Networks to Cultural Mathematics," 26.
3. Kittler, *Platz der Luftbrücke*, 63–64.
4. I am drawing on and extending material published elsewhere. See Winthrop-Young, *"De Bellis Germanicis"* and *Kittler and the Media*.
5. Kittler, "Gleichschaltungen," 256.
6. Kittler, *Gramophone, Film, Typewriter*, xxxix.
7. Kittler, "Synergie von Mensch und Maschine," 102.
8. Kittler, *Gramophone, Film, Typewriter*, 95.
9. Siegert, *Cultural Techniques*, 4.
10. Siegert, *Cultural Techniques*, 4.
11. Kittler, *Discourse Networks*, 368.
12. Note that the formula is *not*: Discursive orders change because *media* change. Though the switch to analog media was fundamental for the switch from the Discourse Network 1800 to the Discourse Network 1900, media technologies in the conventional sense of the word played no part in the preceding switch from Kittler's "Scholars' Republic" (Foucault's classical episteme) to the Discourse Network 1800 (Foucault's modern episteme). In terms of gadgetry and hardware, from writing utensils to printing equipment, people wrote and published in 1800 as they had in 1750. What fundamentally changed was the ways in which they learned to speak and write, including the ways in which they spoke and wrote about speaking and writing. While the technologies of writing were

more or less the same, their cultural construction as well as their legal encoding changed drastically. Kittler was never the media theorist he was said to be, and he certainly does not deserve the moniker *techno-determinist*. Even the frequently invoked term *materialities of communication* does not quite cut it. Kittler began and ended as a theorist of cultural techniques and increasingly technologized culture.

13 Eldredge and Gould, "Punctuated Equilibria." For a helpful philosophical take on punctuated equilibrium, see Turner, *Paleontology*, 37–57.
14 Kittler, *Optical Media*, 30.
15 Note that Kittler explicitly states in "De Nostalgia" that he uses the word *deconstruction* "for the first and last time" (chapter 15, this volume). So much for calling him the "Derrida of the digital age."
16 Kittler identifies the martial origins of nostalgia by tying it to Johannes Hofer's 1688 dissertation, which describes the homesickness of Swiss mercenaries (see Hofer, "Medical Dissertation"), but he leaves it at that. The analysis could be extended to the martial habitat of the later temporalization of nostalgia (looking back in time rather than looking home from abroad), since the latter is associated with the adjustment difficulties experienced by post-Waterloo veterans of Napoleon's Grande Armée. For a recent history see Dodman, *What Nostalgia Was*.
17 Kleist, *Battle of Herrmann*, 15, lines 287–90. All following quotes are cited by page and line number. Note that throughout this introduction the name *Herrmann* is rendered as the more established *Hermann*.
18 Kleist, *Battle of Herrmann*, 18, lines 377–81.
19 Kleist, *Battle of Herrmann*, 18, lines 386–88.
20 Kleist, *Battle of Herrmann*, 42, lines 932–34.
21 Kleist, *Battle of Herrmann*, 42, line 937.
22 The quote is from Kleist, *Battle of Herrmann*, 42, line 937.
23 Kleist, *Battle of Herrmann*, 75, lines 1613–20.
24 Kleist, *Battle of Herrmann*, 122, lines 2632–36.
25 See Schmitt, *Writings on War*, 30–74.
26 Quoted in Roberts, *Napoleon the Great*, 423.
27 Clausewitz, *On War*, 165.
28 Vismann, *Files*, 120.
29 Wehler, *Deutsche Gesellschaftsgeschichte*, 397.
30 Clark, *Iron Kingdom*, 338.
31 Clark, *Iron Kingdom*, 338.
32 Harari, *Ultimate Experience*, 193.
33 Condell and Zabecki, "Editors' Introduction," 4.
34 Citino, *German Way of War*, 308.
35 Kant, *Anthropology*, 92.
36 Engelsing, *Analphabetentum und Lektüre*.
37 On the exclusion of the body from reading, see Kittler's "Authorship and Love," which revolves around a Foucauldian contrast between the premodern, physical

reading intercourse in canto 5 of Dante's *Inferno* and the more spiritual joint reading communions in Goethe's *Sorrows of Young Werther*. First, texts hack and program bodies; then they hack and create souls. For a more detailed analysis, see Winthrop-Young, "On Friedrich Kittler's 'Authorship and Love.'"

38 The release of the reader is superseded by the release of the signifier, commonly associated with the work of Jacques Derrida, which gave rise to similar anxieties caused by the renewed prospect of a harmful untethering of meaning. Once again, Kittler is playing a different game and should not be associated with this variant of so-called poststructuralism (a term he rarely used). Regardless of how others may define discourse analysis, for Kittler it was an idiosyncratic variant of one of the twentieth century's great theory dreams: the quest to identify generative rules determining the production of larger texts and utterances as effectively and systematically as phonetic, lexical, and syntactic rules determine the production of sounds, words, and sentences. This is not a release but an information-theoretical containment of the signifier.

39 One powerful reader-domestication mechanism is the author function, which serves to attract and bind reading trajectories. Rogue reading is in part prevented by the new convention that the text has to be read mindful of authorial intention. The great trick, discussed in depth in Kittler's *Discourse Networks*, is the strange effect that every single reader among a potentially infinite number of readers can receive the messages personally, as if they were addressed to her in particular. Authorship, in other words, has a paranoid tinge: these messages, though written to all, appear to be *for me*. The extreme case, chillingly presented in Stephen King's *Misery*, is the reader who claims ownership over the messages and does not shrink from mutilating the author's body if the messages are not to her liking.

40 The quotation is from Citino, *German Way of War*, 18.

41 Kittler, *Platz der Luftbrücke*.

42 Quoted in Kittler, "De Nostalgia," this volume.

43 Nietzsche, "Case of Wagner," 619.

44 For a recent critique of the binary between revolutionary soldiers and old-regime soldiers, see Berkovich, *Motivation in War*.

45 Quoted in Roberts, *Napoleon the Great*, 643.

46 Heine, *Romantic School*, 246. Of course, the real originator is none other than Schiller, with his notion of replacing socially calamitous street-based uprisings with aesthetically and morally uplifting spectacles on theater stages. The weather was already bad around 1800 and revolutions had better take place indoors.

47 Kittler and Maresch, "Wenn die Freiheit wirklich existiert," 95.

48 "Antirevolution" is from Wehler, *Deutsche Gesellschaftsgeschichte*, 397.

49 Singer and Brooking, *Like War*, 206. See also Andriukaitis, "Russia Uses Fake Rape Stories."

50 Kittler, "Take-Off of the Operators," 70.

51 Cronin, "Cyber-Mobilization," 77. Note the use of the verb *emerge*. Mobilization, enmity, and war are not simply the result of deliberate manipulation and toxic

partisan communication; they are an emergent property, in much the same way as the eddies and swirls of a river, once the flow rate is increased, transform into turbulence.

52 Cronin, "Cyber-Mobilization," 79. In a similar feedback loop, as Lisa Gitelman has shown in her book *Scripts, Grooves, and Writing Machines*, Thomas Edison received thousands of so-called idea letters from an admiring public following the Civil War, thus in effect mobilizing the collective imagination of Americans interested and invested in technological advance and, in turn, envisioning the conditions of possibility for advanced forms of mass communication. Mapping a historically specific "climate of representation" (63), which would accrue in Edison's "Private Idea Notebook" (including "ink for the blind" and an "electrical pen" [72, 161]), Edison (and other members of the blue-ribbon Naval Consulting Board) eventually actively solicited input from the public about war technologies following America's entry into World War I. See Gitelman, *Scripts, Grooves, and Writing Machines*, esp. 62–81. Observes Gitelman: "During and after 1917 thousands of letters poured in with ideas for weaponry and other war *matériel*" (77).
53 Guilhaumou, *La langue politique*, 151–56.
54 Cronin, "Cyber-Mobilization," 81.
55 Clausewitz, *On War*, 75 (emphasis in the original).
56 Clausewitz, *On War*, 77.
57 Sun Tzu, *Art of War*, 79.
58 Speer, *Inside the Third Reich*, 56.
59 Kershaw, *Hitler*, 527–89.
60 Speer, *Inside the Third Reich*, 614–15.
61 Armitage, "From Discourse Networks to Cultural Mathematics," 27 (emphasis in the original).
62 Citino, *German Way of War*, xiii.
63 Nolan, *Allure of Battle*, 12.
64 Citino, *German Way of War*, 306.
65 On killer drones, with many nods to Kittler, see Karppi, Böhlen, and Granata, "Killer Robots"; also Packer and Reeves, *Killer Apps*.
66 See chapter 8, "When the Blitzkrieg Raged," in this collection.
67 For a thorough account see Frieser, *Blitzkrieg Legend*.
68 Citino, *German Way of War*, 305.
69 Kittler, *Gramophone, Film, Typewriter*, 111.
70 Kittler, "Synergie von Mensch und Maschine," 90.
71 On this point see Ohler, *Blitzed*, and Kamienski, *Shooting Up*, 104–16.
72 Citino, *German Way of War*, 302. For a different take, see the recent contribution by David Stahel, *Retreat from Moscow*. German frontline commanders retained a greater degree of independence than previously thought and were able to turn the Stellungskrieg against the advance of the Red Army in the winter of 1941/42 into a strategic German success.
73 It is impossible to discuss all this without lapsing into sarcasm. After 1945, German generals developed great expertise in writing winning books about the war

they lost. The basic message is: We could have won, and it's Hitler's fault that we didn't. As Citino remarks, blaming Hitler is safe and convenient: "He had the perfect credentials. He was dead, first of all, and therefore incapable of defending himself; and second, he was Hitler." Citino, *German Way of War*, 269. But this self-cleansing operation would not have worked so well had it not met with the approval of former enemies. The postwar "identification with the Wehrmacht on the Eastern front" (290), based on the expectation that NATO was about to take on the same Red Army, promoted a positive appreciation of those who had gained a lot of experience fighting the Soviet Union a decade earlier—an identification still at work in video games decades later. For an account of the Western romance of the eastern front, see Smelser and Davies, *Myth of the Eastern Front*; for a recent evaluation of Hitler's checkered performance as commander in chief, see Fritz, *First Soldier*.

74 Citino, *German Way of War*, 303.
75 Theweleit, *Tor zur Welt*, 56–58.
76 No doubt Kittler's veneration for Pink Floyd also relates to the way many songs foreground war as a historical, psychological, and technological ground that gives rise to rock music as an abuse of army equipment. In the case of Roger Waters, hailed in "When the Blitzkrieg Raged" as "Britain's greatest modern poet," the ties that bind war and rock allow for a poignant intergenerational switch, hinted at in some of the most famous lyrics in the most famous Pink Floyd song. Addressing himself, the son, Roger Waters, imprisoned in his fame, appears as the replacement of his father, Eric Fletcher Waters, killed in the Battle of Anzio in February 1944: "Did you exchange / A walk-on part in the war / For a lead role in a cage?" Pink Floyd, "Wish You Were Here."
77 Kittler, *Gramophone, Film, Typewriter*, 140.
78 Kittler, *Gramophone, Film, Typewriter*, 258–59.
79 Neufeld, *Rocket and the Reich*, 273–74.
80 Petersen, *Missiles for the Fatherland*, 171.
81 See Neufeld, *Rocket and the Reich*, 274–75.
82 Kittler, *Gramophone, Film, Typewriter*, 259.
83 Zuse, *Computer—My Life*, 91–94. That Zuse was forced to use his parents' basement because he was unable to procure any support from the German military or any other source has been used as an argument against Kittler's claim that war fuels technological advance. Peace would have been better for Zuse and the German computer.
84 Hodges, *Alan Turing*, 299.
85 Armitage, "From Discourse Networks," 26.
86 Armitage, "From Discourse Networks," 25–26. See also Kittler, *Platz der Luftbrücke*, 18–19.
87 Kittler, *Platz der Luftbrücke*, 19.
88 Pynchon, *Gravity's Rainbow*, 701.
89 Pynchon, *Gravity's Rainbow*, 722.
90 Pynchon, *Gravity's Rainbow*, 521 (emphasis in the original).

91 For example, in "De Nostalgia," there are two extensively commented-on quotes from one scene of Schiller's *Wilhelm Tell* and roughly ten quotes from selected scenes of Kleist's *Hermann*, while the whole last third of the essay is a veritable pastiche of Pynchon, with Kittler frequently briefly paraphrasing the many quotes. For an excellent summary of the (Lacanian) paranoia at work in Kittler's theory production, see Schmidgen, "Successful Paranoia."

92 Pynchon, *Gravity's Rainbow*, 520 (emphasis in the original).

93 Kittler, *Truth of the Technological World*, 199.

94 Neufeld, *Rocket and the Reich*, 274.

95 Gumbrecht, *Truth of the Technological World*, 406.

96 Kittler, *Gramophone, Film, Typewriter*, 259.

97 See Pöhlmann, *Panzer*, 491–504.

98 For instance, see Knaack, *Kunst-Schatz des Führers*.

99 There are no fewer than six contradictory accounts of Kammler's death, which has led some to assume that no single one can be trusted. Since at the end of the war nobody knew more about Germany's secret weapons production, speculations abound that Kammler struck a secret deal with the Americans, shared his knowledge with them, and died in captivity. See also Döbert and Karlsch, "Hans Kammler."

100 Petersen, *Missiles for the Fatherland*, 167. For Kammler's role as a building inspector, see the analysis of the "Kammler sequence" in Ingrao, *Promise of the East*, 139–55.

101 "Auschwitz-theoretical" is from Kittler, *Platz der Luftbrücke*, 22.

102 Rubin, *Do It*, 234.

103 Pinchevski, *Transmitted Wounds*, 63. In this context, Pinchevski's contribution is required reading. Making use of Kittler, it is the first study to pursue the historically shifting medial a priori of trauma concepts.

104 Quoted in Blumenberg, *Work on Myth*, 11.

105 Schneider, "Freud-Träume," 139 (emphasis in the original).

106 Schmitt, "Historiographia in Nuce."

107 Koselleck, "Transformations of Experience," 83.

108 Koselleck, "Transformations of Experience," 83.

109 Kittler 1999, *Gramophone, Film, Typewriter*, 115.

110 "Laboratory" is from Pynchon, *Gravity's Rainbow*, 49.

111 Pynchon, *Gravity's Rainbow*, 336, 265 (emphasis in the original).

112 Pynchon, *Gravity's Rainbow*, 566.

Chapter 1. Free Ways

1 [*Trans. note*: See Müller, *Explosions of a Memory*, 129 (translation amended). "Volokolamsk" refers, by way of Heiner Müller's poem "Volokolamsk Highway," which draws on Alexandr Bek's eponymous 1944 novel, to events that occurred during the failed German advance on Moscow in late 1941.]

2 Pynchon, *Gravity's Rainbow*, 755.

3 Pynchon, *Gravity's Rainbow*, 767.
4 Pynchon, *Gravity's Rainbow*, 756.
5 [*Trans. note:* The acronym HAFRABA originally stood for Hamburg-Frankfurt-Basel, the name of the association founded in 1926 to prepare for the construction of a motorway connecting these cities. The first two letters, HA, later came to refer to Hanseatic cities (*Hansestädte*), in order to include Bremen and Lübeck.]
6 [*Trans. note:* Kittler provides no reference.]
7 [*Trans. note:* In German, *Verkehr* can refer both to traffic and to (sexual) intercourse.]
8 Lacan, *Écrits*, 417.
9 Doumenc, *Les transports automobiles*, 57.
10 Quoted in Gailor, "American Ambulance," 90.
11 [*Trans. note:* Kittler provides no reference.]
12 [*Trans. note:* Kittler provides no reference.]
13 Guderian, "Die Lebensader Verduns," 28.
14 Guderian, "Die Lebensader Verduns," 28.
15 [*Trans. note*: A reference to the 1974 Kraftwerk hit "Autobahn" featuring the refrain "Wir fahren fahren fahren auf der Autobahn" ("We drive drive drive on the autobahn").]
16 [*Trans. note:* Kittler provides no further reference.]
17 [*Trans. note:* Fritz Todt (1891–1942) was appointed inspector general for German roadways in 1933.]
18 [*Trans. note:* Kittler provides no reference.]
19 [*Trans. note*: An ironic reference to the opening lines of Joseph von Eichendorff's romantic poem "The Hunters' Farewell" ("Der Jäger Abschied"): "Oh beautiful forest so high above, / who put you there?" (Wer hat dich, du schöner Wald, / Aufgebaut so hoch da droben?).]
20 See Picker, *Hitlers Tischgespräche*.

Chapter 2. A Short History of the Searchlight

1 [*Trans. note:* In the German original, Kittler mistakenly attributes the words to Nibelung.]
2 Wagner, *Ring of the Nibelung*, 24.
3 Foucault, *"Society Must Be Defended,"* 70.
4 [*Trans. note:* A reference to Goethe's lines "Wär nicht das Auge sonnenhaft, / Die Sonne könnt' es nie erblicken" (If the eye weren't sun-like, / it could never catch sight of the sun).]
5 [*Trans. note:* An editor, writer, and experimenter, Paul Eduard Liesegang (1838–1896) was an active contributor to the early development of photography.]
6 See Schmitt, *Theory of the Partisan*, 61.
7 [*Trans. note:* A reference to the Meininger Ensemble, the court theater of Georg II, Duke of Saxe-Meiningen, which toured Europe in the latter half of the nineteenth century and was renowned for its realistic stagecraft.]

8 [*Trans. note:* Kittler provides no citation for this source.]
9 *Meyers großes Konversations-Lexikon*, 17:727.
10 Proust, *In Search of Lost Time*, 83.
11 Proust, *In Search of Lost Time*, 84.
12 [*Trans. note:* On Doumenc and Verdun, see chapter 1, "Free Ways," in this volume.]
13 [*Trans. note:* See the stage directions for the final scene of *Schlageter*, a Nazi play exalting Albert Leo Schlageter (1894–1923), a member of the German Freikorps executed by the French after he led sabotage operations against the French occupation of the Ruhr region. Johst, *Schlageter*, 134–35.]
14 Speer, *Inside the Third Reich*, 69.
15 [*Trans. note:* "By using special materials and by applying certain principles of statics, we should be able to build structures which even in a state of decay, after hundreds or (such were our reckonings) thousands of years would more or less resemble Roman models." See Speer, *Inside the Third Reich*, 56. For more on this quote, please also see chapter 17, note 14.]
16 Speer, *Inside the Third Reich*, 343.
17 Zhukov, *Reminiscences and Reflections*, 364.

Chapter 3. Fragments of a History of Firearms

1 See Burkert, *Lore and Science*.
2 [*Trans. note:* As Gargantua Senior put it to his son in a letter: "Printing likewise is now in use, so elegant and so correct that better cannot be imagined, although it was found out but in my time by divine inspiration, as by a diabolical suggestion on the other side was the invention of ordnance." Rabelais, *Gargantua and Pantagruel*, 161.]
3 See Rossi, *Birth of Modern Science*.
4 Rossi, *Birth of Modern Science*.
5 See Mersenne, *Harmonie universelle*, 1:30–35.
6 See Mersenne, *Harmonie universelle*, 1:30.
7 See Mersenne, *Harmonie universelle*, 3:198.

Chapter 4. Tanks

1 [*Trans. note:* Kittler's "Tanks" is packed with allusions, mostly to German and European history and literature, beginning with a reference to the former Day of German Unity (Tag der Deutschen Einheit), June 17, an official holiday in the Federal Republic from 1954 to 1990.]
2 [*Trans. note:* Hailing from Saxony, like Kittler himself, Müller is often seen as the most important German dramatist after Brecht. Müller wrote *Wolokolamsker Chaussee I–V* (*Volokolamsk Highway I–V*) as a didactic play in 1985–87, when the political reforms of Soviet premier Mikhail Gorbachev, especially glasnost and perestroika, laid the groundwork for a renewed protest movement in the Eastern Bloc and, eventually, for the reunification of Germany.]

3 [*Trans. note:* As Churchill put it in his letter to Prime Minister Herbert H. Asquith on January 5, 1915: "It would be quite easy in a short time to fit a number of steam tractors with small armoured shelters, in which men and machine guns could be placed, which would be bullet-proof. . . . The caterpillar system would enable trenches to be crossed quite easily, and the weight of the machine would destroy all wire entanglements." See Churchill, *World Crisis*, 74.]
4 [*Trans. note:* Kittler is referring to Brecht's dramatic fragment "Der Untergang des Egoisten Johann Fatzer" (Downfall of the egotist Johann Fatzer), which focuses on a group of deserting World War I soldiers hiding out in the German town of Mühlheim and hoping for a revolution.]
5 Deighton, *Blitzkrieg*, 153.
6 [*Trans. note:* "Male fantasies" is an allusion to Klaus Theweleit's two-volume *Male Fantasies*, a study of prefascist paramilitary troops—returning World War I soldiers who organized into volunteer armies called Freikorps—targeting perceived political enemies of the state in the early days of the Weimar Republic.]
7 [*Trans. note:* Count Helmuth Karl Bernhard von Moltke (1800–1891)—also known as Moltke the Elder to distinguish him from his nephew commanding the German Army at the outbreak of World War I—was a legendary German field marshal and chief of the General Staff of the Prussian Army. A disciple of Carl von Clausewitz, the notorious theorist of modern warfare, Moltke is often considered one of the fathers of modern troop direction and logistics.]
8 Creveld, *Sword and the Olive*, 160.
9 [*Trans. note:* Nikolai Fyodorovich Vatutin led the Red Army to victory during the Battle of Kursk, one of the largest tank battles in history (July–August 1943).]
10 Deighton, *Blitzkrieg*, 2013–14.
11 [*Trans. note:* Kittler refers to the term *Ereignis*, which enters Heidegger's language in his later work, especially *Contributions to Philosophy*.]
12 [*Trans. note:* An allusion to the massacre at Tiananmen—the Mandarin word for "Gate of Heavenly Peace"—on June 4, 1989.]
13 See Friedrich Hölderlin's poem "Remembrance." Hölderlin, *Hymns and Fragments*, 107–9.
14 [*Trans. note:* Vasily Ivanovich Chuikov was the Soviet commander of the Sixty-Second Army (not the Fifty-Second, as Kittler mistakenly states) during the Battle of Stalingrad (August 1942–February 1943), the major battle on the eastern front often regarded as the most strategically decisive battle of World War II, when heavy German losses tilted the balance of power toward the Allied forces. Chuikov's tank forces were also involved in the Battle of Berlin in the spring of 1945 and had encircled the city by the end of April. Chuikov was the first Allied officer to learn of the suicide of Adolf Hitler and—as an officer of the First Belorussian Front—accepted the city's surrender from the commander of the Berlin Defense Area, General Helmuth Weidling, on May 2, 1945.]
15 The necessity of replacing carbon compounds, or mortalities, with silicon compounds, or immortalities, has already been anticipated by Thomas Pynchon. See *Gravity's Rainbow*, 580.

16 [*Trans. note*: While Albert Speer and his team were working on lighter tank designs (such as the Panther) to achieve greater agility on the front, Hitler had a strong preference for large and heavily armored tanks. "By way of pleasing and reassuring Hitler, Porsche also undertook to design the superheavy tank which weighed over a hundred tons and hence could be built only in small numbers, one by one. For security purposes this new monster was assigned the codename Mouse." Speer, *Inside the Third Reich*, 234.]

Chapter 5. Noises of War

1 Dietrich Behrens and Magdalena Karstien's 1925 collection *Geschütz und Geschosslaute im Weltkrieg* (Noises of shells and projectiles in the world war).
2 [*Trans. note*: This etymological jump is also invoked in chapter 9, "Animals of War," in this volume.]
3 [*Trans. note*: Goethe, *Collected Works*, 5:652. The *Collected Works* translation omits the claim to "universality" in Goethe's original statement: "eine neue Epoche in der Weltgeschichte."]
4 Goethe, *Collected Works*, 5:651–52.
5 Stendhal, *Charterhouse of Parma*, 52.
6 Stendhal, *Charterhouse of Parma*, 47–48.
7 Hegel, "Jena Lectures," 171.
8 Hegel, "Jena Lectures," 171.
9 Grabbe, *Napoleon*, 463.
10 Creveld, *Command in War*, 18.
11 Schlieffen, "War Today, 1909," 198.
12 Liliencron, "Sommerschlacht," 27.
13 D. Winter, *Death's Men*, 107. With thanks to Sabine Brand.
14 Jünger, *Storm of Steel*.
15 D. Winter, *Death's Men*, 175.
16 Quoted in Behrens and Karstien, *Geschütz- und Geschosslaute*, 8–9.
17 Quoted in Behrens and Karstien, *Geschütz- und Geschosslaute*, 9.
18 See W. Kittler, *Die Geburt des Partisanen*.
19 Behrens and Karstien, *Geschütz- und Geschosslaute*, 7.
20 Hellingrath, *Hölderlin-Vermächtnis*, 254. Thanks to Bernhard Siegert.
21 Quoted in Fussell, *Great War*, 171.
22 Pessler, "Das historische Museum," 100. "The limits of such a program are naturally built into the very limits of a museum itself. Among all the senses, only the eyes will really be given their due. Whether vivid audio-impressions of war ought to be preserved for posterity at least in part through real-life recordings (that is, in nonverbal form) is a question worth answering. The momentous din of a battle, especially in a world war, is presumably the acoustic event leaving the greatest impression. Innumerable sounds coalesce and interfere with one another: the thunder of the cannons, the swooshing,

hissing, and explosion of the grenades, the crackle of machine guns, the singing of rifles, the clanging of sabers, the signals of drums and trumpets, the galloping of horses, the jingle of the harnesses and drays, and the commandos. Perhaps a sample from such a momentous cacophony, especially from a decisive battle, could be replayed on a phonograph installed in a special room of the museum. What a war museum can offer the eye, however, is infinitely more." (At the very least, the last sentence demonstrates Pessler's ignorance.)

23 See Fussell, *Great War*, 226–30.
24 See Schramm, *Geheimdienst im Zweiten Weltkrieg*, 324.
25 Schramm, *Geheimdienst im Zweiten Weltkrieg*, 324.
26 [*Trans. note:* Jones, *Most Secret War*, 75. "There was a doctrine that radio wavelengths of the order of 10 centimeters could not be generated by electronic valves because the time taken by the electrons to pass through the valve was much too great. This argument was fallacious, but was accepted by many scientists and engineers because we had become almost congenitally inclined to accept such 'postulates of impotence' in basic science."]
27 Jones, *Most Secret War*, 76.
28 See Deighton, *Blitzkrieg*, 163–64.
29 With thanks to Daniel Gethmann.
30 [*Trans. note:* The Junkers Ju 87 (soon followed by the twin-engine Junkers Ju 88) was known as the Stuka, an abbreviation of the German *Sturzkampfflugzeug*, meaning "dive bomber."]
31 Edwards, *Closed World*, 211.
32 Edwards, *Closed World*, 211.
33 Edwards, *Closed World*, 216–17.
34 Edwards, *Closed World*, 214.
35 [*Trans. note:* This closing dictum alludes to a public appeal by Friedrich Wilhelm Graf von der Schulenburg-Kehnert to the citizens of Berlin following the Battle of Jena-Auerstedt, when Prussian troops suffered a severe loss against the armies of Napoleon (1806). Following the defeat, Schulenburg-Kehnert—in his capacity as minister and advisor to Frederick Wilhelm II—famously decreed: "The King has lost a battle. Now remaining calm is the first civic duty. I ask the citizens of Berlin to abide by that. The King and his brothers are alive!" Quoted in Schoeps, *Preußen*, 99.]

Chapter 6. Playback. A World War History of Radio Drama

1 Nietzsche, *Thus Spoke Zarathustra*, 118.
2 [*Trans. note:* The Flight across the Ocean was inspired by Charles Lindbergh's 1927 autobiographical account of his transatlantic flight, *We* (1927). In 1950 Brecht added a prologue and removed Lindbergh's name from the title and the text of the play because of the aviator's Nazi sympathies and his wartime anti-interventionism. See also Brecht, *Bertolt Brecht on Film and Radio*, 38–41.]

3 Groos, *Play of Man*, 19–21.
4 Groos, *Play of Man*, 19–21.
5 [*Trans. note:* Funkspiel (radio play) also referred to a World War II Nazi counter-intelligence practice, when the Gestapo forced captured radio operators in France to send false messages to British Intelligence, thus in effect signaling their allegiance to the French resistance, communicating misinformation, and intercepting classified Allied information.]
6 [*Trans. note:* Kittler provides no reference.]
7 [*Trans. note:* While Kittler provides no specific reference, this quote, widely used in military literature, is commonly attributed to Soviet Admiral Sergei G. Gorshkov (e.g., see "Joint Publication 3-85 "Electromagnetic Spectrum Operations," I-1.) https://www.jcs.mil/Portals/36/Documents/Doctrine/pubs/jp3_85.pdf?ver=2020-04-09-140128-347.]
8 Hüsmert, "Die letzten Jahre," 46.
9 Hüsmert, "Die letzten Jahre," 43.
10 Nietzsche, *Richard Wagner in Bayreuth*, 51.
11 Wagner, *Ring of the Nibelung*, 329.
12 [*Trans. note:* Großdeutscher Rundfunk—loosely translating as "All-German Radio" or "Great-German Radio"—was the designation for the national socialist radio program of the German Reich. The term was suggested by Reich minister of propaganda Joseph Goebbels in 1939 and signaled the party-controlled centrality of patriotic and typically war-related broadcasts. Kittler refers to the final performance of the Berlin Philharmonic, which was broadcast live on April 12, 1945, shortly before the final collapse of the Reich. As the concert concluded with the finale of *Götterdämmerung* (*Twilight of the Gods*), members of the Hitler Youth distributed baskets of cyanide capsules to the audience and to members of the party elite in attendance.]
13 Wagner, *Ring of the Nibelung*, 326.
14 Wagner, *Ring of the Nibelung*, 40.
15 Wagner, *Ring of the Nibelung*, 40.
16 Wagner, *Ring of the Nibelung*, 41.
17 [*Trans. note:* Chapter 7 of Arnheim's theory of radio is titled "In Praise of Blindness: Emancipation from the Body." See Arnheim, *Radio*, 133–202.]
18 [*Trans. note:* Schlieffen, "War Today, 1909," 198. The sentence "Auch mit dem besten Fernglas würde er nicht viel zu sehen bekommen" (Even with field glasses he wouldn't get to see much) is missing from the published English translation of Schlieffen's essay.]
19 Fussell, *Great War*, 51–63.
20 Meier, "Erstes Rundfunkkonzert," 168.
21 Hughes, "Birth of Radio Drama," 146.
22 Brecht, *Bertolt Brecht on Film and Radio*, 42.
23 Brecht, *Bertolt Brecht on Film and Radio*, 41.
24 Brecht, *Bertolt Brecht on Film and Radio*, 37.
25 See Hoffmann, "Vom Wesen des Funkspiels," 374.

26 [*Trans. note:* Kittler provides no reference to Johannsen's and Moeller's work.]
27 [*Trans. note:* Kittler provides no reference.]
28 [*Trans. note:* In the shorter English version of this talk, Kittler added, "Or, in literary terms, until a whole radio drama drowned in static. Long before Pynchon's *Gravity's Rainbow*, literature turned into a feedback of world wars. On the novel's last page, in 1973, the V-2 rocket hits a movie theater in Los Angeles."]
29 Marconi, quoted in Dunlap, *Marconi*, 353.
30 [*Trans. note:* In the English version, Kittler glosses the Gleiwitz incident as follows: "Welles' radiophonic feat to simulate wars against radio stations was, to be sure, another feed forward of World War Two. As you may know, the German propaganda machine disguised the Wehrmacht's attack on Poland as an act of self-defense. The night before, some twenty SS men clothed in Polish uniforms simulated a raid against a local German radio station situated near the two countries' border. The station microphone transmitted gun shots and foreign sounds before its very operation, just as in Welles' fiction, came to a sudden end. Next morning, the Führer was cunningly entitled to a radio speech which called the Wehrmacht's attack a defensive retaliation."]
31 Welles and Koch, in Gosling, *Waging "The War of the Worlds,"* 193.
32 Marconi, quoted in Dunlap, *Marconi*, 267.
33 [*Trans. note:* This is a reference to mathematician John von Neumann's book *Theory of Games and Economic Behavior* (Princeton, NJ: Princeton University Press, 1944), which he coauthored with the Austrian economist Oskar Morgenstern. The book is generally considered the foundational text that created the interdisciplinary research field of game theory.]
34 See Geyer, "German Strategy."
35 Welles and Koch, in Gosling, *Waging "The War of the Worlds,"* 204. The text has "State Militia," but "Signal Corps" officers are "attached to the State Militia."
36 Gosling, *Waging "The War of the Worlds,"* 206. The missiles are also called "rocket machines."
37 Gosling, *Waging "The War of the Worlds,"* 218.
38 Gosling, *Waging "The War of the Worlds,"* 210.
39 Gosling, *Waging "The War of the Worlds,"* 211.
40 [*Trans. note:* A reference to Syberberg's 442-minute-long magnum opus, *Hitler, ein Film aus Deutschland* (1977)—released as *Hitler: A Film from Germany* in Great Britain and as *Our Hitler* in the United States—which includes several original World War II broadcasts and speeches.]
41 [*Trans. note:* Fessenden's widow, Helen, describes her husband's idea as follows: "The manufacture of ten thousand airplanes, each capable of carrying four 100-pound, high-explosive bombs, to be built in Canada by mass production methods and to be delivered at the front by May 1, 1915. The most important feature of the plan was that these airplanes were to be used as airplanes had never been used before—IN MASS. This was an absolutely new concept in warfare; but it was practical. Because of their high speed of maneuver airplanes

by the hundred or by the thousand could fly in column or in echelon; each distinct from its neighbor, yet passing a given point so rapidly as to maintain a continuous shower of bombs on that point. This meant that for the first time it was possible to end the war by some other means than the destruction of man-power. Using aircraft in mass, and striking again and again at the lines of communication and depots, the enemy in the front lines would be kept without food, ammunition or reinforcements until they were ready to give up." To which she adds, at the bottom of the page: "It is interesting to see how literally the recommendations of this memorandum are being carried out in the present war." Fessenden, *Fessenden*, 231.]

42 [*Trans. note:* Bergson, "Meaning of War," 36. On December 12, 1914, Bergson delivered the presidential address to the Académie des Sciences Morales et Politiques.]
43 Bachmann, *Cicadas*, 117.
44 [*Trans. note:* Kittler provides no reference.]
45 Eich, *Dreams*, 92.

Chapter 7. Operation Valhalla

1 Wagner, *Ring of the Nibelung*, 107–8.
2 [*Trans. note:* Issued by Frederick William III on April 13, 1813, the Landsturm edict called on all adult male Prussians who were not already members of the regular army to resist the occupying French forces by any means possible. Further see "De Nostalgia," chapter 15 in this collection.]
3 [*Trans. note:* Kittler does not provide a page reference.]
4 [*Trans. note:* The name Siegfried contains *Sieg*, the German word for "victory."]
5 [*Trans. note:* Henry Bessemer (1813–98) was an English inventor and industrialist who pioneered the cheap nineteenth-century manufacture of steel. Heir to the eponymous steel empire founded by his father, Friedrich Krupp, in the early nineteenth century, Alfred Krupp became the arms manufacturer for the Kingdom of Prussia in 1859 and, later, for the German Empire.]
6 [*Trans. note:* A reference to the trilogy *Die Nibelungen* by German playwright Friedrich Hebbel (1813–63). At the beginning of his career, Kittler wrote a study of Hebbel that was not published for several decades. See Kittler, *Hebbels Einbildungskraft*.]
7 [*Trans. note:* Kittler does not provide a reference.]
8 [*Trans. note:* Literally translating as "fountain (or source) of life," Lebensborn was an SS-supported association committed to raising the birth rate of Aryan children, frequently by means of prearranged extramarital relations and abductions of "racially superior" children from German-occupied territories.]
9 Wagner, *Ring of the Nibelung*, 156.
10 [*Trans. note:* Kittler does not provide the exact reference.]
11 [*Trans. note:* Kittler does not provide the exact reference.]
12 Wagner, *Ring of the Nibelung*, 107.

Chapter 8. When the Blitzkrieg Raged

1 [*Trans. note:* Lyrics from the Rolling Stones, "Sympathy for the Devil."]
2 [*Trans. note:* A reference to Karl Marx's "A Contribution to the Critique of Hegel's Philosophy of Right": "Every sphere of German society must be shown as the partie honteuse of German society: these petrified relations must be forced to dance by singing their own tune to them!" Kittler was fond of this statement, as it appears to argue for resistance by feedback. See Kittler, *Gramophone, Film, Typewriter*, 110; Marx, "Contribution to the Critique," 45.]
3 [*Trans. note:* Founded in 1980, *Spex* was a prominent German rock and pop culture magazine which ceased publication in 2018.]
4 [*Trans. note:* Lyrics from the Rolling Stones, "No Expectations," on *Beggars Banquet*.]
5 Fussell, *Wartime*, 268.
6 [*Trans. note:* Lyrics from the Rolling Stones, "Stray Cat Blues," on *Beggars Banquet*.]
7 [*Trans. note:* An allusion to Robbe-Grillet's 1959 *nouveau roman*, In the Labyrinth (*Dans le labyrinthe*), in which the region, or town of, Reichenfels provides the war-torn setting.]
8 [*Trans. note:* Unidentified source.]
9 [*Trans. note:* A reference to a famous line in Hölderlin's poem "Friedensfeier" (Celebration of peace). See Hölderlin, *Poems*, 65: "Viel hat von Morgen an, / Seit ein Gespräch wir sind und hören voneinander, / Erfahren der Mensch; bald sind wir aber Gesang." (Man has learned much since morning, / For we are a conversation and we can listen / To one another. Soon we'll be song.)]
10 [*Trans. note:* A popular song in wartime Japan. See Fussell, *Wartime*, 185.]

Chapter 9. Animals of War. A Historical Bestiary

1 [*Trans. note*: In the original German, Kittler uses for "humans" the intriguing *Nebenmenschen*, a word with an impressive Freudian and Lacanian pedigree that is normally not translated. However, it is likely that he also used it with a view toward its less esoteric nineteenth-century usage, where it occasionally served as a less emphatic, more practical alternative to *Mitmenschen* (fellow human beings). Nebenmenschen are, as it were, not fully human humans as they appear in the military animal-human composites under discussion here.]
2 [*Trans. note:* The etymological jump from *spit* to *spirit* is about as trustworthy as Kittler's switch, in the original German version, from *Geifer* (frothing saliva, slobber) to Geist. See also chapter 5, "Noises of War," in this volume.]
3 [*Trans. note:* Kittler provides no reference.]
4 [*Trans. note:* A reference to Frank Wisbar's 1959 Stalingrad movie *Hunde, wollt ihr ewig leben?* (*Dogs, Do You Want to Live Forever?*), based on Fritz Wöss's 1958 novel of the same name. At the Battle of Kolin (1757) Frederick the Great is said to

have cursed his fleeing troops with the words, "Ihr verfluchten Racker, wollt ihr denn ewig leben?" (You damned rascals, do you want to live forever?).]

5 [*Trans. note:* Kittler provides no further reference.]

6 [*Trans. note:* Kittler provides no reference to a specific gospel.]

7 [*Trans. note:* Kittler is paraphrasing Hegel's Jena Lectures here. See Hegel, *Hegel and the Human Spirit*, 171. The same passage is quoted in chapter 5, "Noises of War," in this volume.]

Chapter 10. On Modern Warfare. A Conversation with Alexander Kluge

1 [*Trans. note:* A reference to the Battle of Valmy (September 20, 1792), the first victory of the new French citizen army against the invading troops of the First Coalition. Among Germans and Germanists, the battle is remembered primarily because the poet Goethe, who was a witness on the losing side, tried to lift the spirits of the defeated soldiers by assuring them that they had participated in a momentous event: "From this place and from this day forth commences a new era in the history of the world, and you can all say that you were present at its birth." Quoted in Lewes, *Life of Goethe*, 377. See also "Noises of War," chapter 5 in this volume.]

2 [*Trans. note:* According to legend, Holy Roman Emperor Frederick I "Barbarossa" (1122–90), after whom the 1941 German invasion of the Soviet Union is named, lies asleep in a secret chamber underneath the Kyffhäuser hills in Thuringia.]

3 [*Trans. note*: See Kant, *Anthropology*, 92: "The domestic or civil servant under orders needs only to have understanding. The officer, to whom only a general rule is prescribed, and who is then left on his own, needs judgement to decide for himself what should be done in a given case. The general, who must consider potential future cases and who must think out rules on his own, must have Reason."]

4 [*Trans. note:* Kittler provides no further reference.]

5 [*Trans. note:* See "Il fiore delle truppe scelte," in Kittler, *The Truth of the Technological World*.]

6 Geyer, "German Strategy," 527–97.

7 [*Trans. note:* The Kaiserstuhl is a fertile range of hills in the Upper Rhine Plain in southwestern Germany known for its wines. Kittler's claim that its loess layer is of African origin sounds fanciful; it is more likely the result of the erosion and displacement of the Rhine sediments.]

8 [*Trans. note:* "Knight" is a chess reference. In German the knight is called *Springer* (literally, "jumper").]

9 [*Trans. note:* Felix Steiner (1896–1966) was a former army officer who rose to the rank of general in the Waffen-SS (for which he became a prominent postwar apologist). In April 1945 the so-called Army Group Steiner failed to carry out Hitler's order to launch a counterattack against the Soviet assault on Berlin.]

10 [*Trans. note:* Kluge is referring to the Battle of Frankenhausen (May 15, 1525), the last major engagement of the German Peasants' War. The rebellious peasants were defeated by mercenaries; their leader, the charismatic preacher Thomas Müntzer, was captured, put on trial, and executed. Kluge then invokes the old German saying "Geh nicht zu deinem Fürst, wenn du nicht gerufen wirst."]

11 [*Trans. note:* As on several other occasions, Kittler is referring to Albert Speer's final statement at the Nuremberg Trials. Speer described the Third Reich as the "first dictatorship of an industrial state in this age of modern technology," in which "telephone, teletype, and radio made it possible to transmit the commands of the highest level directly to the lowest organs where because of their high authority they were executed uncritically." Speer, *Inside the Third Reich*, 614.]

12 [*Trans. note:* The following paragraph refers to the *mankurt* passage in the novel *The Day Lasts More Than a Hundred Years* by Chingiz Aitmatov (1928–2008). While Kittler's summary comes with a few exaggerations (e.g., there is no mention of children being buried for several years), the basic torture technique is rendered correctly. According to the novel's retelling of Kyrgyz legends, the nomadic Zhuan'zhuan used to shave the heads of young men captured in battle and tightly wrap them in the skin of camel udders. Fitted with a wooden shackle and with their hands and feet tied, the victims were left without food or water in the searing sun for several days. The pain and pressure of the contracting udder skin resulted in brain damage, including a total loss of memory, that turned the few survivors into docile mindless slaves, or mankurts. It is interesting to note that the novel uses this nomadic technique to illustrate the state politics of cultural obliteration imposed by the Soviet system on many of its ethnic minorities. See Aitmatov, *Day Lasts More*, 124–46.]

Chapter 11. Of States and Their Terrorists

1 Lacan, *Écrits*, 662.

2 [*Trans. note:* That Kittler should throw in a reference to Freiburg, the town in which he spent over twenty years, comes as no surprise. Erfstadt, located a few miles southwest of Cologne, is an arcane historical reference: before being assassinated on October 18, 1977, Hanns Martin Schleyer, the most prominent victim of the Red Army Faction, or RAF, was held captive in Erfstadt-Liblar.]

3 [*Trans. note:* Kittler is playfully inserting an iconic Goethe quote (which, incidentally, also serves to support the martial dimension of his lecture). See chapter 5, "Noises of War," and chapter 10, "On Modern Warfare," in this volume. The reference is to the Battle of Valmy (September 20, 1792), the first victory of the new French citizen army against the invading troops of the First Coalition. Among Germans and Germanists, the battle is remembered primarily because the poet Goethe, who was a witness on the losing side, tried to lift the spirits of the defeated soldiers by assuring them that they had participated in a momentous event: "From this place and from this day forth commences a new era in

the history of the world, and you can all say that you were present at its birth." Quoted in Lewes, *Life of Goethe*, 377.]

4 [*Trans. note:* Kittler refers to Oswald Wiener's novel of 1969, *Die Verbesserung von Mitteleuropa* (The Improvement of Central Europe). No English translation exists.]

5 [*Trans. note:* Kittler's use of "herald" is a pun on Horst Herold, president of the BKA from 1971 to 1981. *Herold* happens to be the German word for "herald." For an analysis of Kittler's account of Herold, see Winthrop-Young, "Hunting a Whale of a State."]

6 [*Trans. note:* this is a reference to the high-security Stammheim Prison in Stuttgart, which housed the leading RAF terrorists between 1975 and 1977.]

7 [*Trans. note:* Kittler is referring to a tactic devised by Herold known in German as *negative Rasterfahndung*. The police knew that terrorists were renting apartments in the Greater Frankfurt area under false names, but the information was of little help since it was logistically impossible to scrutinize hundreds of thousands of tenants. Herold correctly surmised that the terrorists would prefer to pay their electric bills in cash, which reduced the number of possible suspects to eighteen thousand. He then fed list after list of legitimate names—officially registered tenants, vehicle owners, student loan recipients, pensioners, insurance holders—into his database of cash-paying customers, thus gradually removing all the legitimate names until only two fake names remained: a drug dealer and the terrorist Rolf Heissler, later named as one of the assassins of Hanns Martin Schleyer.]

8 Kipling, "A Sahib's War," in *Traffic and Discoveries*, 55–71.

9 Belloc, *Modern Traveller*, n.p.

10 See Kipling, *Kim*, 7. To quote one of the most beautiful openings in the history of the novel: "He sat, in defiance of municipal orders, astride the gun Zam-Zammah, on her old platform, opposite the old Ajaib-Gher—the Wonder House, as the natives called the Lahore Museum. Who hold Zam-Zammah, that 'fire-breathing dragon,' hold the Punjab, for the great green-bronze piece is always first of the conqueror's loot." In just two sentences Kipling manages to jump from a cheeky, unnamed half blood to the world-historical "Land of Five Waters."

11 Hillgruber, *Der Zweite Weltkrieg*, 118.

12 [*Trans. note:* A swipe at former 1968 student activist Joschka Fischer, who served as German foreign minister from 1998 to 2005. *Tennō* is a Japanese word for the Emperor of Japan.]

13 [*Trans. note:* See Sophocles, *Antigone*, 17. Kittler is referring to the second, agrarian part of the famous description of man by the Theban chorus: "Of the many strange wonders, / none is more wondrous than man. / He sails across the gray sea / through stormy south winds, / engulfed by the waves. / He tills Gaia year after year, / plowing with mules, / wearing down / eternal, inexhaustible Earth, / the oldest of gods."]

14 Potratz, *Die Skythen in Südrussland*, 87.

15 Nietzsche, *Anti-Christ, Ecce Homo*, 145.

16 [*Trans. note:* Schmitt, *Theory of the Partisan*, 76 (translation amended). See also chapter 8, "When the Blitzkrieg Raged," in this volume.]
17 Schmitt, *Theory of the Partisan*, 80.
18 [*Trans. note:* A reference to an iconic (and ironic) Warhol quotation: "The most beautiful thing in Tokyo is McDonald's. The most beautiful thing in Stockholm is McDonald's. The most beautiful thing in Florence is McDonald's. Peking and Moscow don't have anything beautiful yet." Warhol, *Philosophy*, 71.]
19 [*Trans. note:* For security reasons Herold had to relinquish his home residence and spend decades living in the protected residence Kittler refers to, which he left only after the death of his wife in 2017. He used to say of himself, "I am the last prisoner of the RAF." Jürgs, "Gefangen in der Vergangenheit."]

Chapter 12. Manners of Death in War

1 [*Trans. note:* A reference to Clausewitz's landmark book *On War*, unfinished at the time of his death, in which he draws upon his experiences fighting in the French Revolution and Napoleonic Wars, as well as his military studies at the Prussian Kriegsakademie (War Academy).]
2 [*Trans. note:* Heidegger, *Being and Time*, 243. A reference, the first of many in this chapter, to Martin Heidegger's reflections on death in *Being and Time*, esp. div. II, pt. 1, sec. 46–53.]
3 [*Trans. note:* Bachmann did not write a dissertation on *Being and Time* but on the critical reception of Heidegger.]
4 Pynchon, *Gravity's Rainbow*, 105.
5 Hegel, "Jena Lectures," 171.
6 [*Trans. note:* In the Battle of Jena-Auerstedt (October 14, 1806), the armies of Napoleon scored a decisive victory against outdated Prussian and Saxon troops. In the German original, Kittler plays on the title of Hegel's book *Jenaer Realphilosophie* (Hegel's philosophy of the real, developed in Jena) to suggest that Hegel's philosophical speculations were answered by Napoleon's "Jenaer Realbeweis," his "real-life" conquest of the town. See also chapter 5, "Noises of War," in this volume.]
7 See Hegel, *Phenomenology of Spirit*, 19.
8 *Meyers großes Konversations-Lexikon*, 20:704.
9 Grimmelshausen, *Simplicissimus*, 176–77.
10 [*Trans. note:* See, for example, Herold, *Age of Napoleon*, 437. Napoleon made this pronouncement at age twenty-two, as a young lieutenant of the artillery, during a speech competition given at the Academy of Lyon on the theme of happiness and education.]
11 Benn, *Gesammelte Werke*, 3:427. [*Trans. note:* Benn, "The Poems."]
12 Clausewitz, *On War*, 258.
13 [*Trans. note:* A reference to Charles Marie René Leconte de Lisle, a French poet of the Parnassian movement (1866), commonly known only by his surname, Leconte de Lisle.]

14 [*Trans. note:* Pynchon, *Gravity's Rainbow*, 219. See also chapter 7, "Operation Valhalla," chapter 9, "Animals of War," and chapter 15, "De Nostalgia," in this volume.]
15 Wagner, *My Life*, 3.
16 [*Trans. note:* Reference unclear.]
17 [*Trans. note:* In *The Rhinegold*, the first of four music dramas that constitute *The Ring of the Nibelung*, Wotan's servant Loge is a demigod of fire often acting as a guide and negotiator on behalf of his master. For the following see also chapter 7, "Operation Valhalla," in this volume.]
18 Wagner, *Ring of the Nibelung*, 107–8.
19 See Dunant, *Origins of the Red Cross*.
20 Meyers, "Kriegsanitätwesen," in *Meyers großes Konversations-Lexikon*, 11:677.
21 [*Trans. note:* Shortly before moving to Basel in 1869, Nietzsche renounced his Prussian citizenship but served as a medical orderly in the Prussian Army during the Franco-Prussian War (1870–71).]
22 Schlieffen, "War Today, 1909," 195. (Thanks to Philipp V. Hilgers.) [*Trans. note:* Kittler seems to misread the original passage.]
23 [*Trans. note:* For the song mentioning the Yasukuni Shrine, see Fussell, *Wartime*, 185. See also chapter 8, "When the Blitzkrieg Raged," in this volume.]
24 Schlieffen, "War Today, 1909," 195–96.
25 [*Trans. note:* Upon Germany's mobilization in 1914, and following two previous incarnations, Field Marshal Paul von Hindenburg assumed control of what became known as the Third Supreme Army Command (Dritte Oberste Heeresleitung) in 1916. While ceding most military decisions to the general of infantry Erich Ludendorff, Hindenburg and his deputy increasingly dictated the terms of the German war effort, including the 1918 Spring Offensive on the western front (a.k.a. the Ludendorff Offensive or Kaiserschlacht).]
26 [*Trans. note:* Max Hermann Bauer and Georg Bruchmüller were German officers noted for their development of modern artillery logistics and tactics during World War I. Both were advocates of total war and were involved in the strategies of Ludendorff's 1918 Spring Offensive. Soldiers nicknamed Bruchmüller *Durch-bruchmüller* to play on his name and his ramrod-style strategy of achieving a quick breakthrough (*Durchbruch*) of enemy lines.]
27 [*Trans. note:* Kittler provides no further reference.]
28 [*Trans. note:* An allusion, among others, to Ernst Jünger's *In Stahlgewittern* (1920; first English translation in 1929 as *The Storm of Steel*), a graphic memoir based on his experiences on the Western Front in World War I.]
29 Heidegger, *Being and Time*, 243.
30 Ott, *Martin Heidegger*, 104.
31 Grimmelshausen, *Simplicissimus*, 434.
32 Heidegger, *Being and Time*, 242.
33 Heidegger, *Being and Time*, 242.
34 Heidegger, *Being and Time*, 242.

35 Heidegger, *Being and Time*, 352.
36 [*Trans. note*: Kittler alludes to Heidegger's lecture-turned-essay *The Question concerning Technology* (1954), published almost three decades after *Being and Time* (1927).]
37 [*Trans. note*: Heidegger, *Off the Beaten Track*, 82. In the German original, Heidegger's "setting-upon" (*Angriff*) is close to the notion of attack.]
38 Heidegger, *Off the Beaten Track*, 217.
39 [*Trans. note*: Operation Sichelschnitt, developed by Lieutenant General Erich von Manstein, was the principal attack plan of the Wehrmacht during the Battle of France in 1940. Also referred to as the Manstein Plan, Operation Sichelschnitt describes Manstein's strategy of invading the northeastern part of France through the Ardennes, followed by a high-speed advance to the coast. Vaguely reminiscent of the cut and curvature of a sickle blade—*Sichelschnitt* is the literal German translation of "sickle cut" (with perhaps additional overtones of the Grim Reaper)—the catchy phrase was used by Winston Churchill and in documents of German officers. See especially Frieser, *Blitzkrieg Legend*, 60.]
40 Pynchon, *Gravity's Rainbow*, 521.
41 See Engels, *Herr Eugen Dühring's Revolution*, 102.
42 [*Trans. note*: See also chapter 4, "Tanks," and chapter 8, "When the Blitzkrieg Raged," in this volume.]
43 Fussell, *Wartime*, 270.
44 [*Trans. note*: See Kittler, "Ein Herr namens Luhmann," 183.]
45 See Riedesser and Verderber, *Aufrüstung der Seelen*.
46 See Creveld, *Sword and the Olive*.
47 See Berndt, *Die Zahl im Kriege*.
48 See Derrida, *Cinders*.
49 Grimmelshausen, *Simplicissimus*, 177.

Chapter 13. Ottilie Hauptmann

1 Borges, "Tlön, Uqbar, Orbis Tertius," 12.
2 Goethe, *Collected Works*, 11:147.
3 Goethe, *Collected Works*, 11:99.
4 Thus Gottfried Benn, paraphrasing Ottilie in his 1932 speech for the Prussian Academy. See Benn, *Gesammelte Werke*, 1:435. "We will never be one mummy under / the ancient desert and the happy palms," wrote Mallarmé. See Mallarmé, *Poems*, 15.
5 [*Trans. note*: Hence the title "Ottilie Hauptmann."]
6 See W. Kittler, "Goethes *Wahlverwandtschaften*," 52.
7 [*Trans. note*: The German word translated as "committed" would more literally mean "appropriated" (*vereignet*).]
8 [*Trans. note*: See, for instance, Joshua Trachtenberg's 1939 study *Jewish Magic and Superstition: A Study in Folk Religion* on beliefs regarding "spirit possession." Trachtenberg, *Jewish Magic*, 51–52.]

9. Goethe, *Collected Works*, 11:113.
10. See Foucault's interview with Paolo Caruso: "I in fact consider that from now on morality may be reduced entirely to politics and to sexuality, which itself may be reduced to politics: this is why the moral is the political." Foucault, *Religion and Culture*, 100.
11. [*Trans. note:* Here, Kittler is referring to Friedrich Schiller—from 1773 to 1780 student number 447 at the Hohe Karlsschule, an academy founded and closely watched over by Duke Karl Eugen of Württemberg (1728–93)—and his tutor Jacob Friedrich Abel, who drawing on his experiences as an educator wrote one of the first German handbooks on psychology. See Kittler, "Carlos als Carlsschüler," 256.]
12. Goethe, *Collected Works*, 11:208.
13. See Riemer, *Mitteilungen über Goethe*, 309–10.
14. [*Trans. note:* "In place of 'sociology': a theory of the forms of domination" (An Stelle der "Sociologie" eine Lehre von den Herrschaftsgebilden). Nietzsche, *Will to Power*, 255.]
15. [*Trans. note:* A school for "higher daughters" is an educational institution reserved for young women from the ranks of the nobility and upper middle classes.]
16. [*Trans. note:* Kittler is referring to Nathan's adoptive daughter in Lessing's *Nathan the Wise*.]
17. See Goethe, *Collected Works*, 11:109.
18. [*Trans. note:* In the German original: "auf polnische Art" (going Dutch). Here Kittler draws on Jens Schreiber's argument in "Die Zeichen der Liebe," published in the same volume as the first version of "Ottilie Hauptmann" in Bolz, *Goethes Wahlverwandtschaften*.]
19. Goethe, *Collected Works*, 11:108, 11:109.
20. See Petrat, *Schulunterricht*.
21. Goethe, *Collected Works*, 11:108.
22. Goethe, *Collected Works*, 11:108.
23. Goethe, *Collected Works*, 11:109.
24. See Foucault, *Discipline and Punish*.
25. Goethe, *Collected Works*, 11:208.
26. Goethe, *Collected Works*, 11:118.
27. [*Trans. note:* A private gymnasium for female educators founded in 1811 in Berlin.]
28. Quoted in Blochmann, *Das "Frauenzimmer,"* 116.
29. Niethammer, in Goethe, *Briefe an Goethe*, 1:528.
30. [*Trans. note:* Niethammer, *Streit des Philanthropinismus und Humanismus*, 345. Kittler returns to this exact quote in *Discourse Networks* (62).]
31. Benjamin, "Goethe's Elective Affinities," 337.
32. "It is a terrible duty to imitate the inimitable." Goethe, *Collected Works*, 11:262.
33. Goethe, *Collected Works*, 11:251.
34. Goethe to Joseph Stanislaus Zauper, in Goethe, *Briefe an Goethe*, 2:8; Goethe, *Collected Works*, 11:210.

35 Goethe, *Collected Works*, 11:167.
36 Goethe, *Collected Works*, 11:167.
37 See Geerdts, "Goethes Roman *Die Wahlverwandtschaften*," 286.
38 See Geerdts, "Goethes Roman *Die Wahlverwandtschaften*," 286.
39 See Petrat, *Schulunterricht*, 58.
40 Goethe, *Collected Works*, 11:218.
41 See W. Kittler, "Goethes *Wahlverwandtschaften*."
42 Goethe, *Collected Works*, 11:204.
43 [*Trans. note:* Once again, Kittler deviates from the text: "She did not recognize him, but she thought she could hear the voice of her teacher from her boarding school." Goethe, *Collected Works*, 11:205.]
44 Goethe, *Collected Works*, 11:232.
45 See Hörisch, "Das Sein der Zeichen."
46 [*Trans. note:* Goethe, *Collected Works*, 11:243 (translation amended).]
47 See Foucault, *History of Sexuality*, vol. 1.
48 See Nemec, *Die Ökonomie der Wahlverwandtschaften*, 187.
49 Goethe, *Collected Works*, 11:162.
50 Goethe, *Collected Works*, 11:233.
51 Goethe, *Collected Works*, 11:237.
52 Goethe, *Collected Works*, 11:230.
53 Goethe, *Collected Works*, 11:226.
54 Goethe, *Collected Works*, 11:227.
55 Goethe, *Collected Works*, 11:230.
56 According to the interpretation proposed in Barnes, *Goethe's Die Wahlverwandtschaften*, 197.
57 Goethe, *Collected Works*, 11:225. See W. Kittler, "Goethes *Wahlverwandtschaften*," 230.
58 Goethe, *Collected Works*, 11:225.
59 Goethe, *Collected Works*, 11:228, 11:225.
60 According to Benjamin's commentary on André François-Poncet's reading of the novel. See Benjamin, "Goethe's Elective Affinities," 337.
61 See W. Kittler, *Die Geburt des Partisanen*.
62 François-Poncet, *Les affinités électives de Goethe*.
63 Goethe, *Collected Works*, 11:111.
64 Goethe, *Collected Works*, 11:241.
65 See Turk, "Goethes *Wahlverwandtschaften*," 216.
66 Lacan, *Seminar*, 32.
67 [*Trans. note:* "There is thus the male way of revolving around it, and then the other one . . . the female way." According to Lacan, the masculine *ratage* of the sexual relationship corresponds to the phallus, whereas the feminine modality relates to lack in the Other. See Lacan, *Seminar*, 57. I am employing Joan Copjec's reading of Lacan's formulation here. See Copjec, "Sex," 19. Throughout this passage Kittler alludes to Lacan's arguments and terminology in *Seminar*, book 20: "This botching (*ratage*) is the only way of realizing (the sexual relationship)." Lacan, *Seminar*, 58.]

68 Goethe, *Collected Works*, 11:227. Psychoanalysis has treated this delirium in nosological fashion and decoded it as hysteria.
69 [*Trans. note*: Here, Kittler chooses not to follow Lacan's capitalization method and implications: "the Other" thus becomes simply "the other."]
70 Fink, "Goethes *Wahlverwandtschaften*," 457.
71 Goethe, *Collected Works*, 11:207.
72 Goethe, *Collected Works*, 11:110; and Goethe to Carl Friedrich Zelter, in Goethe, *Briefe an Goethe*, 1:369.
73 See also Zons, "Ein Denkmal voriger Zeiten," 334.
74 Goethe, *Collected Works*, 11:199.
75 Goethe, *Collected Works*, 11:123.
76 [*Trans. note*: The original has "Schweizer Ordnung." Goethe, *Collected Works*, 11:123 (translation amended).]
77 Goethe, *Collected Works*, 11:111.
78 Geerdts, "Goethes Roman *Die Wahlverwandtschaften*," 289.
79 "As long as there is still one beggar around, there will still be myth." Benjamin, *Arcades Project*, 400.
80 Goethe, *Collected Works*, 11:124.
81 Goethe, *Collected Works*, 11:155.
82 Goethe, *Collected Works*, 11:155, 11:175.
83 Kaiser, *Wandrer und Idylle*, 76.
84 See Borges, *Selected Poems*, 93.
85 Heinemann, *Schule*, 116.
86 Heinemann, *Schule*, 126.
87 Goethe, *Collected Works*, 11:142.
88 [*Trans. note*: Kittler's original version of the essay in the 1981 volume edited by Norbert W. Bolz did not contain the following section on Müffling representing the second historical "candidate" (after Rochow) for the portrayal of the Captain in the novel. A decade later, in *Dichter, Mutter, Kind*, Kittler adds the Müffling insert (in the German volume, pages 134–47) without further commentary. To mark this abrupt addition to what thus becomes a "weaponized second version" of the essay (see Winthrop-Young's introduction to this volume), the editors have opted to set this section in bold.]
89 Eckermann, *Conversations of Goethe*, 289.
90 Biedermann, *Goethes Gespräche*, 2:62.
91 See Biedermann, *Goethes Gespräche*, 1:528.
92 Biedermann, *Goethes Gespräche*, 1:528.
93 Müffling, *Passages from My Life*, 4.
94 Müffling, *Passages from My Life*, 4.
95 Müffling, *Offizier, Kartograph, Politiker*, 41. See also Görlitz, *Kleine Geschichte des Deutschen Generalstabes*, 61: "During the nineteenth and twentieth centuries, the majority of the leading officers in the General Staff come from wealthless or impoverished families."

96 [*Trans. note:* Müffling, *Offizier, Kartograph, Politiker*, 48. "Der kleine Krieg," or "la petite guerre," is a part of classic eighteenth-century combat tactics: a warfare of "outposts, patrols, ambushes, raids, the constructions of entrenchments and the attack and defense of fortified places" theorized by Gerhard von Scharnhorst and Carl von Clausewitz. See Paret, *Clausewitz in His Time*, 19.]
97 See Tümmler, *Carl August von Weimar*, 107.
98 Müffling, *Offizier, Kartograph, Politiker*, 53.
99 Goethe, *Collected Works*, 11:105.
100 Müffling, *Passages from My Life*, 3.
101 Müffling, *Offizier, Kartograph, Politiker*, 57. On the relations between Müffling and Gauß, who also made a career under the protection of an old-fashioned yet progressively minded military commander, namely, the Duke of Brunswick, see Grossmann, "Niedersächsische Vermessungsgeschichte."
102 See Clausewitz, *On War*; and Giehrl, *Der Feldherr Napoleon*.
103 [*Trans. note:* The Gotha Observatory on top of the hill Seeberg.]
104 Müffling, *Offizier, Kartograph, Politiker*, 256.
105 Goethe, *Collected Works*, 11:95.
106 Goethe, *Collected Works*, 11:106, 11:110.
107 Goethe, *Collected Works*, 11:106.
108 Goethe, *Collected Works*, 11:107.
109 Goethe, *Collected Works*, 11:125.
110 Goethe, *Collected Works*, 11:233.
111 See Tümmler, *Carl August von Weimar*, 200.
112 See Müffling, *Passages from My Life*, 19. See also Müffling, *Offizier, Kartograph, Politiker*, 63.
113 Müffling, *Passages from My Life*, 18. See also Görlitz, *Kleine Geschichte des Deutschen Generalstabes*, 63.
114 Goethe, *Collected Works*, 11:97.
115 Goethe, *Collected Works*, 11:94.
116 Müffling, *Offizier, Kartograph, Politiker*, 70.
117 Müffling, *Offizier, Kartograph, Politiker*, 70.
118 Goethe, *Collected Works*, 11:95.
119 Müffling, *Offizier, Kartograph, Politiker*, 70.
120 [*Trans. note:* Goethe married his companion Christiane Vulpius just a few days after the Battle of Jena-Auerstedt, on October 19, 1806. See Schwartz, "Why Did Goethe Marry."]
121 Tümmler, *Carl August von Weimar*, 151.
122 Müffling, *Passages from My Life*, 20.
123 Goethe, *Collected Works*, 11:20.
124 Müffling, *Offizier, Kartograph, Politiker*, 71.
125 Müffling, *Offizier, Kartograph, Politiker*, 71.
126 Goethe, *Collected Works*, 11:20.
127 Goethe, *Collected Works*, 11:142.

128 Goethe, *Collected Works*, 11:155.
129 [*Trans. note*: Kittler provides no reference.]
130 Goethe, *Collected Works*, 11:155.
131 Goethe, *Collected Works*, 11:173–74.
132 Müffling, *Offizier, Kartograph, Politiker*, 72.
133 All quotes from Müffling, *Passages from My Life*, 30.
134 Görlitz, *Kleine Geschichte des Deutschen Generalstabes*, 63.
135 [*Trans. note*: That is to say, March 21, 1933, when the symbolic handshake between Reich President and former Field Marshal Paul von Hindenburg and newly appointed Reich Chancellor Adolf Hitler marks the de facto co-option of the military under Nazi rule.]
136 Görlitz, *Kleine Geschichte des Deutschen Generalstabes*, 62–64.
137 Goethe to Carl Friedrich Naumann, in Goethe, *Briefe an Goethe*, 1:179. [*Trans. note*: As translated in Vasco, *Diderot and Goethe*, 41.]
138 [*Trans. note*: The "war game" belonging to Georg Heinrich von Reißwitz, Baron von Reißwitz's son, "warmly recommended" by Müffling to the army "for training purposes," was "truly a simulation: . . . based on probability calculations, it simulated all combinations of terrain resistance, movement speeds, accuracy of fire and death rates." Pias, "Action, Adventure, Desire," 144.]
139 Priesdorff, *Soldatisches Führertum*, 322.
140 [*Trans. note*: Kittler sets up this entire last section in the form of a theoretical dialogue, represented in this English translation as an imaginary conversation between A and B.] Lacan, *Seminar*, 4.
141 Goethe, *Collected Works*, 11:213.
142 [*Trans. note*: A reference to Goethe's meeting with Napoleon in Erfurt on October 2, 1808.]
143 Lacan, *Écrits*, 242.
144 Goethe, *Collected Works*, 11:212.
145 [*Trans. note*: Benjamin, "Goethe's Elective Affinities," 355: "There echoes at the end of the book that 'How beautiful' in the ears of the dead, who, we hope, awaken, if ever, not to a beautiful world, but to a blessed one." Kittler once more goes against the grain of Benjamin's reading, proposing Lacanian desire over messianic hope, and fiction as protocol over the "semblance of reconciliation" as aesthetic blessing.]

Chapter 14. On a Novel That Would Not Only Be Fiction . . .

1 [*Trans. note*: See Hegel's discussion on the subject of romantic fiction in the *Aesthetics*: "For the end of such apprenticeship consists in this, that the subject sows his wild oats, builds himself with his wishes and opinions into harmony with subsisting relationships and their rationality, enters the concatenation of the world, and acquires for himself an appropriate attitude to it." Hegel, *Aesthetics*, 593.]
2 Pynchon, "Togetherness," 6.
3 Siegel, "Who Is Thomas Pynchon," 170.
4 Siegel, "Who Is Thomas Pynchon," 172.

5 [*Trans. note:* U.S. Army Major Robert B. Staver was the chief of the Jet Propulsion Section of the Research and Intelligence Branch of the U.S. Army Ordnance Corps during World War II. One of his tasks (first entitled Operation Overcast) was to interview German scientists involved in weapons development in the final months of the war. Later, Staver urged the evacuation of German scientists and their families to the United States (known as Operation Paperclip), thus ushering in not only the missile developments of the Cold War but eventually also America's space program. Not surprisingly, Wernher von Braun, the chief rocket scientist at Peenemünde and a fixture in *Gravity's Rainbow*, was at the top of Staver's "black list," while Russia offered headhunting money to bring von Braun into their postwar sector. The transition from cannon fodder to Cape Canaveral was in the works. See Ordway and Sharpe, *Rocket Team*, 278, 290.]

6 [*Trans. note:* Kittler is referring to this volume's chapter 16, "Media and Drugs in Pynchon's Second World War," written at about the same time, and Kammler also briefly appears in chapter 17, "Biogeography," also in this volume. Hans Kammler was a civil engineer and high-ranking SS officer responsible for the construction of various concentration camps and secret weapons projects, including manufacturing plants and testing sites. Kittler is referring to the transfer of responsibility for the mass production of the V-2 from the German Army Ordnance Office (Heereswaffenamt) to Kammler following the Allied bombing raids on Peenemünde in August 1943. Kammler relocated these facilities underground to the so-called Mittelwerk, attached to which was a concentration camp complex that served as a labor pool for the production lines of the V-2. Working with demonic dedication and asking the same of his associates—especially as high-speed missile production was considered to be of the essence in 1944–45—Kammler had no regard for the living and working conditions of the enslaved inmates. As he reportedly put it, "Don't worry about the victims. The work must proceed ahead in the shortest time possible" (quoted in Bornemann and Broszat, "Das KL Dora-Mittelbau," 165). Impressed by Kammler's terrible efficiency, Hitler in the spring of 1945 transferred major responsibilities for aircraft support and maintenance from his deputy, Hermann Göring, to Kammler, culminating in his eventual designation as "the Fuehrer's general plenipotentiary for jet aircraft" (Kroener, Müller, and Umbreit, *Germany and the Second World War*, 390).]

7 Pynchon, *Gravity's Rainbow*, 843.

8 See Kennedy, *Vengeance Weapon 2*, 72.

9 Pynchon, *Gravity's Rainbow*, 350.

10 [*Trans. note*: See Jones, *Most Secret War*, 446–47. In Kittler's typescript, the bibliographic information and specific pagination are blank, suggesting that he had yet to finish work on this essay.]

11 [*Trans. note:* The opening lines of *Vineland*, to which Kittler refers, beyond indicating the ostensible oscillation between (so-called) fact and fiction, continue the military and informational discourse of much of Pynchon's work: "Later than usual one summer morning in 1984, Zoyd Wheeler drifted awake in sunlight through a creeping fig that hung in the window, with a squadron of blue jays

stomping around on the roof. In his dream these had been carrier pigeons from someplace far across the ocean, landing and taking off again one by one, each bearing a message for him, but none of whom, light pulsing in the wings, he could ever quite get to in time." Pynchon, *Vineland*, 3.]

12 Pynchon, *Gravity's Rainbow*, 594.

Chapter 15. De Nostalgia

1 [*Trans. note*: Throughout this essay, the German *Heimat* is retained when Kittler uses the word emphatically; in all other cases, it is translated as *home*.]
2 [*Trans. note*: A well-known but untranslatable pun: in modern German, *Elend*, once the designation for being abroad, has come to mean *misery*.]
3 [*Trans. note*: A reference to Hansgünther Heyme's controversial 1984 Stuttgart production of Schiller's *Wilhelm Tell*, which drew parallels between the events depicted in the play and later nationalist and fascist German insurrections.]
4 Schiller, *Wilhelm Tell*, 41.
5 Schiller, *Wilhelm Tell*, 39.
6 Schiller, *Wilhelm Tell*, 39.
7 Schiller, *Wilhelm Tell*, 40, 37.
8 Schiller, *Wilhelm Tell*, 39.
9 Goethe and Schiller, *Correspondence*, 474 (translation amended).
10 Gerschmann, "Johannes Hofers Dissertation," 83.
11 [*Trans. note*: For an English translation, see Hofer, "Medical Dissertation on Nostalgia."].
12 "Nullum admittat remedium, praeter reditum in patriam." Hofer, quoted in Gerschmann, "Johannes Hofers Dissertation," 84.
13 Schmitt, *Theory of the Partisan*, 3.
14 Quoted in Schmitt, *Theory of the Partisan*, 4.
15 Schmitt, *Theory of the Partisan*, 43.
16 Gneisenau, *Schriften*, 260.
17 Quoted in G. Winter and Vaupel, *Reorganisation des preußischen Staates*, 88. See also Haase, *Kleists Nachrichtentechnik*, 100–118.
18 Schmitt, *Theory of the Partisan*, 7. [*Trans. note*: As noted in the introduction, we are throughout using the modern spelling *Hermann*.]
19 Kleist, *Battle of Herrmann*, 15.
20 Kleist, *Battle of Herrmann*, 122.
21 Trevor-Roper, *Hitler's War Directives*, 207.
22 On the objections raised by German industry against the directive, see Herbst, *Der totale Krieg*, 403.
23 Kleist, *Battle of Herrmann*, 18; and Trevor-Roper, *Hitler's War Directives*, 206.
24 [*Trans. note*: A famous quote: "Into the dust with all the enemies of Brandenburg" (In Staub mit allen Feinden Brandenburgs) is the last line of Heinrich von Kleist's play *The Prince of Homburg*.]

25 [*Trans. note:* A reference to Claus Peymann's renowned 1982 production of Kleist's play. Given its incendiary content, and following a surfeit of productions in the Third Reich, *The Battle of Herrmann* had rarely been performed in either West or East Germany.]
26 Kleist, *Battle of Herrmann*, 40.
27 Kleist, *Battle of Herrmann*, 52.
28 Kleist, *Battle of Herrmann*, 67.
29 Kleist, *Battle of Herrmann*, 67.
30 Kleist, *Battle of Herrmann*, 43.
31 Kleist, *Battle of Herrmann*, 75.
32 Pynchon, *Gravity's Rainbow*, 219.
33 [*Trans. note:* The Battle of Velikiye Luki took place from November 1942 to January 1943. Overshadowed by the Battle of Stalingrad, which took place at the same time, the capture of Velikiye Luki was of great strategic importance for the subsequent advance of the Red Army westward.]
34 Kleist, *Battle of Herrmann*, 14. As Richard Samuel shows, Hermann is echoing Gneisenau himself. Samuel, *Aufsätze und Essays*, 423–25.
35 Kleist, *Battle of Herrmann*, 87.
36 [*Trans. note:* A minor mistake. Bolshaya narodnaya voyná translates as "the Great People's War." "The Great Patriotic War" is Velíkaya Otéchestvennaya voyná.]
37 Clausewitz, *On War*, 350. See also Glucksmann, *Le discours de la guerre*.
38 Goerlitz, *History of the German General Staff*, 59.
39 Schmitt, *Theory of the Partisan*, 76.
40 Pynchon, *Gravity's Rainbow*, 245. This quote is for Ute Holl, Lothar Leininger, and others.
41 [*Trans. note:* Kittler attributes the quote to Hölderlin without providing any reference.]
42 Pynchon, *Gravity's Rainbow*, 549–51.
43 Schmitt, *Theory of the Partisan*, 70–71. [*Trans. note:* See also Kittler, "Media and Drugs," chapter 16 in this volume.]
44 Pynchon, *Gravity's Rainbow*, 701.
45 Pynchon, *Gravity's Rainbow*, 76, 105.
46 Pynchon, *Gravity's Rainbow*, 521.
47 Pynchon, *Gravity's Rainbow*, 243.
48 Pynchon, *Gravity's Rainbow*, 148.
49 See Douhet, *Command of the Air*, 10.
50 Pynchon, *Gravity's Rainbow*, 75.
51 Pynchon, *Gravity's Rainbow*, 41.
52 Pynchon, *Gravity's Rainbow*, 41.
53 Pynchon, *Gravity's Rainbow*, 325.
54 Pynchon, *Gravity's Rainbow*, 39.
55 Schmitt, *Theory of the Partisan*, 79.
56 Pynchon, *Gravity's Rainbow*, 639.
57 Pynchon, *Gravity's Rainbow*, 698 (emphasis in the original).

58 Pynchon, *Gravity's Rainbow*, 699.
59 Pynchon, *Gravity's Rainbow*, 303. See also Bornemann, *Geheimprojekt Mittelbau*, 39.
60 Pynchon, *Gravity's Rainbow*, 297, 324.
61 Pynchon, *Gravity's Rainbow*, 293. On the motorized 485th *Abteilung*, see Kennedy, *Vengeance Weapon 2*, 38. See also the depiction of a rocket mascot on page 57, though this one dates from the postwar period of the British Operation Backfire.
62 Schmitt, *Theory of the Partisan*, 80.
63 Pynchon, *Gravity's Rainbow*, 77.
64 Pynchon, *Gravity's Rainbow*, 79. See also Fussell, *Great War*, 131–35.
65 See the furious finale in Fussell, *Great War*, 328–35.
66 Pynchon, *Gravity's Rainbow*, 316.
67 Pynchon, *Gravity's Rainbow*, 566, 265.
68 See Schmitt, *Theory of the Partisan*, 70.
69 Pynchon, *Gravity's Rainbow*, 338. See also Haffner, *Meaning of Hitler*, 17–19, 156–60.
70 Pynchon, *Gravity's Rainbow*, 519.
71 Pynchon, *Gravity's Rainbow*, 520 (emphasis in the original).
72 See Virilio, *War and Cinema*, 69–70.
73 See Pynchon, *Gravity's Rainbow*, 520.
74 Pynchon, *Gravity's Rainbow*, 521.
75 Pynchon, *Gravity's Rainbow*, 525.
76 Pynchon, *Gravity's Rainbow*, 760.

Chapter 16. Media and Drugs in Pynchon's Second World War

1 *Frankfurter Allgemeine Zeitung*, November 3, 1983, 12.
2 [*Trans. note*: About the strategies of autobahns since World War I, see chapter 1, "Free Ways," in this volume.]
3 See also Bergaust, *Wernher von Braun*, esp. 81–82.
4 [*Trans. note*: About World War II and postwar fantasy, see Pink Floyd, *The Final Cut*, side 1.]
5 Pynchon, *Gravity's Rainbow*, 39, 56.
6 Pynchon, *Gravity's Rainbow*, 480, 539, 626, 642, passim.
7 Pynchon, *Gravity's Rainbow*, 96, 312. See the memoirs of von Braun in Ruland, *Wernher von Braun*, 141.
8 Ruland, *Wernher von Braun*, 268.
9 Pynchon, *Gravity's Rainbow*, 304, 559, 706. About Nordhausen, the largest known subterranean factory, see Bornemann, *Geheimprojekt Mittelbau*.
10 Pynchon, *Gravity's Rainbow*, 522, 388.
11 [*Trans. note*: On UHF, see Pynchon, *Gravity's Rainbow*, 325. See also Pynchon's reference to the "'Telefunken radio control'" (207). As Steven Weisenburger glosses, "According to [Walter] Dornberger," from whose memoirs Kittler quotes as well, "the Telefunken Radio Company worked on a centrimetric guidance beam that would have delivered V-2 rockets over a distance of a

hundred and fifty miles and with 'a dispersion of less than a thousand yards.' If the system had gone operational, which it did not, the rockets would have been devastatingly accurate." Weisenburger, *"Gravity's Rainbow" Companion*, 114.]

12 Pynchon, *Gravity's Rainbow*, 76, 105.
13 Pynchon, *Gravity's Rainbow*, 521.
14 [*Trans. note:* Pynchon, *Gravity's Rainbow*, 258. About the birth of the computer from the spirit of espionage, see Kittler's essay "Das Gespenst im Computer." At the time Pynchon was writing *Gravity's Rainbow*, the fact that information machines had already displaced agents at Bletchley Park in 1943 was still hidden away in secret files.]
15 Pynchon, *Gravity's Rainbow*, 509.
16 Following are the words of the *Zahme Xenien* that describe the introduction of a general draft, not militarily or ideologically, but in terms of discourse analysis: "Formerly, somebody could communicate his sufferings to others; he could recount his war experience in old age. These days misery is universal; the individual can no longer lament anymore. Everybody must be on the battlefield—who is there to listen when warriors tell their tales?" [*Trans. note:* as translated in Tabbi and Wutz, *Reading Matters*, 171.]
17 [*Trans. note:* See chapter 7, "Operation Valhalla," in this volume.]
18 See Carl Schmitt's *Theory of the Partisan* on absolute enmity, total mobilization, and Kleist's "partisan poetry."
19 [*Trans. note:* See Fussell, *Great War and Modern Memory*.]
20 See Jünger on World War I as the "strangler of our literature." See Jünger, *Kampf als inneres Erlebnis*, 98, 92.
21 Jünger, *Kampf als inneres Erlebnis*, 12, 28, 50, 107.
22 In the case of the V-2, the time lapse was sixteen seconds. See Ruland, *Wernher von Braun*, 221.
23 Kamper, "Atlantis."
24 Pynchon, *Gravity's Rainbow*, 25.
25 Pynchon, *Gravity's Rainbow*, 28.
26 [*Trans. note:* Fortress Europe (*Festung Europa*) was a military propaganda term in common use by both sides during World War II and referred to the areas of Continental Europe occupied by Nazi Germany as opposed to the United Kingdom. For the Nazi propaganda machine, the term signified Hitler's intent to make all of occupied Europe into a bulwark against British troops attacking from across the Channel. To that effect, between 1942 and 1944, he constructed an extensive system of defenses and fortifications along the coastline(s) of Continental Europe and Scandinavia—often referred to as the Atlantic Wall—including a shield of air defenses. As such, the term circulated widely and entered the discourse of World War II journalism and history. For the British, by contrast, Fortress Europe came to be a battle honor, or special citation, accorded to the Royal Air Force and Allied squadrons for missions flown from British soil against targets in Germany or German-occupied Europe following the fall of France in June 1940.]

27 See also Stevenson, *Man Called Intrepid*, as well as Joseph Borkin's insufficient monograph on IG Farben, *Crime and Punishment of I.G. Farben*, esp. 76–94.
28 Pynchon, *Gravity's Rainbow*, 582.
29 See Foucault, "Fantasia of the Library," 157–77.
30 See Freud, *Complete Psychological Works*, 14:204; and Morris, *Theory of Signs*, 67.
31 Pynchon, *Gravity's Rainbow*, 207.
32 About Staver, see Ruland, *Wernher von Braun*, 249. Here are some further name games that confuse fact and fiction: Höhler, the architect of Nordhausen's Mittelwerke (Bornemann, *Geheimprojekt Mittelbau*, 23), becomes Ölsch (*Gravity's Rainbow*, 298–300); Enzian, the code name for a rocket project in Peenemünde (Ruland, *Wernher von Braun*, 261), becomes the name of the head of the fictitious Waffen-SS Hereros. Finally, "Max" and "Moritz," the two engineers present during the launching of the manned V-2 (*Gravity's Rainbow*, 757–58), quote from von Braun's A-2 of November 1934 (Ruland, *Wernher von Braun*, 89). Readers are asked to keep searching. . . .
33 [*Trans. note*: Pynchon, *Gravity's Rainbow*, 453. As another sign of Pynchon's labyrinthine sourcing or informational camouflage, he most likely used the English translation of the *A4-Fibel* (1944)—the *A-4/V-2 Rocket Instruction Manual* (1957)—to describe the launch sequence of the V-2 (*Gravity's Rainbow*, 316, passim). However, as Weisenburger puts it, "if he used the English version (virtually the only publicly available one), he also chose to use the German terms." Weisenberger, *"Gravity's Rainbow" Companion*, 177. Then again, Pynchon may have had access to the original *Fibel* while writing the novel.]
34 See Pynchon, *Gravity's Rainbow*, 587.
35 Pynchon, *Gravity's Rainbow*, 582.
36 Pynchon, *Gravity's Rainbow*, 582.
37 Pynchon, *Gravity's Rainbow*, 216.
38 [*Trans. note*: An allusion to the famous "Little Albert" experiment in psychology conducted by behaviorist John B. Watson and graduate student Rosalie Rayner around 1919 at Johns Hopkins University.]
39 Pynchon, *Gravity's Rainbow*, 84.
40 Pynchon, *Gravity's Rainbow*, 287; see also 623.
41 Pynchon, *Gravity's Rainbow*, 712; see also 285.
42 Pynchon, *Gravity's Rainbow*, 742.
43 Pynchon, *Gravity's Rainbow*, 434; see also 703.
44 See Shannon and Weaver, *Mathematical Theory of Communication*, 22.
45 [*Trans. note*: A reference to British astronomer Sir Arthur Eddington's notion of the Arrow of Time, or Time's Arrow (most likely from *The Nature of the Physical World* [1928]) in which he essentially argued for a "one-way direction" or "asymmetry" of time in thermodynamic processes. In this work Eddington stated that the second law of thermodynamics could be seen as a case study of such irreversibility, as entropy, understood as a measure of microcosmic disorder within a closed system, increases over time. In such a system, the flow

of time is asymmetrical—that is, nonreversible—because of the irreversible, one-directional increase in disorder within it, eventually leading to the system's energetic standstill.]

46 Pynchon, *Gravity's Rainbow*, 56.
47 Pynchon, *Gravity's Rainbow*, 139.
48 Pynchon, *Gravity's Rainbow*, 139.
49 Pynchon, *Gravity's Rainbow*, 164; see also 167.
50 Pynchon, *Gravity's Rainbow*, 112, 745.
51 Pynchon, *Gravity's Rainbow*, 560. See Virilio, *War and Cinema,* esp. 55, for Speer's theorem that all architecture must anticipate its future "ruin value."
52 Pynchon, *Gravity's Rainbow*, 521.
53 See Howe, *Black Game*.
54 Pynchon, *Gravity's Rainbow*, 93–94, 112.
55 Pynchon, *Gravity's Rainbow*, 388; see also 275.
56 Pynchon, *Gravity's Rainbow*, 878. After viewing this film about a flight to the moon, one of Pynchon's figures observes, "Real flight and dreams of flight go together" (159). See Ruland, *Wernher von Braun*, 57–61, on Universum Film AG (UFA) and Professor Oberth's first liquid-fuel rocket projects; and Virilio, *War and Cinema*, 58, on *Frau im Mond* and the power of film: "The film came out on 30 September 1929, but without the intended publicity of a real rocket launch from the beach of Horst in Pomerania to an altitude of forty kilometers. By 1932 jet technology . . . was set to become one of the major military secrets in the Third Reich, and the German authorities of the time seized Lang's film on the grounds that it was *too close to reality*. A decade later, on 7 July 1943, von Braun and Dornberger presented Hitler with film of the real launch of the A4 rocket. The Führer was in a bitter mood: 'Why was it I could not believe in the success of your work? If we'd had these rockets in 1939 we'd never have had this war.'" More persuasive evidence of the power of film hardly exists: Hitler, the cineast, who was bored by all the real-life demonstrations of the V-2 (Dornberger, *V-2*, 73–77, 99–101), becomes convinced through film.
57 See Virilio, *War and Cinema*, esp. 11 and 68, on Étienne-Jules Marey's chronophotographic gun; see also Aichinger, "Spiegelgeschichte."
58 See Jones, *Most Secret War*, for the relevant confessions of the head of this subdivision.
59 Pynchon, *Gravity's Rainbow*, 301.
60 Pynchon, *Gravity's Rainbow*, 407; see also 567.
61 Pynchon, *Gravity's Rainbow*, 407. See Giedion, *Mechanization Takes Command*, 21, for a picture and description of the function of Marey's gun.
62 Pynchon, *Gravity's Rainbow*, 407.
63 Pynchon, *Gravity's Rainbow*, 422.
64 See Kittler's essay "Romantik—Psychoanalyse—Film" for details.
65 Pynchon, *Gravity's Rainbow*, 588. See Virilio, *War and Cinema*, 137.
66 Dornberger, *V 2*, 239. For Kammler's building activities (including Nordhausen) in the SS Main Economic and Administrative Office, see Georg, *Die wirtschaftlichen*

Unternehmungen der SS, 37, as well as Bornemann, *Geheimprojekt Mittelbau*, 43, 82, 125. For his career until 1932 (Border Patrol East; Sturmabteilung Rossbach; Settlement Office, Danzig; Ministry of Labor), see Kammler, "Zur Bewertung von Geländeerschliessungen." If readers can provide additional information . . .

67 See Ruland, *Wernher von Braun*, 170, though he does not discuss Kammler's motivations. In *Gravity's Rainbow*, however, Pynchon asks his readers, "Is that who you are, that vaguely criminal face on your ID card, its soul snatched by the government camera as the guillotine shutter fell?" (134).

68 Pynchon, *Gravity's Rainbow*, 401.

69 Pynchon, *Gravity's Rainbow*, 416. As a model for the conversation between Weissmann and Pökler, one should read the long dialogue between Dornberger and Dr. Steinhoff, Peenemünde's electrician, in Dornberger, *V 2*, 135–37.

70 [*Trans. note*: As Weisenburger observes, "Sometime between the early thirties and 1944, when we meet him in Holland, Weissmann has evidently been 'busted' from major back to captain," his rank earlier in the novel. Weisenburger, *"Gravity's Rainbow" Companion*, 195.]

71 Pynchon, *Gravity's Rainbow*, 322.

72 See, for example, Dornberger, *V 2*, 266: "Kammler refused to believe in an imminent collapse. He dashed to and fro between the Dutch and Rhineland fronts and Thuringia and Berlin. He was on the move day and night. Conferences were called for 1 o'clock in the morning somewhere in the Harz Mountains, or we would meet at midnight somewhere on the Autobahn and then, after a brief exchange of views, drive back to work again. We were prey to terrific nervous tension. Irritable and overworked as we were, we didn't mince words. Kammler, if he got impatient and wanted to drive on, would wake the slumbering officers of his suite with a burst from his tommy-gun."

73 See Pynchon, *Gravity's Rainbow*, 667. "Since SS General Kammler, Hitler's envoy for V-weapons, cannot be located [after the war], London wants to put Dornberger on trial in his stead. Nobody knows at that time what has become of Kammler. Only several years later do the facts come to light: on May 4, 1945, Kammler arrives in Prague by plane. On May 9 he and 21 SS men defend a bunker against 600 Czech partisans. Kammler leaves the bunker in triumph and fires his automatic weapon at the attacking Czechs. Kammler's aide-de-camps, Sturmbannführer Starck, has been ordered months ago not to let his boss fall into enemy hands. He must walk behind him at a distance of ten steps—'within shooting range.' Now, in this hopeless situation, Starck pumps a round of bullets from his automatic weapon into the back of the SS General's head." Ruland, *Wernher von Braun*, 282. [*Trans. note*: For differing accounts of Kammler's death, see the introduction to this volume by Geoffrey Winthrop-Young.]

74 Pynchon, *Gravity's Rainbow*, 463, 670.

75 Pynchon, *Gravity's Rainbow*, 389; see also 348, 702–4.

76 Pynchon, *Gravity's Rainbow*, 760.

77 Pynchon, *Gravity's Rainbow*, 347.

78 Pynchon, *Gravity's Rainbow*, 703.

79 Pynchon, *Gravity's Rainbow*, 452.
80 Pynchon, *Gravity's Rainbow*, 701; see also 250.
81 Pynchon, *Gravity's Rainbow*, 452.
82 Pynchon, *Gravity's Rainbow*, 527.
83 Pynchon, *Gravity's Rainbow*, 691.
84 Pynchon, *Gravity's Rainbow*, 690–92.
85 Pynchon, *Gravity's Rainbow*, 703.
86 Pynchon, *Gravity's Rainbow*, 738.
87 Pynchon, *Gravity's Rainbow*, 738.
88 Pynchon, *Gravity's Rainbow*, 61.

Chapter 17. Biogeography

1 [*Trans. note:* Kittler was born on June 12, 1943, the day British forces occupied the island of Lampedusa, located between Africa and Sicily. The underbelly of Fortress Europe had in fact first been breached the day before with the Allied occupation of the larger island Pantelleria.]
2 [*Trans. note:* Kittler merges two poems from opposing ends of the political spectrum, thus introducing the collapse and conflation of geopolitical and geographical distinctions that runs through his essay. The first and the third line are from the well-known left-wing anthem and campfire song "Spaniens Himmel" (Spain's sky) by German composer Paul Dessau (music) and his wife, Gudrun Kabisch (lyrics). The second and fourth lines are from "Es zittern die morschen Knochen" (The rotten bones are trembling) by Nazi poet Hans Baumann, a Hitler Youth anthem and one of the most ubiquitous official songs in the Third Reich.]
3 [*Trans. note:* On the role of Karl von Müffling in Goethe's novel *Elective Affinities*, see chapter 13, "Ottilie Hauptmann," in this volume.]
4 [*Trans. note:* The Mittelmark is a region in eastern Germany between the Oder and Neisse rivers. Kittler later recalled that the vacations in Usedom took place in 1953, 1954, 1956, and 1958. At the end of the last vacation, the family fled to West Germany. Thanks to Susanne Holl for supplying this information.]
5 [*Trans. note:* A reference to Operation Hydra, the Royal Air Force bombing of Peenemünde on the night of August 17–18, 1943.]
6 [*Trans. note:* Kittler provides no reference.]
7 [*Trans. note:* An ironic reference to Martin Heidegger's 1933 radio lecture "Creative Landscape: Why Do We Stay in the Provinces?," in which he explained why he had turned down a professorship in Berlin (unlike Kittler, who accepted one in 1993).]
8 [*Trans. note:* Constance Babington Smith (1912–2000), the photo interpreter credited with discovering the v-1 flying bomb at Peenemünde (not, as Kittler notes, the v-2), describes her work for the RAF's Central Interpretation Unit in *Evidence in Camera: The Story of Photographic Intelligence in the Second World War* (1958). In an interview Kittler treated Babington Smith's poem much as she herself had

treated aerial reconnaissance photos: "As a final act of literary scholarship, I would love to execute an interlinear reading of this poem and of each of these so-called places. For example, Oberpfaffenhofen would be the German society for air and space flight; Kreising, I don't know yet; Wismar Sea is of course clear, it's the Baltic Sea. The poem is much longer and contains many more place names, strange villages where German technology withdrew from the threat of the Royal Air Force bombers." Quoted in Rickels, "Spooky Electricity," 69–70.]

9 [*Trans. note:* Pynchon, *Gravity's Rainbow*, 551. See also the conclusion of chapter 15, "De Nostalgia," in this volume.]

10 [*Trans. note:* Hertha Benn, second wife of the poet Gottfried Benn, committed suicide in 1945 shortly before the arrival of the Red Army.]

11 [*Trans. note:* Major General Werner Mummert (1891–1950), commander of the Panzer-Division Müncheberg, formed in March 1945, died five years after the end of the war in Soviet captivity. Kittler provides no reference for the journalist.]

12 [*Trans. note:* Pynchon, *Gravity's Rainbow*, 517.]

13 [*Trans. note:* See Speer, *Infiltration*, 219. On the theory of ruin value, see Speer, *Inside the Third Reich*, 56: "By using special materials and by applying certain principles of statics, we should be able to build structures which even in a state of decay, after hundreds or (such were our reckonings) thousands of years would more or less resemble Roman models." Historians and biographers now agree that this is yet another legend (or lie) in Speer's rich cabinet of questionable claims. He first mentioned the ruin value theory in his autobiography (originally published in German in 1969), but there is no documentary evidence that he had already developed it back in the 1930s, either on his own or in collaboration with Hitler. In all likelihood Speer appropriated an idea put forward in 1933 by art historian Felix Alexander Dargel. See also Welzbacher, "'Ruinenwert' und 'Reichsehrenmal,'" as well as Fuhrmeister and Mittig, "Albert Speer."]

14 [*Trans. note:* As mentioned in the introduction, Kittler—for reasons related in part to his view of the "real" dimensions of World War II—clung to the belief that Zuse's Z4, one of the world's first computers, had been used in the construction of the A4 a.k.a. V-2.]

15 [*Trans. note:* On SS General Hans Kammler (1901–?), who after upgrading the crematoria facilities in Auschwitz became responsible for the V-2 production program, see the introduction and chapter 16, "Media and Drugs in Pynchon's Second World War," in this volume.]

16 [*Trans. note:* Kittler draws together wartime and postwar (and Eastern and Western) rocket projects. Niedersachswerfen is in the vicinity of the V-2 manufacturing site; Baikonur (formerly Leninsk and also known as Zvezdograd, or "Star City") was one of the centers of the Soviet space program.]

17 [*Trans. note:* Kittler provides no source.]

18 [*Trans. note:* Karl Küpfmüller (1897–1977) was one of Germany's leading electrical engineers. From 1941 to 1945, he was head of research and development at Siemens.]

19 [*Trans. note:* Here Kittler refers to Franz Josef Strauss (1915–88), longtime chairman of the Christian Social Union (CSU) and minister-president of Bavaria. Strauss is mentioned by name at the end of the following paragraph in the same context. For this particular quote, see the opening of chapter 16, "Media and Drugs in Pynchon's Second World War," in this volume.]
20 [*Trans. note:* Pynchon, *Gravity's Rainbow*, 495.]
21 [*Trans. note:* Kittler likely refers to Adolph von Menzel's illustrations in Franz Theodor Kugler's *History of Frederick the Great* (1840; English translation 1844).]
22 May Roger Waters pardon the emending or modernizing of his "ships" into "chips." [*Trans. note:* See Waters, "The Post War Dream," on Pink Floyd, *Final Cut*.]

Chapter 18. Theology

1 [*Trans. note:* Kittler provides no source, but he likely refers to Ferdinand Lassalle's post-Hegelian study of Heraclitus, *Die Philosophie Herakleitos des Dunklen von Ephesos*, 188.]
2 [*Trans. note:* A direct reference to the section "On Apostates" in the third part of Friedrich Nietzsche's *Thus Spoke Zarathustra*: "It has been over for the old gods for a long time now—and truly, they had a good cheerful gods' end! They did not 'twilight' themselves to death—that is surely a lie! Instead, they just one day up and *laughed* themselves to death! This happened when the most godless words were uttered by a god himself—the words: 'There is one god. Thou shalt have no other gods before me!'—an old grim-beard of a god, a jealous one who forgot himself in this way: And all the gods laughed then and rocked in their chairs and cried: 'Is godliness not precisely that there are gods but no God?'" Nietzsche, *Thus Spoke Zarathustra*, 146; emphasis in the original.]
3 [*Trans. note:* For a critical take on the political implications of the philhellenism of Kittler's later work, see Breger, "Gods, German Scholars," and Winthrop-Young, *Kittler and the Media*, 102–10. The specter of cultural anti-Semitism arises with Kittler's stark and programmatic contrast between the pure and privileged Greek vowel alphabet and the inferior Semitic (Phoenician) script it was modelled on.]
4 [*Trans. note:* On the derivation of *spirit* from *spit*, see chapter 9, "Animals of War," and chapter 5, "Noises of War," in this volume.]

A4-Fibel. 1944. https://archive.org/details/A4-Fibel_1944_167p/mode/2up

A-4/V-2 Rocket Instruction Manual. Translated by John A. Bitzer and Ted A. Woerner. Redstone Arsenal, AL: Army Ballistic Missile Agency, 1957.

Aichinger, Ilse. "Spiegelgeschichte." In *The Bound Man and Other Stories*, translated by Eric Mosbacher. London: Secker and Warburg, 1955.

Aitmatov, Chingiz. *The Day Lasts More Than a Hundred Years*. Translated by John French. Bloomington: Indiana University Press, 1983.

Anderson, Mark. *In the Storm of Roses: Selected Poems by Ingeborg Bachmann*. Lockert Library of Poetry in Translation. Princeton, NJ: Princeton University Press, 1986.

Andriukaitis, Lukas. "Russia Uses Fake Rape Stories to Create Hostility to NATO Troops." StopFake.org, May 11, 2018. https://www.stopfake.org/en/russia-uses-fake-rape-stories-to-create-hostility-to-nato-troops/.

Armitage, John. "From Discourse Networks to Cultural Mathematics: An Interview with Friedrich A. Kittler." *Theory, Culture and Society* 23, no. 7/8 (2006): 17–38.

Arnheim, Rudolf. *Radio*. Translated by Margaret Ludwig and Herbert Read. London: Faber and Faber, 1936.

Bachmann, Ingeborg. *The Cicadas*. In *Three Radio Plays*, by Ingeborg Bachmann, translated by Lilian Friedberg, 55–117. Riverside, CA: Ariadne, 1999.

Bardmann, Theodor M., and Dirk Baecker, eds. *Gibt es eigentlich den Berliner Zoo noch? Erinnerungen an Niklas Luhmann*. Konstanz: UVK Verlagsgesellschaft, 1999.

Barner, Wilfried, E. Lämmert, and N. Oellers, eds. *Unser Commercium: Goethes und Schillers Literaturpolitik*. Stuttgart: Cotta, 1984.

Barnes, H. G. *Goethe's 'Die Wahlverwandtschaften': A Literary Interpretation*. Oxford: Clarendon, 1967.

Behrens, Dietrich, and Magdalena Karstien. *Geschütz- und Geschosslaute im Weltkrieg: Eine Materialsammlung aus deutschen und französischen Kriegsberichten*. Giessener Beiträge zur Romanischen Philologie, Zusatzheft 2. Giessen: Selbstverlag des Romanischen Seminars, 1925.

Belloc, Hilaire. *The Modern Traveller*. London: E. Arnold, 1898.

Benjamin, Walter. *The Arcades Project*. Translated by Howard Eiland and Kevin McLaughlin. Cambridge, MA: Harvard University Press, 1999.

Benjamin, Walter. "Goethe's Elective Affinities." Translated by Stanley Corngold. In *Selected Writings*, vol. 1, 1913–1926, edited by Marcus Bullock and Michael W. Jennings, 297–360. Cambridge, MA: Belknap Press, 1996.

Benn, Gottfried. *Gesammelte Werke*. Edited by Dieter Wellershoff. Vols. 1 and 3. Wiesbaden: Limes, 1959–60.

Benn, Gottfried. "The Poems." In *Gottfried Benn Poems*, translated by Martin Travers. Accessed December 10, 2016. https://gottfriedbennpoems.com/the-poems/.

Bergaust, Erik. *Wernher von Braun: The Authoritative and Definitive Biographical Profile of the Father of Modern Space Flight*. Washington, DC: National Space Institute, 1976.

Bergson, Henri. *The Meaning of the War: Life and Matter in Conflict*. Introduction by H. Wildon Carr. London: T. Fisher Unwin, 1915.

Berkovich, Ilya. *Motivation in War: The Experience of Common Soldiers in Old-Regime Europe*. Cambridge: Cambridge University Press, 2017.

Berndt, Otto. *Die Zahl im Kriege: Statistische Daten aus der neueren Kriegsgeschichte in graphischer Darstellung*. Vienna: G. Freytag und Berndt, 1897.

Biedermann, Flodoard von, ed. *Goethes Gespräche*. Leipzig: Biedermann, 1909–11.

Blochmann, Elisabeth. *Das "Frauenzimmer" und die "Gelehrsamkeit": Eine Studie über die Anfänge des Mädchenschulwesens in Deutschland*. Heidelberg: Quelle und Meyer, 1966.

Blumenberg, Hans. *Work on Myth*. Translated by Robert M. Wallace. Cambridge, MA: MIT Press, 1988.

Bolz, Norbert W., ed. *Goethes Wahlverwandtschaften: Kritische Modelle und Diskursanalysen zum Mythos Literatur*. Hildesheim: Gerstenberg, 1981.

Borges, Jorge Luis. *Selected Poems*. Edited by Alexander Coleman. New York: Viking Penguin, 1999.

Borges, Jorge Luis. "Tlön, Uqbar, Orbis Tertius." In *Labyrinths: Selected Stories and Other Writings*, edited by Donald A. Yates and James E. Irby, 3–18. New York: New Directions, 2007.

Borkin, Joseph. *The Crime and Punishment of I.G. Farben*. New York: Free Press, 1978.

Bornemann, Manfred. *Geheimprojekt Mittelbau: Die Geschichte der deutschen V-Waffen-Werke*. Munich: J. F. Lehmanns, 1971.

Bornemann, Manfred, and Martin Broszat. "Das KL Dora-Mittelbau." In *Studien zur Geschichte der Konzentrationslager*, 154–98. Stuttgart: De Gruyter, 1970.

Brecht, Bertolt. *Bertolt Brecht on Film and Radio*. Translated and edited by Marc Silberman. London: Methuen, 2000.

Brecht, Bertolt. *Der Ozeanflug*. Frankfurt am Main: Suhrkamp, 1980.

Breger, Claudia. "Gods, German Scholars and the Gift of Greece: Friedrich Kittler's Philhellenic Fantasies." *Theory, Culture and Society* 23, nos. 7–8 (2006): 111–34.

Burkert, Walter. *Lore and Science in Ancient Pythagoreanism*. Translated by Edwin L. Minar Jr. Cambridge, MA: Harvard University Press, 1972.

Churchill, Winston. *The World Crisis 1915*. London: Thornton Butterworth, 1927.

Citino, Robert M. *The German Way of War: From the Thirty Years' War to the Third Reich*. Lawrence: University Press of Kansas, 2005.

Clark, Christopher. *Iron Kingdom: The Rise and Downfall of Prussia, 1600–1947*. Cambridge, MA: Harvard University Press, 2008.

Clausewitz, Carl von. *On War*. 1832. Edited and translated by Michael Howard and Peter Paret. Princeton, NJ: Princeton University Press, 1984.

Cohen, Leonard. "The Old Revolution." In *Songs from a Room*. New York: Columbia, 1969.

Condell, Bruce, and David T. Zabecki. "Editors' Introduction." In *On the German Art of War: Truppenführung*, edited by Bruce Condell and David T. Zabecki, 1–14. Boulder, CO: Rienner, 2001.

Copjec, Joan. "Sex and the Euthanasia of Reason." In *Supposing the Subject*, edited by Joan Copjec, 201–36. London: Verso, 1994.

Creveld, Martin van. *Command in War*. Cambridge, MA: Harvard University Press, 1987.

Creveld, Martin van. *The Sword and the Olive: A Critical History of the Israeli Defense Force*. New York: Public Affairs, 2002.

Cronin, Audrey Kurth. "Cyber-Mobilization: The New *Levée en Masse*." *Parameters* 77 (2006): 77–87.

Deighton, Len. *Blitzkrieg: From the Rise of Hitler to the Fall of Dunkirk*. Foreword by Walther K. Nehring. New York: Random House, 1980.

Derrida, Jacques. *Cinders*. Translated by Ned Lukacher. Introduction by Cary Wolfe. Minneapolis: University of Minnesota Press, 2014.

Döbert, Frank, and Rainer Karlsch. "Hans Kammler, Hitler's Last Hope, in American Hands." Cold War International History Project Working Paper no. 91. August 2019. https://www.wilsoncenter.org/publication/hans-kammler-hitlers-last-hope-american-hands.

Dodman, Thomas. *What Nostalgia Was: War, Empire and the Time of a Deadly Emotion*. Chicago: University of Chicago Press, 2018.

Dornberger, Walter. *V-2*. Translated by James Clough and Geoffrey Halliday. New York: Viking, 1954.

Douhet, Giulio. *The Command of the Air*. Translated by Dino Ferrari. Tuscaloosa: University of Alabama Press, 2009.

Doumenc, Joseph Edouard Aimé. *Les transports automobiles sur le front français, 1914–1918*. Paris: Plon-Nourrit et Cie, 1920.

Dunant, Henri. *The Origins of the Red Cross/"Un Souvenir de Solferino."* Translated by David H. Wright. Self-published, CreateSpace, 2016.

Dunlap, Orrin Elmer. *Marconi: The Man and His Wireless*. 1937. 2nd ed. New York: Macmillan, 1941.

Duverger, Alexandre Jacques Veron. *De la condition politique et civile des femmes*, Part 1 (1872). Kessinger, 2010.

Eckermann, Johann Peter. *Conversations of Goethe*. Translated by John Oxenford. London: E. P. Dutton, 1930.

Eddington, Sir Arthur. *The Nature of the Physical World*. Cambridge: Cambridge University Press, 1928.

Edwards, Paul N. *The Closed World: Computers and the Politics of Discourse in Cold War America*. Cambridge, MA: MIT Press, 1996.

Eich, Günter. *Dreams*. Translated by Anselm Hollo. In *German Radio Plays*, edited by Everett Frost and Margaret Herzfeld-Sander, 66–100. New York: Continuum, 1991.

Eldredge, Niles, and Stephen Jay Gould. "Punctuated Equilibria: An Alternative to Phyletic Gradualism." In *Models in Paleobiology*, edited by T. J. M. Schopf, 82–115. San Francisco: Freeman, Cooper, 1972.

Engels, Friedrich. *Herr Eugen Dühring's Revolution in Science*. 1878. Translated by Emile Burns. Moscow: Progress, 1947. https://www.marxists.org/archive/marx/works/download/pdf/anti_duhring.pdf.

Engelsing, Rolf. *Analphabetentum und Lektüre*. Stuttgart: Metzler, 1973.

Exerzir-Reglement für die Infanterie. Berlin, 1812.

Fessenden, Helen S. *Fessenden: Builder of Tomorrows*. New York: Coward-McCann, 1940.

Fink, Gonthier-Louis. "Goethes *Wahlverwandtschaften*: Romanstruktur und Zeitaspekt." In *Goethes Roman "Die Wahlverwandtschaften,"* edited by Ewald Rösch, 429–83. Darmstadt: Wissenschaftliche Buchgesellschaft, 1975.

Foucault, Michel. *Discipline and Punish: The Birth of the Prison*. Translated by Alan Sheridan. New York: Vintage, 1977.

Foucault, Michel. "Fantasia of the Library." In *Language, Counter-Memory, Practice: Selected Essays and Interviews*, edited by Donald F. Bouchard and translated by Donald F. Bouchard and Sherry Simon, 87–112. Ithaca, NY: Cornell University Press, 1980.

Foucault, Michel. *The History of Sexuality*. Vol. 1, *An Introduction*. Translated by Robert Hurley. New York: Vintage, 1990.

Foucault, Michel. *The Order of Things: An Archaeology of the Human Sciences*. Translated by Alan Sheridan. New York: Vintage, 1994.

Foucault, Michel. *Religion and Culture*. Edited by Jeremy Carrette. New York: Routledge, 2013.

Foucault, Michel. *"Society Must Be Defended": Lectures at the Collège de France, 1975–76*. Edited by Mauro Bertani and Alessandro Fontana. Translated by David Macey. New York: Picador, 2003.

François-Poncet, André. *Les affinités électives de Goethe*. Paris: Alcan, 1910.

Freud, Sigmund. *The Standard Edition of the Complete Psychological Works of Sigmund Freud*. Translated by James Strachey et al. Edited by James Strachey. 24 vols. London: Hogarth, 1953–74.

Frieser, Karl-Heinz. *The Blitzkrieg Legend: The 1940 Campaign in the West*. Translated by John T. Greenwood. Annapolis, MD: Naval Institute Press, 2005.

Fritz, Stephen G. *The First Soldier: Hitler as Military Leader*. New Haven, CT: Yale University Press, 2018.

Fuhrmeister, Christian, and Hans-Ernst Mittig. "Albert Speer und die 'Theorie vom Ruinenwert' (1969): Der lange Schatten einer Legende." In *Bunker: Kriegsort, Zuflucht, Erinnerungsraum*, edited by Inge Marszolek and Marc Buggeln, 225–43. Frankfurt: Campus, 2008.

Fussell, Paul. *The Great War and Modern Memory*. New York: Oxford University Press, 1975.

Fussell, Paul. *Wartime: Understanding and Behaviour in the Second World War*. New York: Oxford University Press, 1989.

Gailor, Frank Hoyt. "An American Ambulance in the Verdun Attack." In *Friends of France: The Field Service of the American Ambulance Described by Its Members*, 89–108. Toronto: Thomas Allen, 1916.

Geerdts, Hans Jürgen. "Goethes Roman *Die Wahlverwandtschaften*: Die Hauptgestalten und die Nebenfiguren in ihrer Grundkonzeption." In *Goethes Roman "Die Wahlverwandtschaften,"* edited by Ewald Rösch, 272–306. Darmstadt: Wissenschaftliche Buchgesellschaft, 1975.

Georg, Enno. *Die wirtschaftlichen Unternehmungen der SS*. Vierteljahreshefte für Zeitgeschichte 7. Stuttgart: Deutsche Verlags-Anstalt, 1963.

Gerschmann, Karl-Heinz. "Johannes Hofers Dissertation 'De Nostalgia' von 1688." *Archiv für Begriffsgeschichte* 19 (1975): 83–88.

Geyer, Michael. "German Strategy in the Age of Machine Warfare, 1914–1945." In *Makers of Modern Strategy*, edited by Peter Paret, 527–97. 2nd ed. Princeton, NJ: Princeton University Press, 1986.

Giedion, Siegfried. *Mechanization Takes Command: A Contribution to Anonymous History*. New York: Oxford University Press, 1948.

Giehrl, Hermann. *Der Feldherr Napoleon als Organisator: Betrachtungen über seine Verkehrs- und Nachrichtenmittel, seine Arbeits- und Befehlsweise*. Berlin: Mittler, 1911.

Gitelman, Lisa. *Scripts, Grooves, and Writing Machines: Representing Technology in the Edison Era*. Stanford, CA: Stanford University Press, 1999.

Glucksmann, André. *Le discours de la guerre*. Paris: Editions de l'Herne, 1969.

Gneisenau, Neidhart von. *Schriften von und über Gneisenau*. Edited by Fritz Lange. Berlin: Rütten und Loening, 1954.

Goerlitz, Walter. *History of the German General Staff, 1657–1945*. Translated by Brian Battershaw. Westport, CT: Greenwood, 1975.

Goethe, Johann Wolfgang von. *Briefe an Goethe: Hamburger Ausgabe*. Edited by Karl Robert Mandelkow. Hamburg: Wegner, 1965–67.

Goethe, Johann Wolfgang von. *The Collected Works in 12 Volumes*. Vol. 5. Edited by Thomas P. Saine and Jeffrey L. Sammons. Translated and introduced by Thomas P. Saine. Princeton, NJ: Princeton University Press, 1994.

Goethe, Johann Wolfgang von. *The Collected Works in 12 Volumes*. Vol. 11. Edited by David E. Wellbery. Princeton, NJ: Princeton University Press, 1995.

Goethe, Johann Wolfgang, and Friedrich Schiller. *Correspondence between Goethe and Schiller*. Vol. 2, *1798–1805*. Translated by L. Dora Schmitz. London: George Bell, 1890.

Görlitz, Walter. *Kleine Geschichte des Deutschen Generalstabes*. Berlin: Haude und Spenersche Verlagsbuchhandlung, 1967.

Gosling, John. *Waging "The War of the Worlds": A History of the 1938 Radio Broadcast and Resulting Panic, Including the Original Script*. Radio script by Howard Koch. Jefferson, NC: McFarland, 2009.

Grabbe, Christian Dietrich. *Napoleon oder die hundert Tage*. In *Werke in einem Band*, edited by Walther Vontin. Hamburg: Hoffmann und Campe, 1960.

Grimmelshausen, Hans Jacob Christoffel von. *Simplicissimus*. Translated and introduced by Mike Mitchell. London: Dedalus, 1999.

Groos, Karl. *The Play of Man*. Translated by Elisabeth Baldwin. New York: Appleton, 1901.

Grossmann, Walter. "Niedersächsische Vermessungsgeschichte im 18. und 19. Jahrhundert." In *C. F. Gauss und die Landesvermessung in Niedersachsen*, edited by the Niedersächsische Vermessungs und Katasterverwaltung, 17–59. Hannover: Niedersächsisches Landesvermessungsamt Hannover, 1955.

Guderian, Heinz. "Die Lebensader Verduns." *Beilage zum Militär-Wochenblatt* 4 (1925): 28–31.

Guilhaumou, Jacques. *La langue politique et la Révolution française: De l'événement à la raison*. Paris: Méridiens Klincksieck, 1989.

Gumbrecht, Hans Ulrich, ed. *The Truth of the Technological World*. Stanford, CA: Stanford University Press, 2015.

Haase, Frank. *Kleists Nachrichtentechnik: Eine diskursanalytische Untersuchung*. Opladen: Verlag für Sozialwissenschaften, 1986.

Habermas, Jürgen. *The Theory of Communicative Action*. Vol. 1, *Reason and the Rationalization of Society*. Translated by Thomas McCarthy. Boston: Beacon Press, 1985.

Haffner, Sebastian. *The Meaning of Hitler*. Translated by Ewald Osers. London: Weidenfeld and Nicolson, 1979.

Harari, Yuval. *The Ultimate Experience: Battlefield Revelations and the Making of Modern War Culture, 1450–2000*. New York: Palgrave Macmillan, 2008.

Hegel, Georg Wilhelm Friedrich. *Aesthetics: Lectures on Fine Art*. Translated by T. M. Knox. Vol. 1. Oxford: Oxford University Press, 1975.

Hegel, Georg Wilhelm Friedrich. *Hegel and the Human Spirit: A Translation of the Jena Lectures on the Philosophy of Spirit (1805–6) with Commentary*. Edited and translated by Leo Rauch. Detroit: Wayne State University Press, 1983.

Hegel, Georg Wilhelm Friedrich. *The Phenomenology of Spirit*. Translated by A. V. Miller. Foreword by J. N. Findlay. Oxford: Oxford University Press, 1976.

Heidegger, Martin. *Being and Time*. Translated by Joan Stambaugh. Albany: State University of New York Press, 1996.

Heidegger, Martin. *Off the Beaten Track*. Edited and translated by Julian Young and Kenneth Haynes. Cambridge: Cambridge University Press, 2002.

Heidegger, Martin. *On the Way to Language*. Translated by P. D. Hertz and J. Strambaugh. New York: Harper and Row, 1982.

Heidegger, Martin. *The Question concerning Technology and Other Essays*. Translated and with an introduction by William Lovitt. New York: Harper, 1977.

Heine, Heinrich. *The Romantic School and Other Essays*. Edited by Robert Holub. New York: Continuum, 2006.

Heinemann, Manfred. *Schule im Vorfeld der Verwaltung: Die Entwicklung der preußischen Unterrichtsverwaltung von 1771–1800*. Göttingen: Vandenhoeck und Ruprecht, 1974.

Hellingrath, Friedrich Norbert Theodor von. *Hölderlin-Vermächtnis*. Edited and introduced by Ludwig von Pigenot. 2nd enlarged edition. Munich: Bruckmann, 1944.

Herbst, Ludolf. *Der totale Krieg und die Ordnung der Wirtschaft: Die Kriegswirtschaft im Spannungsfeld von Politik, Ideologie und Propaganda, 1939–1945*. Stuttgart: Deutsche Verlags-Anstalt, 1982.

Herold, Christopher J. *The Age of Napoleon*. Boston: Houghton Mifflin/Mariner, 2002.
Hillgruber, Andreas. *Der zweite Weltkrieg, 1939–1945*. Stuttgart: Kohlhammer, 1996.
Hodges, Andrew. *Alan Turing: The Enigma*. London: Burnett, 1983.
Hofer, Johannes. "Medical Dissertation on Nostalgia (1688)." Translated by Carolyn Kiser Anspach. *Bulletin of the Institute of the History of Medicine* 2, no. 6 (1934): 376–91.
Hoffmann, Wilhelm. "Vom Wesen des Funkspiels." In *Literatur und Rundfunk, 1923–1933*, edited by Gerhard Hay, 373–74. Hildesheim: Gerstenberg, 1975.
Hölderlin, Friedrich. *Hymns and Fragments*. Translated and introduced by Richard Sieburth. Princeton, NJ: Princeton University Press, 1984.
Hölderlin, Friedrich. *Poems of Friedrich Hölderlin: The Fire of the Gods Drives Us to Set Forth by Day and by Night*. Selected and translated by James Mitchell. 2nd ed. San Francisco: Ithuriel's Spear, 2007.
Hörisch, Jochen. "Das Sein der Zeichen und die Zeichen des Seins: Marginalien zu Derridas Ontosemiologie." In *Die Stimme und das Phänomen: Maginalien zu Derridas Ontosemiologie*, 7–50. Frankfurt am Main: Suhrkamp, 1979.
Howe, Ellic. *The Black Game: British Subversive Operations against the Germans during the Second World War*. London: Joseph, 1982.
Hughes, Richard. "The Birth of Radio Drama." *Atlantic Monthly*, December 1957, 145–50.
Hüsmert, Ernst. "Die letzten Jahre von Carl Schmitt." In *Schmittiana: Beiträge zu Leben und Werk Carl Schmitts*, edited by Peter Tommisson, 40–54. Berlin: Duncker and Humblot, 1988.
Ingrao, Christian. *The Promise of the East: Nazi Hopes and Genocide, 1939–43*. Translated by Andrew Brown. Cambridge, UK: Polity, 2019.
Jones, Reginald V. *Most Secret War: British Scientific Intelligence, 1939–1945*. London: Hamish Hamilton, 1978.
Jünger, Ernst. *Der Kampf als inneres Erlebnis*. Berlin: E. S. Mittler und Sohn, 1922.
Jünger, Ernst. *On the Marble Cliffs*. 1939. Translated by Stuart Hood. London: Penguin, 1984.
Jünger, Ernst. *The Storm of Steel*. Translated by Basil Creighton. London: Chatto and Windus, 1929.
Jürgs, Michael. "Gefangen in der Vergangenheit: Ein Besuch bei Horst Herold."*Der Tagesspiegel*, September 22, 2007.
Kafka, Franz. "The Burrow." In *The Great Wall of China*, edited by Max Brod and Hans Joachim Schoeps. Translated by Willa and Edwin Muir. London: Martin Secker, 1933.
Kaiser, Gerhard. *Wandrer und Idylle: Goethe und die Phänomenologie der Natur in der deutschen Dichtung von Geßner bis Gottfried Keller*. Göttingen: Vandenhoeck und Ruprecht, 1977.
Kamienski, Lukasz. *Shooting Up: A Short History of Drugs and War*. Oxford: Oxford University Press, 2016.
Kammler, Hans. "Zur Bewertung von Geländeerschliessungen für die großtädtische Besiedlung." Engineering Doctoral Thesis, Technische Hochschule Hannover, 1932.

Kamper, Dietmar. "Atlantis—vorgeschichtliche Katastrophe, nachgeschichtliche Dekonstruktion." Unpublished typescript, 1984.

Kant, Immanuel. *Anthropology from a Pragmatic Point of View*. Translated by Victor Lyle Dowdell. Revised and edited by Hans H. Rudnick. Carbondale: Southern Illinois University Press, 1978.

Karppi, Tero, Marc Böhlen, and Yvette Granata. "Killer Robots as Cultural Techniques." *International Journal of Cultural Studies* 21, no. 2 (2018): 107–33.

Kennedy, Gregory P. *Vengeance Weapon 2: The V-2 Guided Missile*. Washington, DC: Smithsonian Institution Press, 1983.

Kershaw, Ian. *Hitler, 1889–1936: Hubris*. London: Allen Lane, 1998.

Kipling, Rudyard. *Kim*. Harmondsworth, UK: Penguin, 1994.

Kipling, Rudyard. "A Sahib's War." In *Traffic and Discoveries*, 55–71. Harmondsworth, UK: Penguin Classics, 1987.

Kittler, Friedrich A. "Authorship and Love." *Theory, Culture and Society* 32, no. 3 (2015): 15–47.

Kittler, Friedrich A. "Carlos als Carlsschüler." In *Unser Commercium: Goethes und Schillers Literaturpolitik*, edited by Wilfried Barner, Eberhard Lämmert, and Norbert Oellers, 241–73. Stuttgart: J. G. Cotta, 1984.

Kittler, Friedrich A. *Dichter, Mutter, Kind*. Munich: Fink, 1991.

Kittler, Friedrich A. *Discourse Networks, 1800/1900*. Translated by Michael Metteer with Chris Cullens. Stanford, CA: Stanford University Press, 1990.

Kittler, Friedrich A. "Das Gespenst im Computer: Alan Turing und die moderne Kriegsmaschine." *Überblick* 9 (1984): 46.

Kittler, Friedrich A. 1998. "Gleichschaltungen: Über Normen und Standards der elektronischen Kommunikation." In *Geschichte der Medien*, edited by M. Fassler and W. Halbach, 255–67. Munich: UTB.

Kittler, Friedrich. *Grammophon Film Typewriter*. Berlin: Brinkmann und Bose, 1986.

Kittler, Friedrich A. *Gramophone, Film, Typewriter*. Translated and introduced by Geoffrey Winthrop-Young and Michael Wutz. Stanford, CA: Stanford University Press, 1999.

Kittler, Friedrich A. *Hebbels Einbildungskraft—die dunkle Natur*. New York: Peter Lang, 1999.

Kittler, Friedrich A. "Ein Herr namens Luhmann." In *Gibt es eigentlich den Berliner Zoo noch? Erinnerungen an Niklas Luhmann*, edited by Dirk Baecker and Theodor M. Bardmann, 183–86. Konstanz: UVK Verlagsgesellschaft, 1999.

Kittler, Friedrich A. *Platz der Luftbrücke: Ein Gespräch mit Stefan Banz*. Nuremberg: Verlag für Moderne Kunst, 2011.

Kittler, Friedrich A. "Romantik—Psychoanalyse—Film: Eine Doppelgängergeschichte." In *Eingebildete Texte*, edited by Jochen Hörisch and Christoph Tholen, 118–35. Munich: Fink, 1985.

Kittler, Friedrich A. "Synergie von Mensch und Maschine." In *Kunst machen? Gespräche über die Produktion von Bildern*, edited by F. Rötzer and S. Rogenhofer, 83–102. Munich: Boer, 1993.

Kittler, Friedrich A. "Take-Off of the Operators." In *Inscribing Science: Scientific Texts and the Materiality of Communication*, edited by Timothy Lenoir, 70–77. Stanford, CA: Stanford University Press, 1998.

Kittler, Friedrich A. *The Truth of the Technological World: Essays on the Genealogy of Presence*. Edited by Hans Ulrich Gumbrecht. Translated by Erik Butler. Stanford, CA: Stanford University Press, 2013.

Kittler, Friedrich A. "Zu Thomas Pynchons *Against the Day*." In *Rekursionen: Von Faltungen des Wissens*, edited by Philipp von Hilgers and Ana Ofak, 239–44. Munich: Wilhelm Fink, 2010.

Kittler, Friedrich A., and Rudolf Maresch. "Wenn die Freiheit wirklich existiert, dann soll sie doch ausbrechen." In *Am Ende vorbei*, edited by Rudolf Maresch, 95–129. Vienna: Turia und Kant, 1994.

Kittler, Wolf. *Die Geburt des Partisanen aus dem Geist der Poesie: Heinrich von Kleist und die Strategie der Befreiungskriege*. Freiburg: Rombach, 1987.

Kittler, Wolf. "Goethes *Wahlverwandtschaften*: Soziale Verhältnisse symbolisch dargestellt." In *Goethes Wahlverwandtschaften: Kritische Modelle und Diskursanalysen zum Mythos Literatur*, edited by Norbert W. Bolz, 230–59. Hildesheim: Gerstenberg, 1981.

Kleist, Heinrich von. *The Battle of Herrmann*. Translated and introduced by Rachel MagShamhráin. Würzburg: Königshausen und Neumann, 2008.

Kleist, Heinrich von. *The Prince of Homburg*. Translated by Bernard Sahlins. Chicago: I. R. Dee, 1990.

Knaack, Kristian. *Der Kunst-Schatz des Führers: Die Kammler-Akte*. Tübingen: Grabert, 2010.

Koselleck, Reinhart. "Transformations of Experience and Methodological Change." In Reinhart Koselleck, *The Practice of Conceptual History: Timing History, Spacing Concepts*, translated by Todd Samuel Presner et al., 45–83. Stanford, CA: Stanford University Press, 2002.

Lacan, Jacques. *Écrits: The First Complete Edition in English*. Translated by Bruce Fink. New York: Norton, 2006.

Lacan, Jacques. *The Seminar of Jacques Lacan. Book XX: On Feminine Sexuality, the Limits of Love and Knowledge (Encore)*. Edited by Jacques-Alain Miller. New York: Norton, 1999.

Lassalle, Ferdinand. *Die Philosophie Herakleitos des Dunklen von Ephesos*. Berlin: Franz Duncker, 1858.

Lewes, George Henry. *The Life of Goethe*. London: Smith, Elder, 1890.

Liliencron, Detlev von. "Eine Sommerschlacht." 1895. In *Collected Works*, vol. 1, 24–42. Berlin: Schuster und Loeffler, 1921. https://archive.org/details/gesammeltewerkeho7liliuoft/page/24/mode/2up.

Lindbergh, Charles A. *We*. New York: G. P. Putnam's Sons, 1927.

Mallarmé, Stéphane. *Poems*. Translated by C. F. MacIntyre. Berkeley: University of California Press, 1957.

"The Marseillaise." 1792. Ministère de l'Europe et des Affaires Étrangères: France Diplomacy. https://www.diplomatie.gouv.fr/en/coming-to-france/france-facts/symbols-of-the-republic/article/the-marseillaise.

Marx, Karl. "Contribution to the Critique of Hegel's Philosophy of Right." In Karl Marx and Friedrich Engels, *On Religion*, 41–58. Mineola, NY: Dover, 2008.

Meier, Eduard. "Erstes Rundfunkkonzert . . . eine Erinnerung aus dem Schützengraben." *Funk* 1 (1924): 168.

Mersenne, Marin. *Harmonie universelle: Contenant la théorie et la pratique de la musique.* Paris, 1636.

Meyers Großes Konversations-Lexikon. 6th ed. Leipzig: Bibliographisches Institut, 1902–8.

Morris, Charles William. *Foundations of the Theory of Signs.* Chicago: University of Chicago Press, 1938.

Müffling, Friedrich Karl Ferdinand. *Offizier, Kartograph, Politiker (1775–1851): Lebenserinnerungen und kleinere Schriften.* Edited by Hans-Joachim Behr. Cologne: Böhlau, 2003.

Müffling, Friedrich Karl Ferdinand. *Passages from My Life: Together with Memoirs of the Campaign of 1813 and 1814.* London: R. Bentley, 1853.

Müller, Heiner. *Explosions of a Memory.* Edited and translated by Carl Weber. New York: PAJ, 1989.

Nemec, Friedrich. *Die Ökonomie der Wahlverwandtschaften.* Munich: Fink, 1973.

Neufeld, Michael J. *The Rocket and the Reich: Peenemünde and the Coming of the Ballistic Missile Era.* New York: Free Press, 1995.

Niethammer, Friedrich Immanuel. *Der Streit des Philanthropinismus und Humanismus in der Theorie des Erziehungs-Unterrichts unsrer Zeit.* Jena: Friedrich Frommann, 1808.

Nietzsche, Friedrich. *The Anti-Christ, Ecce Homo, Twilight of the Idols, and Other Writings.* Edited by Aaron Ridley and Judith Norman. Translated by Judith Norman. Cambridge: Cambridge University Press, 2005.

Nietzsche, Friedrich. "The Case of Wagner." In *The Basic Writings of Nietzsche*, edited and translated by Walter Kaufmann. New York: Modern Library, 1992.

Nietzsche, Friedrich. *On the Genealogy of Morals and Ecce Homo*, edited and translated by Walter Kaufmann. New York: Vintage, 1989.

Nietzsche, Friedrich. *Richard Wagner in Bayreuth.* 1909. Translated by Anthony M. Ludovici. London: Dodo, 1980.

Nietzsche, Friedrich. *Thus Spoke Zarathustra: A Book for All and None.* Edited by Adriano del Caro and Robert Pippin, translated by Adriano del Caro. Cambridge: Cambridge University Pres, 2006.

Nietzsche, Friedrich. *Untimely Meditations.* Edited by Daniel Breazeale, translated by R. J. Hollingdale. Cambridge: Cambridge University Press, 1997.

Nietzsche, Friedrich. *Will to Power.* Edited by Walter Kaufmann. New York: Vintage, 1968.

Nolan, Cathal J. *The Allure of Battle: A History of How Wars Have Been Won and Lost.* Oxford: Oxford University Press, 2019.

Ohler, Norman. *Blitzed: Drugs in Nazi Germany.* Harmondsworth, UK: Penguin, 2017.

Ordway, Frederick I., and Mitchell R. Sharpe. *The Rocket Team.* Boston: MIT Press, 1982.

Ott, Hugo. *Martin Heidegger: A Political Life.* Translated by Allan Blunden. New York: Basic Books, 1993.

Packer, Jeremy, and Joshua Reeves. *Killer Apps: War, Media, Machine.* Durham, NC: Duke University Press, 2020.

Paret, Peter. *Clausewitz in His Time: Essays in the Cultural and Intellectual History of Thinking about War*. New York: Berghahn, 2015.

Pessler, Wilhelm. "Das historische Museum und der Weltkrieg." *Museumskunde* 12, no. 2/3 (1916): 91–104.

Petersen, Michael B. *Missiles for the Fatherland: Peenemünde, National Socialism, and the V-2 Missile*. Cambridge: Cambridge University Press, 2009.

Petrat, Gerhardt. *Schulunterricht: Seine Sozialgeschichte in Deutschland, 1750–1850*. Munich: Ehrenwirth, 1979.

Pias, Claus. "Action, Adventure, Desire: Interaction with PC Games." In *Interactive Dramaturgies: New Approaches in Multimedia Content and Design*, edited by Heide Hagebölling, 133–47. Berlin: Springer, 2004.

Picker, Henry. *Hitlers Tischgespräche im Führerhauptquartier*. Munich: Propyläen, 2003.

Pinchevski, Amit. *Transmitted Wounds: Media and the Mediation of Trauma*. Oxford: Oxford University Press, 2019.

Pink Floyd. *The Final Cut: A Requiem for the Post War Dream*. London: Columbia Records, 1983.

Pink Floyd. *Wish You Were Here*. London: Columbia Records (Harvest), 1975.

Pöhlmann, Markus. *Der Panzer und die Mechanisierung des Krieges: Eine deutsche Geschichte 1890 bis 1945*. Paderborn: Schöningh, 2016.

Potratz, Johannes. *Die Skythen in Südrussland: Ein untergegangenes Volk in Südosteuropa*. Basel: Raggi, 1963.

Preyer, Wilhelm. "Elemente der reinen Empfindungslehre." In *Sammlung physiologischer Abhandlungen*, edited by Wilhelm Preyer, vol. 1., 537–637. Jena: Hermann Dufft, 1877.

Priesdorff, Kurt von, ed. *Soldatisches Führertum*. Vol. 7. Hamburg: Hanseatische Verlagsanstalt, 1937.

Proust, Marcel. *In Search of Lost Time*. Vol. 6, *Time Regained*. Translated by Andreas Mayor and Terence Kilmartin, revised by D. J. Enright. London: Vintage, 2000.

Pynchon, Thomas. *The Crying of Lot 49*. New York: Harper Perennial, 2006.

Pynchon, Thomas. *Gravity's Rainbow*. New York: Viking Penguin, 1987.

Pynchon, Thomas. "Togetherness." *Aerospace Safety* 16, no. 12 (1960): 6–8.

Pynchon, Thomas. *Vineland*. New York: Little, Brown, 1990.

Rabelais, François. *Gargantua and Pantagruel*. Translated by Sir Thomas Urquhart and Pierre Le Motteux, with an introduction by Michael Randall. New York: Barnes and Noble Books, 2005.

Rickels, Laurence. "Spooky Electricity: An Interview with Friedrich Kittler." *Artforum*, December 1992, 66–70.

Riedesser, Peter, and Axel Verderber. *Aufrüstung der Seelen: Militärpsychiatrie und Militärpsychologie in Deutschland und Amerika*. Cologne: Dreisam, 1991.

Riemer, Friedrich Wilhelm. *Mitteilungen über Goethe: Aufgrund der Ausgabe von 1841 und des handschriftlichen Nachlasses*. Edited by Arthur Pollmer. Leipzig: Insel, 1921.

Robbe-Grillet, Alain. *In the Labyrinth*. Translated by Christine Brooke-Rose. London: Alma Classics, 2008.

Roberts, Andrew. *Napoleon the Great*. London: Allen Lane, 2014.

Rolling Stones. *Beggars Banquet, R.S.V.P. Songbook*. New York: Decca Records, 1968.

Rossi, Paolo. *The Birth of Modern Science*. The Making of Europe. London: Blackwell, 2001.

Rossi, Paolo. *Philosophy, Technology, and the Arts in the Early Modern Era*. New York: Harper and Row, 1970.

Rubin, Jerry. *Do It*. New York: Simon and Schuster, 1970.

Ruland, Bernd. *Wernher von Braun: Mein Leben für die Raumfahrt*. Offenburg: Burda, 1969.

Samuel, Richard. *Aufsätze und Essays*. Edited by Walter Müller-Seidel. Darmstadt: Wissenschaftliche Buchgesellschaft, 1967.

Schiller, Friedrich von. *Wilhelm Tell*. Translated by William F. Mainland. Chicago: University of Chicago Press, 1972.

Schlieffen, Alfred von. "War Today, 1909." In *Alfred von Schlieffen's Military Writings*, edited by Robert T. Foley, 194–205. London: Frank Cass, 2003.

Schmidgen, Henning. "Successful Paranoia: Friedrich Kittler, Lacanian Psychoanalysis, and the History of Science." *Theory, Culture, and Society* 36, no. 1 (2019): 107–31.

Schmitt, Carl. "*Historiographia in Nuce*: Alexis de Tocqueville (August 1946)." In *Ex Captivitate Salus: Experiences, 1945–47*, translated by Matthew Hannah, with an introduction by Andreas Kalyvas and Federico Finchelstein, 25–31. Cambridge, UK: Polity, 2017.

Schmitt, Carl. *Theory of the Partisan: Intermediate Commentary on the Concept of the Political*. Translated by G. L. Ulmen. New York: Telos, 2007.

Schmitt, Carl. *Writings on War*. Edited and translated by Timothy Nunan. Cambridge, UK: Polity, 2011.

Schneider, Manfred. "Freud-Träume in fünf Gangarten." *Neue Rundschau* 127 (2017): 139–47.

Schoeps, Hans-Joachim. *Preußen: Geschichte eines Staates*. Berlin: Propyläen, 1966.

Schramm, Wilhelm von. *Geheimdienst im Zweiten Weltkrieg: Operationen—Methoden—Erfolge*. 3rd ed. Munich: Langen-Müller, 1979.

Schreiber, Jens. "Die Zeichen der Liebe." In *Goethes Wahlverwandtschaften: kritische Modelle und Diskursanalysen zum Mythos Literatur*, edited by Norbert W. Bolz, 308–22. Hildesheim: Gerstenberg, 1981.

Schwartz, Peter J. "Why Did Goethe Marry When He Did?" *Goethe Yearbook* 15 (2008): 115–30.

Shannon, Claude E., and Warren Weaver. *The Mathematical Theory of Communication*. Urbana: University of Illinois Press, 1949.

Siegel, Jules. "Who Is Thomas Pynchon . . . and Why Did He Take Off with My Wife?" *Playboy* 34 (March 1977): 97, 122, 168–174.

Siegert, Bernhard. *Cultural Techniques: Grids, Filters, Doors, and Other Articulations of the Real*. Translated by Geoffrey Winthrop-Young. New York: Fordham University Press, 2015.

Singer, P. W., and Emerson T. Brooking. *Like War: The Weaponization of Social Media*. Boston: Eamon Dolan, 2018.

Smelser, Ronald, and Edward J. Davies II. *The Myth of the Eastern Front: The Nazi-Soviet War in American Popular Culture*. Cambridge: Cambridge University Press, 2008.

Smith, Constance Babington. *Evidence in Camera: The Story of Photographic Intelligence in the Second World War*. London: Chatto and Windhus, 1958.

Sophocles. *Antigone*. Translated and edited by Diane J. Rayor. Cambridge: Cambridge University Press, 2011.

Speer, Albert. *Infiltration*. Translated by Joachim Neugroschel. New York: Macmillan, 1981.

Speer, Albert. *Inside the Third Reich*. Translated by R. and C. Winston. New York: Macmillan, 1970.

Spengler, Oswald. *The Decline of the West*. Authorized translation with notes by Charles Francis Atkinson. New York: Knopf, 1939.

Spengler, Oswald. *Man and Technics*. Translated by Charles Francis Atkinson. New York: Alfred Knopf, 1932.

Stahel, David. *Retreat from Moscow: A New History of Germany's Winter Campaign, 1941–1942*. New York: Farrar, Straus and Giroux, 2019.

Stendhal. *The Charterhouse of Parma*. Edited by Roger Pearson. Translated by Margaret Mauldon. Oxford: Oxford World's Classics, 1999.

Stevenson, William. *A Man Called Intrepid: The Secret War*. New York: Ballantine, 1977.

Syberberg, Hans-Jürgen, dir. *Hitler: Ein Film aus Deutschland*. 1977. http://www.syberberg.de/Syberberg2/Events_2003/uncut.html.

Theweleit, Klaus. *Male Fantasies*. Vol 2, *Male Bodies: Psychoanalyzing the White Terror*. Translated by Erica Carter and Chris Turner, in collaboration with Stephen Conway. Foreword by Anson Rabinbach and Jessica Benjamin. Minneapolis: University of Minnesota Press, 1989.

Theweleit, Klaus. *Das Tor zur Welt: Fußball als Realitätsmodell*. Cologne: Kiepenheuer und Witsch, 2004.

Trachtenberg, Joshua. *Jewish Magic and Superstition: A Study in Folk Religion*. 1939. Philadelphia: University of Pennsylvania Press, 2004.

Trevor-Roper, Hugh, ed. *Hitler's War Directives, 1939–1945*. London: Sidgwick and Jackson, 1964.

Tümmler, Hans. *Carl August von Weimar, Goethes Freund*. Stuttgart: Klett-Cotta, 1978.

Turk, Horst. "Goethes *Wahlverwandtschaften*: Der doppelte Ehebruch durch Phantasie." In *Urszenen: Literaturwissenschaft als Diskursanalyse und Diskurskritik*, edited by Friedrich Kittler and Horst Turk, 202–22. Frankfurt am Main: Suhrkamp, 1977.

Turner, Derek. *Paleontology: A Philosophical Introduction*. Cambridge: Cambridge University Press, 2011.

Tzu, Sun. *The Art of War*. Translated and introduced by Samuel B. Griffith. London: Oxford University Press, 1971.

Vasco, Gerhard. *Diderot and Goethe: A Study in Science and Humanism*. Bibliothèque de la Revue de littérature comparée 119. Geneva: Slatkine, 1978.

Virilio, Paul. *War and Cinema: The Logistics of Perception*. Translated by Patrick Camiller. London: Verso, 1989.

Vismann, Cornelia. *Files: Law and Media Technology*. Translated by Geoffrey Winthrop-Young. Stanford, CA: Stanford University Press, 2008.

Wagner, Richard. *My Life*. Edited by Mary Whittall. Translated by Andrew Gray. Cambridge: Cambridge University Press, 1983.

Wagner, Richard. *The Ring of the Nibelung*. Translated by Andrew Porter. New York: Norton, 1977.

Warhol, Andy. *The Philosophy of Andy Warhol (From A to B and Back Again)*. Orlando, FL: Harcourt, 1975.

Waters, Roger. "The Post War Dream." On Pink Floyd, *The Final Cut*. London: Columbia Records, 1983.

Wehler, Hans-Ulrich. *Deutsche Gesellschaftsgeschichte*. Vol. 1, *Vom Feudalismus des Alten Reiches bis zur defensiven Modernisierung der Reformära (1700–1815)*. Munich: C. H. Beck, 1989.

Weisenburger, Steven. *A "Gravity's Rainbow" Companion*. Athens: University of Georgia Press, 1988.

Welzbacher, Christian. 'Ruinenwert' und 'Reichsehrenmal': Albert Speer, Wilhelm Kreis und der Kunsthistoriker Felix Alexander Dargel." *Kritische Berichte: Zeitschrift für Kunst und Kulturwissenschaften* 33, no. 2 (2005): 69–72.

Wiener, Oswald. *Die Verbesserung von Mitteleuropa*. Reinbek bei Hamburg: Rowohlt, 1969.

Winter, Denis. *Death's Men: Soldiers of the Great War*. London: Penguin, 1978.

Winter, Georg, and Rudolf Vaupel, eds. *Die Reorganisation des preußischen Staates*. Vol. 1, *Allgemeine Verwaltungs- und Behördenreform*. Leipzig: Hirzel, 1931.

Winthrop-Young, Geoffrey. "De Bellis Germanicis: Kittler, the Third Reich, and the German Wars." *Cultural Politics* 11, no. 3 (2015): 361–75.

Winthrop-Young, Geoffrey. "Hunting a Whale of a State: Kittler and His Terrorists." *Cultural Politics* 8, no. 3 (2012): 399–412.

Winthrop-Young, Geoffrey. *Kittler and the Media*. Cambridge, UK: Polity, 2011.

Winthrop-Young, Geoffrey. "On Friedrich Kittler's 'Authorship and Love.'" *Theory, Culture and Society* 32, no. 3 (2015): 3–13.

Wisbar, Frank, dir. *Hunde, wollt ihr ewig leben? (Dogs, Do You Want to Live Forever?)*. Stalingrad: Deutsche Film Hansa, 1959.

Wöss, Fritz. *Hunde, wollt ihr ewig leben*. Vienna: Paul Zsolnay Verlag, 1958.

Zhukov, Georgy Konstantinovich. *Reminiscences and Reflections*. Vol. 2. Moscow: Progress Publishers, 1985.

Zons, Raimar. "Ein Denkmal voriger Zeiten: Über die *Wahlverwandtschaften*." In *Goethes Wahlverwandtschaften: Kritische Modelle und Diskursanalysen zum Mythos Literatur*, edited by Norbert W. Bolz, 323–52. Hildesheim: Gerstenberg, 1981.

Zuse, Konrad. *The Computer—My Life*. Foreword by F. L. Bauer and H. Zemanek, translated by P. McKenna and J. A. Ross. Berlin: Springer, 1993.

INDEX

acoustic simulation, 87–88
Aitmatov, Chingiz, 134–35, 251n12
Altenstein, Karl vom Stein zum, 202
Arditi, 129–31
Arnheim, Rudolf, 96
Augustus, 10–11, 202
autobahn, 54–55, 107, 207, 211, 228–29, 266n32, 266n33, 267n56, 269n8; Battle of Verdun and, 57–58; Hitler and, 59–60; Kammler and, 261n6, 267n56, 270n15; martial a priori of, 33; V-2 rocket and, 222

Babbage, Charles, 64, 66
Bachmann, Ingeborg, 108, 151, 161
Bacon, Francis, 70–71
Bar-le-Duc, 57, 66
Battle of Herrmann, The (Kleist), 3, 9, 13, 24, 202, 204, 213
Bauer, Max, 159, 161–62
BBC, 99, 107
Being and Time (Heidegger), 151, 161–62
Benjamin, Walter, 63, 128, 172, 178
Benn, Gottfried, 154, 229, 270n10
Bergson, Henri, 107
Berlin, 27, 59–60, 67, 90, 102, 106, 171, 193, 228–30; AVUS and, 54–55; flak tower 67–68; Müffling and, 180, 187–89; tank exhibition pieces in 73, 75; Zuse and, 39
Birth of Tragedy from the Spirit of Music, The (Nietzsche), 158, 161

blitzkrieg, 1, 3, 16, 31, 34, 61, 89, 144, 163, 209, 221; aesthetics and, 60; failure of, 32; against France, 59; Guderian and, 119, 133; planning and tactics of, 58, 65, 74, 90, 105, 116, 132; Rolling Stones, The and, 117–120; technology and, 103, 107; trauma and, 45;
Bonaparte, Napoleon, 7, 9, 11, 15, 55, 82, 90, 152, 187–88, 198–99, 201, 204; Age of Napoleon, 3; and general staff, 84; and women as mothers, 115, 124, 158; Battle of Jena-Auerstedt and, 14, 183; optical telegraph and, 189; prefigured by Augustus, 10, 202; comments on Prussian army, 14, 22; compared to Wotan, 156–57
Borges, Jorge Luis, 166, 228
Braun, Wernher von, 39, 93, 208, 212, 221–22, 228
Bruchmüller, Georg, 159
Brunswick, Karl Wilhelm Ferdinand von, 80–81, 181, 183
Burrow, The (Kafka), 85, 98
Bush, George W., 13, 62, 142, 145; and 9/11, 13, 141

cable, 7–8, 28, 94, 97–98, 109, 139; trans-atlantic, 8, 94, 155, 195
Cadmus, 45
Campaign in France (Goethe), 81
CBS, 104–7
Cervantes, Miguel de, 193
Chappe, Claude, 25

Choltitz, Dietrich von, 188
Chuikov, Vasily Ivanovich, 75
Churchill, Winston, 74, 120, 165, 196
Citino, Robert M., 29–30, 32, 34;
Clark, Christopher, 14, 35;
Clausewitz, Carl von, 14, 22, 26, 33, 56, 151, 181, 188, 205
Comedy of Danger (Hughes), 99, 102, 105
Command of the Air, The (Douhet), 206
computer, 3, 38, 40, 43, 75, 93, 107, 128, 130, 134, 146, 147, 213, 233; analog computer, 196; animation and, 93; Colossus in World War II, 108; Turing and, 3; Zuse (Z4) and, 39–40, 231
Coppola, Francis Ford, 66, 125
Creveld, Martin van, 83
Cronin, Audrey Kurth, 25
creeping barrage, 85, 159–60
Crown Prince Wilhelm, 54, 56
Crying of Lot 49, The (Pynchon), 195
cultural techniques, 6, 19
culture, 6, 73, 119–20, 139, 164, 168–69, 174, 184, 234; communication culture, 25; determined by conflict, 5; distinction between good and bad, 142–43; Greek, 135; military culture, 28, 34; nature and, 188; Prussian Ministry of, 201; technology and, 65
cyberspace, 25

D'Annunzio, Gabriele, 129–31
Dasein, 161–162
Decline of the West, The (Spengler), 47
Deleuze, Gilles, 73, 124, 143
Derrida, Jacques, 194, 236n15, 237n38
Descartes, René, 71–72, 123, 125, 144
"Die letzten Jahre" (Schmitt), 246n8, 246n9
Discourse Networks (Kittler), 6, 20
Dominik, Hans, 193
Dornberger, Walter, 44, 221–22, 232, 264n11, 267n56, 268n69
Douhet, Giulio, 206
Doumenc, Aimé, 56–58, 66; and route nationale, 109, 57

Dresden, 1–2, 40
Duke of Saxe-Weimar-Eisenach, 80, 82, 181–86. *See also* Karl August
Dunant, Henri, 158
Duvall, Robert, 21

Ecce Homo (Nietzsche), 143
Eddington, Sir Arthur, 217
Eldredge, Niles, 6
Elective Affinities, The (Goethe), 171, 177, 179–82, 184, 186–88
Engelsing, Rolf, 19
Enigma, 4, 118–19
"Essay concerning Poor Relief Societies and the Abolition of Mendicity" (Rochow), 179

Facebook, 24
Falkenhayn, Erich von, 56–57
Faust (Goethe), 2, 65
Fellgiebel, Erich, 106, 234
Fessenden, Reginald, 4, 93, 106–7
Files: Law and Media Technology (Vismann), 14
film, 7, 88, 212; in *Gravity's Rainbow*, 217–24; lanterns as precursors to, 63; literature and, 213–14
"First Concert Broadcast . . . A Memory from the Trenches" (Meier), 98
First World War. *See* World War I.
Flight across the Ocean, The (Brecht), 92, 101
FM (radio), 74, 107
"Fortress Europe," 1, 106, 215, 227
Foucault, Michel, 5–6, 9, 62–63, 112, 142, 168, 217, 234

Gauß, Carl Friedrich, 181, 189
gender, 15, 20, 172, 177, 206
general staff, 15, 54, 55, 58, 74, 97, 129, 190. 198, 228; attrition rates and, 164; communications technology and, 97, 100–101, 205; development of new weapons and tactics and, 74, 131, 159;

Müffling and, 189; Napoleon and, 83; and reorganization of Prussian Army, 15, 201–3
German Way of War, The (Citino), 29–30, 38
Germany, 18, 23–24, 35, 48, 107, 132, 137, 146, 169, 182, 184, 203, 209, 218, 221; autobahn and, 60; in *Gravity's Rainbow*, 48, 207, 224; and necessity for short wars, 29–30, 32; World War I and, 47, 102, 139; World War II and, 1–3, 32, 38, 42–43, 209, 218
Geyer, Michael, 129
Gneisenau, August Neidhart von, 14, 16, 21, 113, 115, 188, 201–2
Goebbels, Joseph, 13, 112, 202, 220
Goethe, Johann Wolfgang von, 2, 9, 63, 145, 169, 171, 213, 227, 241n4, 244n3, 251n3; at Battle of Valmy, 80–83, 250n1; and Schiller, 9, 200
Gould, Stephen Jay, 6
Goya, Francisco, 63, 67
Götterdämmerung (Wagner), 94–5, 102, 106
Gramophone, Film, Typewriter (Kittler), 39
Gravity's Rainbow (Pynchon), 5, 40–44, 163, 193–6, 205–10, 211–24, 226n67, 264n14, 266n33, 267n56
Greece, 124, 136, 142
Gribeauval, Jean-Baptiste Vaquette de, 82
Grimmelshausen, Johann Jacob Christoffel von, 153–54, 161
Groos, Karl, 92
Großdeutsche Rundfunk, 95–96, 106–7
Guattari, Félix, 73, 124, 143
Guderian, Heinz, 32–33, 58–59, 74–75, 119, 133; and blitzkrieg, 60, 65; and VHF, 107, 212
Guilhaumou, Jacques, 25

Hegel, Georg Wilhelm Friedrich, 5, 83, 126, 152, 193
Heidegger, Martin, 37, 48, 75, 102, 161–62, 269n7

Heimat, 10, 20, 24, 198, 200–201, 203–5, 207–8, 210
Heimatliteratur, 198, 202, 205
Heine, Heinrich, 23
Hellingrath, Norbert von, 87
hermeneutics, 202
Herold, Horst, 138, 146–47, 252n5, 252n7, 253n19
Heyme, Hansgünther, 199, 262n3
high command: German High Command, 34, 59, 132, 144, 205, 212, 228, 231; British High Command, 106; French High Command, 119; Rommel's division and, 34
Hitler, Adolf, 1, 13, 27–28, 29, 35, 43, 118, 132, 199, 221, 222; Autobahn and, 54, 59–60; edelweiss as favorite flower, 27, 39; "Nero Decree" and, 13, 202–3; performance as military commander, 34, 87, 94, 239n73; 250n9; 265n26; tanks and, 76, 244n16; theory of ruin value and, 209, 270n13; V-2 and, 41, 54, 212, 261n6; 267n56; 268n73
Hodges, Andrew, 40
Hofer, Johannes, 200
Hoffmann, Wilhelm, 102
Homer, 124, 135, 146
Horkheimer, Max, 4, 35
Hughes, Richard, 99
Husserl, Edmund, 86

Ibsen, Henrik, 21
Iliad (Homer), 135
In Search of Lost Time (Proust), 45, 66, 107
Inside the Third Reich (Speer), 27–28, 34, 133, 238n58, 238n60, 242nn14–15, 242n16, 251n11
intelligence, 92; 104, 128, 130, 133, 216; Allied intelligence, 214; British intelligence service, 88; German intelligence service, 56; Martian intelligence, 105
Iron Kingdom, The (Clark), 14

Jacobins, 26
Jena Lectures on the Philosophy of Spirit (Hegel), 83, 152
Jones, Reginald V., 88–89
Junkers Ju 87, 89

Kafka, Franz, 73, 85–86, 98, 120, 182
kamikaze, 88, 120, 164, 223
Kammler, Hans, 44, 54, 60, 195, 218, 221–22, 230–31, 240n99, 240n100, 261n6, 268n72, 268n73, 270n15; and Dora-Mittelbau, 231; and Speer, 232
Kant, Immanuel, 17–18, 23, 36, 45, 129, 168
Karl August, 80, 180–81, 183–87; and Goethe, 81; and Napoleon, 15. *See also* Duke of Saxe-Weimar-Eisenach
Kershaw, Ian, 27
Kipling, Rudyard, 32, 139–40, 144
Kittler, Friedrich Adolf: 1–11, 13, 15–21, 23–26, 28–48, 127, 233. *See also* writing
Kleist, Heinrich von, 3, 9, 20, 38, 56, 180; Napoleon and, 202; Penthesilea and, 114; rape, 206–7
Kluge, Alexander, 31, 33–34, 75, 118, 127
Koselleck, Reinhart, 46–47
Krupp, Alfred, 114, 209
Kuhn, Thomas, 6

Lacan, Jacques, 23, 36, 57, 115, 137, 193, 204, 215–16
Lang, Fritz, 208, 218–19
language, 9, 25, 41, 82, 90, 101, 147, 188; human subjectivity and, 36–37; programming languages, 108; psychoanalysis and, 45
Leibniz, Gottfried Wilhelm, 80, 219
levée en masse, 16, 25–26, 35, 201
Liesegang, Paul Eduard, 63
Liliencron, Detlev von, 84
Lilienstern, August Otto Rühle von, 180, 188

Lindbergh, Charles, 100
Ludendorff, Erich, 112, 116, 159–60, 162
Luhmann, Niklas, 92, 164

machine gun 68, 84, 85, 140, 160; Battle of Omdurman, 65; stormtrooper tactics and, 129. *See also* Maxim gun
Macho, Thomas, 73, 124, 154
madness, 222
Man and Technics (Spengler), 9
Manstein, Erich von, 118
Marconi, Guglielmo, 93, 97, 103–4
Marey, Étienne-Jules, 220, 222
mass media, 4, 208
Maxim gun, 65, 139–40
Maxwell, James Clerk, 93, 104
McLuhan, Marshall, 107, 147
media technologies, 4, 48; and war, 20, 27, 34, 36, 43, 79, 124, 222–23
media theory, 4, 30
Meier, Eduard, 98–99, 102
Meininger ensemble, 65, 241n7
Mersenne, Marin, 71–72
missile, 37–38, 43, 163, 206, 215, 218, 229; ballistic, 38, 48, 196, 231; intercontinental, 89, 222; Minuteman, 194; nuclear, 43, 147, 172, 174, 177, 188, 206, 211, 231; Stinger, 144; subjects as, 3, 36. *See also* V-2
Moltke, Count Helmuth Karl Bernhard von (the Elder), 14, 74, 84, 126, 189
Moltke, Helmut von (the Younger), 55–56
Most Secret War (Jones), 206
mothers, 20, 113, 139, 155, 171; discourse network 1800 and, 20, 169, 171; in *Elective Affinities*, 173–74, 178, 190; in *Gravity's Rainbow*, 204, 207; Napoleon and, 115, 124, 156, 158
Müffling, Friedrich Karl Ferdinand von (Baron), 180–89, 227, 234
Mummert, Werner, 230, 270n11

music, 22, 35, 66, 69, 72, 98, 119, 224; Richard Wagner and, 21–22, 89, 94, 96. See also rock and roll
My Life (Wagner), 156, 180, 254n15

nature, 105, 158, 161, 185, 188, 208; accelerated evolution and, 6–7
Nazism, 27, 35
Niethammer, Friedrich Immanuel, 171
Nietzsche, Friedrich, 72, 91–92, 94, 98, 142–43

On the Marble Cliffs (Jünger), 123
On War (Clausewitz), 21, 33, 188, 205
Operation Barbarossa, 30, 32, 127
Operation Citadel, 118
Operation Desert Storm, 128, 163
Operation Sickle Cut, 87, 120, 133, 163
Operation Valhalla, 20–21, 110, 112, 114–15, 157
Order of Things, The (Foucault), 5–6, 8, 108

panzer, 30, 56, 59, 205; in campaign against France, 30, 59; Panther panzer at Battle of Kursk, 118, 124; 244n16; Rommel's division and, 34, 43; war crimes and, 43. See also tanks
Pax Americana, 146, 194
Pessler, Wilhelm, 87
Peymann, Claus, 203, 263n25
philosophy, 20, 32, 79, 151, 185, 188, 206; history of war and, 142, 144; replacing revolution, 23; stormtrooper tactics and, 162
phonograph, 87
Pierce, Charles Sanders 214
Pinchevski, Amit, 44
Plato, 70
Porsche, Ferdinand, 76
Preyer, Wilhelm, 92
Prince of Homburg, The (Kleist), 9, 262n24
prototype, 65, 76, 107–8, 171, 199
Proust, Marcel, 66

psychoanalysis, 45, 207
Pynchon, Thomas, 3, 10, 58, 89, 152, 156, 193–96, 207, 210, 228–30, 232, 240n91; 264n11, 264n14, 266n33, 267n56, 268n67; depiction of World War II, 41–44, 89, 152, 163, 195–96, 205–10, 211–24, 229; impact on Kittler, 40–41, 228; mothers in *Gravity's Rainbow*, 204, 207

Quarrel between Philanthropism and Humanism (Niethammer), 171
Question Concerning Technology, The (Heidegger), 162

Rabelais, François, 70
radar, 63, 68, 92, 107, 212
radio, 91–94, 96–104, 100, 101, 103, 106–9; radio technology, 4, 74, 101, 119; and war, 20, 27, 34, 36, 43, 79, 124, 222–23
Red Army Faction (RAF), 23, 147, 203, 251n3, 252n6, 253n19
Reign of Terror, 7
Rhinegold (Wagner), 62, 110
"Ride of the Valkyries" (Wagner), 22, 125
Ring of the Nibelung (Wagner), 21–22, 62, 110–12, 115–16, 156–58, 241nn1–2, 246n11, 246nn13–16, 248n1, 248n6, 248n9, 248n12, 254n18
Rochow, Friedrich Eberhard von, 179
rock and roll, 33, 35, 106–7
Rommel, Erwin, 34, 38, 119, 132
Royal Air Force, 40, 67, 88, 218, 228–29
Rubin, Jerry, 44

Scharnhorst, Gerhard von, 14, 186–87
Schiller, Friedrich: 9–12, 65, 199–200, 202–3, 240n91
Schlieffen, Alfred Count von: 30, 32, 38, 55–56, 161, 234; Guderian, 58; Schlieffen Plan, 30, 32, 38, 55–56, 58, 132, 146, 213; "War Today, 1909," 97, 158–59, 246n18, 252n22, 252n24

Schmitt, Carl: 13, 63, 93, 114, 136, 145, 201–2, 205, 207, 209; and Tocqueville, 46, 240n106
Schneider, Manfred, 45
Second World War, 211. *See also* World War II
Seeckt, Hans von, 58
Shannon, Claude, 68, 217
Siegert, Bernhard, 4
Siemens, 64, 66, 119, 231
Simplicissimus (Grimmelshausen), 161
Singer, P. W., 120
Smith, Constance Babington, 229
social media, 3, 24–25
software, 18, 108, 131, 147
Sophocles, 53, 143
Sorrows of Young Werther, The (Goethe), 19, 237n37
speech, 136, 234; Guderian, 59; noise, 79, 82; orders of speech, 5, 18; radio drama, 91–92, 99, 107; Woman and, 170
Speer, Albert, 195, 203, 242n15; theory of ruin value, 67, 209, 218, 230, 232, 270n13
Spengler, Oswald, 9, 47
Staver, Robert B., 195, 216
Steiner, Felix, 132, 250n9
stereo, 33, 61, 107–8, 119
Storm of Steel (Jünger), 84
Strauss, Franz Joseph, 211, 232, 271n19
Structure of Scientific Revolutions, The (Kuhn), 6
Stülpnagel, Heinrich von, 188
Sun Tzu, 16, 26
Syberberg, Hans-Jürgen, 106, 228
"Sympathy for the Devil" (The Rolling Stones), 32, 117

tactics: animals and, 124; *Auftragstaktik*, 17, 24; autobahn, 58; barrage, 159, 163; in *The Battle of Herrmann*, 202; *Bewegungskrieg*, 31; blitzkrieg, 27, 60, 65, 90; Free Corps and, 132; maps and, 181, 189; mission tactics, 16–18, 129, 154; psychoanalysis, 45; searchlight and, 65; technical innovations, 8, 74; Wagner, 113–16
tanks, 31–33, 43, 53, 58–59, 68, 73–76, 87, 97, 100, 105, 116, 118, 125, 155, 164–65, 198, 219, 228–29, 242n1; and battle, 118, 243n9; blitzkrieg and, 120; commanders and, 59; Guderian and, 133; Kittler and, 43; Martian, 105–6; Maus (codename), 76, 244n16; microtanks, 76; radio-equipped, 32–33, 89; Sherman tanks 119; tank division, 75, 89, 119, 163, 205; Tiger tanks, 124; Wehrmacht and, 107
Tannhäuser (Wagner), 65
tape recorder, 107
technological media, 95, 218–19
teleology, 43
telephone, 28, 97–98, 102, 133
telephony, 109; wireless: 2, 8, 93, 97–98, 100–103, 109, 234
teleprinter, 119
teletype, 28
Theory of the Partisan (Schmitt), 143, 201, 241n6, 253nn16–17, 262nn13–14, 262n15, 262n18, 263n39, 263n55, 264n68
Theweleit, Klaus, 35, 229
Thus Spoke Zarathustra (Nietzsche), 142–43
Tocqueville, Alexis de, 46–47
"Togetherness" (Pynchon), 194, 196
"Transformations of Experience and Methodological Change" (Koselleck), 46
Treaty of Tilsit, 14
Tristan (Wagner), 84
Trotsky, Leon, 22, 162
Tucholsky, Kurt, 22–23
Turing, Alan, 3, 40, 119
Twain, Mark, 21
typewriter, 39, 84

UHF (radio), 107, 212
Ulbricht, Walter, 229–30
United States, 58; British Empire and, 139, 141; commercial radio and, 100, 104; German-American technology transfer, 194–97, 212, 215–16, 224; impact on Kittler, 228–29; post-9/11, 145–47; Schmitt and, 46; Spanish-American War, 97; world dominance and, 141–42. *See also* V2 (V-2) rocket

Vineland (Pynchon), 196–97, 261n11
V2 (V-2) rocket, 3, 38, 60, 68, 105, 228–231; Dora-Mittelbau, 38, 208, 230; in *Gravity's Rainbow*, 53, 89, 194–97, 206–10, 211–24; guidance system, 197; Peenemünde Army Research Center and, 38–41, 43–44, 195–96, 207, 212, 220–22, 229, 232
Valkyrie, The (Wagner), 21–22, 110–112, 114–15, 125, 157
Vatutin, Nikolai, 75
Verdun, 53, 56–59, 87; fortress of, 66; Doumenc and, 242n12
VHF (radio), 32–33, 107–8, 212
Virilio, Paul, 2, 35, 65, 219, 221
Vismann, Cornelia, 14
Voss, Johann Heinrich, 201

Wagner, Richard, 89, 163; media technology and, 66; Nietzsche and, 22, 94, 237n43, 246n10; *Ring* and radio drama, 94–96
War and Cinema (Virilio), 35, 219
warfare, 68, 74–75, 93, 99, 101–2, 112, 118, 212, 221; animals in, 123–26; blitzkrieg, 27–38, 60–61, 65, 90, 103, 133, 163; Clausewitz and, 14, 22, 26, 151, 205, 236n27, 238nn55–56, 263n37; death, 151–65; and information, 24–26, 37, 83–84, 103, 108, 138, 163, 189, 196, 213–14, 216–17, 219; *Introduction to Electronic Warfare*, 93; mechanized, 25, 32, 34, 41, 108; mobilization and, 7, 18, 25–6, 31, 41, 97, 101, 119; modern, 7, 11, 20, 28, 33–36, 42, 45, 57, 80–83, 86, 101–2, 123, 126, 155, 158–59, 163, 200; modern subjectivity and, 13–18; modern engineering and, 94, 185; noise and, 79–90; sandbox and, 56, 189, 227, 228; telegraphy and, 25, 55, 97, 139, 155, 189; trench, 56, 66, 74, 84–86, 94, 98, 102, 114–16, 118, 120, 129, 133, 158–59, 161, 208, 213–14; women and, 9, 12–13, 15, 20–21, 24, 114–15, 171–74. *See also* Pynchon; radio; tactics; World War I; World War II
Waters, Roger, 118, 138, 146, 176–77, 204, 239n76
Wehler, Hans-Ulrich, 14
Weimar Republic, 58, 100
Welles, Orson, 75, 103–4, 106; "War of the Worlds," 103–5, 107
white noise, 94, 101, 218
Wiener, Norbert, 68, 138
Wilhelm Tell (Schiller), 9, 11, 199
Winter, Denis, 58, 87, 204
Wolf, Friedrich, 80, 101–2, 108, 123–24, 147
Woman in the Moon (Lang), 208, 219
women, 9, 130, 134, 200, 213; in battle, 112–4; in *The Battle of Herrmann*, 12–13, 200, 202–4, 206–7; Berlin women's organization, 27; in *Elective Affinities*, 171–74; modern nuclear family and, 177; motherhood and, 155–58, 169–74, 176, 207; as self-motivated subjects, 15, 19–21
World War I, 3, 8, 22, 227, 229, 231; *Auftragstaktik*, 17; blitzkrieg, 31–33; noise, 79, 83–84, 86, 88; radio drama, 93–94, 97, 99, 102; road construction, 55–58, 66; Spengler, 47; tanks, 74, 76. *See also* warfare
World War II, 120, 139, 152, 157, 198, 205, 208, 212, 222–23, 228; hidden history, 1–3, 28–29, 195; Hitler as commander,

World War II (*continued*) 34; as macrotechnological event, 43, 47; noise, 86–92; radio drama, 92–93, 104–6, 108; searchlights, 67–8; speed, 33, 38, 124–5, 132; tanks, 74–5, 118, 124, 133; United States 139, 141, 145–46. *See also* Pynchon; V2 (V-2) rocket

writing, 219; Frederick the Great and, 154; Kittler and, 2, 9, 20, 35, 38–44, 170, 183, 189, 233; literature as writing and command, 213–14, 217; sound and, 82, 84, 91

Z4, 39–40, 43, 270n14
zeitgeist, 37
Zhukov, Georgy, 68, 118, 228
Zuse, Konrad, 39–40, 43, 231, 239n83, 270n14

Chapter 1. Free Ways
Originally published as "Auto Bahnen," in *Der Technikdiskurs in der Hitler-Stalin-Ära*, edited by Wolfgang Emmeric and Carl Wege (Stuttgart: Metzler, 1995), 114–22; and translated by Geoffrey Winthrop-Young in *Cultural Politics* 11, no. 3 (2015): 376–83. A shorter version of the same essay appeared in *Kulturrevolution: Zeitschrift für angewandte Diskurstheorie* 5 (1984): 44–47.

Chapter 2. A Short History of the Searchlight
Originally published as "Eine Kurzgeschichte des Scheinwerfers," in *Der Entzug der Bilder: Visuelle Realitäten*, edited by Michael Wetzel and Herta Wolf (Munich: Fink, 1999), 83–89; and translated by Geoffrey Winthrop-Young in *Cultural Politics* 11, no. 3 (2015): 384–90.

Chapter 3. Fragments of a History of Firearms
Originally published as "Bruchstücke einer Geschichte der Feuerwaffen," in *Feuer: Elemente des Naturhaushalts II*, edited by Bernd Busch with Johann Georg Goldammer and Andreas Denk (Cologne: Wienand, 2001), 560–62.

Chapter 4. Tanks
Originally published as "Panzer," in *100 Wörter des Jahrhunderts*, edited by Wolfgang Schneider (Frankfurt am Main: Suhrkamp, 1999), 195–99.

Chapter 5. Noises of War
Originally "Geräusche des Krieges" (unpublished lecture manuscript in German first presented in Basel in June 1994).

Chapter 6. Playback. A World War History of Radio Drama
Originally "Playback: Weltkriegsgeschichte des Hörspiels" (unpublished lecture manuscript in German presented in June 1999) and "Radio Drama" (a second shorter and also unpublished version in English).

Chapter 7. Operation Valhalla
Originally published as "Unternehmen Walhall," in *Die Nibelungen: Bilder von Liebe, Verrat und Untergang*, edited by Wolfgang Storch (Munich: Prestel, 1987), 62.

Chapter 8. When the Blitzkrieg Raged
Originally published under the same title in *Sympathy for the Devil*, edited by Albert Kümmel-Schnur (Munich: Fink, 2009), 137–41.

Chapter 9. Animals of War. A Historical Bestiary
Originally published as "Die Tiere des Krieges: Ein historisches Bestiarium," in *Das Tier in mir: Die animalischen Ebenbilder des Menschen*, edited by Johannes Bilstein and Matthias Winzen (Cologne: Walther König, 2002), 143–59; and translated by Geoffrey Winthrop-Young in *Cultural Politics* 11, no. 3 (2015): 391–94.

Chapter 10. On Modern Warfare. A Conversation with Alexander Kluge
Originally published as "Über moderne Kriegsführung," in Friedrich Kittler, *Short Cuts*, edited by Peter Gente and Martin Weinmann (Frankfurt am Main: Zweitausendeins, 2002), 211–26.

Chapter 11. Of States and Their Terrorists
Originally published as "Von Staaten und ihren Terroristen," in Étienne Balibar, Friedrich Kittler, and Martin van Creveld, *Vom Krieg zum Terrorismus? Humboldt-Universität zu Berlin, Mosse-Lectures 2002/2003* (Berlin: Humboldt-Universität zu Berlin, 2003), 33–50; and translated by Geoffrey Winthrop-Young in *Cultural Politics* 8, no. 3 (2012): 385–97.

Chapter 12. Manners of Death in War
Originally "Todesarten im Kriege" (unpublished manuscript in German presented in June 1999).

Chapter 13. Ottilie Hauptmann
Originally published in Friedrich Kittler, *Dichter, Mutter, Kind* (Munich: Fink, 1991), 119–48. A shorter version of the same essay appeared in *Goethes Wahlverwandtschaften: Kritische Modelle und Diskursanalysen zum Mythos Literatur*, edited by Norbert W. Bolz (Munich: Gerstenberg, 1981), 260–75.

Chapter 14. On a Novel That Would Not Only Be Fiction . . .
Originally "Über einen Roman, der nicht bloß Fiktion wäre" (unpublished manuscript with handwritten corrections, in German).

Chapter 15. De Nostalgia
Originally published under the same title in *Literatur und Provinz: Das Konzept Heimat in der neueren Literatur*, edited by Hans-Georg Pott (Paderborn: Ferdinand Schöningh, 1986), 153–68; and translated by Geoffrey Winthrop-Young in *Cultural Politics* 11, no. 3 (2015): 395–405.

Chapter 16. Media and Drugs in Pynchon's Second World War
Originally published as "Medien und Drogen in Pynchons Zweitem Weltkrieg (*Gravity's Rainbow*)," in *Narrativität in den Medien*, edited by Rolf Kloepfer and Karl-Dietmar Möller (Münster: MAkS Publikationen, 1985), 231–52. This is a revised version of the translation by Michael Wutz and Geoffrey-Winthrop Young published in *Reading Matters: Narrative in the New Media Ecology*, edited by Joseph Tabbi and Michael Wutz (Ithaca, NY: Cornell University Press, 1997), 157–72.

Chapter 17. Biogeography
Originally published as "Biogeographie," in *Ein deutscher Traum: Zyklus auf das Jahr 1990*, edited by Wolfgang Storch (Berlin: Hentrich, 1990), 63–71.

Chapter 18. Theology
Originally published as "'Theologie," in *Götter und Schriften rund ums Mittelmeer*, edited by Peter Berz, Peter Weibel, Susanne Holl, Gerhard Scharbert, Joulia Strauss, and Friedrich Kittler (Munich: Fink, 2017), 411.

www.ingramcontent.com/pod-product-compliance
Lightning Source LLC
Chambersburg PA
CBHW051049230426
43666CB00012B/2623